Selected Musical Plays by Noël Coward

Selected Musical Plays by Noël Coward:
A Critical Anthology

This Year of Grace
Bitter Sweet
Words and Music
Pacific 1860
Ace of Clubs
Sail Away
The Girl Who Came to Supper

Edited by
ARIANNE JOHNSON QUINN

methuen | drama
LONDON • NEW YORK • OXFORD • NEW DELHI • SYDNEY

METHUEN DRAMA
Bloomsbury Publishing Plc
50 Bedford Square, London, WC1B 3DP, UK
1385 Broadway, New York, NY 10018, USA
29 Earlsfort Terrace, Dublin 2, Ireland

BLOOMSBURY, METHUEN DRAMA and the Methuen Drama logo are trademarks of
Bloomsbury Publishing Plc

First published in Great Britain 2022

Copyright © NC Aventales AG, 2022
Introduction and Commentary © Arianne Johnson Quinn, 2022

The authors asserted their right under the Copyright, Designs and Patents Act, 1988,
to be identified as authors of this work.

Cover design by Rebecca Heselton
Cover image: Elaine Stritch and Noel Coward of *Sail Away*
© Bettmann/ Contributor/ Getty Images

All rights reserved. No part of this publication may be reproduced or transmitted in any form or by any means, electronic or mechanical, including photocopying, recording, or any information storage or retrieval system, without prior permission in writing from the publishers.

Bloomsbury Publishing Plc does not have any control over, or responsibility for, any third-party Websites referred to or in this book. All internet addresses given in this book were correct at the time of going to press. The author and publisher regret any inconvenience caused if addresses have changed or sites have ceased to exist, but can accept no responsibility for any such changes.

No rights in incidental music or songs contained in the work are hereby granted and performance rights for any performance/presentation whatsoever must be obtained from the respective copyright owners.

All rights whatsoever in this play are strictly reserved and application for performance etc. should be made before rehearsals to Alan Brodie Representation Ltd of Paddock Suite, The Courtyard, 55 Charterhouse Street, London EC1M 6HA. No performance may be given unless a licence has been obtained. No rights in incidental music or songs contained in the Work are hereby granted and performance rights for any performance/presentation Whatsoever must be obtained from the respective copyright owners.

A catalogue record for this book is available from the British Library.

A catalog record for this book is available from the Library of Congress.

ISBN: HB: 978-1-3502-3469-7
PB: 978-1-3502-3468-0
ePDF: 978-1-3502-3470-3
eBook: 978-1-3502-3471-0

Typeset by RefineCatch Limited, Bungay, Suffolk

To find out more about our authors and books visit www.bloomsbury.com
and sign up for our newsletters.

Contents

Introduction vi

PART I
1920s and 1930s: The Cochran Revue

This Year of Grace 3
Bitter Sweet 77
Words and Music 143

PART II
Post-war Musical Plays

Pacific 1860 217
Ace of Clubs 287

PART III
Broadway Plays of the 1960s

Sail Away 357
The Girl Who Came to Supper 447

Introduction

This anthology centres on the musical theatre works of Noël Coward (1899–1973) that were staged between the 1920s and the 1960s, incorporating new archival evidence and supporting critical material. These works span multiple genres that are significant to the development of the British and American musical, including revue, musical comedy and operetta. Part I includes the scripts of revues from the 1920s and 1930s produced by impresario Charles B. Cochran: *This Year of Grace* (1928) and *Words and Music* (1932). It explores these works in the context of both Coward's musical style in the 1920s and 1930s and that of his rivals including Cole Porter. Part II contains the scripts of his post-war musical plays, including *Pacific 1860* (1946) and *Ace of Clubs* (1949). These scripts allow us to reconsider his post-war musical plays as a vital part of the theatrical landscape through the inclusion of critical reception history. Finally, Part III explores the history of Coward's Broadway legacy and reconsiders his lasting cultural impact on American musical theatre. The scripts for *Sail Away* (1961) and *The Girl Who Came to Supper* (1963) reveal another aspect of Coward's writing and his connection to the Broadway stage at the height of the 'Golden Age' American musical.

Although Coward's work as playwright, songwriter and actor of stage and screen has long been celebrated, his contributions to the British musical have largely been forgotten. This lack of attention is due in part because of the idiosyncratic nature of the works themselves that imitates the creative nature of Coward himself. Like many theatre creators, songwriters and playwrights of his day, Coward wrote musical works that spanned a variety of styles, from revue to musical comedy to operetta.[1] This wide range of styles was also a direct result of the fact that his work was created for multiple producers in a global theatre market, beginning with his collaboration with producers André Charlot and Charles B. Cochran and ending with his Broadway plays. Not all of his musical plays were commercially successful but, as we see from the examples in this volume, there is much to learn from the 'flop', and the ways in which it reflects Coward's creative development (Mendelbaum, 1991). This multiplicity of style demonstrates his adaptability, the extent of his creativity, and the myriad styles and genres that constituted the British and American musical.

The works in this volume provide a critical introduction to the wide range of Coward's musical plays, illustrating the breadth and depth of his lyrical creativity, and highlighting the diverse identities of the collaborators and performers with whom he worked. Though the style of these works varies, they are linked together by his creative thread, and his ability to craft barbed and witty observations of his social world. Given the frequent performances of many of Coward's works, including *Private Lives* (1930), *Blithe Spirit* (1941) and *Present Laughter* (1942), this volume is a timely portrait of Coward's oeuvre and its lasting influence on the wider world of musical theatre.

---

1   Dominic McHugh, 'Noël Coward: Sui Generis'. In *The Oxford Handbook of the British Musical.* (Oxford: Oxford University Press, 2017).

Introduction   vii

Part I: 1920s and 1930s: The Cochran Revue

This Year of Grace (1928)

This Year of Grace, also known as *Cochran's 1928 Revue*, represents the pinnacle of the style of the Charles B. Cochran revue. The show opened on 28 February 1928 at the Palace Theatre in Manchester, UK, and was one of Coward's only shows to successfully transfer to Broadway. An anonymous critic remarked on the 'all British company' which Cochran took over to New York, stating: 'The revue, which is of a peculiarly British character in all its aspects, will be reproduced in its entirety without any concession to New York tastes. This is the first time such a thing has been attempted for several years.'[2] While in New York, Coward met Aimee McPherson, the American evangelist who was captivated by Coward's work and remarked that 'Dance, Dance, Little Lady' reminded her of one of her sermons.

Consisting of performances by four lead performers and considerable ensemble including Cochran's 'Young Ladies' it comprises sketches and musical numbers that reflect London life in the late 1920s. Sketches include 'A Tube Station' and 'The Theatre Guide', with lush dance numbers and comic solos and duets interspersed, including the hit song 'World Weary'. Staged by Frank Collins, with stage and costume design by Gladys Calthrop and Doris Zinkeisen, and with several dances choreographed by Max Rivers, the production also featured several dances choreographed by Tilly Losch. Taken together, these sketches with barbed social observations (explained to modern readers through critical notes), song lyrics and description provide a portrait of one of the most enduring theatrical genres in British theatre.

Bitter Sweet (1929)

Bitter Sweet is the pinnacle Coward's musical achievement with producer Charles B. Cochran.[3] The British production opened on 2 July 1929 at the Palace Theatre in Manchester, before going on to a London run of 697 performances, as well as a modest Broadway transfer produced by Florenz Ziegfeld (1867–1932). It has been subsequently revived several times and was adapted into a moderately successful Hollywood film starring Jeanette MacDonald and Nelson Eddy in 1940. The style of the work, which he termed an 'operette', was Coward's unique contribution to musical theatre form, and was meant to evoke the idea of the operetta whilst focusing on the style of playwriting and character-driven narratives that otherwise defined his work. Although the form may have been unique to this work, the focus on character-driven narratives was reminiscent of his earlier works.

In a uniquely Coward style, it brings the world of late nineteenth-century Europe to life with the aesthetic sensibilities of the Gay Nineties and melodramatic dialogue.[4]

---

2   Anonymous, '*Bitter Sweet*', *Northampton Chronicle and Echo*, Tuesday 16 1929.
3   See, for instance, Charles B. Cochran's memoir, *A Showman Looks On* (London: J.M. Dent & Sons, 1945).
4   See Vernon Woodhouse, 'English Actress's Big Success in U.S.A.', *The People*, Sunday 27 October 1929 (Charles B. Cochran Collection, Scrapbook 60, GB/THM/97/60).

Actress Peggy Wood recalled: 'I have known Noël for ten years ... He is saying in *Bitter Sweet* what he has always said. He points a finger of scorn at a certain section of contemporary society and cries "look at it; isn't it awful!" then he shows us another generation which had a sense of dignity and knew romance.'[5] It is narrated through a series of dramatic flashbacks spun out through various musical styles, as the protagonist Sarah (who is later called Sari) recalls her relationship with music teacher Carl Linden.

Bitter Sweet is Coward's most conventional operetta-style musical play, replete with a Ruritanian setting, lush waltz numbers, extended chorus numbers and romantic duets that charmed audiences with its sentimental musical style. Although the story of the work came easily to Coward, his friend and secretary Cole Lesley remembered: 'Noël finished the book of *Bitter Sweet* with no trouble, but the score would not come so easily; try as he might the one big waltz number, always so necessary to him in his musicals, refused to materialize.'[6] Nevertheless, each of the musical styles in the work calls to mind the Austro-German operetta that was so popular during Coward's childhood.

Words and Music (1932)

The height of Coward's revue style for Charles B. Cochran, *Words and Music* consists of sketches and musical numbers that showcase the world of performance and upper-crust society in which Coward lived, whilst simultaneously exposing the cracks in their sparkling world. This revue was also an artistic response to the Cochran revues of Cole Porter (1891–1964), the American sophisticate who had gained a foothold in London theatre. Porter's revue of 1929 entitled *Wake Up and Dream* had been written on the heels of Coward's *This Year of Grace*, leading to a comparison between the two creators. An anonymous critic argued of *Wake Up and Dream*: 'The show isn't *quite* so good as *This Year of Grace* ...'[7] Still, Porter and Cochran would go on to collaborate on more than half a dozen revues and large-scale productions before Coward's professional dispute led to the dissolution of his working relationship with Cochran.

In this revue we see Coward's comic lyric style in such numbers as 'Mad Dogs and Englishmen', 'Mad About the Boy' and 'The Party's Over Now', all of which became commercial hits for Coward as well as countless cover versions. Replete with ballet scenes, a Victorian-style tableau, appearances by female heroines of days past – including Restoration theatre star Nell Gwynn (1650–87) – a series of comic poems, a farcical setting of *Journey's End* and a sketch about socially aware youngsters, this revue embodied the creative and innovative spirit of 1930s London. The musical numbers, sketches and descriptions that follow give us a better understanding of the overarching aesthetic of the witty and glamorous 1930s Coward revue.

---

5 Anonymous, 'Noël Coward at Rehearsals: Peggy Wood Talks About *Bitter Sweet*', *The Era*, Wednesday 31 July 1929, p. 9.
6 Cole Lesley, *Remembered Laughter* (New York: Alfred Knopf Publishers, 1976), 125.
7 Anonymous, '*Bitter Sweet*', *The Tatler*, no. 1452, Wednesday 24 April 1929.

The diverse elements in this production were bolstered by an equally varied group of creators who took part in the work's development. They include the Black choreographer Buddy Bradley (1905–72), whom Cochran recruited from America. Although nothing remains of Bradley's choreography, it is likely that he oversaw much of the dance collaborations and musical choices made by Coward and Cochran's musical mistress and Coward's amanuensis, Elsie April (1884–1950).[8]

Words and Music opened in London at the Adelphi Theatre on 16 September 1932, after a brief Manchester try-out in August of that year. It ran for 164 performances, with a cast of forty-seven and a large ensemble. Coward's godson and biographer Sheridan Morley notes that Coward also directed the production, demonstrating his artistic involvement in the production.[9] It starred Cochran luminaries Ivy St Helier, Joyce Barbour, Romney Brent, John Mills and Coward's later longtime partner, young Graham Payn, in a small role.[10] Although this was not the longest-running Cochran revue for Coward, it demonstrates his skills as a multifaceted composer and playwright, and the comic style we see in later works such as *Blithe Spirit* (1941) or *Present Laughter* (1942).

Part II: Post-war Musical Plays

Pacific 1860 (1946)

Pacific 1860, set in a fictional British colony in the Pacific during the reign of Queen Victoria, features intermingled portraits of imperialism and cultural nostalgia. With a cast of twenty-five, including eighteen female roles and seven male roles, this work is a stylistic combination of operetta and musical comedy. Operatic prima donna Elena Salvador, originally portrayed by Mary Martin, navigates snobbery from the island's social establishment as she balances romance and career amidst the lush backdrop of Pacific island life. The show was the first to play at the newly reopened Theatre Royal, Drury Lane, which had been badly damaged during the Second World War, on 19 December 1946 and ran for 129 performances.

Ace of Clubs (1949)

Set in a nightclub in London, this book musical is Coward's response to the Beatnik generation of the late 1940s. The show brought to life characters found in the gritty

---

8 Cochran's employment and naming of Bradley during a time in which Black creators were so rarely credited demonstrates his commitment to innovative entertainment while indicating that his theatres were likely some of the most progressive in 1920s and 1930s London. For more on the contributions of Bradley, see Sean Mayes and Sarah K. Whitfield, *An Inconvenient Black History of British Musical Theatre, 1900–1950* (London: Bloomsbury Methuen Drama, 2021).
9 Sheridan Morley, *Noël Coward* (London: Haus Publishing), 54.
10 According to Barry Day, after Payn performed 'Nearer My God to Thee' whilst tap dancing Coward declared, 'We've got to have the kid in the show' (Barry Day, *The Letters of Noël Coward* (London: Bloomsbury Methuen Drama, 2007), 280).

world of a Soho nightclub include gangsters, juvenile delinquents, detectives and nightclub performers, with some of his most recognizable songs, including 'I Like America'. Written, composed and directed by Coward, the cast includes nineteen female roles and twenty-one male roles. The show opened at the Cambridge Theatre in London on 7 July 1950 after a Manchester try-out, and ran for 211 performances, starring Graham Payn, Pat Kirkwood, Sylvia Cecil and Myles Eason.

The show is largely forgotten today; however, it included several of his most popular songs, including 'Chase Me, Charlie', 'I Like America' and an early version of 'Sail Away'. Although it has long been painted as a flop, in fact it enjoyed a successful three-week try-out in Manchester before playing Birmingham on its way to London. It opened under a great deal of secrecy, as was typical of a Coward show of the era. As the *Manchester Evening News* noted: 'There have been lockings of stage doors and rehearsals and a steady refusal to "let anyone in on" the new musical play.'[11] Coward's comical yet cynical examination of London's darker side remains as an example of his experimentation and creativity in the 1940s and 1950s. This was Coward's first foray in musical theatre into the darker side of life, combining characteristic comedy with moments of seduction and violence.

Part III: Broadway Plays of the 1960s

Sail Away (1961)

The last work for which Coward wrote both book and music, *Sail Away* opened on Broadway on 3 October 1961, running for 167 performances, followed by a West End staging with a run of 252 performances at the Savoy Theatre in 1962. Critic Sam Zolotow stated that the musical has been 'marking time since 1959', noting that it was originally intended to be called *Later than Spring*. Coward once again assumed the majority of creative direction for the play, providing music, lyrics and book, as well as serving as the play's director.[12] This had long been part of the Coward 'brand', his ability to work across multiple areas and exert precise artistic control over all aspects of his work.

The musical tells the story of American divorcee Mimi Paragon, played by Elaine Stritch, who works on a British cruise ship as a whacky, larger-than-life hostess, where she meets the dashing younger Johnny Van Mier. Coward expressed his concerns about working with Stritch, whom he described as 'wildly enthusiastic and very funny', but noted: 'However, I think I shall be able to manage her. If I can, all will be fine and dandy, if not ze scenes will be terrible [*sic*]. I must engage an expert understudy.' Later Stritch shot back with, 'Not only didn't he get an expert understudy, but I ended up playing both parts.'[13] One wonders if he recalled his earlier interactions with other troublesome stars like Mary Martin and Gertrude Lawrence.

---

11 Anonymous, '*Ace of Clubs*', *Manchester Evening News*, Tuesday 16 May 1950.
12 Sam Zolotow, 'Coward Musical Slated for Fall; "*Sail Away*" Is Planned for October', *New York Times*, 30 March 1961.
13 Mel Gussow, 'Finding Fame Wittily, with Coward as Guide', *New York Times*, 2 November 1999.

In addition to casting complications, the musical style of the work combines Coward's penchant for social comedy with the musical style of the 1960s Broadway musical. The cast included twenty-one female roles and twenty-two male roles. Musical highlights include Coward's distinctive bite in 'Why Do the Wrong People Travel?' and 'Where Shall I Find Him?' sung here by Coward. *Sail Away* could have been mistaken for a pre-war musical, were it not for Joe Layton's choreography which struck a contemporary note. Yet it was not a hit in New York. Coward lamented: 'It is perfectly possible that I *am* out of touch with the times. Have I really ... reached the crucial moment when I should retire from the fray and spend my remaining years sorting out my memories and sentimentalizing the past at my expense', clearly anxious that he was past his creative prime.[14]

Despite the lacklustre critical response, Coward's lyrics still pushed the limits of what a musical play could do, including controversial enough lyrics to receive the censure of the BBC ban. *New York Times* noted: 'Four saucy songs from the Noël Coward Broadway show *Sail Away* have been banned from British radio. They are thought to offend on the ground of general taste,' said a spokesman for the British Broadcasting Corporation.[15] The offending songs in question included 'The Passenger's Always Right', its reprise 'The Customer's Always Right', 'Useful Phrases' and 'Why Do the Wrong People Travel?'. The latter became a signature tune for Elaine Stritch.

The Girl Who Came to Supper (1963)

The second of Coward's trio of late Broadway works, *The Girl Who Came to Supper*, is the last work for which he composed the complete score. With music and lyrics by Coward and book by Harry Kurnitz, the story draws from playwright Terence Rattigan's 1953 play *The Sleeping Prince* – a work which Broadway producer Herman Levin had long desired to see in musical form. Set in London during George V's coronation in 1911, this romantic musical comedy centres on the story of American chorus girl Mary Morgan who falls in love with Balkan archduke Charles after he sees her performance in a West End musical called *The Coconut Girl*.

The play opened in New York at the Broadway Theatre on 8 December 1963, running for 112 performances, with orchestrations by Robert Russell Bennett, who contributed so much to creating create the twentieth-century Broadway sound. The cast reflects the lavish style of the 1960s musical, including twenty-four male roles and twenty-one female roles, with the cast doubling several minor roles with the chorus. Although the musical style of the work reflects a different approach to musical theatre for Coward, it nevertheless aligns with the style of the large-scale West End musicals and their American imitations from this era. This includes shows such as Lionel Bart's *Oliver!* (1960), Anthony Newley and Leslie Bricusse's *Stop the World – I Want to Get Off* (1961) and *Baker Street* (1965) produced by Harold Prince; all of which capitalized on the American fascination with nostalgic portraits of British culture.

---

14 Philip Hoare, *Noël Coward: A Biography* (Chicago: University of Chicago Press, 1998), 472.
15 Anonymous, 'British Bar "Sail Away" Songs', *New York Times*, 19 June 1962.

References

Anonymous. 'A Dainty Ballet: British Prima Ballerina's Success in *Coppélia*'. *The Daily Chronicle*, 10 November 1924.
Anonymous. '*Ace of Clubs*'. *Manchester Evening News*, Tuesday 16 May 1950.
Anonymous. 'Aid for Songwriters: Leslie Boosey at P.R.S. Lunch'. *The Stage*, Thursday 2 July 1953.
Anonymous. 'Among the Newer Leading Ladies in Broadway Musicals'. *New York Times*, 5 January, 1964.
Anonymous. '*Bitter Sweet*'. *Northampton Chronicle and Echo*, 16 Tuesday 1929.
Anonymous. '*Bitter Sweet*'. *The Tatler*, no. 1452, Wednesday 24, 1929.
Anonymous. 'British Bar "*Sail Away* Songs"'. *New York Times*, 19 June 1962.
Anonymous. 'The Cambridge: *Ace of Clubs*'. *The Stage*, Thursday 13 July 1950.
Anonymous. 'Cochran'. *The Evening News*, 9 November 1924.
Anonymous. 'Coward Explains – It's Only Satire'. *Birmingham Daily Gazette*, Friday 30 June 1950.
Anonymous. 'Coward Show Lost'. *Daily Herald*, Wednesday 17 September 1947.
Anonymous. 'Death of the Oldest Postmistress in Britain'. *Aberdeen Press and Journal*, Monday 21 February 1910.
Anonymous. 'Drury Lane: *Pacific 1860*'. *The Stage*, Thursday 26 December 1946.
Anonymous. 'Drury Lane Premiere', *Yorkshire Post and Leeds Intelligencer*, Friday 20 December 1946.
Anonymous. 'Greeting *Words and Music*', *The Tatler*, no. 1631, 28 September 1932, p. 32.
Anonymous. 'London Theatre: *This Year of Grace*'. *The Stage*, Thursday 29 March 1928.
Anonymous. 'Mary Martin, of *Pacific 1860*: An American Star at Drury Lane'. *The Tatler*, Wednesday 25 December 1946.
Anonymous. 'Noël Coward at Rehearsals: Peggy Wood Talks About *Bitter Sweet*'. *The Era*, Wednesday 31 July 1929, p. 9.
Anonymous. 'Noël Coward Records His Own Songs'. *Market Harborough Advertiser and Midland Mail*, Friday 18 November 1932.
Anonymous. 'Noël Coward's New Lead – Mary Martin'. *The Sketch*, Wednesday 11 December 1946.
Anonymous. 'Sacked for Political Views'. *Todmorden Advertiser and Hebden Bridge Newsletter*, 1932.
Anonymous. 'The London Theatres: Noel Coward's "*Ace of Clubs*"'. *The Scotsman*, Monday 10 July 1950.
Anonymous. 'The Principal of "Mr. Cochran's Young Ladies"'. *Illustrated Sporting and Dramatic News*, Saturday 7 April 1928.
Anonymous. '*This Year of Grace*'. *The Sketch*, Wednesday 11 April 1928.
Anonymous. '*This Year of Grace*'. The *Tatler*, Wednesday 11 April 1928.
Anonymous. 'Unemployment in 1932'. *Aberdeen Press and Journal*, Friday 7 April 1933, pg. 6.
Anonymous. Untitled article. *Glasgow Bulletin*, 8 December 1924 (Cochran Collection Scrapbook 42, GB 71 TGM/97 misc. 1924–29).
Anonymous. '*Words and Music*'. *Belfast Newsletter*, Thursday 22 September 1932.
Anonymous. '*Words and Music*'. *The Era*, Wednesday 21 September 1932.
Anonymous. '*Words and Music*'. *Nottingham Journal*, Saturday 17 September 1932, p. 7.
Cochran, Charles B. *A Showman Looks On*. London: J.M. Dent & Sons, 1945.
Day, Barry. *The Letters of Noël Coward*. London: Bloomsbury Methuen Drama, 2007.
'Fidelio'. 'The London Stage Turns the Corner.' *The Sphere*, Saturday 1 December 1928.
Grein, J. T. 'The Stage'. *The Sketch*, Wednesday 28 September 1932.

Gussow, Mel. 'Finding Fame Wittily, with Coward as Guide'. *New York Times*, 2 November 1999.
Hoare, Philip. *Noël Coward: A Biography*. Chicago: University of Chicago Press, 1998.
Lesley, Cole. *Remembered Laughter*. New York: Alfred Knopf Publishers, 1976.
Lewin, David. 'But the Backstage Party Was Ecstatic'. *The Daily Express*, 2 November 1951.
London, Louise. *Whitehall and the Jews, 1933–1948: British Immigration Policy, Jewish Refugees and the Holocaust*. Cambridge: Cambridge University Press, 2001.
Mayes, Sean and Sarah K. Whitfield. *An Inconvenient Black History of British Musical Theatre, 1900–1950*. London: Bloomsbury Methuen Drama, 2021.
McHugh, Dominic. 'Noël Coward: Sui Generis'. In *The Oxford Handbook of the British Musical*. Oxford: Oxford University Press, 2017.
Morley, Sheridan. *Noël Coward*. London: Haus Publishing.
Riis, Thomas L. 'The Experience and Impact of Black Entertainers in England, 1895–1920.' *American Music* 4, no. 1 (1986): 50–8.
Taubman, Howard. 'Theatre: Girl Who Came to Supper in Premier: José Ferrer is Star of Musical at Broadway'. *New York Times*, 9 December 1963.
Toynbee, Jason and Catherine Tackley. 'Black British Jazz: Routes, Ownership and Performance'. *American Music* 4, no. 1 (1986): 50–8.
Wattslondon, Stephen. 'Sturdy Traditions: Tessie O'Shea's Local Triumph Stirs Memories of English Music Halls'. *New York Times*, 16 February 1964.
Wilson, John S. 'International Romance: An International Romance Set to Music Coward's Score'. *New York Times*, 8 December 1963.
Woodhouse, Vernon. 'English Actress's Big Success in U.S.A.', *The People*, Sunday 27 October 1929.
Zolotow, Sam. 'Coward Musical Slated for Fall: "Sail Away" Is Planned for October'. *New York Times*, 30 March 1961.

PART I
1920s and 1930s: The Cochran Revue

This Year of Grace

Critics' Notes

Critics remarked on Coward's unique style in crafting the revue. One critic noted:

> Coward has shown his versatility, his sense of the stage, his powers of satire, and his skill in fashioning effective musical numbers as author and composer of Mr Cochran's *1928 Revue* . . . [it] is indeed a splendid show from beginning to end . . . Mr Coward has a hit at the flocks of shepherded queuers-up, one of the bequests of the war, together with the equally ridiculous army of straphangers, right on to the second finale . . . In between we have a number of clever and commendably brief skits on various phases of modern life, such as the dancing craze and the holiday habit, and as the Eternal Triangle, treated very succinctly, and not in the long and tedious manner to be noted in so many revues. Mr Coward's music if jazzish now and then, does not disdain some lively and well-turned tunes . . .[1]

The primary draw for the production was the cast, including Jessie Matthews, praised by the *Illustrated Sporting and Dramatic News* for 'making this revue one of the best London has ever seen'.[2] *The Tatler* remarked that the stars were supported by Cochran's female ensemble of which were 'what Americans would call a "bunch" of pretty "buds". Altogether a very important part of the show which everyone in London is going to see.'[3] The work was also highly praised in the United States as one of the few successful transfers from the London stage. According to *The Sphere*: 'So much has been written about *This Year of Grace*, the Noël Coward revue which Charles B. Cochran produced at the Pavilion, that it is better to consider the remarkable fact that its duplicate production in New York the other night was not only received with a torrent of praise, but was the first English musical show which the Americans had seen for years.'[4] On both sides of the Atlantic, it was clear that the production set the standard for the 1920s Cochran revue, and exemplified the Noël Coward brand of sparkling entertainment.

Original Cast

Part I

1. A Tube Station

Fred (*a bookstall attendant*)   Fred Groves[5]

Female Passengers: Madeline Gibson, Florita Fey, Greta Taylor, Marjorie Robertson, Betty Davis, Gladys Godby, Peter May, Marjorie Browne, Peggy Wynne, Marie

---

1 Anonymous, 'London Theatre: This Year of Grace', *The Stage*. Thursday 29 March 1928.
2 Anonymous, 'The Principal of "Mr Cochran's Young Ladies"', *Illustrated Sporting and Dramatic News*, Saturday 7 April 1928.
3 *The Tatler*, Wednesday 11 April 1928.
4 'Fidelio', 'The London Stage Turns the Corner', *The Sphere*, Saturday 1 December 1928.

Masters, Rosalind Wade, Nancy Barnett, Decilia Monbray, Doreen Austin, Nancy Fielder, Isla Bevan, Nora Olive, Kathleen Coram

An office boy   Tommy Hayes[6]

Male passengers: Arthur Warren, Syd Shields, Eddie Grant, Edward Coventry, Charles Farey, Frank Fox, Richard Hadyon, Fred Le Roy, Fred Herries

Bank Clerk	Sonnie Hale[7]
Lift Man	Billy Shaw[8]
Lady Gwendolyn Verney	Madge Aubrey[9]
Hon. Millicent Bloodworthy	Ann Codrington[10]
Harry (*a booking clerk*)	Lance Lister[11]
Charles	Douglas Byng[12]
Mary	Jessie Matthews[13]
1st Girl	Sheilah Graham[14]
2nd Girl	Moya Nugent[15]

Song 'Waiting in a Queue'   Sonnie Hale

2. 'Mary Make Believe'

Jessie Matthews and Mr Cochran's Young Ladies

3. The Theatre Guide

Announcer	Lance Lister
Page	Nora Olive[16]

---

5 Fred Groves (1880–1955) was a British actor known for his appearances in such woks as Coward's *Cavalcade*.
6 Unknown actor and singer
7 John Robert 'Sonnie' Hale-Monro (1902–59), was an actor, screenwriter and director who was known early on for his revue performances, including Cole Porter's *Wake Up and Dream* (1929).
8 Billy Shaw was a revue performer known for minor roles in such works as Rodgers and Hart's *Lido Lady* (1927).
9 Madge Aubrey (1902–70) was an English stage actor, who made her first professional stage appearance in *The Fatal Wedding* (1912).
10 Ann Codrington (1894–1982) was an English stage and film actor, known for such films as *No Place for Jennifer* (1950).
11 Lance Lister was a revue performer known for minor roles in such works as *Looking at You* (1929).
12 Douglas Coy Byng (1893–1987) was an English comic singer and songwriter, known for his female impersonations. He appeared in Charles B. Cochran and Coward's *On with the Dance* (1925) and was also a noted pantomime dame.
13 Jessie Matthews (1907–81) was an English stage and film actress, dancer and singer, who starred in both Cochran revues and films including *First a Girl* (1935).
14 Sheilah Graham (1904–88) was a British-born American gossip columnist, and part-time actor, known for her relationship with F. Scott Fitzgerald.
15 Moya Nugent (1901–54) was a British stage actor, known for her performances in Cole Porter's West End revues and Noël Coward works including *Cavalcade*, *Words and Music*, *Operette* and *Pacific 1860*.
16 Nora Olive (?) was a London revue performer. Other stage credits include Charles B. Cochran's *One Dam Thing After Another* (1927).

6   This Year of Grace

A. 'The Trial of Mary Dugan'
The Judge Melville Cooper[17]
Mary Dugan Moya Nugent
Mrs Rice Ann Codrington
District Attorney Fred Groves[18]
Mary's Brother Fred Le Roy[19]
Two Policemen Eddie Grant[20]
Edward Coventry[21]

A Luncher Syd Shields[22]

B. 'Show Boat'
Joe Snowball[23]

C. 'Young Woodley'
Two Schoolboys Lance Lister
Douglas Byng

D. 'Any Noël Coward Play'
The Leading Lady Madge Aubrey
Her Support Ann Codrington
Arthur Warren[24]
Nancy Fieldera[25]
Cecil Stafford

E. 'The Squeaker'
Bill Anerley Fred Groves
Jim (*his son*) Syd Shields

4. 'Mad About You'

Sheilah Graham, William Cavanagh and Mr Cochran's Young Ladies

Speciality Dance Jean Barry[26]
Jack Holland[27]

---

17 Melville Cooper was a London revue performer. Other stage credits include Charles B. Cochran's *One Dam Thing After Another* (1927).
18 Fred Groves was a revue performer known for minor roles in works including *Autumn Fire* (1926) and *Do You Remember?* (1929).
19 Fred Le Roy was known for works such as *Tip-Toes* (1926) and *The Blue Train* (1927).
20 Eddie Grant was an actor and singer known for minor revue performances, including the revues of Charles B. Cochran.
21 Edward Coventry was a London revue performer.
22 Syd Shields was a London revue performer.
23 Edwin 'Snowball' Harris was a Black American performer who appeared in New York, Paris and London. Not much is known about his life and work.
24 Unknown actor and singer.
25 Nancy Fielder was a revue performer for Charles B. Cochran. Other credits include Cole Porter's *Wake Up and Dream* (1929).
26 Unknown actor and singer.
27 Unknown actor and singer.

5. 'The "Bus Rush"'

The People: Maisie Gay, Madge Aubrey, Tommy Hayes, Robert Algar, Betty Shale, Moya Nugent, Betty Davis, Ann Coddrington, Nancy Fielder, Arthur Warren, Cecil Stafford

6. 'Lorelei'

Singers	Paul Ruby[28]
	Sonnie Hale
Lorelei	Lauri Devine[29]
Sailor	William Cavanagh[30]

7. Snowball

8. 'Ignorance Is Bliss'

A. 1890

Mrs Blake (*Proprietress of Private Hotel*)	Maisie Gay
Husband	Sonnie Hale
Wife	Jessie Matthews
Annie (*a Servant*)	Moya Nugent

B. 1928

Reception Clerk	Douglas Byng
Husband	Lance Lister
Wife	Madge Aubrey
Page	Tommy Hayes

9. The Golfers

Billy Shaw, Frank Fox, Arthur Warren, Charles Farey, Eddie Grant, Syd Shields

10. 'A Room with a View'

Jessie Matthews, Sonnie Hale and Paula Ruby

11. Griffith Bros. and Miss Lutie[31]

Present their famous Performing Horse, 'Pogo'

12. 'Teach Me to Dance Like Grandma'

Jessie Matthews and Mr Cochran's Young Ladies

---

28 Unknown actor and singer.
29 Unknown actor and singer.
30 William Cavanagh was a revue performer. Other credits include *Looking at You* (1929).
31 A variety act for Cochran. Other credits include Cole Porter's *Wake Up and Dream* (1929).

8   This Year of Grace

Polka   Nancy Barnett[32]
Mazurka   Nancy Barnett
                                                       Sonnie Hale

Polka Children: Gladys Godby, Marie Masters, Betty Davis, Decilia Mobray, Isla Bevan, Nora Olive, Kathleen Coram, Doreen Austin

Young Ladies: Peter May, Florita Fey, Greta Taylor, Marjorie Browne, Peggy Wynne, Madeline Gibson, Jean Barnes, Marjorie Robertson

Young Gentlemen: Arthur Warren, Edward Coventry, Billy Shaw, Frank Fox, Richard Haydon, Charles Farey, Fred Herries, Fred Le Roy

The Three Graces:
Taglioni   Jessie Matthews
Grisi   Sheilah Graham
Ellsler   Moya Nugent
Waltz   Jean Barry
                                                       Jack Holland

Finale   The Entire Company

Part II

13. The Lido Beach

The Contessa   Betty Shale
Lady Fenchurch   Norah Howard
Lady Saltwood   Ann Condrington
Lady Verlap   Lauri Devine
Sir John Verlap   Robert Algar
Sir Frederick Saltwood   Sonnie Hale
The Conte   Fred Groves
Sir Charles Fenchurch   Lance Lister
Young Man   William Cavanagh
Baroness Kurdle   Douglas Byng
Mr Clark   Cecil Stafford
Violet   Jessie Matthews
Ruth   Sheilah Graham
Jane   Madge Aubrey
Ivy   Moya Nugent

Opening Chorus 'Little Women'
Jessie Matthews, Sheilah Graham, Madge Aubrey, Moya Nugent

---

32   Nancy Barnett was a revue performer for Cochran. Other credits include Cole Porter's *Wake Up and Dream* (1929).

14. The English Lido Beach

Announcer	Lance Lister
Mr Freeman	Fred Groves
Mrs Freeman	Ann Codrington
Alice	Moya Nugent
Frankie	Tommy Hayes
Official	Melville Cooper
Madge	Sheilah Graham
Doris	Marjorie Browne[33]
Mr Harris	Sonnie Hale
Mrs Harris	Norah Howard
Vi	Kitty Jacobs[34]
George	Jack Kosky[35]
Mrs Clark	Madge Aubrey
Phyllis	Lolita Hudson[36]
Mrs Jones	Betty Shale
Daisy Kipshaw	Maisie Gay

Opening Chorus 'Mother's Complaint'

Ann Codrington, Norah Howard, Madge Aubrey, Betty Shale

'Britannia Rules the Waves'
Maisie Gay and Company

15. Ballet 'The Legend of the Lily of the Valley'

Announcer	Sonnie Hale
Flannelette	Luisi Blackburn
Berganot	Lauri Devin

Fairies: Florita Fey, Marjorie Robertson, Gladys Godby, Marjorie Browne, Nora Olive, Madeline Gibson

Female Courtiers: Betty Davis, Marie Masters, Nancy Barnett, Nancy Fielder, Isla Bevan, Kathleen Cowan

Male Courtiers: Arthur Warren, Charles Farey, Edward Coventry, Richard Haydon, Fred Le Roy, Fred Herries

Marquis de Poopinac	Douglas Byng

---

33 Marjorie Browne was a revue performer for Cochran. Other credits include *One Dam Thing After Another* (1927).
34 Unknown actor and singer.
35 Unknown actor and singer.
36 Lolita Hudson was a stage actor known for Shakespeare and the revues of Charles B. Cochran.

16. 'Rules of Three'

Announcer	Lance Lister

A. Barrie
The Wife	Moya Nugent
The Lover	Melville Cooper
The Husband	Fred Groves

B. Lonsdale
The Wife	Jessie Matthews
The Lover	Sonnie Hale
The Butler	William Cavanagh
The Husband	Lance Lister

C. Wallace
The Wife	Ann Codrington
The Lover	Douglas Byng
The Husband	Robert Algar

17. 'Dance Little Lady'   Sonnie Hale

The Little Lady	Lauri Devine

Dancers: Betty Davis, Gladys Godby, Peter May, Marjorie Browne, Nora Olive, Kathleen Coran, Billy Shaw, Arthur Warren, Syd Shields, Eddie Grant, Edward Coventry, Frank Fox

18. 'Chauve Souris'

The Great Man	Lance Lister

Singers: Maisie Gay, Fred Groves, Sonnie Hale, Douglas Byng, Robert Algar

19. 'Gothic'

Luise Blackburn[37]
Lauri Devine

Music by Johann Sebastian Bach

20. 'Try to Learn to Love'

Jessie Matthews, Sonnie Hale and Mr Cochran's Young Ladies

21. 'It Doesn't Matter How Old You Are'

Maisie Gay

---

37 Luise Blackburn was a London revue performer. Other credits include *Shake Your Feet* (1927) and *Morning, Noon and Night* (1929).

22. A Spanish Fantasy

Jean Barry and Jack Holland

23. 'Law and Order'

Policewoman Pellet	Douglas Byng
Matchseller	Betty Shale
Young Girl	Moya Nugent
Young Man	Edward Coventry
Policewoman Wendle	Maisie Gay

Scene by Marc Henri and Laverdet

24. Finale   The Entire Company

Crew:
Orchestral Direction	Ernest Irving
Pianist	Elsie April
General Stage Manager	Frank Collins
Stage Director	Sidney C. Sinclair

Act One

Scene One

Characters

Bank Clerk
Lift Man
Fred
Harry
Lady Gwendolyn Verney
Hon. Millicent Bloodworthy
Charles
Mary
1st Girl
2nd Girl – etc.
Urchin

Opening Scene – The Tube

The scene is the booking-office of an underground railway station.

There is a newspaper stand on the left and on the right on an angle upstage are the lift gates which are closed.

Three people come on quite quietly – buy papers and tickets at the slot machines, then take their stand by the lift. They open their papers and read them – a dirty little **Urchin** *enters, gets a ticket and also takes his stand, then gradually two by two and in groups the entire company come on (with the exception of a few principals required in the ensuing scene). Everyone is completely preoccupied and dressed in ordinary work-a-day clothes, and there should be no sound at all but the click of the slot machine and the rustle of newspapers. Suddenly the little* **Urchin** *who has been unable to afford a paper begins to whistle through his teeth – quite softly at first. One or two people lower their papers and regard him rather impatiently for a moment – the tune he is whistling is a very definite dance rhythm – he whistles a little louder – a woman a few feet away from him, without looking up, begins to shuffle her feet – then the woman starts again – gradually as the* **Urchin**'s *whistle gets louder, everyone starts moving slightly – the* **Man** *at the bookstall takes up the tune and hums it carelessly, then almost imperceptibly at first, the orchestra takes up the tune – it swells louder until everybody is dancing hard. At this moment a young* **Bank Clerk** *rushes in hurriedly, buys a ticket and a paper – looks at everyone jigging about – recognizes the tune and sings it.*

Bank Clerk *sings one verse, one chorus.* **Bank Clerk** *and* **Chorus** *sing one chorus, and into dance as arranged.*

'Waiting in a Queue'

Verse:

In a rut
In a rut
In a rut
We go along
Nothing but
Nothing but
The same old song,
To those who view us lightly
We must seem slightly
Absurd,
We never break the ritual
One habitual
Herd.

Refrain:

Waiting in a queue
Waiting in a queue
Everybody's always waiting in a queue,
Fat and thin
They all begin
To take their stand – it's grand – queuing it.
Everywhere you go
Everywhere you go
Everybody's always standing in a row,
Short and tall
And one and all
The same as sheep – just keep – doing it.
No one says why
No one says how
No one says what is this for,
No one says no
No one says go
Non one says this is a bore,
If you want to do
Anything that's new,
If you're feeling happy, furious or blue,
Wet or fine
You get in line
For everybody's waiting in a queue.

At the end of the number the lift comes up – the **Attendant** *dances out and everyone dances in, the* **Bank Clerk** *and the* **Attendant** *last.*

The gates close and the lift disappears and the **Man** *in the bookstall stops humming as the rhythm dies away in the orchestra.*

Enter first entrance right **Lady Gwendolyn Verney** *and the* **Hon. Millicent Bloodworthy***, elaborately and expensively dressed. They look round, slightly bewildered.*

Lady Gwendolyn   What do we do now, darling?

Millicent   Get our tickets, I suppose.

Lady Gwendolyn   Yes, but where? Life's agony, isn't it?

Millicent   Torture, dear – but it's no use grumbling – we can't possibly use our cars with all the roads up – We must just be brave and do what the common people do.

Lady Gwendolyn   It all seems very complicated. (*Turns and sees ticket machines.*) Look at these funny grey things!

Millicent   Those must be the ticket machines.

Lady Gwendolyn   My dear, how delicious! We must put in some pennies, or something.

Millicent   I haven't any change.

Lady Gwendolyn   Neither have I. We'll get it at the bookstall.

Millicent (*crosses to news-stand*)   Have you got *Vogue*?

Fred *is in front of newspaper stand.*

Fred   'Ave I got wot?

Millicent   *Vogue*.[38]

Fred   Wot's that?

Lady Gwendolyn   It's a paper, I'm afraid.

Fred   I got *Tit-Bits Answers*,[39] an' all the 'dailies'.

Millicent   Have you change for a pound?

Fred   Mostly in pennies, mum.

Lady Gwendolyn   How divine – we can buy things with them.

Fred   I shouldn't do that, ma'am, if I was you. I should send them to the British Museum as curiosities.

---

38 American fashion magazine since 1892.
39 A weekly magazine geared towards young adults, published from 1888 to 1948.

Goes to back of stall and gets change.

Millicent   Here's the pound.

Fred (*counting out change*)   There y'are, lady. There's three-and-six in coppers, five and five's ten, and ten's a pound.

Millicent   Thank you a thousand times.

Fred   It's a pleasure, so 'elp me God.

Lady Gwendolyn   Come along, darling. (*Crosses to machines.*)

Millicent (*putting a penny in the ticket machine*)   It's really quite an adventure, isn't it?

The ticket comes out.

Lady Gwendolyn   I'm thrilled – we must have some more.

She puts in several pennies.

Millicent (*also cramming pennies in*)   What tremendous fun!

Fred   'Ere, 'ere, 'ere, wot you think you're doing?

He comes over to the machine.

Lady Gwendolyn   I'm afraid it's stuck.

Fred   This ain't Wembley,[40] you know. (*He shakes the machine.*)

Millicent   There now – I've got fourteen. How many have you, darling?

Lady Gwendolyn   I've got tons.

Fred   Wot's the idea? That's what I want to know. Wot's the idea? Where d'yer want to go?

Lady Gwendolyn   Well, we want ultimately to get to the Ritz.

Fred (*crosses to right shouting*)   'Arry, 'Arry, come 'ere!

Harry   'Allo!

Harry, *the booking-clerk, comes out of his office and comes to centre.*

What's the matter?

Fred   'Ere's a couple of bejewelled duchesses bunging up one of the ' 'ow-d'yer-do's'.

Harry (*shaking the machine*)   What d'you want to come mucking about 'ere for? You ought to be at home looking after your children.

Millicent   We happen to be unmarried.

---

40 Wembley Stadium in London.

Fred   I shouldn't 'ave thought you'd let a little thing like that stand in yer way.

Lady Gwendolyn   Horrible brute!

Fred   Who's 'orrible?

Millicent   Come away, Gwen dear, they're insulting us.

Goes off first exit left

Lady Gwendolyn   There are your ridiculous tickets.

She throws them over both the men and goes out grandly first exit left

Harry   Well, I'll be damned!

Fred   There you are – that's class.

Harry   Class, phew! If my old woman made up 'er eyes like that, I'd lock 'er in the scullery!

Fred   Wot do they want to come nosing round 'ere for – bloated aristocrats?

Harry   You know the trouble with you, Fred, is you're a bit Bolshie.[41]

Fred   No, all this democracy makes life 'ellish uncomfortable.

Harry   What we want in England is more and better birth control.

Fred   Oh no, we don't

Harry   Oh yes, we do.

Fred   It's men like you as is responsible for the birth-rate falling.

Harry   Well, if you're responsible for it rising, you ought to be ashamed of yourself. This country's overpopulated.

Enter **Charles**, *a very exquisite young man. Crosses to centre, looks at them and then goes up to ticket machines.*

Fred   No, it ain't. It's all right – you've won. I'm all for birth control.

Charles *puts a penny in the slot machine and cannot work it.*

Charles   I say! – attendant – it's stuck.

Lift rises.

Fred   Give it a shake.

Charles *shakes it gently.*

Charles   I'm afraid it's still stuck.

---

41 Slang for Bolshevik, referring to an aggressive stereotype of far-left soldiers.

Lift doors open. Exit two people right and left.

Fred   I said shake it – not stroke it! 'Ere! (**Fred** *comes over to machine.*) Where d'you want to go – anyhow?

Charles   Queen's Gate.

Fred *gives the machine a violent shake – gets ticket out, gives it to* **Charles**, *then pushes him into the lift.*

Fred   Take him away, Hubert – 'e's breaking my 'eart.

Attendant   Right!

The lift goes down.

Fred   'Arry, that's wot the Russian Ballet's[42] done for England.

Mary *enters first entrance right She is charmingly dressed and she is reading a book in which she is so engrossed that she collides with* **Fred**, *who has crossed to right centre.*

Mary   Oh, I *am* so sorry.

Fred   That's all right, miss.

Mary   Could you tell me the time, please?

Fred   About eleven o'clock.

Mary   Thank you. It doesn't matter if I wait here for a little, does it? (*Crosses to centre.*)

Fred   You can wait here as long as you like.

Two Girls *come on from first entrance left, buy tickets and wait for the lift.*

Mary   I'm expecting a friend.

Fred   Boy friend, I'll be bound.

Mary   You're quite right.

1st Girl *suddenly sees* **Mary** *and crosses to left of her.*

1st Girl   Mary!

Mary   Hallo!

1st Girl   What are you doing here?

Mary   I'm waiting for Jack Burton.

2nd Girl   Jack! We've just left him –

---

42   Reference to Sergei Diaghilev's ballet company the Ballets Russe, which toured London several times between 1909 and 1929.

Mary   Oh! Perhaps I mistook the time –

1st Girl   Didn't you have a row with him last night?

Mary   Yes – but not a serious one.

2nd Girl   Are you sure?

1st Girl   You're so difficult, you know – you won't be content with men as they are – you're always trying to alter them.

Mary   Only because they never seem a bit like what they're made out to be in books.

1st Girl   Books! Who cares about books?

Mary   I do.

Lift rises.

2nd Girl (*crosses to right*)   Life comes first, duckie. If I were you, I'd step out of my beautiful dreamland and face a bit of reality – it's more comforting in the long run.

Mary   You think I'm a fool, don't you?

Lift doors open – exit two people.

2nd Girl   Not exactly – but you're always pretending things are what they're not.

1st Girl   Here's the lift. Good-bye, Mary.

Mary   Good-bye.

They enter lift and it goes down.

Close no. tabs.

'Mary Make-Believe'

Verse:

> I have been reading in this book of mine
> About a foolish maiden's prayer
> And every gesture, word and look of mine
> Seems to be mirrored there.
> She had such terribly pedantic dreams
> That her romantic schemes
> Went all awry
> Her thoughts were such
> She claimed too much
> And true love passed her by.

Refrain:

> Mary make-believe
> Dreamed the whole day through

Foolish fancies
Love romances
How could they come true?
Mary make-believe
Sighed a little up her sleeve
Nobody claimed her
They only named her
Mary make-believe.

Counter-melody (to be sung by **Chorus**):

She's just a girl who's always blowing mental bubbles
Till she's quite out of breath – quite out of breath
She seems to have the knack of magnifying troubles
Till they crush her to death – crush her to death.
She's just a duffer of the ineffective kind
She's bound to suffer from her introspective mind
Her indecisions quite prevent her visions – coming true.
Imagination is a form of flagellation
If a sensitive child – lets it run wild
It dims the firmament till all the world is permanently blue.

She's simply bound to make a bloomer
Until she's found her sense of humour
If love should touch her ever
She'll never, never see it through.

And **Mary** *sing the refrain at the same time* **Chorus** *sing counter-melody.*

Dane *as arranged. As* **Chorus** *exit – eight* **Girls** *right and eight* **Girls** *left* **Mary** *is in centre of stage. Fade out as* **Girls** *exit.*

Close tabs on **Mary**'s *last note.*

The Theatre Guide Announcement

The **Announcer** *enters from first entrance right.*

Announcer   Ladies and gentlemen, the fact that the theatre advertisements in the daily newspapers are extremely inadequate has for a long while been a source of great sorrow to Mr Cochran;[43] he feels that the public are not sufficiently warned as to what they are to expect, by the bare unilluminating titles of plays, so therefore we propose in this revue to give you nightly a brief impression of the current dramatic successes of London – we will first condense into as brief a space as possible the general theme

---

43 Reference to producer Charles B. Cochran.

and trend of each important play running at the moment, so that before rushing blindly to Keith Prowse to book seats, you will have some idea as to what you are going to see.

The four plays given here are examples only. This scene must be kept up-to-date with current successes. Between each of the following scene a sign bearing the name of the play is shown to the audience by a **Girl** *in page's dress. She enters from first entrance left and exits same place.*

The Trial of Mary Dugan

Scene: **Judge**'s *high desk up left. Table and one chair right on which is seated an* **Old Man**. *Chair right on which is seated a* **Widow**. *Chair left on which is seated* **Mary**. **Brother** *is standing behind* **Old Man**. **Counsel** *at back of table. As curtains open all the characters are speaking at the same time.*

Judge   Objection overruled. Object sustained.

He bangs front of desk with small hammer every time he speaks.

Counsel   You killed Edgar Rice. (*Pointing at* **Mary**.)

Brother   She's my sister. (*Appealing to* **Audience**.)

Widow *opens veil several times and screams every time she does it.* **Old Man** *is discovered seated at table eating a sandwich, which he finishes, then brushes crumbs off table, puts his hat on and exits right. When he starts to go everybody stops till he is off, then starts speaking again.*

Policeman   Order in court! (*Repeating this all the time.*)

The Silver Cord

A **Young Man** *in a dressing-gown is pacing up and down thinking and smoking a cigarette. Suddenly outside the door is heard a terrible crash, followed by some shots and screams, a motor horn, a siren, a police whistle and another appalling crash.*

Young Man   What's that?

A charming **Elderly Woman** *puts her head round the door.*

Elderly Woman   It's only Mother!

Blackout.

Young Woodley

Scene: School blackboard and easel at back. Small bench in front of blackboard.

Boy (*standing behind bench*)   How do babies come?

Boy (*seated on bench sharpening a pencil*)   I will tell you.

Any Noël Coward Play

Six people are discovered standing on stage when the curtains open, **Principal** *in centre with large bunch of flowers. She comes forward. Loud applause and cries of 'Speech'.*

Principal   Ladies and gentlemen, this is the happiest moment of my life.

Boos and catcalls.

Blackout.

Dance Duet (Boy and Girl)
'Mad About You'

Boy *and* **Girl** *enter –* **Boy** *right and* **Girl** *left.*

He
>Dear, your personality
>Is bad for my morality
>It's more than I can bear.

She
>Tho' I surmise it isn't wise
>To set my cap at you
>I've lost all control and on the whole
>I can't live through a single minute
>Dear, without your image in it.

He
>When you are inclined to be
>Encouraging and kind to me
>I simply walk on air
>Maybe I'll wake up soon and break my heart
>To find that you – aren't here.

Refrain:

He
>I'd like to tell you that I'm mad about –
>Mad about you – mad about you

She
>But there is one thing that I'm sad about
>Sad about – sad about too.

He
>When you met me you swore
>You were essentially nice
>But I wasn't so sure
>When we had kissed once or twice.

She
>For all I know you're just a gadabout
>Gadabout – gadabout who
>Is always eager to exchange old love for new.

Both
>I've a feeling – you've been concealing
>A thousand or two
>Mad about, mad about, mad about you!

They exit first exit left.

Eight **Tap Dancers** *enter second exit left. Dance as arranged and exit second exit left.*

Eight **Toe Dancers** *enter second entrance left. Dance as arranged and exit second exit left.*

Speciality Dancers *(***Holland** *and* **Barry***).*

At end of number:

Close tabs.

Eight **Tap Dancers** *cross in front, followed by the eight* **Toe Dancers***, followed by the two* **Speciality Dancers***.*

Blackout.

The Bus Rush

Scene: Park railings cloth, with an ordinary bus sign right centre down on footlights.

Principal, a middle-aged **Lady** *with several parcels and balloons, enters from first entrance left. She has been shopping. She crosses to sign, looks at it and takes up her position waiting for a bus.*

Enter from first entrance right **Working Man***,* **Wife** *and small* **Child***. They look at bus sign; then take up their position right of* **Lady** *and wait.*

Enter from first entrance left, a **Middle-Class Woman***, looks at sign and stands in front of* **Lady***.* **Lady***, annoyed, comes in front of her and waits.*

Enter from first entrance left, three **Girls***. They look at sign, and stand in front of* **Lady***. She comes around them and stands in front of them.*

Enter from first entrance left, two **Men** *and one* **Girl***. They cross to sign, look at it and stand in front of* **Lady***. She, very much annoyed, comes round in front of them. At this moment a motor horn is heard off right. They all look out front, eyes slowly travelling*

Act One   23

around till they get to prompt side. They all rush off prompt side and the two **Men** *and one* **Girl** *go right off. There is an altercation with the* **Bus Conductor**. *Bus bell rings and they all come slowly back on stage to their former positions by sign.*

A motor horn is heard. Exactly the same business as before, all looking round house and rushing off. This time the three **Girls** *go right off.*

Working Man, **Wife** *and* **Child** *and* **Middle-Class Woman** *come on and take up positions by sign.* **Lady** *comes on, looks at them, and waits left centre of stage.*

Middle-Class Woman *sees this, crosses in front of* **Lady** *and takes up position left of her.* **Working Man**, **Wife** *and* **Child** *cross in front of them and take up positions to left of* **Middle-Class Woman**. *Motor horn off right. They all rush to right. When they get to sign, bus bell heard off left. They all stop – same business as before, all looking round house and rushing off. Motor horn off right. Same business as before. Altercations with* **Bus Conductor** *and the* **Lady** *comes to centre, very much beraged (sic) and parcels all crushed and pulled to pieces.*

Lady *whistles and calls: 'TAXI! TAXI!'*

Blackout.

'Lorelei'[44]

Scene: Full set.

Singer *comes on first entrance right and takes up position by floats, sings one verse and one refrain.*

Verse 1:

> When the day
> Fades away
> Twilight dies
> Sirens rise
> Combing their hair with cool green fingers
> Crooning out their song
> Let him beware who loves and lingers
> Over-long.

Refrain 1:

> Lorelei, Lorelei,
> Call to sailors drifting by
> Cooo, cooo, come hither,
> While they're sailing a voice is wailing
> A beckoning tune.
> No use prating they'll all be paying

---

44 Myth of a siren called 'Lorelei' who lured men to their downfall, made famous by German poet Heinrich Heine's 1824 poem, which sparked dozens of musical settings by Franz Liszt and others.

A reckoning soon
Under the moon.

Tabs open: **Mermaid** *discovered bus: of appealing to* **Sailors** *on ships passing.*

One small schooner passes from left to right.

One submarine passes from left to right.

One large schooner passes from left to right.

When in centre it belches forth a large column of smoke all over the **Mermaid**. *She turns and faces audience with face all covered with black. While this business is on the* **Man Singer** *is singing the 2nd refrain.*

2nd Refrain:

> Lorelei, Lorelei,
> Sit around and weep and cry
> Days are so long
> Everything's wrong
> Completely.
> All the sirens in these environs
> Are sorry they spoke
> Coaling steamers are belching streamers
> Of horrible smoke
> Making them choke.
> Lorelei, Lorelei,
> Sadly sigh and wonder why
> Every new ship
> Gives them the slip
> So neatly.
> What could be more obscene
> Than vamping a submarine
> Pity the languid left-alone Lorelei.

Blackout.

Snowball

Snowball *was a little Black boy who played the banjo.*

Ignorance Is Bliss

Scene One

Scene: The scene is a hotel bedroom of the Nineties.

Act One 25

A young **Husband** *and* **Wife** *are ushered in by a very fat* **Proprietress** *– a* **Chambermaid** *comes in after them with their luggage. The furniture is ugly and heavy and on the right is a large double brass bed.*

Proprietress   Put the things down over there, Annie.

Chambermaid *puts bags at the end of the sofa.*

Proprietress   Come this way, please.

They come on and across to front of sofa.

I think you'll be very comfy here. (*Shakes up bed.*)

Husband   Thank you.

Wife (*with an effort*)   I'm sure we shall.

Proprietress   Married to-day?

Together:

Husband   Oh no!
Wife   Oh yes!

Proprietress (*rubbing her hands*)   Now, now, now now! You mustn't be shy. (*To* **Chambermaid**.) Don't stand there gaping, Annie – run away.

Chambermaid   Yes'm.

She crosses back of sofa and exits door centre.

Proprietress   Do you know Worthing well?

Crosses to window opposite prompt side.

Husband   No.

Proprietress   You can get a lovely view of the sea from this window 'ere – here.

Wife (*gulping*)   How nice.

Proprietress (*archly*)   But I don't suppose you'll be looking out of the window much, will you? (*Crosses to centre.*)

Wife   Oh, Harry!

Husband   That will be all now, thank you, Mrs Blake.

Proprietress (*crosses up to door centre*)   If you want anything you've only got to ring for it, you know.

Husband   Thanks – thanks very much.

Proprietress   Not at all – a pleasure – I like to see young things standing on the threshold of life, as it were.

She stands and looks at them smiling. There is a long pause.

Husband   Quite.

Proprietress (*conversationally, coming downstage*)   I was born 'ere, you know, born and married and widowed all in Worthing.[45]

Wife (*nervously*)   How nice.

Proprietress   It's the close season now – but it's very gay in the summer.

Husband   It must be. (*Puts coat down on sofa.*)

Proprietress   Last year we had no less than twenty-seven honeymoon couples – they all 'ad this room – separately, of course.

Wife   Oh, Harry!

Husband   That will be all now, thank you, Mrs Blake.

Proprietress   Well – ring if you want anything, you know.

Husband   Yes – thank you.

Proprietress (*roguishly*)   I don't suppose you'll ring much though, will you?

Wife   Oh, Harry!

Husband   Oh, good night.

Proprietress (*laughing gaily*)   It's me as should be saying that to you – Sir.

She goes out, door centre.

Wife   Oh, Harry! (**Wife** *sits on sofa.*)

This whole scene to be played in an agony of embarrassment. **Husband** *sits on sofa.*

Husband   Well – here we are.

Wife   Yes – here we are.

Husband   Quite a nice room, isn't it?

Wife   Delightful.

Husband   It all went off very well, didn't it?

Wife   Yes.

Husband   Yes, and now – er – we – here we are.

Husband *gets up from sofa.*

Wife   Yes – here we are.

---

45   Seaside town in West Sussex, England.

Husband When we've unpacked, we can put the bags under – the – (*he looks in agony at the bed*) sofa.

Wife Yes – we can, can't we?

Husband Yes – we can, can't we? Who's going to unpack first, you or me?

Wife I don't know.

Husband We'll toss up – tails you do – heads I do.

Wife Oh, Harry! (*Gets up from sofa – crosses to* **Harry**.)

Husband (*throwing coin*) It's heads – that's you!

Wife Oh!

Husband I'll – er – go downstairs and order breakfast for the morning – while you – er – get into – er – start to unpack.

Wife Very well.

Husband (*kissing her hurriedly*) Cheer up, dear.

Wife Oh, Harry!

He goes out quickly.

She falls on her knees by the sofa.

(*Wailing.*) Oh, mother – oh, mother – oh, mother!

Scene Two

A very modern hotel bedroom.

A **Husband** *and* **Wife** *are ushered in by the* **Booking Clerk**. *A* **Page Boy** *enters with the luggage.*

Proprietor I hope you'll be comfortable here.

Wife Oh yes – divine. (*She thumps the bed with her fist.*) Bed feels all right.

Husband Got a stinker on you?

Wife Yes, here – (*She gives him one.*)

Husband (*to* **Clerk**) Send up two dry Martinis, will you?

The **Wife** *opens a portable gramophone and puts on a dance record. Then starts to undress.*

Wife Here, Harry – unhook me.

Husband (*doing so*) Right – Ouch!

Wife What is it?

Husband   I always scratch myself with this damned hook!

Blackout.

Hands Number

Miss Losch.

This was an exquisite creation by **Tilly Losch***, in which she only used her hands.*

Duet: 'A Room with a View'

Scene: A window flat.

Boy *and* **Girl** *behind centre of tabs. They open tabs and are discovered in each other's arms.*

Verse:

He
>I've been cherishing
>Through the perishing
>Winter nights and days
>A funny little phrase
>That means
>Such a lot to me
>That's you've got to be
>With me heart and soul
>For on you the whole
>Thing leans.

She
>Won't you kindly tell me what you're driving at
>What conclusion you're arriving at?

He
>Please don't turn away
>Or my dream will stay
>Hidden out of sight
>Among a lot of might –
>Have-beens!

He
>A room with a view – and you
>And no one to worry us
>No one to hurry us – through
>This dream we've found
>We'll gaze at the sky – and try
>To guess what it's all about

Then we will figure out – why
The world is round.

She
We'll be as happy and contented
As birds upon a tree
High above the mountains and the sea

Both
We'll bill and we'll coo – ooo – oo
And sorrow will never come
Oh, will it ever come – true
Our room with a view.

Tabs open. Window discovered.

Boy *exits right* **Girl** *left.*

They go round and appear in window, which they open.

Verse 2:

She
I'm so practical
I'd make tactical
Errors as your wife
I'd try to set your life
To rights.
I'm upset a bit
For I get a bit
Dizzy now and then
Following your mental flights.

He
Come with me and leave behind noisy crowds,
Sunlight shines for us above the clouds.

She
My eyes glistened too
While I listened to
All the things you said
I'm glad I've got a head
For heights.

Refrain 2:

She
A room with a view – and you
And no one to give advice
That sounds a paradise – few
Could fail to choose

With fingers entwined we'll find
Relief from the preachers who
Always beseech us to – mind
Our P's and Q's.

He

We'll watch the whole world pass before us
While we are sitting still
Leaning on our own window-sill.

Both

We'll bill and we'll coo – ooo – oo,
And maybe a stork will bring
This, that and t'other thing – to
Our room with a view.

Gipsy *enters first entrance right, crosses to centre with* **Boy**, *humming 2nd refrain. She sees them in window and asks for money. He gives her money. She spreads four cards on stage, then holds up four fingers to* **Boy** *and* **Girl** *in window, indicating for babies, and rocks arms as if rocking baby, picks up cards and waves good-bye and exits first exit left.*

Both

We'll bill and we'll coo – ooo – oo,
And maybe a stork will bring
This, that and t'other thing – to
Our room with a view.

He slowly takes her in his arms. She turns her back to audience – sees that they are exposed to passers-by. They slowly close windows. They kiss. Shadow shows on window. They close curtains.

Blackout.

Griffiths Brothers

Horse Pogo.

[The **Griffiths Brothers** *were in reality father and son. I forget which was the front legs of Pogo and which was the back, but whichever way which the result was to make Pogo not only a pantomime horse but a very definite character.]*

'Teach Me to Dance Like Grandma'

Scene: Pink velvet curtains.

Principal *enters from right as tabs open.*

Verse:

I'm getting tired of jazz tunes

Monotonous
They've gotten us
Crazy now.
Tho' they're amusing as tunes
Music has gone somehow.
I hear the moaning – groaning of a saxophone band
It simply shakes me – makes me – want to play a lone head.
Please understand
I want an age that has tunes
Simple and slow
I'm feeling so
Lazy now.

Refrain:

Teach me to dance like Grandma used to dance
I refuse to dance – Blues.
Black Bottoms,[46] Charlestons,[47] what wind blew them in
Monkeys do them in zoos.
Back in the past the dancing signified just a dignified glow.
They didn't have to be so strong
Tho' they revolved the whole night long.
Teach me to dance like Grandma used to dance
Sixty summers ago!

Eight **Girls** *enter from first entrance left.*

They sing one refrain and dance and bus: to three refrains and exit first exit left with **Principal**.

Finale: Act One

Scene: Full set, silver cyclorama, etc.

Curtains open.

Dancer *discovered up stage centre, in old-fashioned polka dress.*

Dance: *Polka – to tune of 'Grandma's Days' as in score. End of dance.*

Man *enters first entrance left in old-fashioned dress. They dance – mazurka (as in score), twice through. End of dance.*

---

46 A dance that originated in the American South. It became famous in London after Black dancer Edith Wilson performed it in Lew Leslie's *Blackbirds*, also produced by Cochran.
47 A dance that likely originated near Charleston, South Carolina. It became popularized by Black songwriter James P. Johnson's 'The Charleston' seen in the Black Broadway show *Runnin' Wild* (1924), produced by George White.

He exits first exit left. She exits first exit left.

Four Little Girls *and* **Four Little Boys** *enter second exit left. They dance Polka as arranged, 'Brie-à–Brae' as in score.*

Exit second exit right.

The **Three Graces**: *First one enters enter second exit left, comes down centre. Second one enters second exit right, comes down right. Third one enters second exit left, comes down left.*

Dance as arranged in score.

Portions of ballet from 'Robert the Devil'.

They exit right and left.

Valse: Holland and Barry Speciality

Enter third entrance left. Dance as arranged.

Finale. Full company. Valse.

Eight Small Girls *enter second entrance left. When they are all on* **Eight Big Girls** *and* **Eight Big Boys** *enter from first entrance right and valse around* **Small Girls** *who are waltzing in middle of stage.*

Ten Couples of Principals *enter from first entrance left and valse around outer edge of other dancers till curtain – then they reverse.*

Curtains open – they waltz round once more.

Curtain.

Waltz refrain: 'Teach Me to Dance' as in score.

Act Two

The Lido Beach

Characters

The Contessa
Lady Fenchurch
Sir Charles Fenchurch
Young Man
Baroness Kurdle
Mr Clark
Lady Millicent
Lady Saltwood
Lady Verlap
Violet
Jane
Baby
Grace

Opening.

The scene is the Lido beach. There should be a back-cloth with 'Excelsior Hotel' on it up against bright blue sky. In the foreground a row of cabanas with coloured striped awnings and coloured mattresses and cushions. When the curtain rises the **Chorus** *is discovered in a straight line across the stage, with their hands on their knees looking out front. Some are in bathing dresses, and some in gaily coloured pyjamas. There is a general air of sunshine and colour and gaiety.*

Opening **Chorus.**

All
    A narrow strip of sand
    Where Byron used to ride about,
    While stately ships would glide about
    The sea on either hand.
    But now the times have changed,
    For civilised society
    With infinite variety
    Has had it rearranged.
    No more the moon
    On the still Lagoon
    Can please the young enchanted,
    They must have this
    And they must have that
    And they take it all for granted.

    They hitch their star
    To a cocktail bar

Which is all they really wanted,
That narrow strip of sand
Now reeks with assininity
Within the near vicinity
A syncopated band
That plays the blues – all the day long –
And all the old Venetians say
They like a nice torpedo
To blow the Lido away.

Chorus go upstage and form several groups.

*Two **Wives** enter top entrance right and two top entrance left and come down to footlights.*

Wives
Beneath the blue skies
Of sunny Italy,
We lie on the sand
But please understand
We're terribly grand.
We firmly married
The old nobility,
But we can spend happy days here,
Take off our stays here,
Tarnish our laurels,
Loosen our morals.
Oh! you'll never know
The great relief it is
To let our feelings go,
We're *comme il faut*[48]
You see and so
It doesn't matter what vulgarity
We show!

*Two **Husbands** enter top right and two top left come down and take up positions on left of each **Wife**.*

Husbands
Ladies of abundant means
And less abundant minds,
Although we're not romantic
We crossed the cold Atlantic
To choose a few commercial queens
Of different sorts and kinds.
Returning with a cargo
Of girlhood from Chicago,
Tho' we regret it more from day to day

We think it only fair to you to say
It wasn't for your beauty that we married you,
It wasn't for your culture or your wit,
It wasn't for the quality that Mrs Glyn[49] describes
As 'It', just it.
It wasn't your position in society
That led us on to making such a fuss.

Four **Wives** *start going off left. Four* **Husbands** *start going off right singing the last three lines.*

Forgive us being frank,
But your balance in the bank
Made you just the only wives for us.

At exit of **Husbands** *and* **Wives**, **Chorus** *form a straight line across stage and sing this verse*:

All
This narrow strip of sand
Makes something seem to burst in us,
Brings out the very worst in us,
But kindly understand

We've got the blues all the day long
And every year we always say
We'd like a nice torpedo
To blow the Lido away!

Half exit right. Half exit left.

At the end of the opening chorus there is a general buzz of conversation. Four people playing outside a cabana on the left are quarrelling furiously.

Lady Millicent *is lying on mattress right.*

Contessa   What did you play that for?

Sir Charles Fenchurch   Because it seemed to me the most suitable card to play.

Contessa   I've always thought you a dreary old fool, Charles.

Lady Fenchurch   Darling Contessa – don't be so tiresome.

Contessa   We're playing bridge – not animal grab.

A **Young Man** *in a bathing suit approaches the table first entrance left.*

Young Man   Are we lunching upstairs dressed, or down here undressed?

---
48 Behaving in the necessary manner demanded by etiquette.
49 Elinor Glyn (1864–1943) was a British novelist and scriptwriter, known for her romantic fiction, who popularized the concept of the 'It Girl'.

Contessa   Mind your own business!

Young Man   It is my business. I'm paying for lunch.

Lady Fenchurch   Upstairs then, dear – it's more expensive.

Young Man   Look – here comes a photographer.

Everybody at once screams and rushes eagerly off the stage. **Sir Charles** *stops and looks at cards and then rushes off. After a moment they return smiling with satisfaction. The* **Young Man** *lies down at bottom of mattress right.*

Sir Charles Fenchurch   Well, I double.

The **Baroness Kurdle**, *an elderly woman, comes out of her cabana in a dressing-gown – she is large and extremely feminine. She is followed by* **Mr Clark** *from top entrance left.*

Lady Millicent   Who's this? I'm new to the Lido.

Contessa   That's the Baroness Kurdle. Just an Austrian girl.

Baroness Kurdle   Where iss my oil?

Lady Millicent   Your what, dear?

Baroness Kurdle   Oil – somebody have pinched him.

Mr Clark   Pinched who?

Baroness Kurdle   My oil. It iss my hour for sunburn.

Lady Millicent (*holding up bottle*)   Is this it?

Mr Clark *pulls mattress down stage.*

Baroness Kurdle   Ach yes – Mr Clark, you will please rub my back – I, my front can do myself –

Lady Millicent   I never know, Baroness, why you go to all this trouble, anyhow.

Baroness (*taking off her dressing-gown and displaying a slightly inadequate bathing costume*)   Sunburn is very becoming – but only when it is even – one must be careful not to look like a mixed grill. (*She undoes her shoulder-straps of her bathing suit and lies face downwards on a mattress.*) Mr Clark, you will please begin.

Mr Clark *dutifully begins to rub her back with oil.*

Lady Millicent   Look – there's a photographer.

Baroness   My wrap – my God! My wrap – my God!

Everybody at once rushes off all entrances left. The **Baroness Kurdle** *is the last one off the stage.*

Violet, **Jane**, **Baby** *and* **Grace** *enter top entrance right. They are all exquisitely dressed.*

Violet   What's that crowd over there?

Jane   Only a camera-man.

Baby   Really, the way these people rush after publicity is disgusting – we don't go on like that.

Grace   They're amateurs, dear – and we're professionals.

They come downstage to footlights.

Quartette: 'Little Women'

Violet, **Jane**, **Baby** *and* **Grace**.

Verse 1:

Business as arranged.

All
>We're little girls of certain ages
>Fresh from London Town,
>Like an instalment plan of Drage's[50]
>We want so much down.
>We have discovered years ago
>That flesh is often clay,
>We're not a new sin
>We're on the loose in
>Quite the nicest way.
>We have renounced domestic cares
>For ever and for aye,
>We're not so vicious,
>Merely ambitious,
>If there must be love
>Let it be free love.

Refrain:

>We're little women,
>Alluring little women,
>Cute but cold fish
>Just like goldfish
>Looking for a bowl to swim in.
>We lead ornamental
>But uncreative lives,

---

50 A department store in early twentieth-century London.

We may be little women
But we're not good wives.

Violet

I am just an ingénue
And shall be till I'm eighty-two
At any rude remark my spirit winces,
I've a keen religious sense
But in girlish self-defence
I always have to put my faith in princes.

All

Do not trust them, gentle maiden,
They will kick you in the pants.

Ruth

I'm not a type that is frequently seen
I wear my hair in a narrow bang,
I have remained at the age of eighteen
Since I left home in a charabanc[51]
Tho' men all pursue me
When they woo me
They construe me as innocent,
But when I hear things suggestively phrased
I'm not unduly amazed.

All

It takes far more than that to wake
Sweet wonder in her eyes.

Jane

I waste no time on things
That other girls are arch about,
I much prefer to march about alone.
I'm a baby vamp,
I'd take a postage stamp,
I just believe in grabbing
Anything that's offered me.
If Mother Hubbard proffered me – a bone
I should not be upset,
Have the darned thing re-set.

All

Much further than the Swanee River
She keeps her old folks at home.[52]

---

51 An early form of a bus.
52 Reference to Stephen Foster's 'Old Folks at Home' (1851).

Ivy

    I am a girl whose soul with domesticity abounds,
    I know a man of six foot three who's worth
    A million pounds (*woops*),
    Tho' he is like a brother
    I haven't told my mother
    He's given me a lovely house and grounds!

All

    Be it ever so humbug
    There's no place like home.

Second refrain:

All

    We're little women,
    Alluring little women,
    Cute but cold fish,
    Just like goldfish
    Looking for a bowl to swim in.
    Tho' we're very clinging
    Our independence thrives
    We may be little women
    But we're not good wives.

They all exeunt first exit left on the last four bars.

The English Lido

Characters

Mr Freeman
Mrs Freeman
Alice
Frankie
Official
Mr Harris
Mrs Harris
Phyllis
Vi
Georgie
Mrs Clark
Mrs Jones
Madge
Doris
Daisy Kipshaw

Hockey Players, Children, Cameraman, Bathers, etc.

Preliminary speech. **Announcer** *comes on in front of tabs.*

Announcer   Ladies and gentlemen, it has been suggested in several newspapers of late that English seaside resorts hold out fewer attractions to visitors than Continental ones. Any true patriotic Englishman naturally resents this reflection on our national gaiety and Mr Cochran perhaps more keenly than anyone – so he has determined to prove conclusively once and for all that no holiday resort in the world can equal in charm, gaiety and light-hearted care-free enjoyment an average watering-place on the shores of the English Channel.

Opening Chorus

All the **Chorus** *are discovered in a straight line across the stage.* **Mr** *and* **Mrs Harris** *in middle of line,* **Mr** *and* **Mrs Freeman** *to the left of them.*

All
   Hooray, hooray, hooray!
   The holidays!
   The jolly days
   When laughter, fun and folly days
   Appear.
   Hooray, hooray, hooray!
   The laity
   With gaiety
   And charming spontaneity
   Must cheer.

Mr Harris
   I've left my bowler hat and rubber collar far behind.

Mrs H
   I wish to God you'd left that awful Panama behind,
   It looks gaga behind.

All
   But never mind because the holidays are here,
   Our tastes are very far from Oriental,
   We have a very fixed idea of fun,
   The thought of anything experimental
   Or Continental
   We shun.
   We take to innovations very badly,
   We'd rather be uncomfortable than not
   In fighting any new suggestion madly
   We'd gladly
   Be shot!
   We much prefer to take our pleasures sadly

Because we're really quite contented with our lot.

The scene is structurally the same as the Lido scene, except that in place of cabanas there are bathing machines. The sky is leaden-grey and there is a violent wind blowing. Some of the characters wear ill-fitting bathing costumes with Burberrys and mackintoshes over them, others are dressed respectably in flannels and blazers and plus-fours and cloth coats and skirts and very rumpled summer dresses. There broods over everything that air of complacent dreariness which is inseparable from any English seaside resort.

When the opening chorus is over, a very well-developed **Woman** *of about thirty runs in from first entrance right to centre.*

Woman   I say, girls, what about a game of beach hockey?

1st Girl   Topping!

2nd Girl   Righto!

3rd Girl   Good egg!

About nine of them go off – leaving the stage empty except for the harassed family on the right. They sit in the two end chairs. And the **Freeman** *family on the left and a few odd people strolling about.* **Mrs Freeman** *is vainly trying to put up a deck-chair right of bathing machine. Finally she sits down. An* **Old Man** *climbs up steps of bathing machine and looks through hole in the door.* **Mr Freeman** *sits down right of bathing machine with a newspaper.*

Mr Freeman   'I, come on out of it, nosy!

Old Man *goes top exit right.*

Mrs Freeman (*sits down*)   That's the first time over been 'ot for ten days. (*Is knitting.*)

Mr Freeman   What are you grumblin' about?

Mrs Freeman   I'm not grumblin', but it's my belief this place isn't as bracing as they said it was. I feel awful.

Mr Freeman (*wearily*)   Oh, what's the matter with you?

Mrs Freeman   Well, I'll tell you – I've got a cold, wind under the 'eart, I feel sick and me feet hurt!

Mr Freeman   What d'you think you are – a medical magazine?

Mrs Freeman   Well, if you 'and't 'ad hiccoughs all night I might 'ave got a bit of sleep and felt better.

Mr Freeman   Where's Alice?

Mrs Freeman   'Elping Frankie on with his bathing things – 'e loves the water.

Shrill screams of rage come from inside the bathing machine.

Mr Freeman   Yes, it sounds like, don't it?

*Alice, a girl of about sixteen, in a very voluminous bathing-gown comes out of the bathing machine leading **Frankie**, a little boy of ten, clad only in striped bathing drawers – he is yelling loudly. Cross to right.*

Mr Freeman   Can't you keep the child quiet, yer ma's not feeling well.

Alice   'E found a beetle in 'is bucket.

Mr Freeman *goes over to* **Frankie**.

Mr Freeman   'Ere, 'ere, 'ere, Frankie, stop it – you're getting a big boy now – making all that fuss about a poor innocent beetle.

Mrs Freeman   That child's been a bundle of nerves ever since we took him to see 'Chang'.

*An **Official** in uniform walks on and taps **Mr Freeman** on the shoulder.*

Official   Excuse me, this little lad must have a top to 'is bathing dress.

Mr Freeman   Why – what for?

Official   Corporation's rules.

Mrs Freeman *gets up from chair and comes downstage.*

Mrs Freeman   Lot of nonsense – the child's under age.

Official   Can't 'elp that, madam.

Alice   'E 'asn't got a top.

Official   The Corporation's very strict about indecent exposure.

Mr Freeman   Well, it's coming to something if a child of ten can't enjoy a state of nature without giving a lot of old ladies ideas.

Official   England don't 'old with states of nature.

Mrs Freeman   'Ere – 'e'd better 'ave my crochet sports jacket. (*Crosses to right. She gives it to **Alice**, who drapes it round **Frankie**.*) Will that do?

Official   Yes – sorry to 'ave troubled you.

He goes off second exit left.

Mr Freeman   Well, I'm damned!

Alice   Come on, Frankie.

Takes him off first exit right.

Mr Freeman   That boy looks effeminate. You going to have a bathe this morning?

Mrs Freeman   Not unless you want me to die this afternoon.

Mr Freeman   I'm off to 'ave a paddle. (*Cross to right.*)

Mrs Freeman   Mind you take plenty of soda with it.

Mr Freeman *is going off and collides with* **Madge** *and* **Doris** *on the way. They are crossing from right to left.*

Mr Freeman   Pardon.

Doris *and* **Madge** *stroll across.*

Madge   Where was I?

Doris   He was just holding your hand and the band was playing the *Mikado*.[53]

Madge   Oh, yes – well, dear – I said, keep your hands to yourself and he said, why? and I said, you know why, and he said, come off it, Miss High and Mighty, and I said, don't be saucy, and he brought me some nougat and I didn't get home till two in the morning.

They go off.

Mrs Harris (*reading the paper*)   Fred!

Harris (*who has been sleeping*)   'Allo!

Mrs Harris   That murderer's been caught.

Harris   Which one?

Mrs Harris   Last Tuesday's.

Harris   Oh!

Mrs Harris   You can go and see the 'ouse where it 'appened. It's quite near 'ere. Mabel went yesterday and said it was lovely – blood all over everything.

Harris   Coo! We might take the children this afternoon.

Mrs Harris   All right. I'll cut some sandwiches.

Two children, **Georgie** *and* **Vi**, *come running in screaming from first entrance right. They go to their Mother.*

Harris   What's up now?

Vi   Georgie hit me with his iron spade.

Georgie   No, I never!

Vi   Yes, he did!

Georgie   No, I never!

Mrs Harris   Come 'ere, Georgie – that's the third time you've 'it Vi in two days – I'll teach you.

She bends him across her knee and smacks him – the noise is deafening.

Harris   Can't you leave the blighter alone?

Mrs Harris   Don't you tell me 'ow to bring up me own children!

---

53   This is a reference to Gilbert and Sullivan's *The Mikado* (1885).

Harris The poor little bloke didn't mean it.

Vi Yes, 'e did.

Harris You shut up, you – (*He slaps her. She sets up a terrible howl.*)

Vi (*screaming*) Ow ow ow! Father 'it me!

Mrs Harris You great brute, you! (*Getting up and taking* **Vi** *in her arms.*)

Harris Brute, am I?

Mrs Harris Be quiet, Vi – stop that noise!

Harris I can't stand this – I'm going to get drunk –

Goes off top exit left.

Mrs Harris That'll be a change –

A harassed mother, **Mrs Clark**, *enters pushing a screaming child in front of her. They get to centre.*

Mrs Clark I brought you 'ere to enjoy yourselves and enjoy yourselves you're going to! Now go on – paddle.

She smacks her hard and the **Child** *goes off screaming,* **Georgie** *and* **Vi** *follow first exit right.*

Mrs Clark *sits down exhausted next to* **Mrs Freeman** *right.*

Mrs Clark I'll never come to this place again as long as I live.

Mrs Freeman I don't think I shall live long enough to be able to.

Mrs Harris *is fanning herself with her paper.*

Mrs Jones, *a weary-looking woman, comes on top entrance right and sits down next to her.*

Mrs Jones Good morning, Mrs Harris.

Mrs Harris Good morning.

Mrs Jones I've just come from the 'ospital, my little Albert fell off a rock yesterday and cut 'is 'ead open –

They all come downstage.

'Mother's Complaint'

We're all of us mothers
We're all of us wives,
The whole depressing crowd of us
With our kind assistance
The Motherland thrives.
We hope the nation's proud of us

For one dreary fortnight
In each dreary year
We bring our obstreperous families here.
We paddle and bathe while it hails and it rains
In spite of anaemia and varicose veins,
Hey nonny, ho nonny, no no no.
Our lodgings are frowzy
Expensive and damp.
The food is indigestible
We sit on the beach
Till we're tortured with cramp
And life is quite detestable.
The children go out with a bucket and spade
And injure themselves on the asphalt parade,
There's sand in the porridge and sand in the bed,
And if this is pleasure, we'd rather be dead,
Hey nonny, ho nonny, no no no!

Vi, **Phyllis** *and* **Georgie** *rush on from first entrance right.*

Vi   Mum, mum, Cissie Parker's seen a whale.

Mrs Harris   Don't you tell such lies, Violet Harris.

Phyllis   It's true, it's true – I saw it too – look there!

Alice *and* **Frankie Freeman** *rush on.*

Alice   Mother – mother – a great big whale.

Mrs Freeman   May God forgive you, you wicked little fibber.

Several other **Children** *rush on screaming, and all the* **Chorus**: '*A whale, a whale.*' *Also grown-ups – finally the* **Official** *re-enters top entrance left and comes to centre of stage.*

Official   'Ere, 'ere, 'ere – what's all this noise?

Mrs Harris   There's a whale – my Vi's seen a whale. Look, there it is!

Lots more people rush on. The **Official** *produces some glasses and looks through them.*

Official   That's not a whale – that's Daisy Kipshaw, the Channel swimmer. She gets 'ere regularly every Friday morning from Boulogne.

Everybody cheers. **Three Men** *come on with cameras and finally* **Daisy Kipshaw**, *a very large woman in a bathing suit, enters from first entrance left. The* **Three Men** *with cameras take photos of her, one as she turns to pick up her cloak which she has dropped on getting to centre of stage. As she enters all the* **Chorus** *take up lines across stage on* opposite prompt *side.*

Finale and number for **Daisy Kipshaw**.

She comes centre.

Chorus
    Hail, Neptune's daughter
    The pride of Finsbury Park,[54]
    Behold a modest clerk
    Is goddess of the water.
    Hail, pioneer girl
    Tho' rain and wind have come
    You've swum and swum and swum
    You really are a dear girl.

Daisy
    Kind friends, I thank you one and all
    For your delightful greetings.
    I merely heard my country's call
    At patriotic meetings.

Chorus
    Just think of that,
    Just think of that,
    She got her inspiration at
    A patriotic meeting.
    Oh, tell us more,
    Oh, tell us more,
    Oh, tell us what you do it for,
    It must be overheating.

Daisy
    King friends, I thank you all again
    And since you ask me to
    I will explain.

Song: 'Britannia Rules the Waves'

Daisy
    Like other chaste stenographers
    I simply hate photographers
    I also hate publicity.

Chorus
    She lives for sheer simplicity.

Daisy
    For any woman more or less
    A photo in the daily press
    Is horribly embarrassing.

---

54 A public park in the London neighbourhood of Harringay, known during the First World War as a location for pacifist meetings.

Chorus
It must be dreadfully harassing.

Daisy
The British male
May often fail,
Our faith in sport is shaken,
So English girls awaken
And save the nation's bacon.

Refrain 1:

Sung by **Daisy** *alone first.*

Up girls and at 'em,
And play the game to win,
The men must all give in
Before the feminine.
Bowl 'em and bat 'em
And put them on the run,
Defeat them every one
Old Caspar's work is done,
We'll do out bit till our muscles crack
We'll put a frill on the Union Jack,
If Russia has planned
To conquer us and
America misbehaves,
Up girls and at 'em,
Britannia rules the waves!

Business with chorus as arranged.

Refrain 2:

Daisy & Chorus
Up girls and at 'em,
And play the game to win,
The men must all give in
Before the feminine.
Bowl 'em and bat 'em,
And put them on the run,
Defeat them every one
Old Caspar's work is done.

Daisy
We'll do our bit till our muscles crack

Chorus
We'll put a frill on the Union Jack.

Daisy
If Russia has planned

To conquer us and
America misbehaves,
Up girls and at 'em,
Britannia rules the waves!

Refrain 3:

Up girls and at 'em,
Go out and win your spurs,
For England much prefers
Applauding amateurs.
Man is an atom
So break your silly necks
In order to annex
Supremacy of sex.
Valiantly over the world we'll roam
Husbands must wait till the cows come home.
The men of to-day
Who get in our way
Are digging their early graves,
Up girls and at 'em,
Britannia rules the waves.

Refrain 4:

Daisy & Chorus

Up girls and at 'em,
And play the game to win,
The men must all give in
Before the feminine.
Bowl 'em and bat 'em,
And put them on the run,
Defeat them every one
Old Caspar's work is done.
We'll do our bit
Till our muscles crack,
We'll put a frill
On the Union Jack.

Daisy

Here's to the maid
Who isn't afraid
Who shingles and shoots and shaves.

Chorus

Up girls and at 'em,
Britannia rules the waves.

Business of **Chorus Boys** *getting in her way. They lift her up. As they all drop on stage –*

Blackout.

'The Legend of the Lily of the Valley'
Dress Plot

Flannelette *Beaded Shaftesbury Avenue evening frock, necklace of ping-pong balls – brown leather aviator's cap, cricket pads and bare feet.*

Bergamot *American Union two-piece bathing suit, bare legs; boots with spats and an admiral's hat – bow and arrow.*

Female Courtiers *Pink flannel drawers, lace camisoles, Russian boots. The framework of hoop skirts composed of gas piping – headdress with traditional of eighteenth century with dolls' furniture festooned in the hair.*

Male Courtiers *Jaeger long-legged combinations – football boots – brass-studded leather belts with small jewelled swords – small gold crowns on elastic.*

Fairies *Burberrys, bowler hats, long tope wigs reaching to the floor – gossamer wings – pink satin ballet shoes.*

Marquis de Poopinac *Plus-fours – Harlequin shirt with spangles, tight-fitting cap with a celluloid windmill. Bare legs with carpet slippers.*

Scene: The scene should be angular with factory chimneys and wheels turning. The choreography should be almost entirely posturing in the most unattractive attitudes possible.

Introductory Speech

Ladies and gentlemen, as a sop to those of you who are bored and satiated with usual superficialities of light musical entertainments, Mr Cochran has asked me to announce the production of a short ballet in which beauty, austerity and intellectuality are blended together with that spirit of progressive modernity which we have learned to demand and expect from the striking performances of Diaghelieff's Russian Ballet.[55] We live in an age of Revolution in Art and perhaps the most vital and tremendous movement in this revolution is the stern reversion to bare primitive simplicity.

The ballet we are about to present is entitled *The Legend of the Lily of the Valley*. The atmosphere is definitely early eighteenth-century French, smacking of gently undulating country life, and then again, smacking ever so slightly of the debauched life at court. The actual legend is simplicity itself. Flannelette, a dainty shepherdess of the period, is guarding her flock, occasionally she dances to them, but they pay no heed – suddenly from over the hill comes striding Bergamot, a shepherd who loves her. They execute what is technically described as a Pas de Deux, which leaves Flannelette exhausted – Bergamot plays his pipe to her for a moment and then goes sadly away. Flannelette is left dreaming on the grass, during which the love theme is repeated in the orchestra for three flutes and the cophatican.[56] Then six fairies enter

---
55 A reference to the Ballets Russes, which toured throughout Britain in the 1910s and 1920s.
56 Unknown instrument.

and execute with considerable spirit a Pas du Tout – Flannelette starts up amazed – Suddenly a bugle call is heard. The fairies rush off and a coach drives by – stops, and disgorges the evil and depraved Marquis de Poopinac with several court ladies whose tinkling false laughter sounds strangely incongruous in such sylvan surroundings. This jarring note is brought out in the music with astounding effect by a muted oboe and six clavabaladalas.[57] The Marquis, observing Flannelette, is immediately inflamed by her beauty. He flirts with her and she, flattered by his attention, accompanies him to a neighbouring coppice, during which the courtiers dance a stately Pavanne[58] which is interrupted by the re-entrance of Bergamot, who is searching wildly for Flannelette – he questions each of the courtiers in mime, or dumb show, but they only laugh mockingly – suddenly a cry is heard. Flannelette comes running in with her fichu extremely ruffled, followed by the Marquis. Bergamot attacks him and the Marquis runs him through with his sword, and the story closes to music of transcendental beauty.

Open Blue with Music

Rules of Three Announcement

Announcer   Ladies and gentlemen, there has been a good deal of argument in the papers lately as to the general staleness of the English drama. There have been bitter complaints to the effect that there *are no new* ideas any more. We now intend to demonstrate to you *our* point of view on the matter, which is that new ideas are not necessary, and that it is only the *treatment* that is important. We propose to show a perfectly commonplace situation as it would be handled by three celebrated dramatists. The situation is the Eternal Triangle. A wife is surprised during a scene with her lover by the unexpected entrance of her husband.

Moves to prompt side.

First of all as Sir James Barrie would write it.

Exit first exit left.

1. Sir James Barrie[59]

Characters

The Wife
The Husband
The Lover

---

57 Percussion instrument.
58 A stately sixteenth-century court dance, known for a slow duple rhythm.
59 Sir James Matthew Barrie (1860–1937) was a Scottish novelist and playwright, best known for *Peter Pan* (play 1904, novel 1911).

Act Two 51

The **Wife** *is darning socks by the fire.*

Wife (*pensively*)   Ah me – I often wonder if all the little pink toes of all the little pink babies in the world were counted, how many there would be.

Enter left the **Lover**.

Lover   Jeannie!

Wife (*rising, comes downstage right centre*)   Why have you come?

Lover   I heard your voice in the wood.

Wife   You couldna' have heard any such thing, James MacTagget, and it's a great fanciful fool you are.

Lover   Jeannie!

Wife   Whisht man – away with you.

Lover   I love you, Jeannie. I've loved you since ever I was a bairn no higher than a hiccough!

Wife   Are you forgetting that I am a wife, James?

Lover   Nay, I'm remembering it. The wife of a man who doesna' love or understand your ways.

Wife   Ah, but you're wrong – John's well enough – my ways are not so difficult to grasp – I'm naught but a little shrivelled nut of a woman –

Lover   You're a pixie to me.

Wife   Thank you, James – a pixie's a chancy thing to be.

Lover (*passionately*)   I had a mind to be a great poet once, but the fairies made mock of me and I became an insurance agent.

Wife   A great big brown insurance agent.

Lover   Behind each of the company's policies I hear your laugh, and a winsome, cuddlesome sort of laugh it is. It seems to say, come away, James MacTagget, and learn how not to grow up. I'll teach you. I'll teach you.

Wife   I *could* teach you that.

Lover   Will you?

Wife   Listen now – do you know how many babies there are in the world?

Lover   No.

Wife   Them multiply the answer by seven and you'll make a rainbow.

Lover   Jeannie – come with me. (*He crushes her to him.*)

Wife   No, no!

Lover   Don't send me to the workhouse of might-have-beens.

Enter the **Husband** *right.*

Husband   Jeannie!

Wife   Oh!

Husband   What does this mean?

Wife (*laughing*)   What a solemn face – sit down while I get your tea – you'd better be going, James.

Husband   Tea – I'll not taste your tea.

Wife   Go, James.

Husband   Stay.

Wife   Go – what fools men are –

Husband   Stay!

Wife   Vera well, stay – you great quarrelsome schoolboys, if I were the mother of either of you, I'd spank you and put you to bed – come, shake hands now.

Lover   I'll not shake hands – I love Jeannie, John, and I'll make no bones about it. Good-bye.

He goes out left.

Husband   Is this true?

Wife   Yes.

Husband   Why did you not go with him?

Wife (*putting her head on* **Husband**'*s shoulder*)   Because it's you I love – you with your great laugh and your great hands and the tenderness in your eye when you see a baby having its bath and the gentleness in your voice when you take me in your arms and call me Mrs Woodlesome Whatnot.

Husband (*taking her in his arms*)   Mrs Woodlesome Whatnot!

Blackout. Close tabs.

Announcer *comes on first entrance left.*

2. Frederick Lonsdale[60]

The **Wife** *is discovered dancing to a gramophone. The* **Lover** *enters left.*

Lover   Duchesses don't dance as well as they used to.

---

60   Frederick Lonsdale (1881–1954) was a British playwright, known for works such as *The Maid of the Mountains* (1917).

Wife No, my dear, but much more.

Lover Where's Johnnie?

Wife (*stopping the gramophone*) Still in the House of Lords, I think.

Lover My God, Jean, you look chic.

Wife It isn't difficult to look chic nowadays. One only needs line and lipstick.

Lover I saw the Duke of Belgravia at lunch.

Wife I thought he was dead.

Lover He is, but he won't life down.

Wife Do you think it was quite decent of you to come here?

Lover Decency be damned, I love you.

Wife As a man loves a woman or as a gentleman loves a gentlewoman?

Lover All four.

The **Butler** *enters with cocktails right.*

Wife I've got a new cocktail for you.

Lover What's it called?

Wife The Debrett Dollop![61]

Lover Do you like being a butler, Finsbury?

Butler Very much, your Grace. We are the only class left with any manners.

Lover What about the Upper Ten?

Butler They only have bedside manners.

He goes out right.

Wife I don't know what the lower orders are coming to.

Lover You're a silly woman, Jean, with the brains of a louse.

Wife Dear James, you're drunk – you must have been lunching with your mother.

Lover Nevertheless, I love you.

Wife (*surrendering herself to him*) Kiss me like you did last Wednesday in the Royal Enclosure at Ascot.[62]

He kisses her violently.

The **Husband** *enters right.*

---

61 Debrett refers to *Debrett's Peerage*, a list of the British aristocracy.
62 A horse-racing course in Britain, known as a society spot for London's upper crust.

Husband My dear Jean – you might have left the door open.

Lover (*looking up*) Hullo, Johnnie.

Husband By God, Jimmie, you're an awful swine – is there any cocktail?

Wife Not a drain. I love Jimmie, you know.

Husband Of course I know – everybody knows. it makes a damned good story – I've been dining out on it for weeks.

Lover What shall we do about it?

Husband What is there to do? I can't divorce her because I have to have a mistress for my father's old place.

Wife Don't discuss me so cold-bloodedly – I'm not an electric hare.

Lover Well, we'd better go on as we are, I suppose.

Husband All right. (*Crosses to centre.*) Here's an extra latch-key.

Lover Thanks, cheerio!

Exits left.

Husband Nice fellow.

Wife Johnnie, I'm awfully fond of you.

Husband Why?

Wife Because you're a very great gentleman.

Husband What is a very great gentleman?

Wife I don't know. I go to so few theatres.

Blackout. Close tabs.

French Farce[63]

Characters

Jeanne
Jacques
Jean
Annette

*The scene is **Jeanne**'s bedroom. This whole episode must be played at lightning speed.*

The telephone rings.

---

63 A French farce is a comic genre that originated in the fifteenth century, characterized by exaggerated elements, ridiculous gestures and the absurd.

Annette *runs on.*

Annette (*at telephone*)   'Allo yes, m'sieu – no m'sieu – yes, m'sieu – no, m'sieu – certainly, m'sieu –

She rushes off.

Jeanne *rushes on in highly coloured pyjamas.*

Jeanne (*at telephone*)   Jacques – darling – yes, angel.

No, angel – quickly, quickly – (*Makes kissing noise.*)

Yes, yes – darling, darling – (*She hangs up telephone.*)

Annette – Annette

Annette *rushes in.*

Annette   Yes, madame.

Jeanne   My peignoir, quickly.

Annette   Yes, madame.

She rushes off.

Jeanne *goes to telephone.*

Jeanne (*at telephone*)   Elysée 9468 – yes, yes – no, no – Hallo – Gaston – is it you? – Yes – No, I don't think so – very well – hurry – (*She puts telephone down.*)

Annette *rushes in – a bell rings.*

Quickly, Annette – quickly – it is he – answer the door.

She puts on her peignoir.

Annette *rushes off.*

Jacques *rushes on.* **Jeanne** *flies into his arms.*

They kiss passionately.

Jacques (*between kisses*)   Darling – beloved – angel – previous – saint – divinity –

Annette *rushes on with a pair of pyjamas.*

Annette   Here, m'sieu.

Jacques *rushed off.*

Jeanne   You can go now, Annette.

Annette   Yes, madame.

There is the sound of the front door slamming.

Jeanne   My God, my husband!

Jean *rushes on.*

Jean (*clasping her in his arms*) My darling wife – I have returned from Lyons three days earlier than I expected –

Jeanne Jean, Jean – how glad I am – (*She casts an anxious look at the door.*)

Jean You seem worried, my angel.

Jeanne It is the heat – will you go and close the spare room window?

Jean Certainly, beloved.

He rushes off left.

Jacques *rushes on right in pyjamas.*

Jacques (*clasping her in his arms*) My enchantress –

Jeanne (*pushing him back*) Hide quickly, quickly –

Jacques Very well –

He rushes off right.

Jean *rushes on left.*

Jean There is no window in the spare room.

Jeanne My foolish darling – it was a joke – Run and fetch my handbag for me, it is on the piano.

Jean Imperious angel.

He rushes towards right.

Jeanne No, no – on the piano.

Jean How stupid – I'd forgotten the piano was in the bathroom.

He rushes off left.

Jacques *rushes on right.*

Jacques (*taking her in his arms*) Wonderful – wonderful – wonderful –

Jeanne Quick, quick, my husband –

Jacques *leaps into bed.*

Jean *rushes on with a pair of shoes.*

Jean Here are your shoes. They were in the bureau.

Jeanne My darling.

Jean *sees* **Jacques**'*s hat.*

Jean (*furiously*) What is this?

Jeanne It is your mother's. She came here this afternoon.

Jean   Where is she?

Jeanne (*hysterically*)   In there! (*She points right and* **Jean** *rushes off.*)

Jeanne *jumps into bed with* **Jacques**. **Annette** *rushes on in pyjamas, looks round and then beckons.*

Jean *rushes on.*

Annette   It's all right – the coast's clear.

Jean (*clasping her in his arms*)   My darling!

Blackout.

'Dance Little Lady'

Singer *comes on from first entrance right and takes position extreme right.*

Verse:

> Tho' you're only seventeen
> Far too much of life you've seen
> Syncopated child.
> Maybe if you only knew
> Where your path was leading to
> You'd become less wild.
> But I know it's vain
> Trying to explain
> While there's this insane
> Music in your brain.

Open tabs slowly. **Dancer** *discovered in centre of stage. Dance is arranged.*

Refrain:

> Dance, dance, dance, little lady,
> Youth is fleeting – to the rhythm beating
> In your mind.
> Dance, dance, dance, little lady,
> So obsessed with second best
> No rest you'll ever find,
> Time and tide and trouble
> Never, never wait.
> Let the cauldron bubble
> Justify your fate.
> Dance, dance, dance, little lady.
> Leave tomorrow behind

Patter.

Singer *crosses to extreme left.*

> When the saxophone gives a wicked moan

Charleston hey hey,
Rhythms fall and rise
Start dancing to the tune
The band's crooning – for soon
The night will be gone,
Start swaying like a reed
Without heeding the speed
That hurries you on.
N*****[64] melodies
Syncopate your nerves
Till your body curves
Dropping – stooping,
Laughter some day dies
And when the lights are starting to gutter
Dawn through the shutter
Shows you're living in a world of lies.

Six Boys *and* **Six Girls** *– dancers, in masks – enter from first entrance left. Dance as arranged. They dance to three and a half refrain as in score and exit second exit right.* **Dancer** *exits second exit right.* **Singer** *exits first exit left.*

Blackout.

Chauve-Souris[65]

Introduction

Speech before curtain.

Ladies and gentlemen, ass you see I find him verrey deeficult to spik English. There iss an old Russian proberb wheech say that a dead rhinosceros iss nearer to the stars than a leetle child who steecks a peen eento iss old grandmother, all of wheech have no bearing whatever upon the leetle scene wheech my Company weel preesent.

Eet iss a peecneeck een olt Russia. The caviar iss all up eaten and the samovar dry and the peasants play peculiar games weth one another and seeng and seeng and seeng.

Open with Music

'Quintette'

Profile boat – **Four Men** *and* **One Woman** *standing behind it. They are dressed in burlesque Russian costumes.*

---

64 This racial slur has been deliberately obscured throughout the text.
65 Literally translated 'bald mouse' or 'bat'.

Ish con broshka
Whoops dad illoshka
Whoops dad illoshka
Inkle drop vaard.

Ish con broshka
Whoops dad illoshka
Whoops dad illoshka
Inkle drop vaard.

Wheeshka eeglee
Wheeshka bombolom
Wheeska weedlewee
Chock chock wish laa.

Wheeshka eeglee
Wheeshka bombolom
Wheeska weedlewee
Inkle drop vaard.

Tabs close on last note.

Announcer *comes from centre, bows to audience.*

Announcer   I hope you have liked him and will tell all your friends about her – and ask them all to come.

Exits through centre.

'Try to Learn to Love'

Boy *and* **Girl** *enter first entrance right. Dance as arranged.*

Verse 1:

He
   In kindergartens
   In country or town
   Our education begins
   Like little Spartans[66]
   We're taught to crush down
   The inclination to sin.
   When we change to gentle adolescence
   Things get rather strained.
   There's a strange, peculiar effervescence
   No one has explained.

---

66   The Spartans were the strongest army in Ancient Greece.

Chorus 1 (Repeat):
    First you learn to spell a little bit,
    Then, if you excel a little bit,
    Other things as well a little bit
    Come your way;
    Though the process may be slow to you
    Knowledge of the world will flow to you.
    Steadily you grow a little bit,
    Day by day;
    Though you're too gentle, sentimental
    In fact, quite a dreary bore,
    Though you're aesthetic, apathetic,
    To all men but Bernard Shaw,[67]
    Use the velvet glove a little bit,
    Emulate a dove a little
    Try to learn to love a little bit more.

She
    The art of wooing,
    I'm firmly resolved
    For men is terribly crude.
    To be pursuing
    Is not so involved
    As having to be pursued.
    Doubts and fears
    Make woman work much faster
    Tho' they're frail and weak
    Taking years
    Successfully to master
    Feminine technique.

Refrain 2:

    First you droop your eyes – a little bit,
    Then if you are wise – a little bit
    Register surprise – a little bit
    If he's bold,
    Stamp your foot with some celerity,
    Murmur with intense sincerity
    That his immature temerity
    Leaves you cold.
    But when you get him
    You must let him
    Have the joy he's yearning for,
    And whisper sweetly

---

67 George Bernard Shaw (1856–1950) was an Irish playwright, critic and political figure, best known for works such as *Arms and the Man* (1894) and *Pygmalion* (1913).

Indiscreetly
He's the boy that you adore.
Use the moon above a little bit,
Emulate the dove a little bit,
Try to learn to love – a little bit more.

Tabs open.

They dance one chorus and exit second exit left.

Chorus *enter from second entrance right. Sing first refrain as they come on.*
Dance as arranged – exit second exit right.

Boy *and* **Girl** *enter first entrance left. Dance to two choruses as arranged.*
Close tabs at end of dance.

'It Doesn't Matter How Old You Are'

Maisie Gay *before green tabs.*

Verse 1:

Life is just a gamble
And without preamble
I should like to state my case.
I'm no Messalina
I've a slightly cleaner
Outlook on the human race.
Don't imagine that I'm hewn from
Marble or stone,
I'm not entirely immune from
Pangs of my own.
Tho' I'm over forty
I can still be naughty
In an unassuming way.
Beauty doesn't always win the day
I say.

Refrain 1:

It doesn't matter how old you are
If the joys of life are sweet.
It doesn't matter how cold you are
If you've still got central heat.
I've seen raddled wrecks
With false pearls hung round their necks
Get away with lots of sex appeal
And tho' I may have been through the mill
I'm a creature of passion still
It doesn't matter how old you are
It's just how young you feel.

Verse 2:

>Tho' I'm not a gay girl
>I'm a 'come-what-may' girl,
>Nothing in my life is planned.
>Men with love get blinded
>But I'm so broad-minded
>I just smile and understand.
>Men don't always want to marry
>They're not to blame.
>I'm quite certain that Dubarry[68]
>Felt just the same.
>Too much love is nauseous
>One can't be too cautious
>Cupid's such a wily foe,
>Tho' I never let myself quite go,
>I know.

Refrain 2:

>It doesn't matter how old you are
>If your heart can still beat fast,
>It doesn't matter how bold you are
>When the dangerous age is past.
>Tho' my face is lined
>And my outlook too refined
>I shall never let my mind congeal,
>Pompadour found her love a cure
>But I'll go further and fare much worse,
>It doesn't matter how old you are
>It's just how young you feel.

Refrain 3:

>It doesn't matter how old you are
>If you've still the strength to care,
>However naughty you're told you are
>It's entirely your affair.
>Tho' I come a smack
>And go rolling off the track
>It will never be from lack of zeal.
>You may laugh when you look at me
>But watch the papers and wait and see!
>It doesn't matter how old you are
>It's just how young you feel.

---

68 Jeanne Bécu, Comtesse du Barry, or Madame du Barry (1743–93) was ta courtesan and the last mistress of Louis XV of France, made popular in films and novels that focused on her reputation as a seductress.

Spanish Ballet

Five Girls *in Spanish dress discovered. Dance as arranged.* **Two Riding Girls** *and* **One Spanish Girl** *enter from top entrance right and top entrance left.* **Principal** *from centre.*

At the end of dance all exit right.

Speciality Dance (Holland *and* **Barry).**

Enter first entrance left. Dance. Exit first exit left.

Law and Order

The scene is a street in London. This is a cloth painted with park railings and a lamp-post right.

Policewoman Pellet *enters from right – advances to centre of stage, bends and straightens herself in traditional fashion and stands left of lamp-post. An* **Old Woman**, *selling matches, enters from left – walks across and meets* **P.W. Pellet**.

Pellet   Move on – you're loitering.

Old Woman   I can't move any faster – I've got fallen arches. (*Spits.*)

Pellet   Don't argue. Don't argue. You're loitering. Move on. (*Sniffs.*)

The **Old Woman** *goes off first exit right.*

Pellet *sniffs and stands still – a* **Girl** *enters from right, walks to the middle of the stage and stoops down to tie her shoe-lace. A* **Young Man** *enters also from right and bumps into her.*

Young Man   I beg your pardon.

Girl   Not at all.

The **Young Man** *goes off left and* **Policewoman Wendle** *strides on first entrance left.*

Wendle   Now then, now then –

Girl   What d'you mean 'Now then'?

Wendle   None of that.

Girl   None of what?

Wendle   None of what you were thinking of.

Girl   How dare you! (*Crosses to left.*)

Wendle   I've been watching you – flouncing about.

Girl   Don't you talk to me like that or I shall call a policeman.

She marches off with her head in the air.

Wendle Impertinence!

Pellet (*sympathetically*) They're all alike. The girls of to-day – fast, over-dressed, *and* saucy!

Wendle I don't know what London's coming to – the higher the buildings the lower the morals.

Pellet Been in the Force long?

Wendle About three months – my husband went to Australia.

Pellet On business?

Wendle No, on purpose.

Pellet It's the woman who pays, and pays.

Both And pays.

Pellet Men are all alike.

Wendle Only some more than others. I'm not a suspicious woman, but I don't think my husband 'as been entirely faithful to me.

Pellet Whatever makes you think that?

Wendle My last child doesn't resemble him in the least.

Pellet What you must have gone through!

Wendle Bottles and bottles of aspirin.

Pellet (*producing paper bag*) 'Ave a choc?

Wendle Not on duty.

Pellet Come on – there's no one about.

Wendle Well, as long as they 'aven't nut on 'em.

She takes one.

They both munch.

There is a loud bang offstage.

Pellet What was that?

Wendle Only one of them balloon tyres burst.

Pellet I see the Croydon Ramblers beat the Lyons Corner House girls last Tuesday.

Wendle No stamina in that Lyons lot.

Pellet Oh, I don't know – Minnie Packer's a lovely centre-forward.

Wendle She had to leave the field.

Pellet Why?

Wendle Lost 'er bust bodice in a scrum.

Pellet   Go on!

Wendle   Lily Burton finished the game – and you know what she is – all hips and hysteria.

Pellet   I wish I'd been there – I 'ad to do extra duty – Vera Pearn got special leave to go to the white sales.

Wendle   Favourtism.

Pellet   I gave Inspector Rogers a piece of my mind, I can tell you.

Wendle   She's a mean cat, that Inspector Rogers, if ever there was one.

Pellet   And common! – My dear – do you know she –

They draw closer – **Pellet** *whispers.*

Wendle   She *didn't*!

Pellet   She did – right in me face.

Wendle   What did you do?

Pellet   I saluted and swept out – but I couldn't 'elp crying a bit when I got me 'elmet off. But luckily Sergeant Leggat came in and she lent me 'er puff and we got to talking, she told me all about Jessie Lucas.

Wendle   What about her?

Pellet   She's in 'ospital.

Wendle   What – again!

Pellet   No. She was on duty at Victoria Station and got three ribs broken trying to see Adolphe Menjou.[69]

Wendle   Adolphe Menjou?

Pellet   I love Adolphe Menjou – he's so suave.

Wendle   He's suave right enough, but I prefer Ronald Colman[70] – he's more bellicose – don't misunderstand, I mean more up and doing. Did you see that film – John Gilbert[71] and Greta Garbo?[72]

Pellet   My dear! After the first kiss I quivered like as aspurn.

Wendle   They oughtn't to do it, you know – it's past a joke. After all, we're only human –

Both bend.

---

69 Adolphe Jean Menjou (1890–1963) was an American actor, known for films such as Charlie Chaplin's *A Woman of Paris* (1923).
70 Ronald Charles Coleman (1891–1958) was a theatre and silent film actor, who later starred in such Hollywood films as *The Prisoner of Zenda* (1937).
71 John Gilbert (1897–1936) was an American actor, screenwriter and director, known as 'the Great Lover' during the silent film era. The film referenced here is *Flesh and the Devil* (1926), which starred both Gilbert and Garbo, and sparked a wave of rumours about a supposed love affair between them.
72 Greta Garbo (1905–90) was a Swedish-American actor, known for films such as *Ninotchka* (1939).

Pellet   Do you remember that robe de nuit she wore?

Wendle   The one with the black chiffon?

Pellet   Yes, I saw the spitting image of it in Swan and Edgar's.[73]

Wendle   Did you get it?

Pellet (*giggling*)   Well, I know it was terribly naughty of me, but I just couldn't resist it.

Wendle   Is it cut V shape? – too divine! –

Pellet   Well, dear, I must say I 'ad to alter it a bit.

Shouts off right.

Wendle   – See your skin through it –

Their conversation is here lost in a terrible commotion offstage. Shouts and screams of 'Murder!' A **Man** *rushes across the stage clutching a knife, followed by* **Two Women** *screaming and another* **Man** *brandishing a revolver.* **Pellet** *and* **Wendle** *are so engrossed that they don't see them – when the four people have gone off there is suddenly a loud, single scream and a shot.*

Pellet   What was that?

Wendle   Only another one of those tyres burst.

Blackout.

Finale

Scene: Stage door.

Stage Door-Keeper *discovered in box.*

Eight Stage Hands *enter first entrance right and cross stage, singing:*

> We're eight stage hands,
> Weary and winsome,
> Embassy Club be blowed.
> We've got wives and a nice drop of gin
> Somewhere in the Old Kent Road.[74]
> Good night! Good night!

Exit first exit left.

Eight Chorus Girls *enter first entrance right. Some give keys to* **Stage Door-Keeper**. *They come down to footlights and sing:*

> One, two, three, four,
> Five, six, seven, eight
> All going home to bed.

---

73 Swan and Edgar was a department store in Piccadilly Circus from 1837–2013.
74 This is a reference to the British music hall song 'Knocked 'Em In the Old Kent Road' which was written by Albert Chevalier in 1891.

Nobody's asked us to supper,
We wish we were dead.
Tho' we know quite
Well if we are late
Mother will leave the light,
We're feeling depressed
'Cos no one wants us;

They exit first exit left, singing last two lines:

So it would be best
For us to say good night.

Eight Show Girls *enter first entrance right. Spread across stage at footlights.*

You'll never know girls
Nicer than show girls,
For our behaviour
Reeks of Belgravia,[75]
We're so restrained that
Men have complained that

They exit first exit left, singing last two lines:

We've nothing left to show,
Good night, good night, good night.

Smart Parts *enter first entrance right some give keys to* **Stage Door-Keeper**. *Spread across stage at footlights.*

Tho' we hardly speak parts
We support the weak parts
In our unpretentious way.
Now that you have seen us
Kindly choose between us
We shall all be stars some day.

They exit first exit left, singing last two lines.

Good night and in the next revue that Cochran produces
We'll see our talents have more definite uses.

All **Principals** *enter first entrance right, cross to straight line at footlights.*

Now you know our
Personalities
What is it all about?
We're most surprised to discover
You haven't walked out.
We've exhausted
Our vitalities,

---

75 An affluent area of central London.

Sorry we've been so bright,
Just hurry and go
And put your coats on
We've come to the moment
When we say good night,
Good night, good night, good night.

Blackout.

All the **Company** *are discovered in motor-cars.*

We are the cause
Of all the traffic jam in Piccadilly,[76]
Motoring laws
We disregard because they are so silly,
Toot-toot – toot-toot,
Toot-toot – toot-toot – toot-toot.
We're driving home in our
Driving home in our
High-powered cars,
You'd better hurry and take cover
For our knowledge of driving is slight,
Toot-toot – toot-toot,
Toot-toot – toot-toot – toot-toot,
So good good good good night.

You've seen the revue
Right through.
We hope you're applauding too
For it's according to
You – the money speaks.
We hope you can rouse
Keith Prowse[77]
To something sensational,
Their approbation'll
House us here for weeks.
We thought it best to have a try-out,
We're not allowed to shirk,
Please don't let us fly out
Of work.
The best we can do
It's true
May not make you yearn again
Soon to return again to
This dreary revue.

---

76 A street in London's West End.
77 Keith Prowse is a theatre ticket and hospitality agency in London.

Close curtains.

Finale[78]

Announcement   Ladies and gentlemen, Mr Cochran has suddenly arrived, rather tardily I fear, at the realisation that our revue is completely lacking in the two essentials of American musical entertainment – pep and speed – so therefore we propose to remedy these deficiencies as best we can in the short time left to us.

Opening chorus:

> Playing the game
> You have to biff the ball
> And bang the ball
> In playing the game
> You have to whiff the ball
> And whang the ball
> And rah rah – rah rah – rah rah – rah rah – rah rah –
> We're so collegiate – so collegiate –
> You are to blame
> For all the speed of it
> Your need of it
> Is really a terrible shame
> And rah rah – rah rah – rah rah – rah rah – rah rah –
> Everybody plays the game.

At the end of opening chorus dance the **Boys** *and* **Girls** *rush off and* **Helen** *and* **Harry** *rush on from opposite sides of the stage.*

Helen   Oh, Harry!

Harry   How's your prep –

Helen   Oh, Harry!

Harry   Say, girlie, if I win the big game to-day it will be for you.

Helen   Oh, Harry!

Number: 'The Sun, the Moon and You'

At the end of which all the **Boys** *and* **Girls** *rush off and* **Helen** *and* **Harry** *again rush on.*

---

78 From the script: This alternative finale was used in the American production.

Verse 1:

> Little girlie
> Late or early,
> I just dream of you.
> Since that happy Tuesday when we met
> If you only knew,
> One and one are two
> That's a thing you never should forget.

Refrain:

> I want the sun, the moon and you,
> They simply thrill me through and through,
> The little stars that shine above
> Just fill me full of thoughts of love,
> My heart is throbbing,
> For you're robbing
> Me of all my pride,
> So listen, baby,
> Don't say maybe
> You will be my bride.
> Sweetheart, I could never be blue
> With just the sun, the moon and you.

Boys *and* **Girls** *rush off.*

Helen *and* **Harry** *again rush on.*

Harry Say, listen, girlie, I've got a peach of a scheme.

Helen Oh, Harry!

Harry And is you'll just say yes, everything will be jake.

Helen So do do de-o, Harry!

Reprise of 'The Sun, the Moon and You'.

Full chorus and finale.

Duet: 'Lilac Time'

He
> Oh tell me, little maiden pray
> Why should you choose to hide away
> On such a lovely summer's day?

She (*aside*)
> He does not know that I am the Princess, disguised as a beggar maid. Ah me!

To him:
>Kind sir, I know not who you are
>But if you should presume too far
>I shall seek refuge with Mamma.

He (*aside*)
>She does not know that I am the Crown Prince, disguised as a gardener – Ah me!

She
>Spring is the time for folly – Ah ah – ah ah –

He
>Fly away melancholy – ah ah – ah ah –

She
>Spring is the time

He
>Spring is the time

She
>Spring is the time

He
>Spring is the time

She
>For folly

He
>So melancholy fly away –
>For it is spring and life is gay and jolly.

Refrain 1:

Both
>Lilac time, lilac time
>Blossoms are o'er the lea.

He
>Birds are chirruping love's sweet song

She
>Church bells ring-a-ding-ding-ding-dong!

He
>Steal a kiss,
>Just like this

He kisses her.

She
>You are too bold and free (*She slaps him roguishly.*)

Both
> That is why it's lilac time
> Under the chestnut tree.

Verse 2:

She (*holding up a book*)
> I am engrossed as you can see
> In reading some philosophy.

He
> Literature this year must be
> So very much in vogue,
> Why should you bury that dainty nose
> In so much dry and dusty prose?

She
> You're making love to me, I suppose,

He
> You charming little rogue,

She
> A charming little rogue,

Both
> A charming, charming, charming little rogue.

Refrain 2:

Both
> Lilac time, lilac time
> Blossoms are o'er the lea.

He
> Birds are mating near and far

She
> Tra-la-lalala – la, la, la.

He
> Steal a kiss
> Just like this. (*Kisses her.*)

She
> You are too bold and free. (*She slaps him lightly.*)

Both
> That is why it's lilac time
> Under the chestnut tree,
> Ah ah – ah ah –
> Ah ah – ah ah – ah ah ah ah ah ah
> Heigho nin nonny no
> Heigho whack jolly-o

Heigho, lackaday do
That is why it's lilac time
That is why it's lilac time
Ha ha ha ha ha ha ha ha ha ha ha ha ha ha ha!

'World Weary'

Verse 1:

When I'm feeling dreary and blue,
I'm only too glad to be left alone,
Dreaming of a place in the sun,
When day is done, far from a telephone;
Bustle and the weary crowd
Make me want to cry out loud,
Give me something peaceful and grand
Where all the land slumbers in monotone.

Refrain 1:

I'm world weary, world weary,
Living in a great big town,
I find it so dreary, so dreary,
Everything looks grey or brown,
I want an ocean blue, great big trees,
A bird's-eye view of the Pyrenees,
I want to watch the moon rise up
And see the great red sun go down,
Watching clouds go by through a wintry sky fascinates me
But if I do it in the street,
Every cop I meet simply hates me,
Because I'm world weary, world weary,
I could kiss the railroad tracks,
I want to get right back to nature and relax.

Verse 2:

Get up in the morning at eight,
Relentless Fate,
Drives me to work at nine;
Toiling like a bee in a hive
From four to five
Whether it's wet or fine,
Hardly ever see the sky,
Buildings seem to grow so high,
Maybe in the future I will
Perhaps fulfil
This little dream of mine.

Refrain 2:

> I'm world weary, world weary,
> Living in a great big town,
> I find it so dreary, so dreary,
> Everything looks grey or brown,
> I want a horse and plough,
> Chickens too,
> Just one cow
> With a wistful moo,
> A country where the verb to work
> Becomes a most improper noun;
> I can hardly wait
> 'Til I see the great open spaces,
> My loving friends will not be there
> I'm so sick of their God-damned faces,
> Because I'm world weary, world weary,
> Tired of all these jumping jacks,
> I want to get right back to nature and relax.

'I Can't Think'

Verse 1:

> It was early in September
> That we met each other first,
> And my entrance, I remember,
> Was distinctly unrehearsed.
> I had been to buy some butter
> And some raspberries and some eggs,
> When I slipped up in the gutter
> And clasped him round the legs.

Refrain:

> I can't think why he looked at me so queerly,
> I can't think why he scowled and walked away,
> I fell, as I apologised sincerely
> He might have – well, perhaps I shouldn't say.
> I can't think how he managed to resist me,
> Perhaps the wish was father to the thought,
> I can't think why he didn't even kiss me,
> But I *do* think he did nothing of the sort.

Verse 2:

> It was later in October
> When we met – heig-ho! – once more,
> I believe that I was sober,

But I couldn't be quite sure.
It was early in the morning
And the air was pure and sweet,
When I staggered without warning
And fell prostrate at his feet.

Refrain 2:

I can't think why balance so betrayed me,
I can't think why he hiccoughed and then frowned,
I feel as he had not the strength to raise me
He might have least have joined me on the ground.
I can't think why his manners so depressed me,
Perhaps he was too social and refined,
If you think he attempted to molest me,
I *do* think he did nothing of the kind.

Blackout.

Bitter Sweet

Critics' Notes

Critical responses to the work focused on Coward's masterful musical style and character-driven plot, and his direction. A critic for *The Tatler* remarked: 'Genius is a word to be used sparingly, but in his own sphere, and records show how elastic are its dimensions, Mr Coward deserves the epithet. His versatility is positively indecent.'[1] London producer Charles B. Cochran stated: 'I believe Noël Coward has never done better work . . . his direction of the play has been masterly. I know nobody who can get so much from actors by the quietest of methods.'[2] Coward's choice to not only compose, write, and direct the work was unique, although it is worth noting the contributions, including orchestration and arrangement, by pianist Elsie April. Much like earlier works, British critics praised the show's accessible style, including *The Scotsman*, which noted: 'Mr Noël Coward's play *Bitter Sweet* continues to hold its sway over the playgoing public . . .' emphasizing Coward's personal and artistic accessibility for mainstream audiences.[3]

It was not only the musical style, but Coward's all-encompassing creative approach that defined the work's success. As *The Sporting Times* argued:

> In these days it usually takes a battalion of authors, composers, lyric-writers and contributors of extra numbers to concoct a musical entertainment. So it was rather a risk that C. B. Cochran took when he allowed Noel Coward to write *Bitter Sweet* all by himself – libretto, lyrics, music, everything, in fact, except those poignant lines in the programme which tell you that the chewing-gum used in Act II is by Chumpley's Ltd.[4]

On the genre of the work, critic Vernon Woodhouse remarked:

> In what an 'operette' differs from an operetta I really do not know, but the exchange of the final vowel seems to be important, for this production differs in many ways from any English play with music that I have ever seen. It differs still more greatly from any American musical play . . . For once in a way here is a musical play with a charming story which would be good entertainment without one bar of music, and not only is there a story, but real characters carry it on.[5]

Woodhouse further remarked upon the musical 'stage dressing' in which Coward transforms the musical time and place through the inclusion of styles from each era evoked in the historical flashbacks. Finally, Coward's youthful energy captivated critics and audiences. As an anonymous critic for *The Illustrated London News* noted:

> Coward is still the wonder-youth of our theatre, but one who is learning humanity and gaining balance as he continues his extraordinarily successful

---

1   Anonymous, 'The Passing Shows: *Bitter Sweet* at the Lyceum', *The Tatler*, Wednesday 7 August 1929.
2   Anonymous, 'Our London Letter', *Staffordshire Sentinel*, Thursday 27 June 1929.
3   Anonymous, untitled, *The Scotsman*, Monday 27 April 1931.
4   Anonymous, 'One-Man Show', *Sporting Times*, Saturday 27 July 1929, p. 11.
5   Vernon Woodhouse, 'Coward's Triumph and Hardy Hash', *The Bystander*, Wednesday 31 July 1929, p. 14.

career ... his own librettist, his own melodist, his own producer, and scoring in each of these capacities – doing easily off his own bat, in less happy attempts in this kind, has required the efforts of half-a-dozen and more collaborators.[6]

As we see in the following script, Coward's style is at once nostalgic, innovative and romantic; all elements that contributed to the work's commercial success and longevity.

Original Cast

The Marchioness of Shayne (*Sarah Millick*)	Peggy Wood[7]
Dolly Chamberlain	Dorothy Boyd[8]
Lord Henry Jekyll	William Harn[9]
Vincent Howard	Billy Milton[10]
Carl Linden	Georges Metaxa[11]
Mrs Millick	Elaine Inescourt[12]
Hugh Devon	Robert Newton[13]
Victoria	Jose Fearon[14]
Harriet	Masie Drage[15]
Gloria	Rose Hignell[16]
Honor	Isla Bevan[17]
Jane	Eileen Carey[18]
Effie	Mary Pounds[19]
Lotte	Millie Sim[20]

6 Anonymous, 'The Playhouses', *Illustrated London News*, Saturday 27 July 1929, p. 34.
7 Mary Margaret Wood (1892–1978) was an American actor of stage and screen, whose other notable performances include the role of Ruth in the 1941 New York production of *Blithe Spirit*.
8 Dorothy Boyd (1907–96) was born in Surrey, England. Other credits include films such as *Easy Virtue* (1928) and *A Shot in the Dark* (1933).
9 Little is known about British stage actor William Harn.
10 Billy Milton (1905–89) was a British stage, film and television actor. Other credits include the films *A Star Fell from Heaven* (1936) and *Yes, Madam?* (1939).
11 Georges Metaxa (1899–1950) was a Romanian-born American actor of stage and screen. Other London credits include Kurt Weill's ill-fated *A Kingdom for a Cow* (1935). Film credits include *Swing Time* (1936) and *Hi Diddle Diddle* (1943).
12 Elaine Inescourt (1879–1964) was a stage actor, known for roles in such plays as *Androcles and the Lion* (1946).
13 Robert Newton (1905–56) was an actor born in Shaftesbury, England, whose credits include films such as *Treasure Island* (1950).
14 Robert Newton was a minor English character actor.
15 Jose Fearon was a minor stage actor in the West End.
16 Rose Hignell was also Peggy Wood's understudy.
17 Isla Mary Bevan (1908–76) was a London-born actor of stage and screen. Other credits include *The Sign of Four* (1932).
18 Eileen O'Casey (1900–95) was an Irish stage actor who used the surname Carey. Other credits include Max Reinhardt's *The Miracle* (1912).
19 Mary 'Toots' Pounds (1897–1976) was an Australian actress and singer, best known for her solo performances as a concert singer.
20 Millie Sim (1895–1986) was an English stage actor, whose other was the famous 'Millie Hilton' of the five Rudge Sisters.

Freda   Betty Huntley-Wright[21]
Hansi   Marjorie Rogers[22]
Gussi   Norah Howard[23]
Manon (*La Crevette*)   Ivy St. Helier[24]
Captain August Lutte   Austin Trevor[25]
Captain Schnezi   Gerald Nodin[26]
Lieutenant Tranisch   Arthur Alexander[27]
Herr Schlick   Clifford Heatherley[28]
Marquis of Shayne   Alan Napier[29]
Vernon Craft   Arthur Alexander
Cedric Ballantyne   William Harn
Bertram Sellick   Eric Lauriston[30]
Lord Henry Jade   Penryn Bannerman[31]

Directed by Noël Coward
Stage design by G. E. Caltrop and Ernest Stern[32]

Lay Out

---

21 Betty Huntley-Wright (1911–93) was an English actor and singer, who performed in pantomimes, as well as radio and television productions.
22 Marjorie Rogers was a minor stage actor in the West End.
23 Norah Howard (1900–68) was a British actor of stage and screen, whose film credits include *A Cuckoo in the Nest* (1933).
24 Ivy St. Helier (1886–1971) was born in London, and worked as an actor, composer and lyricist.
25 Claude Austin Trevor Schlisky (1897–1978) was a Northern Irish actor, best known for originating the film role of Agatha Christie's Hercule Poirot in *Alibi* (1931).
26 Gerald Nodin (1899–1969) was an English actor, best known for *Over the Moon* (1939).
27 Arthur Alexander was a music hall performer, best known for his drag performances.
28 Clifford Heatherley Lam (1888–1937) was an English actor of stage and screen, best known for such films as *The Constant Nymph* (1928).
29 Alan William Napier-Clavering (1903–88) was an English stage and screen actor who was engaged by the Oxford Players. He was later cast as the first Alfred in the television series *Batman* (1965).
30 Eric Lauriston was a minor stage actor in the West End.
31 Penryn Bannerman was a minor English stage actor; little is known about his life.
32 Gladys Edith Mabel Calthrop (1894–1980) was a stage and set designer who first met Coward in 1921. She designed many of the sets for his productions, including *Private Lives* (1931). Ernest Stern (1876–1954) was born in Bucharest, and worked in the German cabaret world before he worked with Calthrop on *Bitter Sweet*.

Act One

Scene One

Characters: **Marchioness of Shayne, Dolly Chamberlain, Lord Henry Jekyll, Vincent Howard, Nita, Helen, Jackie, Frank, Parker, Guests, Musicians,** *etc. The scene is* **Lady Shayne**'s *house in Grosvenor Square.*[33] *The year is 1929.*

There is a small dance in progress. At the back of the stage in the centre are large double doors leading into the supper room. On the left-hand side is a small jazz band which is playing in front of the open windows. On the right-hand side a smaller door opens into the library. When the curtain rises the stage is crowded with **Dancers**. **Parker** *throws open the double doors at the back and announces supper. Everyone goes in laughing and talking and can be seen taking their places at small tables. The double doors are closed and the members of the band retire on to the balcony for a little fresh air, with the exception of* **Vincent Howard**, *who remains at the piano improvising syncopations softly.*

Dolly Chamberlain *and* **Henry Jekyll** *come in from the library.* **Dolly** *is pretty and attractive, about twenty.* **Henry** *is a trifle older and included to be faintly pompous.*

Dolly   They've all home in to supper – come on.

Henry   It's damned hot.

Dolly   You've been grumbling about one thing and another all the evening.

Henry   Sorry, old darling.

Dolly   Do you think you love me really?

Henry   Of course. Don't be an ass.

Dolly   Enough?

Henry   Enough for what?

Dolly   Oh, I don't know – enough to spend your life with me, I suppose.

Henry   It's a little late to worry about that now – with the wedding next Monday.

Vincent *strikes a chord with some viciousness.* **Dolly** *looks sharply over her shoulder at him.*

Dolly   You're right, it is hot.

Henry   Where's Lady Shayne?

Dolly (*pointing to supper room*)   In there, I expect.

Henry   Strange old girl.

Dolly   I hope I shall be like that when I'm seventy.

---

33   A large garden square in London's upper-class Mayfair district.

Henry   She can't be as much as that.

Dolly   She is – she was at school with my grandmother.

Henry   Good God!

Dolly   It must be funny to look back over so many years. I wonder if she minds.

Henry   Minds what?

Dolly   Being old, of course – to have led such a thrilling life and then to suddenly to realise there's nothing left to look forward to.

Henry   Well, she certainly is a gay old bird.

Dolly   Henry! (*She looks at him almost shocked.*)

Henry   What?

Dolly   How silly that sounds – a gay old bird.

Henry   Well, it's true isn't it? – That's what she is, always travelling around and giving parties and staying up all night – it's almost indecent – I wouldn't like to see my grandmother going on like that.

Dolly   Well, you needn't worry. (*She laughs.*)

Henry   How do you mean?

Dolly   All your relations are too pompous to enjoy anything.

Henry   Dolly!

Dolly   Well, they are – they've all got several feet in the grave, there's no life left in them, if ever there was any, which I doubt – you'll probably be like that too in a few years.

Henry   You think Lady Shayne's life has been thrilling, do you? (*He smiles superciliously.*) That's funny.

Dolly   Yes, I do – I do – and it isn't so funny either.

Henry   Now look here, Dolly, if you knew some of the things about Lady Shayne that *I* know –

Dolly   I know more than you know – I know that she justified her existence – she lived for something –

Henry   She was thoroughly immoral in her youth – lovers and awful second-rate people round her all the time. It was lucky for her she met Shayne and got back.

Dolly   Got back to what?

Henry   Decent people – society.

Dolly   Oh dear. I can laugh now.

Henry   Now, Dolly, my girl – I –

Dolly (*suddenly with vehemence*)   Shut up – shut up – go away from me – you're pompous and silly and I can't bear it –

Henry   Dolly!

Dolly (*wildly*)   Go away – go away!

Henry   You're impossible.

He stamps off into the supper room.

Vincent   Can I stop playing now?

Dolly (*in a stifled voice*)   No – go on.

Vincent   I can't bear it much longer – darling.

Dolly   Vincent – don't.

Vincent   Please come over here and sit close to me.

Dolly   I'd better not, I think.

Vincent   Afraid?

Dolly   Yes. (*She goes over and sits beside him – he goes on playing.*)

Vincent   I love you so.

Dolly   Oh, God! I'm so utterly, utterly miserable. (*She buries her head in her arms.*)

Vincent   Don't cry – you're going to marry a rich man and have rich friends and a rich house and rich food, and some day if you're really rich enough you'll be able to engage me to come and play for you. (*He laughs bitterly.*)

Dolly   How can you be so horrid!

Vincent   You'll be safe anyhow.

Dolly   I don't want to be safe.

Vincent   Come away with me then – I've got no money – nothing to offer you – you'd look fine singing my songs in some cheap cabaret somewhere – and living in third-rate hotels and just – well, earning your living –

Dolly   It sounds marvellous.

Vincent   Don't be a damned fool!

Dolly   Vincent –

Vincent   It's hell – (*He stops playing and goes towards the window.*)

Dolly   Where are you going?

Vincent   To call the boys – we've got to work some more.

Dolly   I shan't see you again until – until – after I'm married.

Vincent   Never mind – safety first.

Dolly   What am I to do? –

Vincent   Good-bye, you poor little kid –

He suddenly takes her in his arms and kisses her. She twines her arms round his neck and they stand there clasped tight. **Lady Shayne** *enters from the supper room. She watches them silently for a moment. She is seventy years old, but her figure is still slim; her hair is snow-white, and her gown is exquisite.*

Lady Shayne   Dolly!

Dolly *and* **Vincent** *break away from one another.*

Lady Shayne   I come on an errand of peace from your fiancé. If it is inopportune I apologise.

Dolly   Oh, Lady Shayne.

Lady Shayne (*to* **Vincent**)   You are the piano player in the band, aren't you?

Vincent   I'm sorry for what happened just now, your ladyship. It – it was an accident.

Lady Shayne   In what way – an accident?

Vincent   I – er – we were saying good-bye.

Lady Shayne   Your drummer is too loud, and I can't bear the man who plays the saxophone.

Dolly   Lady Shayne – I – let me explain.

Lady Shayne   When a man plays off-key the only explanation is that he's a bad musician.

Dolly   Lady Shayne – I love Vincent and – he loves me.

Lady Shayne   And this is Vincent?

Dolly   Yes, of course.

Lady Shayne   And Henry, your future husband, is in there – practically weeping into the cold asparagus.

Vincent   You're laughing at us – your ladyship.

Lady Shayne   I laugh at almost everything now – it's only when one is very old indeed that one can see the joke all the way round.

Dolly   What joke?

Lady Shayne   Life and death and happiness and despair and love. (*She laughs again.*)

Vincent   Don't laugh like that, please – your ladyship.

Lady Shayne   So you're a musician – an amiable. sensitive-looking young man – and you've been making love to this child – or has she been making love to you? – everything seems to have changed round lately.

Vincent   It just happened – we – at least that is – I don't know.

Lady Shayne   Are you a married man?

Vincent   No – of course not.

Lady Shayne   Well, you needn't be so vehement. I merely thought you might have forgotten –

Vincent   My intentions are quite honourable, if presumptuous.

Dolly   Are you angry?

Lady Shayne   Not in the least, my dear. What do you intend to do?

Dolly   I don't know.

Lady Shayne   Well, if I were you I should make up my mind. (*She turns towards the supper room.*)

Dolly   You *are* angry.

Lady Shayne   I detest indecision.

Dolly   I don't understand –

Several people come out of the supper room, including **Nita** *and* **Helen**.

Nita   Dolly – what have you been doing to Henry – he's plunged in gloom.

Helen   He's sending out thought waves of depression and I got the lot, being next to him.

Jackie *rushes out of the supper room with* **Frank** *and several others.*

Jackie   What's happened to the band? Oh, Mr Howard, play something – play something romantic – I want to dance.

Lady Shayne (*laughing*)   Yes – play something romantic.

Vincent (*savagely*)   I'll play anything anybody wants – that's what I'm hired for – (*He goes to the piano.*) Here's romance for you – how's this –

He plays a swift jazz tune. Everyone begins to dance and jig about. **Nita** *Charlestons a few steps, while* **Helen** *and* **Jackie** *clap their hands and sing. Suddenly* **Lady Shayne** *stamps her foot sharply.*

Lady Shayne   Stop – stop – it's hideous – you none of you know anything or want anything beyond noise and speed – your dreams of romance are nightmares. Your conception of life grotesque. Come with me a little – I'll show you – listen – listen –

Frank (*softly*)   Oh, God, what's the old girl up to now.

Dolly   Be quiet.

Lady Shayne *begins to sing – everyone squats down on the floor – some of them giggling furtively.* **Vincent** *and* **Dolly** *stare at her as though transfixed.*

'The Call of Life'

Lady Shayne
  Your romance could not live the length of a day,
  You hesitate and analyse,
  Betray your love with compromise,
  Till glamour fades away;
  All too soon you realise
  That there is nothing left to say.

Chorus
  Hey, hey – hey, hey,
  How does she get that way;
  She'd be more light-hearted
  If she started – to Charleston;[34]
  She's never danced it,
  She's never danced it;
  Perhaps her muscles are disinclined,
  Perhaps she hasn't the strength of mind.

Lady Shayne
  Love that's true can mean naught to you but a name,
  A thing that isn't part of you;
  Can never touch the heart of you;
  It's nothing but a game,
  A fire without a flame.

Men
  We find it difficult to grasp your meaning.

Lady Shayne
  Maybe the past is intervening.

Chorus
  We very much regret that times have changed so,
  Life is more speedily arranged so.

Lady Shayne
  In your world of swiftly turning wheels
  Life must be extremely grey.

Chorus
  We've no time to waste on Love Ideals,
  That which to our sense most appeals
  Is all we can obey.

Lady Shayne
  No – no. Not so;

---

34 The Charleston, which was imported from the United States at the end of the First World War, symbolized modernity, progress and mainstream culture.

There must be something further on,
A vision you can count upon,
To help you to acquire
A memory when Youth is gone
Of what was once your heart's desire.

There is a call that echoes sweetly
When it is spring and Love is in the air;
Whate'er befall, respond to it completely,
Tho' it may bring you sadness and despair;
Fling far behind you
The chains that bind you,
That love may find you
In joy or strife;
Tho' Fate may cheat you,
And defeat you,
Your Youth must answer to the Call of Life.

The lights slowly go out, and through the darkness her voice grows sweeter and younger, until presently the lights go up again and disclose a young girl of about seventeen standing demurely in a prim Victorian room with spring sunlight flooding through the windows behind her. Seated beside her at an Erard grand pianoforte is a young music master, **Carl Linden** *– he is playing the piano, but his eyes are gazing up at her face and he is smiling a trifle wistfully as she comes to the end of the song.*

Scene Two

Characters: **Sarah Millick, Carl Linden, Mrs Millick, Hugh Devon.** *The scene is the* **Millicks'** *house in Belgrave Square. The year is 1875.*

When **Sarah** *finishes singing,* **Carl** *allows his hands to drop from the keys, and still gazing into her eyes, he speaks:*

Carl   That was excellent, Miss Sarah – you are improving in a very marked manner.

Sarah (*demurely*)   Thank you.

Carl   I wrote that song for you when I was sixteen years old.

Sarah   But Mr Linden, that cannot be true – we have only known each other during the past year.

Carl   I mean that I wrote it for someone like you.

Sarah (*quickly*)   Oh!

Carl   Not a real person – just an ideal in my mind, someone young and charming – holding out her arms as you did just now – expectantly.

Sarah   Expectant of what, Mr Linden?

Carl (*hopelessly turning away*)   I don't know.

Sarah I think it is the loveliest song I ever heard.

Carl (*looking at her again*) Do you?

Sarah (*meeting his eyes*) Yes – of course.

Carl You took the high note too much at the back of your throat.

Sarah I'm sorry.

Carl It doesn't matter.

Sarah Oh, but, surely it does.

Carl Nothing matters but just these few moments.

Sarah Why do you say that, Mr Linden?

Carl Because it's spring, and I – I –

Sarah Yes?

Carl I fear I am talking nonsense.

Sarah (*smiling*) Perhaps a little.

Carl We have festivals in the spring in my country – and the young boys and girls dance and their clothes are brightly coloured, glinting in the sun, and the old people sit round under the trees, watching and tapping their sticks on the ground and reviving in their heart's memories of when they, too, were young and in love.

Sarah In love?

Carl Yes – as you are in love with your handsome Mr Devon.

Sarah Oh – Hugh – yes, of course. Tell me more about your country, Mr Linden.

Carl There is nothing to tell really – it seems so very far away – I've almost forgotten.

Sarah You're homesick though, I can see you are.

Carl Can you?

Sarah Perhaps it's the climate here, it *is* depressing –

Carl Yes, a little. (*He sings.*)
   Tho' there may be beauty in this land of yours,
   Skies are very often dull and grey;
   If I could but take that little hand of yours,
   Just to lead you secretly away.
   We would watch the Danube as it gently flows,
   Like a silver ribbon winding free;
   Even as I speak of it my longing grows,
   Once again my own dear land to see.
   If you could only come with me,
   If you could only come with me.

Sarah   Oh, Mr Linden.

Carl   Yes.

Sarah   How very strange everything is to-day.

Carl   Will you forgive me, Miss Sarah, when I tell you that I shall be unable to play at your wedding reception.

Sarah (*disappointed*)   Oh!

Carl   I must go away on that day – to Brussels.

Sarah   Brussels?

Carl (*hurriedly*)   Yes, a concert – I have to play at a concert – it is very important.

Sarah   I understand.

Carl   Do you?

Sarah   Yes – but it is very, very disappointing.

Carl   But I am deeply grateful for the honour you have done me in asking me.

Sarah (*lightly, but turning away*)   This is the last time we shall meet then for ever so long.

Carl   To-night – I am playing to-night for the dance.

Sarah   But that is different. There will be so many people –

Carl   This is indeed the last time we shall be alone together.

Sarah (*looking down*)   Yes.

Carl   You have been a charming pupil – I shall always look back on these months with happiness.

Sarah   Happiness?

Carl   And sadness too.

Sarah   Oh, dear.

Carl   There are tears in your eyes.

Sarah   In yours also.

Carl   I know – I am sorry to be so foolish.

Sarah   Dear Mr Linden –

She gives him her hand, he kisses it fervently, then pulls himself together with a tremendous effort.

Carl   Once more now – your exercises just once more through.

Sarah (*tearfully*)   Very well.

Carl *strikes a chord –* **Sarah** *sings up and down, saying 'Ah'. Suddenly a barrel organ*[35] *strikes up in the street outside a sugary sentimental melody.* **Sarah** *perseveres with her exercises, then* **Carl** *begins to sing to her, accompanied by the orchestra, with the barrel organ as a background.*

'I'll See You Again'

Carl
    Now Miss Sarah, if you please,
    Sing a scale for me.

Sarah
    Ah – Ah – Ah –

Carl
    All my life I shall remember knowing you,
    All the pleasure I have found in showing you
    The different ways
    That one may phrase
    The changing light, the changing shade;
    Happiness that must die,
    Melodies that must fly,
    Memories that must fade,
    Dusty and forgotten by and by.

Sarah
    Learning scales will never seem so sweet again
    Till our Destiny shall let us meet again.

Carl
    The will of Fate
    May come too late.

Sarah
    When I'm recalling these hours we've had
    Why will the foolish tears
    Tremble across the years,
    Why shall I feel so sad,
    Treasuring the memory of these days
    Always?

Carl
    I'll see you again,
    Whenever spring breaks through again;
    Time may lie heavy between,
    But what has been
    Is past forgetting.

---

35 A small, mechanical, portable organ that contains bellows and pipes. It was often used by street performers throughout Europe, particularly in Germany.

Sarah
>This sweet memory,
>Across the years will come to me;
>Tho' my world may go awry,
>In my heart will ever lie,
>Just the echo of a sigh, Good-bye.

Mrs Millick *enters with* **Hugh Devon**. *During the ensuing scene until* **Carl**'s *exit, the love theme should be continued in the orchestra very softly.*

Mrs Millick Darling child – your lesson should have been over a quarter of an hour ago. There is so much to be done – I declare I'm nearly frantic – Hugh has been telling me about his aunt – poor Lady Ettleworth, she developed acute gastritis yesterday evening, and it may mean postponing the wedding, and on the other hand it may not. I'm certain it was the peas she ate at lunch here. They were like bullets. Good – afternoon, Mr Linden.

Carl (*bowing*) Good-afternoon, Mrs Millick.

Hugh Good-afternoon.

Carl (*bowing*) Good-afternoon.

Hugh You look tired, Sarah.

Sarah I am a little – I – it is quite hot to-day.

Mrs Millick I fear I must hurry you away, Mr Linden – Sarah has a dressmaker at four-thirty and there is so much to be done.

Carl I quite understand.

Mrs Millick Doubtless Sarah will resume her lessons with you when she is settled down in her new home.

Sarah Mother – I –

Mrs Millick It will be an occupation – I always believe in young married women having an occupation.

Carl I should have thought being married would be sufficient.

Mrs Millick (*slightly scandalised*) Mr Linden –

Carl (*bitterly*) Your daughter must learn from someone else when she is a young married woman, Mrs Millick. I shall not be here.

Mrs Millick Well, I'm sure I'm very sorry, I –

Carl (*looking fixedly at* **Sarah**) I shall be far away in my own country – but each year when spring comes round again, I shall remember you, Miss Sarah, and what a charming pupil you were, and how, although you sometimes sang your top notes from the back of your throat, and your middle notes through your nose, you always sang your deep notes from your heart.

Mrs Millick My dear Mr Linden!

Carl This is good-bye, Miss Sarah, except for to-night, when there will be so many people – too many people.

He bows abruptly and goes out. The music swells loudly in the orchestra, the theme of 'The Call of Life'. **Sarah** *begins to sing it brokenly.* **Hugh** *advances towards her, but she pushes him away and falls weeping into her mother's arms as the lights fade out.*

Scene Three

Characters: **Sarah Millick, Carl Linden, Mrs Millick, Hugh Devon, Lady Devon, Sir Arthur Fenchurch, Victoria, Harriet, Gloria, Honor, Jane, Effie, Marquis of Steere, Lord Edgar James, Lord Sorrel, Mr Vale, Mr Bethel, Mr Proutie, Four Footmen, Guests, Musicians,** *etc. The scene is the ballroom of the* **Millicks'** *house in Belgrave Square. The year is 1875.*

It is the ballroom of the **Millicks'** *house in Belgrave Square. There are three windows at the back opening on to a balcony overlooking the Square. On the left at an angle are double doors opening on to the landing and staircase. On the light is a small dais upon which the orchestra is playing, conducted by* **Carl Linden.** *Below this double doors lead into the supper room and on the left below the big doors is a small door leading into the drawing room. There are coloured lights festooned over the balcony which look charming against the shadowy trees in the Square.*

When the curtain rises, the ball is nearly over. A mazurka is in progress: the dresses of the guests are almost entirely pastel shades with the exception of a few chaperones in black and grey and purple, who are seated on small chairs and sofas below the orchestra. At the end of the mazurka most of the couples leave the floor; some go out on the balcony, some into the supper room and some into the drawing-room.

Lady Devon, *an imposing dowager, meets* **Mrs Millick** *as she billows in from the supper room.*

Lady Devon Charming, Violet – quite delightful – I congratulate you.

Mrs Millick The young people seem very happy, I think.

Lady Devon I thought Sarah looked radiant but a trifle flushed when she was waltzing with Hugh a little while ago.

Mrs Millick She has been flushed all the evening. I hope she isn't feverish – I feel quite disturbed about her.

Lady Devon I feel sure you have no cause to be – she was positively hilarious in the supper room.

Mrs Millick Unnaturally so.

Lady Devon She is in love, my dear.

Hugh *enters from the supper room.*

Hugh (*in harassed tones*) Oh, there you are.

Lady Devon (*fondly*) Happy boy.

Hugh I am very worried.

Mrs Millick Why – what has happened?

Hugh Sarah is behaving in a most peculiar manner – she upset a full glass of claret cup over Sir Arthur Fenchurch and laughed.

Mrs Millick Laughed!

Lady Devon Sir Arthur – Good heavens!

Sir Arthur *enters, a pompous-looking old gentleman. He is obviously restraining a boiling fury with a great effort. His shirt-front is claret-stained and his manner frigid.*

Sir Arthur (*bowing to* **Mrs Millick** *furiously, but politely*) A delightful evening, Mrs Millick – thank you a thousand times.

Mrs Millick But, Sir Arthur – you mustn't think of going.

Sir Arthur I couldn't think of staying – so many fresh young people enjoying themselves so very thoroughly – I feel out of place.

Lady Devon But, Sir Arthur –

Sir Arthur (*firmly*) Good-night, Lady Devon. Good-night, Mrs Millick. (*To* **Hugh**.) My boy – I sincerely *hope* your marriage will be a happy one.

Mrs Millick Well!

Hugh There now.

Lady Devon How very, very unfortunate.

Sarah *enters from the supper room; she looks lovely, but her manner is strained and almost defiant.*

Sarah Has he gone?

Mrs Millick Sarah – I'm ashamed of you.

Sarah He patted my hand, mamma, then he patted my head. I detest being patted.

Hugh He's one of the most influential men in London.

Mrs Millick And so kind.

Sarah And so pompous.

Lady Devon Sarah!

Mrs Millick The first thing to-morrow morning you shall write him a letter of apology.

She moves away with **Lady Devon**.

Sarah To-morrow is so far away. (*She laughs.*)

Hugh I don't understand you to-night, Sarah.

Sarah   I don't think I quite understand myself.

Hugh   Why did you cry this afternoon in the music room?

Sarah   Are you glad you are going to marry me, Hugh?

Hugh   Why did you cry like that?

Sarah   And will you be kind to me – always?

Hugh   You haven't answered me.

Sarah   And do you love me?

Hugh (*irritably*)   Sarah!

Sarah   Do you?

Hugh   Of course I do – what is the matter with you?

Carl Linden *stands up on the orchestra dais where the band have been regaling themselves with refreshments, and very softly plays on the violin 'I'll See You Again'.* **Sarah** *starts and then begins to laugh hysterically.*

Sarah   Don't look so solemn, Hugh – I'm in love.

Hugh   My dear girl, that's all very well –

Sarah   Is it?

Hugh   But you really must restrain yourself.

Sarah (*almost rudely*)   What a stupid tune, Mr Linden – so dismal –

Hugh   Sarah!

Sarah (*peremptorily*)   Play something gay, please – immediately.

Hugh (*softly*)   Sarah, you must not speak like that – have you taken leave of your senses?

Sarah (*vehemently*)   Let me alone – please go away – let me alone!

Hugh *goes angrily on to the balcony.* **Carl** *strikes up a tremendously gay melody.*

'What Is Love?'

Play something gay for me,
Play for me, play for me;
Set me free,
I am in a trance to-night,
Can't you see
How I want to dance to-night?
Madly my heart is beating,
Some insane melody possessing me,
In my brain thrilling and obsessing me;

How can I leave it to call in vain?
Is it joy or pain?
Live your life, for Time is fleeting,
Some insistent voice repeating;
Hear me – beat me,
How can I leave it to call in vain?
Is it joy or pain?

Refrain:

Tell me – tell me – tell me, what is love?
Is it some consuming flame;
Part of the moon, part of the sun,
Part of a dream barely begun?
When is the moment of breaking-waking?
Skies change, nothing is the same,
Some strange magic is to blame;
Voices, that seem to echo round me and above,
Tell me, what is love, love, love?
Play something gay for me,
Play for me – play for me;
Tell me why
Spring has so enchanted me;
Why this shy
Passion has been granted me;
Am I awake or dreaming?
Far and near
Every lover follows you,
Swift and clear,
Flying as the swallows do;
Leave me no longer to call in vain,
Are you joy or pain?
Leave me not by Love-forsaken,
If I sleep, then let me waken;
Hear me – hear me,
Leave me no longer to call in vain
Are you joy or pain?

Repeat refrain:

Sarah *begins to waltz round the stage by herself, and as she passes the supper room, the library and the balcony,* **Guests** *join her in her dance, until the whole stage is encircled by a wheel of young people laughing and chattering. At the end of this, the band plays 'God Save the Queen'; everyone naturally stands still, and then the party breaks up.* **Sarah** *takes her place at the door with her mother, in order to bid goodbye to the* **Guests**. *The* **Musicians** *are packing up their instruments, and finally all go out, including* **Carl**. **Hugh** *comes in from the balcony.* **Sarah** *leaves her mother talking to some* **Guests** *and runs up to him.*

Sarah I'm sorry, Hugh.

Hugh (*stiffly*) It doesn't matter.

Sarah Oh, but it does – I was unkind and silly.

Hugh It doesn't matter.

Sarah Will you please forgive me?

Hugh There is nothing to forgive.

Sarah I shall be bad again if you are so polite.

Hugh My dear Sarah!

Sarah (*desperately*) Are you always going to be like this – after we are married, I mean – cold and unbending?

Hugh I can only hope you are not often going to behave as you have to-night.

Sarah Oh, dear.

Hugh I don't feel that you realise yet the dignity of the position you will hold as my wife.

Sarah I am not your wife yet.

Hugh I enjoy being high-spirited as much as anyone.

Sarah Do you?

Hugh But there is a time and place for everything.

Sarah Then I can look forward to us being very high-spirited when we are alone – when no one is looking – you might wear a funny hat at breakfast.

Hugh I am very fond of you, my dear, but you must remember I am older than you.

Sarah Not so very much.

Hugh And it is part of my profession to consider appearances.

Sarah Diplomatically speaking.

Hugh Are you laughing at me?

Sarah No, but I'm looking at you – just as though I had never seen you before.

Lady Devon *enters.*

Lady Devon Hugh, *dear.*

Hugh Yes, mother?

Lady Devon I have been waiting for you downstairs. The carriage is at the door. Good-night, Sarah.

Sarah Good-night. I have been telling Hugh I was sorry to have behaved so badly.

Lady Devon (*smiling*) I am afraid you're marrying a tomboy, Hugh.

Sarah No, no – I won't be one any more.

Lady Devon Dear child. (*She kisses her.*) Come, Hugh. (*She moves over to* **Mrs Millick** *at the door.*)

Hugh Good-night, Sarah.

Sarah Good-night, Hugh.

Hugh Will you drive with me to-morrow afternoon in Regent's Park?

Sarah Thank you – that will be delightful.

Hugh Until to-morrow – my dear. (*He looks round carefully and then kisses her chastely and departs with* **Lady Devon**.)

Mrs Millick Well, that's over. Where are the girls?

Sarah Harriet and Gloria?

Mrs Millick Yes.

Sarah Sitting out somewhere with Lord Edgar and Mr Proutie.

Mrs Millick And Effie and Jane and Honor and Victoria?

Sarah They're sitting out, too.

Mrs Millick Come with me – we must find them – really you modern young people have no sense of behaviour at all.

She goes with **Sarah** *into the supper room while the music strikes up the introductory bars of a concerted number.* **Harriet** *and* **Lord Edgar** *peep round the library door and tiptoe out on to the stage.* **Gloria** *and* **Mr Proutie** *do the same from the balcony –* **Effie**, **Jane**, **Honor**, **Victoria** *and* **Mr Vale**, **Lord Sorrel**, **Lord Steere**, **Mr Bethel** *all join them.*

'The Last Dance'

Men
  They've all gone now – have no fear –

Girls
  Sarah's mother may be near,
  If she should hear

All
  She might be rather cross with us,
  Elderly people make too much fuss.

Men
  Always insist on a chaperone,
  Never leave love alone.

Girls
  We feel frightened, if you please
  Don't flirt or tease.

Men
> Gentle and sweet in your purity,
> We give our hearts as security.

Girls
> We shall be scolded a lot for this.

Men
> You won't miss just one kiss.

They all kiss.

Girls
> Think of the consequences, please, you haven't realised
> What an appalling thing for us to be so compromised,
> So dreadfully, dreadfully, dreadfully, compromised.

Men
> Everything's ending,
> The moon is descending,
> Behind the tall trees in the park.

Girls
> Silence falls,
> Slumber calls.

Men
> We men together
> Were wondering whether
> We might have a bit of a lark.

Girls
> No jokes in the dark, please,
> What sort of a lark, please?

All
> Just a slight dance,
> One more dream – of – delight dance;
> Just a sort of good – night dance
> Would be glorious fun.

Men
> Won't you let us, please let us, just stay for a while,
> Won't you, please won't you, be gay for a while?
> All we desire is to play for a while
> Now the party's done.

Girls
> Just a fast waltz,
> Till the world seems a vast waltz
> Very often the last waltz
> Is the birth of Romance.

All
>It's a June night,
>There's a thrill in the moonlight;
>Let's give way to the tender surrender
>Of our last dance.

At the end of the number all the men, with the exception of **Mr Proutie**, *creep out, leaving the* **Girls** *seated demurely on gilt chairs at some distance from one another all round the stage.* **Mr Proutie**, *being very smitten with* **Gloria**, *hides behind the sofa.* **Mrs Millick** *re-enters, looking rather agitated, followed by* **Sarah**.

Mrs Millick   Girls – where have you been?

Harriet   Nowhere, Aunt Violet.

Mrs Millick   Where is Lord Edgar?

Honor   He went hours ago, Mrs Millick.

Mrs Millick   And Lord Steere, Mr Bethel, Mr Vale and Lord Sorrel?

Victoria (*sighing*)   All gone.

Mrs Millick   And Mr Proutie?

Gloria   He was so tired he left early.

Mrs Millick   Come out from behind that sofa, Mr Proutie.

Mr Proutie *comes out, looking very sheepish. All the girls giggle.*

Mr Proutie *is very young and cherubic.*

Mr Proutie   I – I – fell asleep – I apologise.

Mrs Millick   I quite understand.

Mr Proutie (*appealingly to* **Gloria**)   Miss Gloria, I –

Mrs Millick   Good-night, Mr Proutie.

Mr Proutie   Miss Gloria said that –

Mrs Millick (*sternly*)   *Good-night*, Mr Proutie.

Mr Proutie   Er – er – good-night – thank you for having me – er– er good-night.

He goes out, covered with embarrassment.

Mrs Millick   Gloria – what does this mean?

Gloria   Nothing, Aunt Violet.

Mrs Millick   If it were not that this was a festive occasion, I should punish you severely for your deceit.

Harriet   Dear Aunt Violet – don't be cross.

Mrs Millick   To bed with the lot of you.

Effie   Oh, not yet – just ten minutes more.

Mrs Millick   Certainly not – it's nearly one o'clock – fine bridesmaids you'll make on Thursday, if you stay up so late.

Harriet   Won't you let us stay up just a little longer?

Honor   Oh, Mrs Millick, do – please do.

Mrs Millick   No – Sarah's tired –

Sarah   No, I'm not, mother I know I couldn't sleep for ages.

Gloria   Just a short while – please!

They all cluster round her and speak at once – finally she breaks away from them.

Mrs Millick   Very well – ten minutes then and no more. Sarah, come into my room and say good-night.

Sarah   Yes, mother.

Mrs Millick   Remember now – in ten minutes' time I shall tell Parker to come and put out the lights – and don't make too much noise –

Harriet   We won't, we promise.

Gloria   Good-night, Aunt Violet.

Mrs Millick *goes out amid a chorus of 'Good-nights'. The moment the door has closed upon her the girls fling aside their demure manner and dance about the stage.* **Harriet** *jumps on to the orchestra dais and begins to strum the piano.* **Effie**, **Honor** *and* **Sarah** *sing gaily while* **Victoria** *and* **Jane** *dance.*

Honor   Oh, Sarah – I do envy you being married and going to Paris and everything.

Sarah   Do you?

Effie   Aren't you dying of excitement? – I know I should be.

Sarah   No, not exactly. I feel strange somehow.

Gloria   What sort of strange?

Sarah   I don't know – it's difficult to explain – perhaps I'm frightened.

Jane   Nobody could be frightened of Hugh.

Victoria   When I marry, it must be somebody just like Hugh.

Harriet   I shall choose someone taller – more robust, you know.

Effie   How can you, Harriet – Hugh's just the right size.

Gloria   I shall marry Mr Proutie.

All   Gloria! – What do you mean?

Gloria (*calmly*)   He adores me.

Janb   Has he asked you?

Gloria   Of course.

Honor   And you said yes?

Gloria   I said no. But that doesn't matter – he'll ask me again.

Effie   Are you in love with him?

Gloria   No – not a bit.

Honor   How *can* you, Gloria?

Gloria   I'd much rather marry someone I didn't love really.

All   'Gloria!' 'Really!' 'You're dreadful!' 'Why?', etc.

Gloria   Because I could manage him better.

Harriet   I agree with Gloria.

Victoria   So do I.

Sarah   I don't – I want love.

Effie (*giggling*)   So do I – but you'll get it before I do –

They all laugh.

Honor   I mean to have a lot of babies.

Jane   I want someone to protect me always – someone strong that I can look up to –

Harriet   Fiddlesticks!

Victoria   Rubbish!

Gloria   Old-fashioned nonsense!

Jane   Let's play a game.

Sarah   What game?

Effie   Yes, yes – any game.

Honor   Postman's knock.

Sarah   No – no – that means one of us going out –

Jane   How, when and where.

Effie   So does that.

Sarah   Let's play an exciting game – a noisy game.

Harriet   Aunt Violet will hear.

Sarah   No she's two floors up.

Gloria   Blind Man's Buff[36]

Effie   Yes – yes.

---

36   A childhood game that is a variant of tag. The English version contains troubling racial images from Britain's colonial past, including a racial slur which has been marked here.

Sarah That will do –

Victoria Who'll be it –

Jane Eeny meeny miny mo – we must do eeny meeny miny mo –

Finale

Gloria Eeny meeny miny mo

Harriet Catch a n***** by his toe

Victoria If he hollers let him go

All O.U.T. spells out and so

Gloria Out goes she. (*She points to* **Effie**.)

Effie Out goes me. (*Skipping about.*) This is the loveliest, loveliest part of the party.

Gloria Eeny meeny miny mo

Harriet Catch a n***** by his toe

Victoria If he hollers let him go

All O.U.T. spells out and so

Gloria Out goes she. (*She points to* **Harriet**.)

Harriet Out goes me.

She and **Effie** *take hands and twirl around.*

Harriet
Effie } Now we're free who knows who'll be he!

Gloria Eeny meeny miny mo

Victoria Catch a n***** by his toe

Sarah If he hollers let him go

All O.U.T. spells out and so

Victoria Out goes she. (*She points to* **Gloria**.)

Gloria Out goes me. (*She joins* **Effie** *and* **Harriet**.)

Harriet
Effie
Gloria } This is the loveliest, loveliest part of the party.

Act One, Finale   103

Victoria   Eeeny meeny miny mo

Sarah   Catch a n***** by his toe

Jane   If he hollers let him go

Jane   Out goes she. (*Points to* **Victoria**.)

Victoria   Out goes me. (*She joins* **Effie**, **Harriet** *and* **Gloria**.)

All   This is the loveliest, loveliest part of the party.

Effie   ⎱ Only three of them left now we're excited to see
Harriet ⎰ Who is going to be blind man, who's it going to be.

Sarah   I have a strange presentiment it's me.

Jane   Eeny meeny miny mo
Out goes she. (*She points to* **Honor**, *who joins the others*.)
Eeny meeny miny mo
Out goes she. (*She points to* **Jane**.)
I'm HE – it's me. It's me – I'm HE.

Girls   Just get a handkerchief and bind it around her eyes.

Sarah   Not too tight, not too tight.

They blindfold her.

Girls   She mustn't see a thing no matter how much she tries.

Sarah   That's all right – that's all right.

Girls   She will cheat if she can,
That corner's raised a bit,
Turn her round till she's dazed a bit,
Are you ready now,
One, two, three!

Sarah   Since the party began,
Something's been taunting me,
Some presentiment haunting me,
What can it be?

Girls   Start now – start now,
She can see the ground,
She can see the ground.

Sarah   Somehow, somehow,
Some forgotten sound,
Some forgotten sound,
Echoes deep in my heart,
Strangely enthralling me,
Someone secretly calling me,

Like a melody far away.
Oh, for Heaven's sake start,
Here go along with you,
We can see nothing wrong with you
We want to play.

They all dance about and dodge her. The door on the right opens and **Carl Linden** *comes into the room. He moves across to the piano and collects his music and is on his way out when* **Sarah** *clasps him round the neck. All the* **Girls** *laugh.* **Carl** *is staggered for a moment, drops his music, and then completely losing all restraint kisses her on the mouth. She snatches the bandage from her eyes and stares into his face. All the other* **Girls** *are watching aghast.*

Sarah (*softly*)   It's you I love – now and always.

She kisses him, then draws back and they stand there staring at one another oblivious of everything. **Effie** *giggles suddenly and then stops herself.*

Harriet   Sarah –

Gloria   Sarah – don't be silly – Sarah –

Neither **Carl** *nor* **Sarah** *turn their heads.*

Carl   Come with me –

Sarah   Now?

Carl   Yes – now – to-night.

Sarah   I'll come with you – whenever you want me to.

Carl   I love you – do you hear – I've loved you for months – for years really – ever since I was a boy I've known you were waiting for me somewhere – I'll take care of you – live for you – die for you.

Sarah   Don't say that, my darling. (*Singing.*)
Should happiness forsake me,
And disillusion break me,
Come what may,
Lead the way,
Take me, take me.
Although I may discover,
Love crucifies the lover,
Whate'er Fate has in store,
My heart is yours for evermore.

Carl (*singing*)
Oh Lady, you are far above me,
And yet you whisper that you love me,
Can this be true or is it just some foolish dream?

Sarah (*speaking*)   You know it's true, look in my eyes – can't you see?

Carl (*speaking softly*)   Oh, my dear, dear love. (*Singing.*)
  Now tho' your fears are sleeping, Look well before the leaping.
  Love of me
  May be repaid
  By weeping.
  Life can be bitter learning,
  When there is no returning,
  Whate'er Fate has in store,
  My heart is yours for evermore,
  I love you – I love you – I love you.

Gloria
  You cannot realise the things you say.
  You quite forget yourself, please go away.

Harriet   Now leave this all to me, my dear, It's really too absurd.

Effie   It's quite the most romantic thing that I have ever heard!

Victoria (*speaking*)   Effie, be quiet.

Sarah *kisses* **Carl** *again full on the mouth.*

Harriet *rushes up and drags them apart.*

Harriet   Sarah – are you mad? – Mr Linden, please go at once.

Carl (*smiling*)   How can I go?

Gloria   Harriet – leave this to me –

Sarah   Stop – don't say another word.

Effie (*rushing up histerically*)   It's the most wonderfully thrilling thing that ever happened in the world.

Harriet   Don't be an idiot, Effie.

Sarah (*quietly*)   Effie's right, Harriet.

Harriet   I'm going straight upstairs to fetch Aunt Violet.

Effie (*struggling with her*)   You shan't! You shan't! – They love each other – look at them – Honor, Victoria, Jane, help me!

Honor, **Victoria** *and* **Jane** *come to her assistance.*

Sarah *and* **Carl** (*singing*)
  I'll see you again,
  Whenever spring breaks through again,
  Always I'll be by your side,
  No time or tide
  Can part us ever –

Victoria Shhh! Someone's coming – hide – quickly –

They all hide behind sofas and chairs.

Four Footmen *enter pompously to music.*

Footmen Quartette

>Now the party's really ended,
>And our betters have ascended
>All with throbbing heads,
>To their welcome beds,
>Pity us, who have to be up,
>Sadly clearing the debris up,
>Getting for our pains,
>Most of the remains.
>Though the Major-Domo is a trifle tight,
>Though the mistress hiccoughed when she said good-night,
>We in our secluded garret,
>Mean to finish up the claret –
>Cup all right.
>When we've doused the final candles,
>We'll discuss the latest scandals
>We have overheard,
>Pleasure long deferred.
>When the Duke of So and So stares
>At his wife, we know below stairs,
>While she smirks and struts,
>That he hates her guts.
>Though we all disguise our feelings pretty well,
>What we mean by 'Very good' is 'Go to hell'.
>Though they're all so grand and pompous,
>Most of them are now non compos,
>Serve them right,
>Good-night.

They extinguish all the lights and close the windows and go out, closing the doors behind them. All the **Girls** *come out, and lastly* **Carl** *and* **Sarah**. **Sarah** *goes up to* **Harriet**. **Gloria** *lights two candles.*

Sarah Harriet – whatever you do won't be the slightest use – I love Carl – I'm going with him – I don't care where or how – but this is my life, you understand – my whole life – so help me – all you can – please – please –

Harriet Think of Hugh, you're mad.

Sarah Perhaps I am mad, but I'm happy – can't you see – I'm really happy –

Harriet Mr Linden, I appeal to you.

Gloria It's no use, Harriet.

Harriet I feel as if I were in a dream.

Carl You are.

Harriet What are your prospects – have you any money?

Carl None – no money – but I can earn enough.

Sarah So can I – I'll sing –

Victoria Sarah!

Carl Yes – Sarah will sing and I will play and we will make a living – come, Sarah.

Sarah Like this?

Effie Quickly, Jane your bedroom is nearest – your hat and cape.

Jane *and* **Effie** *fly out of the room. 'The Call of Life' theme plays softly.* **Sarah** *runs up to the windows and flings them open, singing.* **Carl** *joins her.*

Sarah *and* **Carl** (*singing*)
 Fling far behind you
 The chains that bind you,
 That Love may find you
 In joy or strife;
 Tho' Fate may cheat you,
 And defeat you,
 Your youth must answer to the Call of Life.

Effie *and* **Jane** *return with a hat and cape. They dress her in them, and she and* **Carl** *go out together. As the orchestra crashes out the final chords, the others rush to the balcony to wave.*

Curtain.

Act Two

Scene One

Characters: **Sari Linden, Carl Linden, Manon** *(La Crevette),* **Lotte, Freda, Hansi, Gussi, Captain August Luttb, Herr Schlick, Waiters, Cleaners, Orchestra,** *etc. The scene is the interior of* **Herr Schlick***'s cafe: in Vienna. The year is 1880.*

It is about twelve o'clock noon, and **Waiters** *in shirt-sleeves are tidying up the tables and polishing brasses. There are also some cleaners and charwomen swabbing the floor.* **Carl,** *in shirt-sleeves, is rehearsing with the orchestra on the orchestra platform at the back,* **Lotte, Hansi** *and* **Freda,** *three ladies of the town, elaborately dressed, are seated at a table down-stage left. The opening chorus is sung in snatches by the* **Waiters, Cleaners,** *etc.*

Waiters
    Life in the morning isn't too bright,
    When you've had to hurry round and carry plates all night;
    And the evening isn't too gay,
    When you know you've got to rise and be at work all day.
    This cafe merely caters
    For a horde of drunken satyrs,
    Why, oh why, we're waiters nobody can say.

Cleaners
    Oh dear, it's clear to see that cleaners lead a worse life,
    Every day we curse life;
    More and more
    The muscles on our brawny arms like iron bands are
    Scrubbing till our hands are sore;
    We scout and polish till our fingers ache,

Waiters (*humming*)
    Hum – hum – !

Cleaners
    Each hour we feel as tho' our backs would break,

Waiters
    Hum – hum!

Cleaners
    We weep and keep our growing families as well,
    Why we're here at all nobody can tell.

Waiters
    Life in the morning isn't too bright,
    When you've had to hurry round and carry plates all night.

Cleaners
    Oh dear, it's clear to see that cleaners lead a worse life.

Waiters
And the evening isn't too gay,
When you know you've got to rise and be at work all day.

Cleaners
You see the reason why each day we want to curse life.

Waiters
For this cafe merely caters

Cleaners
Weary

Waiters
For a horde of drunken satyrs:

Cleaners
Dreary

Waiters
Why, oh why, we're waiters nobody can say.

Cleaners
Every day.

Waiters
Ah – Ah – Ah –

Cleaners
Ah – Ah – Ah –

At the end of it, **Carl** *rests his orchestra for a moment.*

Lotte   He left me at half-past ten, my dear, he kissed my hand, à la grand chevalier, which made me laugh, I *must* say.

Freda   Is that all he left you with – a kiss?

Lotte   Don't be vulgar, Freda, everything was arranged last night in his carriage – we drove round and round the Ringstrasse.[37]

Hansi   I hope it didn't make you too giddy, dear.

Lotte   You none of you understand, this is an 'affaire de cœur'.[38] I'm sure of it.

Fritz, *a waiter, brings* **Lotte** *a bill for the coffee and brioches they have been having.*

Lotte   It's not my turn – Hansi?

Hansi   I paid yesterday.

Lotte   Come along, Freda – no fumbling.

Freda   I wasn't fumbling – I was just trying to count up how many times I've paid during the last month.

---

37 The circular grand boulevard that encircles the historic Innere Stadt district of Vienna, Austria.
38 Affair of the heart.

Hansi   That oughn't to take you long.

Freda (*rather crossly*)   Oh, here you are, then. (*She gives him some money.*)

He nods and goes off.

Lotte   Where was I?

Freda   Driving round the Ringstrasse, my dear, talking business.

Lotte   You can all jeer if you like but just you wait and see. Anyhow, I feel positively exhausted, having had to get up so early.

Hansi   I'm tired too.

Gussi *enters, elaborately dressed and wearing a fur tippet and muff.*

Gussi   Hallo, girls.

Freda   Oh, my God, look at Gussi.

Hansi (*fingering the tippet*)   Where did you get it?

Gussi   Here, leave off, surely you've seen a bit of mink before?

Hansi   Not on you.

Gussi   Well, have a good look now and enjoy it.

Lotte   Who gave it to you?

Gussi (*with great coyness*)   I hardly like to tell you, it was such a delightful surprise – I had been spending the night with my dear old grandmother –

Hansi   I hope she took her spurs off.

They all laugh. **Gussi** *sits down at the table.*

Lotte   Do you want some coffee?

Gussi   No thanks, it would spoil my lunch.

Freda   I'm lunching at Sacher's – I can bring a friend – Hansi?

Hansi   No thank you, dear.

Freda   Lotte?

Lotte   Who are you lunching with, the old ostrich?

Freda   No, he's gone to Warsaw. This is a banker – quite young, but common, no use for dinner – do you want to come?

Lotte   I don't mind.

Hansi   I can't imagine, Freda, why you waste your time with small fry.

Freda   I don't consider any free meal small fry.

Lotte, **Freda** *and* **Hansi** *sing a trio.*

'Ladies of the Town'

Though we're often accused of excessively plastic, drastic sins,
When we're asked to decide on the wrong or the right life,
Night life wins,
We know that destiny will never bring
A wedding ring about.
Our moral sense may really not be quite the thing
To fling about, sing about;
We'll achieve independence before it's too late, and
Wait and see.
What care, what care we?

Refrain:

Ladies of the town, ladies of the town,
Though we've not a confessional air,
We have quite a professional flair,
Strolling up and down, strolling up and down,
We employ quite an amiable system
Of achieving renown,
Though the church and state abuses us,
For as long as it amuses us,
We'll remain, no matter how they frown,
Naughty, naughty, ladies of the town.

We can often behave in a very disarming, charming way,
Which can frequently add to the money we lay by,
Day by day.
If we are told of something on the Stock Exchange[39]
We pry a bit,
And if it's safe we get some kindly banker
To supply a bit, buy a bit,
And if later our helpers may wish to forget us
Set us free,
What care, what care we?

Refrain:

Ladies of the town, ladies of the town,
Though we're socially under a cloud,
Please forgive us for laughing aloud,
Strolling up and down, strolling up and down,
Disapproval may sometimes submerge us,
But we none of us drown,
We have known in great variety
Members of the best society,

---

39 A reference to the London Stock Exchange.

And should we decide to settle down,
We'll be wealthy ladies of the town.

When **Lotte**, **Freda** *and* **Hansi** *have gone off* **Carl** *addresses his orchestra on the dais.*

Carl   It is lacking in colour. Strings, when you take the theme in the first refrain, bring it out, let it live and breathe, and mean something. In the last four bars I've marked a *rallentando*[40] – Now then –

He raises his baton and the orchestra begins La Crevette's song – as the music swells **Manon** *enters briskly. She is, naturally, in day clothes and a hat; she listens for a moment, and then stamps her foot.* **Carl** *stops the orchestra.*

Manon   No, Carl – it must be quicker there.

Carl   When we were working yesterday that was the exact spot you wanted it slower.

Manon   Listen – it starts so – (*She sings.*) 'Lorsque j'étais petite fille en marchant parmi les prés' – swift, staccato like that, then 'J'entendis la voix d'ma tante, qui murmura á côté' – just a leetle slower – not much, you understand –

Carl   Very well. (*He starts the music again.*)

Manon *stops him.*

Manon   No, no, no – you are so stubborn.

Carl   Stubborn?

Manon   Yes – you are a musician, yes, but you know nothing about singers, especially when they have no voice like me.

Carl (*coming down to her*)   You have a beautiful voice, Manon.

Manon (*laughing suddenly*)   Now you are being earnest and sincere, it is so many years since I saw that solemn look in your eyes –

Carl   You can't expect me to pay you compliments often, when you try to quarrel with me all the time.

Manon   I quarrel! Don't be a fool.

Carl (*turning away*)   It's you who are a fool –

Manon (*touching his arm, softly*)   No, Carl – I was once – but I'm not anymore.

Carl   What do you mean?

Manon   Where is Sari – your little English Sarah?

Carl   She will be here soon.

Manon (*mockingly*)   How exciting!

Carl   You do hate her, don't you?

---

40 A gradual decrease in speed.

Manon (*gaily*)   Passionately – I should like to scratch her eyes out and pull her nose off and wring her neck –

Carl   Manon!

Manon   – in a friendly way. (*She laughs again.*)

Carl   Don't laugh like that.

Manon   You used to love my laughter – it was so gay and charming, you said – I think you mentioned once that it reminded you of a bird chirruping, that was a very pretty thought, Carl –

Carl   Please go away now – I must continue my rehearsal.

Manon   Carl –

Carl   Yes.

Manon   I'm only teasing you and irritating you because I'm jealous –

Carl   But, Manon.

Manon (*holding up her hand*)   No, don't protest and say I have no right to be jealous! I know that well – ours was such a silly little affair really, and so long ago, but somehow it was very sweet and it left a small sting behind –

Carl   It was your fault that it ended.

Manon   I know that too – and I'm glad – I was very proud of myself finishing it all suddenly like that – because it was for the best – I'm no good for you really – not faithful enough, and you should be free always, because you're an artist. (*She turns away.*) But now you'll never be free, so my beautiful little sacrifice was all in vain. (*She laughs.*) Go back to your work – I'll run through my words here –

Carl   Manon – I –

Manon   Please – play my music for me – I'm not sure of it yet – I'm not sure of anything.

Carl *looks at her silently for a moment and then goes thoughtfully back to the orchestra.* **Manon** *calls* **Fritz** *and orders herself a drink. He brings it immediately and she sings her song quietly.*

'If Love Were All'

Life is very rough and tumble,
For a humble Diseuse,[41]
One can betray one's troubles never,
Whatever
Occurs,

---

41 A female performer of recitations or monologues.

Night after night,
Have to look bright,
Whether you're well or ill
People must laugh their fill.
You mustn't sleep
Till dawn comes creeping.
Though I never really grumble
Life's a jumble.
Indeed –
And in my efforts to succeed
I've had to formulate a creed –

Refrain:

I believe in doing what I can,
In crying when I must,
In laughing when I choose,
Heig-ho, if love were all
I should be lonely,
I believe the more you love a man,
The more you give your trust,
The more you're bound to lose.
Although when shadows fall

I think if only –
Somebody splendid really needed me,
Someone affectionate and dear,
Cares would be ended if I knew that he
Wanted to have me near.
But I believe that since my life began
The most I've had is just
A talent to amuse.
Heig-ho, if love were all!
Tho' life buffets me obscenely,
It serenely
Goes on.
Although I question its conclusion,
Illusion
Is gone.
Frequently I
Put a bit by
Safe for a rainy day.
Nobody here can say
To what, indeed,
The years are leading.
Fate may often treat me meanly,
But I keenly
Pursue

A little mirage in the blue.
Determination helps me through.

Repeat refrain.

Manon *goes off after song.* **Carl**, *at the end of* **Manon**'s *song, dismisses the orchestra, who go off. He comes down from the dais, putting on his coat, when* **Gussi** *enters.*

Gussi   Hallo, Carl.

Carl (*absently*)   Hallo.

Gussi   Like a drink?

Carl   No, thanks.

Gussi   Are you lunching with anyone?

Carl   Yes, my wife.

Gussi   I might have known it. (*She slips her arm through his.*) Let me know when you feel like being unfaithful to her, won't you?

Carl (*smiling*)   You're bad, Gussi, thoroughly bad – go along with you.

Gussi   Here listen, you know that dark red coat of mine?

Carl   Yes.

Gussi   Would your Sari like it? I've had this given to me. (*She waves her muff.*) I shan't need it any more.

Carl   It's very, very sweet of you, Gussi.

Gussi   You both look so pinched – it depresses me to look at you – bring Sarah along to lunch at my flat –

Carl   Very well.

Captain August Lutte *enters.* **Captain August** *is a debonair, imposing-looking man.*

Gussi   Just a moment, some good news has come in – come at one-thirty, if I'm not back tell Liza to serve you.

Carl   But, Gussi –

Gussi (*firmly*)   Good-bye, dear Carl –

Carl *goes off laughing.* **Gussi** *sidles up to* **Captain August**.

Gussi   Good morning.

Captain August (*bowing stiffly*)   Good morning.

Gussi   Can I do anything for you?

Captain August   I wish to see Herr Schlick.

Gussi (*grimacing*)   How nice.

Captain August (*abruptly*)   You are very pretty.

Gussi (*shrinking away*)   Oh, Captain – my salts – my salts.

Captain August   Perhaps you will make a rendezvous with me for next week?

Gussi   I may be dead next week, what's the matter with now?

Captain August   I fear that I am otherwise engaged.

Herr Schlick *enters, oily and ingratiating.*

Herr Schlick   Captain – forgive me please – I – (*Sees* **Gussi**.) What are you doing here?

Gussi   Just feeding the swans – Good-bye.

She goes off.

Captain August   Herr Schlick, I have a complaint to make.

Herr Schlick   It shall be rectified – before you say it, whatever is wrong is rectified.

Captain August   Among your professional dancing partners you have been careless enough to engage an iceberg.

Herr Schlick   Good God!

Captain August   A beautiful, alluring, unsociable iceberg – her name is Sari.

Herr Schlick   She is new, Captain; she has only been here a few weeks.

Captain August   Even a few weeks is surely time enough to enable her to melt sufficiently to sup with me –

Herr Schlick   She is English, Captain, one must make allowances.

Captain August   I do not come to a cafe of this sort to make allowances – I come to amuse myself and to pay for it.

Manon *re-enters on the dais just above them. She is looking for* **Carl***, but stops on hearing their voices.*

Herr Schlick (*very flurried*)   Captain – I assure you – anything that you wish – I will arrange as soon as possible.

Captain August   I wish for this Sari to sup with me – tonight.

Herr Schlick   She shall, Captain, she shall.

Captain August   You will please have a special supper laid ready in a quiet room – No. 7 is the best, I think –

Herr Schlick   You are sure that you would not rather have Lotte or perhaps Hansi –

Captain August   Quite sure.

Herr Schlick   You see this English girl is the wife of my orchestra leader – they are said to be in love – it will be a little difficult –

Captain August (*rising*)   I hope I have made myself quite clear –

Herr Schlick   But, Captain –

Captain August   You will please arrange things as I have suggested – to-night I wish no allowances to be made.

He bows as he is about to go out, meets **Sari** *coming in. She has grown more poised and mature during the years spent with* **Carl***. She starts visibly on seeing* **Captain August** *– he clicks his heels and bows.*

Captain August   Good morning.

Sari   Good morning.

Captain August   It is a beautiful morning.

Sari   Beautiful.

Captain August   But chilly.

Sari   It is very warm out.

Captain August   Would you honour me by lunching with me?

Sari   I'm so sorry, but I am already engaged.

Captain August   Perhaps a drive, a little later on; we might go up to Cobenzl –[42]

Sari   Please forgive me, but to-day it is impossible.

Captain August   I quite understand. (*He bows again.*) Until to-night, madame.

He goes off.

Herr Schlick (*furiously*)   It may interest you to know that you are losing me one of my most valued clients – I'll deal with you later. Captain – a moment, please – Captain –

He rushes off. **Sari** *looks after him pensively for a moment and then sighs.* **Manon** *comes down from the dais.*

Manon   Sari.

Sari   Oh!

Manon   Don't look so startled –

Sari   I came to find Carl. Have you seen him?

Manon   Yes, I've just been rehearsing with him.

Sari   Oh!

Manon   He's about somewhere.

Sari   I'll find him. (*She turns to go.*)

Manon   I want to speak to you.

---

42   Two mountains in Vienna referred to as the Cobenzl: the Latisberg and the Reisenberg.

Sari (*coldly*) Yes? What is it?

Manon Oh, why do you always look at me like that?

Sari Like what?

Manon Aloof and superior.

Sari I wasn't conscious of being either of those things.

Manon Yes, you were – you know you were – you always are with me. But, listen, never mind about that now – I heard Schlick arranging for you to have supper in a private room with Captain August to-night.

Sari What!

Manon So be careful.

Sari (*incredulously*) You heard Schlick arranging for *me* –

Manon Yes – yes, yes – I thought you might like to know.

Sari How horrible!

Manon Not so horrible as all that; lots of the girls here would be glad of the chance, but as Carl is in love with you and you are apparently in love with him, I thought –

Sari (*rather stiffly*) Thank you, Manon.

Manon Not at all. (*She turns to go.*)

Sari Manon –

Manon (*stopping*) Yes?

Sari I'm sorry.

Manon What for?

Sari If my manner is – well, unkind –

Manon (*patting her arm*) All is well, my dear – I don't love him any more, really, at least I don't think I do, and anyhow you have no reason to be jealous, nothing to be afraid of. Look at me, and then look in the glass. (*She kisses her lightly, and goes off humming a reprise of her former song.*)

Carl *enters from left.*

Sari Carl.

Carl Darling! (*He kisses her fondly.*) How quick you've been dressing. I crept out without waking you.

Sari Yes, I know; you must never do that again.

Carl Why – what's the matter?

Sari I dreamt – something dreadful. I awoke terrified – I came straight here without any coffee or anything – to see if you were safe.

Carl I safe? Why, of course I'm safe – why shouldn't I be?

Sari I don't know, I'm frightened. I hate this place – let's go away. I'd rather go back to singing in the streets again, at least we were independent then and together.

Carl We're together now – always.

Sari (*wildly*) No, no – not here we're not – we're separated by hundreds of things and people – you're the chef d'orchestre[43] and I'm a professional dance partner. I hate it, I tell you – I can't be gay and enjoy it like the other girls, because I love you – I can't feel happy when the cavalry officers put their arms round my waist and dance and flirt with me, because I love you, and because I'm scared.

Carl Why are you scared?

Sari Something horrible will happen if we stay here. I know it, I feel it –

Carl Come along and have a little lunch, then you'll feel better. We're going to Gussi's flat – she's got a present for you – you know that red coat –

Sari Oh, Carl, Carl, you won't understand! –

Carl *takes her in his arms.*

Carl You must take hold of your courage, my sweet – we must both put up with things now in order to be secure later on – no more street singing – it broke my heart to see you hungry – that's all past – you've been so splendid and brave all through – just hold on for a few weeks more until we have enough to start that little cafe –

Sari (*hysterically*) Laugh at me then – laugh everything away, stop me being solemn – we're both too young to be dreary and sentimental – make me forget the present in planning for the future – where will our cafe be? How shall we manage it? Shall I be able to sing your songs there? – One day I might make them famous – I love your music so very much – I want it to be known all over the world, and one day it will be, I'm sure of it – do you think I could help – do you?

Carl (*kissing her*) Darling.

'Little Cafe'

Carl
  We share a mutual ambition
  Which naught can disarrange,

Sari
  Based on the hopeful supposition
  That soon our luck will change.

Carl
  Tho' we very often wonder whether
  Poverty will win the day,

---

43 Orchestral conductor.

Sari
>Just as long as we remain together
>Troubles seem to fade away.

Both
>However hard the bed one lies on
>The same old dreams begin,
>We're always scanning the horizon
>For when our ship comes in.

Refrain:

Carl
>We'll have a sweet little cafe
>In a neat little square,

Sari
>We'll find our fortune
>And our happiness there.

Carl
>We shall thrive on the vain and resplendent

Sari
>And contrive to remain independent.

Carl
>We'll have a meek reputation
>And a chic clientele.

Sari
>Kings will fall under our spell.

Both
>We'll be so zealous
>That the world will be jealous
>Of our sweet little cafe in our square.

Sari
>Can you imagine our sensations
>When we've security?

Carl
>And all our dreary deprivations
>Are just a memory.

Sari
>Tho' we're very often driven frantic,
>Peace is very hard to find.

Carl
>All these dreadful days will seem romantic
>When we've left them far behind.

Both
>Fate needn't be quite such a dragon,
>He knows how tired we are.
>We'll hitch out hopeful little wagon
>On to a lucky star.

Refrain:

Carl
>We'll have a sweet little cafe
>In a neat little square,

Sari
>We'll find our fortune
>And our happiness there.

Carl
>We shall thrive on the vain and resplendent

Sari
>And contrive to remain independent.

Carl
>We'll have a meek reputation
>And a chic clientele.

Sari
>Kings will full under our spell.

Both
>We'll be so zealous
>That the world will be jealous
>Of our sweet little cafe in our square.

At the end of the last refrain **Carl** *takes* **Sari** *in his arms and the curtain falls.*

Scene Two

Characters: **Sari Linden, Carl Linden, Manon** *(La Crevette),* **Captain August Lutte, Lieutenant Tranisch, Herr Schlick, Lotte, Freda, Hansi, Gussi, Six Special Dancers, Officers, Guests, Waiters, Musicians,** *etc.*

The scene is the same, except that the atmosphere has changed from a frowsy daylight squalor to a tinselled gas-light gaiety.

It is about 2 a.m.

When the curtain rises everyone is waltzing. **Carl** *is conducting the orchestra on the dais. Some of the* **Girls** *have* **Male Partners** *and some are dancing with one another. The stage should look as hot and crowded as possible. At the end of the opening waltz*

Carl *stops his orchestra and the theatre orchestra takes up the* **Officers'** *entrance music. About a dozen smart* **Officers** *come marching on in attractive undress uniform. They sing a concerted introductory number with the* **Girls**.

'Officers' Chorus'

Officers
 We wish to order wine, please,
 Expressly from the Rhine, please,
 The year we really don't much care.

Ladies
 Oh dear,
 Now that you're here
 Think of the wear and tear.

Officers
 We hope without insistence
 To overcome resistance
 In all you little ladies fair.

Ladies
 Oh well,
 How can we tell
 Whether you'd really dare?

Officers
 We sincerely hope it's really not a thankless task
 Amusing us,
 Won't you please agree?

Ladies Ah, me!

Officers You could quickly break our hearts by everything we ask
 Refusing us;
 Cruel that would be, ladies, can't you see!
 We're officers and gentlemen,
 Reliable and true,
 Considerate and chivalrous
 In everything we do.

 Though we're gay and drunk a trifle,
 All our laughter we should stifle,
 Were we summoned by a bugle call.
 We're amorous and passionate,
 But dignified and stern,
 Which if you play us false you'll quickly learn.
 Do not let our presence grieve you,
 When we've loved you we shall leave you,
 For we're officers and gentlemen, that's all!

After song. **Captain August** *and* **Lieutenant Tranisch** *enter, and* **Captain August** *and the* **Officers** *sing 'Tokay', of which everyone joins in the last refrain.*

'Tokay'[44]

Officers
    Tokay!

Captain August
    When we're thoroughly wined and dined,
    And the barracks are left behind,
    We come down to the town to find
    Some relief from the daily grind.
    Love is kind,
    Love is blind.

Officers
    Tokay!

Captain A.
    When the thoughts of a man incline
    To the grapes of a sunlit vine,
    On the banks of the golden Rhine,[45]
    Slowly ripening pure and fine,
    Sweet divine,
    Lover's wine.
    Lift your voices till the rafters ring,
    Fill your glasses to the brim and sing:

Refrain:
    Tokay!
    The golden sunshine of a summer day,
    Tokay!
    Will bear the burden of your cares away.
    Here's to the love in you,
    The hate in you,
    Desire in you.

Officers
    Wine of the sun that will waft you along
    Lifting you high on the wings of a song.

Captain August
    Dreams in you,
    The flame in you,
    The fire in you,
    Tokay – Tokay.

---

44 A type of wine from Hungary.
45 The river that flows from Switzerland down through Germany.

Officers
So while forgetfulness we borrow,
Never minding what to-morrow has to say,

Captain August
Tokay!

All
The only call we all obey,
Tokay – Tokay – Tokay!

Some go off to the bar, others seat themselves at tables and order wine. **Sari** *and* **Manon** *come in and sit at a table below the balcony to the right.* **Sari** *is simply dressed in white.* **Manon** *is very gay in scarlet sequins.*

Sari   I'm so tired.

Manon   Well, for heaven's sake don't look as if you were.

Sari   I'm sick of pretending.

Manon   So am I, but it's no use worrying about that. The whole business is pretending. Life's pretending.

Sari   That hateful Captain August – he smiled at me in the bar – an odious smile.

Manon   I hope you smiled back.

Sari   I certainly did not.

Manon   Well, that was very foolish of you – there's nothing so alluring to that type of man as snowy chastity.

Sari   How can you, Manon. (*She smiles.*) I'm so miserable really, it's horrid of you to laugh at me.

Manon   That's better – you're smiling yourself now.

Lieutenant Tranisch *enters from the bar, comes to their table and bows to* **Manon**.

Lieutenant Tranisch   Mademoiselle La Crevette.

Manon   Yes?

Lieutenant Tranisch   We have never spoken before, but I wish to say you are an admirable artiste – you sing like an angel.

Manon (*laughing very loudly*)   You Viennese are so gallant. I sing like a frog.

Lieutenant Tranisch   Will you come to the bar and take a drink with me?

Manon   What is this now – what does this mean? Is it the birth of a romance? I feel so flattered.

Lieutenant Tranisch (*slightly embarrassed*)   Mademoiselle – I –

Manon   Never mind, Lieutenant, I am not deceived – you think I sing well, that is very kind – now tell me – cards on the table – to which of the more attractive women here do you want me to introduce you?

Lieutenant Tranisch Really – you misunderstand me – I –

Manon Come now – tell me – I have no sensibilities.

Lieutenant Tranisch There is a small blonde lady like a kitten in yellow – I will admit to you frankly – she enthrals me strangely.

Manon That would be Gussi. (*She rises.*) Excuse me for a moment, Sari.

Sari Of course.

Lieutenant Tranisch (*clicking his heels and bowing to* **Sari**) Fraulein.

Manon Come along – but let me warn you – Gussi is a collector.

Lieutenant Tranisch Collector?

Manon Yes, of antiques – very enthusiastic – old jewellery for preference. If your acquaintance ripens, let me advise you when walking to keep to the more modem thoroughfares. (*She looks at* **Sari** *smilingly.*) Heigho – if love were all!

She and **Lieutenant Tranisch** *go off to the bar.* **Captain August** *enters and comes to* **Sari***'s table, but as he does so* **Carl** *sees him and comes down from the orchestra.*

Captain August (*bowing*) Madame –

Carl Sari, I want to talk to you. You remember the second movement in the concerto I was scoring yesterday, I have had the most magnificent idea – instead of using strings alone, I shall strengthen it with the zimbale just towards the end where it goes – tum tum tum tum – (*He hums.*)

Sari Yes, I know – *what* a good idea. (*She also hums.*) Tum tum – tum tum tum –

They both hum together, and finally **Captain August**, *finding himself completely ignored, turns on his heel and marches back into the bar.*

Sari (*half laughing*) Oh, Carl – that was wonderful of you.

Carl I was watching – I'm always watching to see that no harm comes to you.

Sari I hate him *so* – he won't leave me alone – he embarrasses me.

Carl Cheer up, my dearest.

Sari I'll try. (*She smiles.*) Oh, Carl, there's something so heavy weighing down on my heart – I felt it this morning, and it's there again now.

Carl (*looking at her*) You're very strange to-night – you've been strange all day – eager and tense like a frightened child. Is there anything the matter really?

Sari Yes – no – I don't know. I feel as though fate were too strong for us, as though our love for one another and our happiness together was making the gods angry. I feel suddenly insecure.

Carl We'll go away, then, to-morrow.

Sari Carl!

Carl   We have a little money saved anyhow. I hate Schlick and this place as much as you do really. To-night is the end of it. We'll go to Frankfurt. Heinrich is there, he'll help us.

Sari   To-night is the end of it.

Carl   You remember Heinrich – with the long brown beard – you laughed at him.

Sari   Yes, he was funny, but I liked him.

Carl   Do you feel happier now?

Sari   Oh yes, much, much happier.

Carl   So do I – we'll be free again – independent – I must get back. Au revoir, my dear love.

Sari   Au revoir.

She kisses her hand to him and goes off. **Gussi** *and* **Lieutenant Tranisch** *come on, followed by* **Hansi** *and* **Preda**, *who are giggling.*

Gussi   Louis Quinze – of course it was only paste, but definitely Louis Quinze.

Lieutenant Tranisch   How interesting.

Gussi   I'll show it to you to-morrow – we can drive there after luncheon.

Lieutenant Tranisch   We haven't had supper yet.

Gussi   No, but we will – we'll sit here – I shall have to dance in a minute – Fritz – Hans –

She sits down with **Lieutenant Tranisch** *at a small table and calls the* **Waiters**. **Freda** *and* **Hansi** *sit down also, but on the opposite side of the stage, at the same table at which* **Carl** *and* **Sari** *played the preceding scene.*

Hansi   I'll tell you one thing here and now, whatever Gussi is talking about is *not* paste.

Freda   I doubt if it's even Louis Quinze.

Sari *comes in.*

Hansi   Here comes the snow queen.

Freda   Hallo, Sari.

Sari   Hallo.

Hansi   Any offers to-night?

Freda   Don't tease her, Hansi – she's in love.

Sari (*smiling*)   No, no offers so far.

Hansi   Do you want a drink?

Sari   Yes – I'd love one.

Hansi   Fritz –

She calls the **Waiter** *and orders wine.*

Freda   That's pretty, that dress – is it new?

Sari   Yes. I made it myself from a pattern.

Freda   It sags a little bit behind – here – look – give me a pin, Hansi.

Hansi   You can have this brooch for the time being, but give it back, it's not valuable, but lucky.

She gives **Sari** *a brooch.* **Sari** *stands up while* **Freda** *fixes the brooch on to the dress.* **Captain August** *comes in and bows ironically to* **Sari**.

Captain August   Will you honour me with this dance, please?

Sari (*jumping slightly*)   Oh – no, I'm sorry – I'm engaged.

Captain August   I fear that is not strictly true.

Freda   I'll dance with you, if you like.

Captain August   Please do not think me impolite, but I have set my heart on dancing with Fraulein Sari.

Sari   Forgive me, Captain, but it's quite impossible.

Captain August   We shall see. (*He bows abruptly and walks across the stage to where* **Herr Schlick** *is standing talking to two other* **Officers**. *He is obviously very angry. He speaks to* **Herr Schlick** *swiftly and angrily.*)

Sari   I hate him – he's always tormenting me.

Freda   You're unwise, my dear – it's best to humour them a little.

Sari   I've tried – I've danced with him, but he presses me too close and whispers humble things to me.

Hansi   He's very rich and, I believe, generous.

Sari   Yes, but that doesn't interest me.

Hansi (*wistfully*)   There's no doubt about it – love is very bad for business.

Herr Schlick *comes to their table.*

Herr Schlick   Sari –

Sari   Yes, Herr Schlick.

Herr Schlick   You are engaged and paid by me as a dancing partner for my clients, are you not?

Sari   Yes.

Herr Schlick   I have received several complaints from Captain August Lutte – he says you persistently refuse to dance with him.

Sari He takes advantage of my position.

Herr Schlick It would be better if you realised once and for all that you have no position – after to-night you may consider your engagement at an end.

Sari (*with spirit*) It is at an end anyhow – my husband and I are leaving Vienna to-morrow.

Herr Schlick Oho – I see. Well, I should like to remind you that you both have a week's salary owing to you, and unless you dance willingly and agreeably with Captain August or any other of the officers when they ask you to, neither you nor your husband will receive a penny of your salary – I run my cafe on business lines, you understand.

Sari But, Herr Schlick, that is unfair – my behaviour has nothing to do with my husband.

Herr Schlick That is enough. I am sick to death of your stupid mincing airs and graces – unless you behave yourself to-night, you will both leave to-morrow without your money, and be damned to you!

He leaves **Sari**, *who sinks miserably into her chair.* **Hansi** *and* **Freda** *try to comfort her and give her some wine.* **Herr Schlick** *advances to the middle of the floor to announce the commencement of the entertainment.*

Herr Schlick Ladies and gentlemen, I crave your kind attention for the most superb musical entertainment ever offered in Vienna.

Everyone applauds.

Thank you. Thank you. My first number will be my six magnificent dancing girls – trained exclusively in the finest ballet schools in the world. Lise, Trude, Fritz, Toni, Greta and Elsa.

Six Girls *rise from their various tables and make a line in the middle of the floor. There is a lot of applause.* **Carl** *strikes up their music and they dance, after which they return to their tables amid cheers.* **Schlick** *again takes the floor.*

Herr Schlick Gentlemen – ladies and gentlemen – I beg attention for my favourite, your favourite, the world's favourite star – Manon La Crevette.

He steps aside and **Manon** *comes running on. She is greeted with vociferous applause. She sings a very saucy French song: 'Bonne Nuit, Merci!' interspersed with a good deal of back-chat and ogling.*

'Bonne Nuit, Merci!'[46]

Manon
    Lorsque j'étais petite fille
    En marchant parmi les prés

---

46 Thank you and good night.

J'entendi la voix d'ma tante
Qui murmura a côté,
'N'oublie pas la politesse
Lorsque viendra un amant
Car tout la bonheur réside là dedans.'

Refrain:

C'est pourquoi clans mes affaires,
Soit de cceur ou soit d'esprit,
C'est pourquoi je tâche de plaire
Toute la foule de mes amis,
Soit qu'ils m'offrent pied-à-terre
Ou me montrent une bonne affaire
J'leurs reponds, 'Vas-y. Bonne Nuit Merci!'

Lorsque je suis v'nue à Paris
J'étais sage de nature,
Mais que faire clans la vie
Etant jeune pour rester pure!
Quand ma politesse m'obligea
Lorsqu'je suivais par hasard
Une adventure dans les boites des boulevards.

Refrain:

Et j'ai rencontré en ville
Un monsieur bien comme il faut,
Il m'a dit, 'Ma petite fille,
Veux-tu faire un p'tit do-do?'
Lorsqu'j'arrive chez lui toute de suite
J'me dit, 'Deshabilles-toi vite!'
J'me suis dis 'Vas'y. Bonnie Nuit. Merci!'

As encore she sings a waltz song in which everybody joins.

Waltz song:

'Tis time that we were parted,
You and I,
However broken-hearted,
'Tis good-bye!
Although our love has ended
And darkness has descended,
I call to you with one last cry:

Kiss me
Before you go away!
Miss me
Through every night and day.

Though clouds are grey above you,
You'll hear me say I love you!
Kiss me
Before you go away!

Parmi les chansons tristes
De l'amour,
Joies et chagrins existent
Tour à tour,
Et presqu'avec contrainte
On risque la douce etreinte
Qui nous separe enfin toujours.

Refrain:

Je t'aime,
Tes baisers m'ont grisée
Même
A l'heure de t'en aller,
La volupté troublante
Brise mes lèvres brûlantes,
Je t'aime,
A l'heure de t'en aller.

At the end of this **Carl** *strikes up another waltz and everybody begins to dance.* **Herr Schlick** *comes over to* **Sari**'s *table and stands behind it; After a moment* **Captain August** *approaches and bows.*

Captain August   Fraulein Sari has perhaps by now forgotten her other engagement.

Sari (*rising agitatedly*)   I – please – I –

Herr Schlick   You are quite right, Captain, she has forgotten.

Sari   Captain August – I am very tired – will you please forgive me just this once?

Captain August   One dance, please.

Herr Schlick   I think you would be well advised to grant Captain August's request.

Sari (*pulling herself together*)   Certainly, Captain, I shall be charmed.

She gives one despairing look at **Carl** *on the dais – he is watching anxiously – then she surrenders herself to* **Captain August**'s *arms and they begin to waltz.* **Carl** *watches all the time. As the dance progresses* **Captain August** *is obviously becoming more and more aggressively amorous.* **Carl**, *with obvious agitation, perceptibly quickens the tempo of the music. Finally the* **Captain August** *waltzes* **Sari** *into the centre of the floor – stops dead, tightens his arms around her and kisses her on the mouth passionately, bending her right back as he does so. She gives one cry.* **Carl** *stops the music dead with a crash and leaps over the railing of the dais on to the middle of the floor. He drags* **Sari** *away from* **Captain August**, *then, springing at him, strikes him in the face. Immediately the buzz of excitement dies down into dead silence.*

Carl (*wildly*)   Swine – filthy, ill-mannered drunken swine!

Sari (*in a whisper*)   Carl!

Manon (*rushing forward*)   Carl – don't be a fool.

Captain August *gives an unpleasant laugh and draws his sword.*

Captain August   Tranisch – look after our foolhardy young friend here, will you?

Lieutenant Tranisch   Not now – not now – wait.

Captain August   I regret – I cannot wait.

Lieutenant Tranisch *draws his sword and hands it to* **Carl** – **Manon** *clutches his arm.*

Carl   Stand back, Manon – look after Sari – please.

Captain August *attacks him and they fight a brief duel, the crowd making a large ring round them. Suddenly* **Captain August** *knocks* **Carl***'s sword from his hand and runs him through. There is a general scream and everyone crowds forward.* **Sari** *silently and madly fights through the crowd and sinks to the ground, taking* **Carl** *in her arms.* **Lieutenant Tranisch** *motions the crowd back. There is silence except for* **Manon***, who is crying loudly and hopelessly.*

Sari (*softly – she is dry-eyed*)   I'll love you always – always – do you hear?

Carl (*weakly*)   Sari – Sari – my sweet, sweet Sari –

His head falls back in her lap, and she kneels there staring before her dazed and hopeless as the curtain falls.

Act Three

Scene One

Characters: **Madame Sari Linden, Marquis of Shayne, Lady James** *(Harriet),* **Mrs Proutie** *(Gloria),* **Mrs Bethel** *(Effie),* **Lady Sorrel** *(Honor),* **Mrs Vale** *(Jane),* **Duchess of Tenterden** *(Victoria),* **Lord James, Mr Proutie, Mr Bethel, Lord Sorrel, Mr Vale, Duke of Tenterden, Hon. Hugh Devon, Mrs Devon, Vernon Craft, Cedric Ballantyne, Bertram Sellick, Lord Henry Jade, Accompanist** *(to* **Madame Linden***),* **Butler, Guests,** *etc.*

The scene is **Lord Shayne***'s house in London. The year is 1895.*

It is the drawing-room of the **Marquis of Shayne***'s house in London. Fifteen years have passed since Act Two, and it is now 1895. When the curtain rises,* **Lord Shayne***, a distinguished old man, is standing a little to the right receiving his guests, who are announced by the* **Butler***.* **Lady Jambs** *(***Harriet***) and* **Mrs Proutie** *(***Gloria***) are announced with their husbands, likewise*

Mrs Bethel *(***Effie***),* **Lady Sorrel** *(***Honor***),* **Mrs Vale** *(***Jane***), and lastly the* **Duchess of Tenterden** *(***Victoria***).*

They are all by now smart middle-aged society matrons. Their entrance and **Lord Shayne***'s reception of them is all part of the opening chorus.*

Opening Chorus[47]

All
    Tarara boom-de-ay,
    Tarara boom-de-ay,
    We are the most effectual,
    Intellectual
    Movement of the day.
    Our moral standards sway
    Like Mrs Tanqueray,
    And we are theoretically
    Most aesthetically
    Eager to display
    The fact that we're aggressively
    And excessively
    Anxious to destroy
    All the snobbery
    And hob-nobbery
    Of the hoi-polloi.
    Tarara boom-de-ay.
    It's mental washing day,
    And come what may

---

[47] From the musical hall number that was first performed in Henry J. Sayer's 1891 *Tuxedo* revue.

We'll scrub until the nation's morals shrink away.
Tarara boom-de-ay!

Exquisites
Though we are languid in appearance,
We're in the vanguard.
We feel we can guard
The cause of Art.
We shall ignore all interference,
For our complacence
With this renaissance
Is frightfully smart.
Please do not think us unrelenting,
Our charming frolic
With the symbolic
Is meek and mild.
We merely spend our time preventing
Some earnest stripling
From liking Kipling[48]
Instead of Wilde.[49]
Now that we find the dreary nineteenth century is closing,
We mean to start the twentieth in ecstasies of posing.

All
Tarara boom-de-ay,
It's mental washing day,
And come what may
We'll scrub until the tiresome bourgeois shrink away.
Tarara boom-de-ay!

Which is concluded by a sextette by **Harriet**, **Gloria**, **Honor**, **Jane**, **Effie** *and* **Victoria**. *Everyone else retires into the supper room, leaving them on the stage.*

'Alas, the Time Is Past'

Alas, the time is past when we
Could frolic with impunity.
Secure in our virginity,
We sometimes look aghast
Adown the lanes of memory,
Alas, the time is past.
Ah, then the world was at our feet,
When we were sweet-and-twenty,
We never guessed that what we'd got,
Tho' not a lot – was plenty.

---

48 Reference to author and journalist Rudyard Kipling (1865–1936).
49 Reference to Irish poet and playwright Oscar Wilde (1854–1900).

We gaily sought some Abelard[50]
To cherish, guard and own us,
But all we know of storm and strife
Our married life – has shown us.
Alas, the time is past when we
Could frolic with impunity.
Secure in our virginity,
We sometimes look aghast
Adown the lanes of memory.
Alas, the time is past.
Alack-a-day me – alack-a-day me!
Ah, then the world was at our feet,
Alas, the time is past.

Harriet What have you done to your hair, Effie? – it strikes me as peculiar.

Effie Nothing in particular.

Gloria I'm afraid you're becoming a little pernickety, Harriet; you must guard against it.

Honor Where's your late husband, Victoria?

Victoria Later than ever, my dear – he's at Boodles,[51] I expect.

Jane Talking too much.

Harriet And drinking much too much.

Victoria You can't upset me by saying that, Harriet dear. I find alcohol one of the greatest comforts of matrimony!

Honor Victoria!

Victoria In a husband, I mean – it leaves one free for one's charities.

Jane A little too free sometimes, my pet.

Harriet Who is this woman?

Effie Which woman?

Harriet The one we've been invited to meet.

Victoria Some strange Hungarian singer – probably very glittering and rather stout.

Honor Oh, I shouldn't think so – Lord Shayne has been pursuing her for ages from capital to capital.

Harriet Central Europe is far too musical, there can be no two opinions about that.

Jane I hear she's very beautiful.

---

50 Reference to French philosopher Peter Abelard (1079–1142)
51 A British luxury jeweller founded in 1798.

Lord Shayne *has entered unobserved from the supper room.*

Lord Shayne She is –

Victoria Good heavens, how you made me jump!

Lord Shayne She is one of the few really beautiful people in the world.

Harriet How very disconcerting!

Honor Do you think we shall like that?

Lord Shayne I shall be very interested to see the effect she has on you – you are all – if I may say so – so very representative.

Victoria Of what, dear Lord Shayne?

Lord Shayne Shall we say '*fin de siecle*'?[52]

Harriet I was afraid somebody would say that before the evening was over.

The **Butler** *announces the* **Hon. Hugh Devon** *and* **Mrs Devon**. **Lord Shayne** *moves over to greet them.* **Hugh** *has developed along the exact lines that one would have expected; he has become a good deal more pompous with the years, and has a tremendously diplomatic manner. His wife is fat and vague.*

Victoria Margaret dear, how are you?

Mrs Devon Shattered, completely shattered! Our cabby was raving mad. He kept saying the oddest things to his horse, at least I hope they were to his horse. I pretended not to understand, one has to think of prestige –

Lord Shayne I hear you're going to Vienna.

Hugh Yes, next week, thank God! I believe Mullins has been making a fearful hash of everything.

Mrs Devon Isn't it exciting! I was so afraid we were going to be sent to Riga or Christiania or somewhere draughty like that.

Harriet Hugh generally gets what he wants.

Mrs Devon As it is, I don't know what I shall do with the children. I can't help feeling that Eva is the wrong age for Vienna.

Lord Shayne No one is the wrong age for Vienna – it's a city of enchantment – magnificent.

Hugh I'm told the plumbing is appalling.

Victoria Lord Shayne has fallen in love again – haven't you, my dear?

Lord Shayne I am always in love with beauty.

Hugh Admirably put, Shayne. I quite agree with you.

---

52 End of the century.

Jane We're all on tenterhooks to see Madame Linden – she's due at any moment.

Mrs Devon What are tenterhooks, I never know.

The **Butler** *throws open the doors and announces* **Madame Sari Linden**. **Sarah** *enters, exquisitely gowned and radiantly beautiful, carrying herself with tremendous poise; her jewels are superb, and the years have invested her with a certain air of decision which is almost metallic as compared with the tremulous diffidence of her youth.* **Lord Shayne** *goes forward and kisses her hand.*

Lord Shayne My dear, how enchanting to see you again. (*He turns with a smile.*) I think you know everyone here.

Harriet Good heavens, Sarah!

Victoria (*astounded*) Sarah!

Effie It can't be – it can't be –

She rushes up and kisses her. There is a babel of surprised and excited conversation. **Hugh** *stands a little apart, looking a trifle embarrassed.*

Honor We heard that you had died, ages and ages ago.

Sari I did die. Fifteen years ago to be exact. Things happened and I couldn't come back. I didn't want to come back, so I thought I'd better die, vaguely and obscurely. It was the only thing to do – it sort of rounded everything off so satisfactorily.

Jane It's unbelievable, Sarah, dear Sarah.

Sari Please don't be quite so pleased to see me. It makes me feel ashamed, particularly with Hugh standing there, looking so stern. How do you do, Hugh?

Hugh I'm delighted to see you again. Margaret, I want you to meet Sarah – Sarah –? (*He looks questioningly at her.*)

Sari Linden – don't say you've forgotten Carl Linden, the man I eloped with, practically under your nose, Hugh?

Hugh I remember perfectly – how is he?

Sari He's dead – I'm so glad to meet you, Mrs Devon. I do hope Hugh is a charming husband and not too embittered – I treated him abominably, you know.

Mrs Devon (*shaking hands with her*) It's all so very surprising – very, very surprising – Hugh told me the whole story, when he heard of your death in Prague or somewhere. He was dreadfully upset, weren't you, Hugh?

Hugh Yes, indeed, I was.

Sari (*smiling and tapping him lightly with her fan*) Dear Hugh, never mind – everything always turns out for the best, doesn't it? At least, almost everything.

Lord Shayne Won't you have a little supper – Sari?

Honor 'Sari' – it does sound pretty, doesn't it – 'Sari'.

Sari   Only a very little, if you want me to sing for you.

They all go into the supper room, chattering and laughing, while the orchestra very softly and lightly plays a reprise of the 'Blindman's Bluff Finale' in Act One. When the supper room doors close behind them, the other doors open and four over-exquisitely dressed young men enter. They all wear in their immaculate buttonholes green carnations. **Vernon Craft**, *a poet,* **Cedric Ballantyne**, *a painter,* **Lord Henry Jade**, *a dilettante, and* **Bertram Sellick**, *a playwright.*

Bertie   It's entirely Vernon's fault that we are so entrancingly late.

Vernon   My silk socks were two poems this evening and they refused to scan.

Henry   It's going to be inexpressibly dreary, I can feel it in my bones.

Cedric   Don't be absurd, Henry, your whole charm lies in the fact that you have no bones.

They sing a quartette: 'We All Wore a Green Carnation'.

'We All Wore a Green Carnation'[53]

Blasé boys are we,
Exquisitely free
From the dreary and quite absurd
Moral views of the common herd,
We like porphyry bowls,
Chandeliers and stoles,
We're most spirited,
Carefully filleted 'souls'.

Refrain:

Pretty boys, witty boys, too, too, too
Lazy to fight stagnation,
Haughty boys, naughty boys, all we do
Is to pursue sensation.
The portals of society
Are always opened wide,
The world our eccentricity condones,
A note of quaint variety
We're certain to provide.
We dress in very decorative tones.
Faded boys, jaded boys, womankind's
Gift to a bulldog nation,
In order to distinguish us from less enlightened minds,
We all wear a green carnation.

---

53 A number that references the green carnation of Oscar Wilde. It has since become a symbol of the British LGBT community.

We believe in Art,
Though we're poles apart
From the fools who are thrilled by Greuze.[54]
We like Beardsley[55] and Green Chartreuse.[56]
Women say we're too
Bored to bill and coo,
We smile wearily,
It's so drearily true!

Refrain:

Pretty boys, witty boys, you may sneer
At our disintegration,
Haughty boys, naughty boys, dear, dear, dear!
Swooning with affectation.
Our figures sleek and willowy,
Our lips incarnadine,
May worry the majority a bit.
But matrons rich and billowy,
Invite us out to dine,
And revel in our phosphorescent wit.
Faded boys, jaded boys, come what may,
Art is our inspiration,
And as we the reason for the 'Nineties' being gay,
We all wear a green carnation.

Refrain:

Pretty boys, witty boys, yearning for
Permanent adulation,
Haughty boys, naughty boys, every pore
Bursting with self-inflation,
We feel we're rather Grecian,
As our manners indicate,
Our sense of moral values isn't strong.
For ultimate completion
We shall really have to wait
Until the Day of Judgment comes along.
Faded boys, jaded boys, each one craves
Some sort of soul salvation,
But when we rise reluctantly but gracefully from our graves,
We'll all wear a green carnation.

They go off. **Lord Shayne** *and* **Sari** *come in from the supper room.*

---

54 Jean-Baptiste Greuze (1725–1805) was a French portrait painter.
55 Aubrey Vincent Beardsley (1872–98) was an English illustrator and author.
56 The only alcohol in the world with a naturally green tint.

Lord Shayne I want to talk to you.

Sari I know.

Lord Shayne You can guess what I am going to say?

Sari Yes, I think so.

Lord Shayne I love you.

Sari (*smiling*) I was right.

Lord Shayne Will you honour me by becoming my wife? You've now refused me in practically every capital in Europe – London is the last on the list.

Sari Why should London prove the exception?

Lord Shayne It's home.

Sari (*sighing*) Yes – I suppose it is.

Lord Shayne It has charm, London – a very peaceful charm, particularly for anyone who is tired like you. You can drive in the Park in the spring and look at the crocuses.

Sari Please don't talk of spring.

Lord Shayne Then there's the autumn, when the leaves fall in the Square, and you can sit on a rickety iron chair and watch the children searching for horse chestnuts.

Sari (*wistfully*) Whose children?

Lord Shayne Just anybody's.

Sari The fogs come in November.

Lord Shayne Fogs can be delightful.

Sari Can they? (*She smiles.*)

Lord Shayne Particularly when you're warm and snug by a crackly fire drinking tea, while from the yellow gloom outside the trees look in at you like ghosts.

Sari I don't like tea or ghosts.

Lord Shayne You're very hard to please.

Sari How do you know I'm tired?

Lord Shayne By your voice, and your eyes.

Sari I'm afraid I don't love you – actually! I think you're kind and understanding and gay and very dear, but you know I've only really loved one man all my life. I know it's tiresome to be so faithful, particularly to a mere memory, but there it is.

Lord Shayne I think perhaps I could make you happy – anyhow happier.

Sari May I think it over a little? I'll let you know a little later.

The supper room doors open and everyone comes noisily into the room.

Victoria   Sarah – aren't you going to sing soon?

Honor   Do you remember our singing lessons at Madame Claire's before you met Carl Linden – I mean – Oh dear –

Sari (*smiling*)   I remember! I do hope my voice has improved since then.

Lord Shayne   Silence, please! Madame Sari Linden will sing us some of Carl Linden's enchanting songs, the songs she has made so famous.

Everyone applauds and arranges themselves comfortably.

Sari   Where is my accompanist, is he here?

A foreign-looking **Young Man** *detaches himself from the crowd.*

Young Man   Here I am.

Sari   What shall we start with?

Young Man   'The River Song?'

Sari   No, that's too difficult to begin with.

Young Man   'Zigeuner'?

Sari   That will do. Ladies and gentlemen, this song needs a slight preface. My husband wrote it when he was only sixteen. He visited Germany for the first time and sailed down the Rhine past forests and castles and gipsy encampments, and they fired his imagination so much that he wrote this song of a lovely flaxen-haired German Princess who fell in love with a Zigeuner gipsy.[57]

The **Young Man** *starts the introduction and* **Sari** *takes her stand by the piano.* **Lord Shayne** *stands pensively near her gazing at her. She sings 'Zigeuner'.*

'Zigeuner'

Once upon a time
Many years ago,
Lived a fair Princess,
Hating to confess
Loneliness was torturing her so.
Then a gipsy came,
Called to her by name.
Woo'd her with a song,
Sensuous and strong,
All the summer long;
Her passion seemed to tremble like a living flame.

Is taken up after the first verse by the orchestra.

Bid my weeping cease,

---

57 A racial slur for a member of the Romany travelling community of Eastern Europe.

Melody that brings
Merciful release,
Promises of peace;
Through the gentle throbbing of the strings.
Music of the plain,
Music of the wild,
Come to me again,
Hear me not in vain,
Soothe a heart in pain,
And let me to my happiness be reconciled.

Refrain:

Play to me beneath the summer moon,
Zigeuner! – Zigeuner! – Zigeuner!
All I ask of life is just to listen
To the songs that you sing,
My spirit like a bird on the wing
Your melodies adoring – soaring,
Call to me with some barbaric tune,
Zigeuner! – Zigeuner! – Zigeuner!
Now you hold me in your power,
Play to me for just an hour,
Zigeuner!

At the end of it everyone applauds. She silences them by raising her hand.

This is a very simple, sentimental little song. I do hope you won't laugh at it – it means a very great deal to me.

She unpins a bunch of white violets from her waist and throws them to **Lord Shayne**. *Then she begins to sing the refrain of 'I'll See You Again'.*

Reprise:

I'll see you again,
I live each moment through again.
Time has lain heavy between,
But what has been
Can leave me never;
Your dear memory
Throughout my life has guided me.
Though my world has gone awry.
Though the years my tears may dry,
I shall love you till I die,
Good-bye!

At the end the lights dim and the orchestra crashes out the melody. When the lights go up again, it is the present day, the same as Act One, Scene One, and she is an old woman singing to a lot of young people sprawling on the floor. When she finishes singing, **Dolly Chamberlain** *springs to her feet.*

Dolly   It is the most thrilling, divine, marvellous thing I've ever heard – Vincent, I'm mad about you – d'you hear – I love you.

She flings herself into his arms. He gently and rather absently disengages himself.

Vincent   What a melody – my God, what a melody!

He goes to the piano and begins to play 'I'll See You Again', softly as a fox-trot. The rest of the band join in and then the orchestra. Everyone gets up 'hey-heying' and Charlestoning and finally, led by **Dolly**, *they all go jazzing and through the double doors, followed by* **Vincent** *and the members of the dance band.* **Lady Shayne** *is left alone, standing quite still. Suddenly she begins to laugh, a strange, cracked, contemptuous laugh; she rises to her feet, and then, suddenly holding out her arms wide, she sings:*

Sari   Though my world has gone awry,
Though the end is drawing nigh.
I shall love you till I die,
Good-bye!

The curtain falls.

Words and Music

Critics' Notes

The height of Coward's revue style for Charles B. Cochran, this revue consists of sketches and musical numbers that showcase the world of performance and upper crust of society in which Coward lived, whilst simultaneously exposing the cracks in their sparkling world. This revue was also an artistic response to the Cochran revues of Cole Porter (1891–1964), American sophisticate who had gained a foothold in London theatre. Porter's review of 1929, entitled *Wake Up and Dream* had been written on the heels of Coward's *This Year of Grace* (1929), leading to a comparison between the two creators. An anonymous critic argued of *Wake up and Dream!*:

> The show isn't *quite* so good as *This Year of Grace*, but quite too wonderful all the same . . . in the absence of Mr Coward and Miss Maisie Gay, what does he (Cochran) do? He chooses the next best thing to Coward in the personage of Cole Porter, and camouflages the lack of broad comedy in a whirlwind of dancing.[1]

Porter and Cochran would go on to collaborate on more than a half dozen revues and large-scale productions for Cochran before Coward's professional dispute led to the dissolution of his working relationship with Cochran.

In this revue we see Coward's comic lyric style in such numbers as 'Mad Dogs and Englishmen,' 'Mad About the Boy,' and 'The Party's Over Now,' all of which became commercial 'hits' for Coward and countless cover version. Coupled with ballet scenes, a Victorian-style tableaux production, appearances by female heroines of days past, including star of the Restoration theatre Nell Gwynn (1650–87), a series of comic poems, a farcical setting of 'Journey's End,' and a sketch about socially-aware youngsters, this revue embodied the creative and innovative spirit of 1930s London. The musical numbers, sketches and descriptions that follow give us better understanding of the overarching aesthetic of the witty and glamourous 1930s Coward revue.

The diverse elements in this production were bolstered by an equally divergent group of creators who took part in the work's development. Coward and Cochran employed a remarkably diverse group of collaborators, including Black choreographer Buddy Bradley (1905–72), whom Cochran recruited from America. Although nothing remains of Buddy's choreography, it is likely that he oversaw much of the dance collaborations and musical choices made by Coward and Cochran's musical mistress and Coward's amanuensis, Elsie April (1884–1950).[2]

Words and Music opened in London at the Adelphi Theatre on 16 September 1932, after a brief Manchester tryout in August of that year. It ran for 164 performances, with a cast of 47 and large ensemble. Coward's godson and biographer Sheridan Morley notes that Coward also directed the production, demonstrating his artistic involvement

---

1   Anonymous, *The Tatler*. Wednesday, April 24, 1929. Number 1452.
2   Cochran's employment and naming of Bradley during a time in which Black creators were so rarely credited demonstrates his commitment innovative entertainment while indicating that his theatres were likely some of the most progressive in 1920s and 30s London. For more on the contributions of Bradley see Sean Mayes and Sarah K Whitfield, *An Inconvenient Black History of British Musical Theatre, 1900–1950*. (London: Bloomsbury, Methuen, 2021).

in the production.³ It starred Cochran luminaries Ivy St. Helier, Joyce Barbour, Romney Brent, John Mills, and Coward's later longtime partner, young Graham Payne in a small role.⁴ Although this was not the longest running Cochran revue for Coward, it demonstrates his skills as a multifaceted composer and playwright, and his sense of comic human nature that we see in later comedies such as *Blithe Spirit* (1941) or *Present Laughter* (1942).

Critical responses to this production highlight the concept of the revue as an ephemeral entity; revues centred on up-to-the-minute cultural satire, references to daily life and politics (within the bounds of the Lord Chamberlain's censorship rules for representation). The *Belfast Newsletter* compared the work to Coward's *Cavalcade* (1931) which had become a symbol of 1930s patriotism only the previous year:

> Mr Noel Coward has a rare gift of capturing passing moods. Nothing could have been better timed than his production of *Cavalcade* a year ago, just when a wave of patriotic feelings was sweeping the country. But in his new revue *Words and Music* Mr Coward shows himself a bit out of date . . . Earlier in the year it was fashionable enough to speak of an impending crash with cheerful pessimism . . . To-day such talk is right out of date.⁵

Other critics, however, praised Coward's balance of modernity and tradition, including J. T. Grein of *The Sketch* who argued: 'To the valiant Mr Noel Coward nothing is sacred, and so he goes to hell for leather for all manner of modern crazes, with side blows at the elder and wiser, who are as dense as the younger generation is "bright" in the maniacal sense of modernity.'⁶ Similarly, *The Era* noted: 'Make no mistake; this is a highbrow revue. Its references are subtle . . . It is a show completely subdued to the method of one high priest of stage art. The rhythm of the thing is perfect; Coward assisted by Cochran's shekels and tactical sagacity, once more proves himself a masterful producer.'⁷ Both Coward and Cochran's creativity are certainly reflected in this work, which remains a standard for aesthetic sensibility, musical style and biting wit of the 1930s revue.

Original Cast

*Ivy St. Helier:*⁸

(1) Dresser   Opening Chorus
(2) Governor's Lady   Mad Dogs and Englishmen
(3) Postmistress   Hall of Fame

---

3 Sheridan Morley, *Noël Coward* (London: Haus Publishing), 54.
4 According to Barry Day, after Graham performed 'Nearer My God to Thee' whilst tap dancing Coward declared: 'We've got to have the kid in the show.' Barry Day, *The Letters of Noël Coward* (London: Bloomsbury, Methuen, 2007), 280.
5 Anonymous, '*Words and Music*', *Belfast Newsletter*, Thursday 22 September 1932.
6 J. T. Grein. 'The Stage', *The Sketch*, Wednesday 28 September 1932.
7 Anonymous, '*Words and Music*', *The Era*, Wednesday 21 September 1932.

(4) Announcer   Journey's End
(5) Betty   Fairy Whispers
(6) Old Lady   Boarding House Ballet
(7) Wife of an Acrobat   (Single)
(8) Mrs Rowntree   Midnight Matinée
(9) Lady Skeffington   The Party's Over Now

Romney Brent:[9]

(1) Missionary   Mad Dogs and Englishmen
(2) Indiarubber Bath man The Hall of Fame
(3) Stanhope   Journey's End
(4) Narrator   Fairy Whispers
(5) Doctor   Crèche Ballet
(6) Stuart Ingleby   Midnight Matinée
(7) Lord Skeffington   The Party's Over Now

Joyce Barbour:[10]

(1) Children of the Ritz
(2) Announcer   The Hall of Fame
(3) Woman of the World   Mad About the Boy
(4) Frou-Frou   Journey's End
(5) Children of the Ritz
(6) Something to Do with Spring
(7) Mrs Draycott Salome Midnight Matinée
(8) Hostess   The Party's Over Now

John Mills:[11]

(1) Let's Live Dangerously (Bobby)
(2) Clergyman   The Hall of Fame
(3) Harry Happy   Journey's End
(4) Roger   Fairy Whispers
(5) Bank Clerk   Boarding House Ballet
(6) Something to Do with Spring
(7) Young Man   The Party's Over Now
(8) Englishman   Mad Dogs and Englishmen

---

8 Ivy St. Helier (1886–1971) was born in London, England, and worked as an actor, composer and lyricist. Among other roles, she played Manon La Crevette in *Bitter Sweet* (1929).

9 Romney Brent (1902–76) was a Mexican actor, director, dramatist and librettist. Amongst other works for the London stage, he collaborated with German composer Kurt Weill on *A Kingdom for a Cow* (1935).

10 Joyce Barbour (1901–77) was an English stage actor whose career began in pantomime in Birmingham. London stage credits include *Present Arms* (1928) and Rodgers and Hart's *Ever Green* (1930) (also produced by Charles B. Cochran).

11 Sir John Mills, CBE (1908–2005) was an English actor who appeared in over 120 films in addition to his stage work. London stage credits include *Cavalcade* (1931) and *Of Mice and Men* (1939).

Namara:[12]

(1) Let's Say Good-Bye
(2) Marie Françoise   Journey's End
(3) Mamma   Younger Generation
(4) Singer   Boarding House Ballet
(5) Finale

Steffi Duna:[13]

(1) Lilli   Let's Live Dangerously
(2) Tart   Mad About the Boy
(3) Raleigh   Journey's End
(4) Matron   Crèche Ballet
(5) Leonora   The Party's Over Now

Doris Hare:[14]

(1) Jane   Let's Live Dangerously
(2) Planter's Wife   Mad Dogs and Englishmen
(3) Servant Girl   Mad About the Boy
(4) Journey's End
(5) Joan   Fairy Whispers
(6) Clergyman's Wife   Boarding House Ballet
(7) Marie   Younger Generation
(8) Young Girl   The Party's Over Now

Joan Clarkson:[15]

(1) 2nd Mother   Let's Live Dangerously
(2) Planter's Wife   Mad Dogs and Englishmen
(3) Life Story   The Hall of Fame
(4) Journey's End
(5) Jane   Fairy Whispers
(6) Invalid   Boarding House Ballet
(7) Westmorsham   Blessington
    Midnight Matinée
(8) Finale

---

12 Marguerite Namara (1888–1974), born Marguerite Evelyn Cecilia Banks, was an American lyric soprano, well known for her interpretations of Gilbert and Sullivan. She adopted the stage name 'Namara' after her mother's maiden name 'McNamara', and made several London appearances, thanks to her close connections with Coward's social set.
13 Steffi Duna (1910–92) was a Hungarian-born film actor and dancer, whose first appearance on the London stage was in *Words and Music*. She later moved to Hollywood in 1932, embarking on a successful career as a character performer.
14 Born in Bargoed, Glamorgan, Wales, Doris Breamer Hare (1905–2000) was a British actor, singer, dancer and comic. During the Second World War she joined Evelyn Laye in a revue of the BBC Forces Programme. She was also part of the Royal Shakespeare Company, and played various television roles.
15 Joan Rosaline Clarkson (1904–82) was born in London. Film credits include *The Mystery of Dr. Fu Manchu* (1923) and *The Sacred Order* (1923).

Norah Howard:[16]

(1) Planter's Wife   Mad Dogs and Englishmen
(2) School Girl   Mad About the Boy
(3) Journey's End
(4) Dotsie   Fairy Whispers
(5) Tennis Girl   Boarding House Ballet
(6) Miss Spence   Joan of Arc
                                     Midnight Matinée

Effie Atherton:[17]

(1) Planter's Wife   Mad Dogs and Englishmen
(2) Holiday Mermaid   The Hall of Fame
(3) Journey's End
(4) Housemaid's Knees
(5) Announcer   Ballets
(6) Lemworth   Nell Gwynn
                                      Midnight Matinée

(7) Finale

Ann Codrington:[18]

(1) 1st Mother   Let's Live Dangerously
(2) Planter's Wife   Mad Dogs and Englishmen
(3) Secretary   Mad About the Boy
(4) Journey's End
(5) Mrs Harrison   Fairy Whispers
(6) Proprietress   Boarding House Ballet
(7) Ponting   Marie Antoinette
                                      Midnight Matinée

(8) Finale

Gerald Nodin:[19]

(1) Governor   Mad Dogs and Englishmen
(2) Shrimp Catcher   The Hall of Fame
(3) General   Journey's End
(4) Clergyman   Boarding House Ballet
(5) Policeman   The Party's Over Now

---

16 Norah Howard (1900–68) was born in London. Stage credits include *Me and My Girl* (1939) and *The Big Noise* (1936).
17 Effie Atherton (1907–2005) was born in Edinburgh. In addition to her stage credits which include Charlot's *1925 Revue*, she also starred in several films, including the musical comedy *Temptation* (1934).
18 Born in Kasuli, India, Ann Codrington (1894–1982) starred in several films, including *I'll Turn to You* (1946) and *Alice's Adventures in Wonderland* (1948).
19 English actor Gerald Nodin (1899–1969) is primarily remembered as a film actor, whose credits include *Over the Moon* (1939) and *Hangman's Wife* (1950).

Millie Sim:[20]

(1) Planter's Wife   Mad Dogs and Englishmen
(2) Friend   Mad About the Boy
(3) Journey's End
(4) Fairy Queen   Fairy Whispers
(5) Spinster   Boarding House Ballet
(6) Hogan   Diane de Poitiers
    Midnight Matinée

(7) Finale

Chorus Parts
Moya Nugent:[21]
Phyllis Harding:[22]
Betty Hare:[23]

(1) Four Little Débutantes Are We
(2) The Gin is Lasting Out
(3) Nuns   Journey's End
(4) Younger Generation
(5) Four Little Débutantes So Tired

	Lay Out
	1st Part:
1. Opening Chorus	Set. Tabs. Cyc.
	Twelve Girls
	Dresser: Ivy St. Helier
	Call Boy
	Twelve Men
2. Débutantes	Tabs. Spotlight
	Moya Nugent
	Phyllis Harding
	Betty Hare
	Pauline Barran
3. Let's Live Dangerously	Set in Two
	1st Mother: Ann Codrington
	2nd Mother: Joan Clarkson

---

20 Born Millie Helen Rosalie Sim (1895–1986), Sim was the daughter of actress Millie Hilton and part of the performance troupe the five Rudge Sisters.

21 Moya Nugent (1901–54) was a British actor and singer, primarily associated with the works of Noël Coward. Over the course of her career she performed in twelve of his works, including *Conversation Piece* (1934).

22 Phyllis Harding (dates unknown) was an actor associated with Coward. She performed in several of his works, including *This Year of Grace* (1929), *Conversation Piece* (1934) and *Point Valaine* (1935).

23 Born Besse Maud Hare (1898–1981) in Treharris, Glamorgan, Wales, Berry Hare performed in numerous stage works, films and television programmes. Credits include *Tread Softly* (1952) and *For the Love of Ada* (1972).

150 Words and Music

	Lilli: Steffi Duna Jane: Doris Hare Bobby: John Mills
4. Children of the Ritz	Tabs Joyce Barbour Eight Show Girls
5. Mad Dogs and Englishmen	Frame Drop in Two Romney Brent Twelve Girls
5. Mad Dogs and Englishmen	*Planter's Wives:* Norah Howard Ann Codrington Doris Hare Effie Atherton Millie Sim Joan Clarkson Two Coolies (explain THIS) Snake Charmer Governor: Gerald Nodin Governor's Lady: Ivy St. Helier Policeman Contortionist Two Englishmen, etc.
6. Débutantes	Tabs. Spotlight Moya Nugent Phyllis Harding Betty Hare Pauline Barran
7. Let's Say Good-bye	Set in Two. Rostrum Gina: Natura Paul:
8. Hall of Fame	Tabs. Drop in Two Ivy St. Helier Effie Atherton Joan Clarkson *Announcer:* Joyce Barbour Gerald Nodin Romney Brent John Mills
9. Mad About The Boy	Drop in One. Four Sets – Tableau Crowd Society Woman: Joyce Barbour Friend: Millie Sim

	School Girl: Norah
	Friend: Joy Sprigg
	Servant Girl: Doris Hare
	Tart: Steffi Duna
	The Boy
	Secretary: Ann Codrington
10. Journey's End	Scrim. Dug Out (Set in Two). Trees Platform. Revolve & Cyc
	Announcer: Ivy St. Helier
	Marie François: Namara
	Stanhope: Romney Brent
	Trotter:
	Raleigh: Steffi Duna
	Frou Frou: Joyce Barbour
	Harry Happy: John Mills
	General: Gerald Nodin
	The Emperor:
	Six Show Girls
	Six Dancing Boys
	Full Company
	Six Typists
	Six Generals
	Four Nuns (Drabs)
	2nd Part
11. Housemaid's Knees	Number One Tabs
	Twelve Chorus Girls
	Effie Atherton
12. Fairy Whispers	Two Sets
	(1)
	Mr Harrison:
	Mrs Harrison: Ann Codrington
	Molly: Joy Spring
	Joan: Doris Hare
	Cuthbert
	(2)
	Betty: Ivy St. Helier
	Dotsie: Norah Howard
	Jane: Joan Clarkson
	Roger: John Mills
	Narrator: Romney Brent
	Fairy Queen: Millie Sim
	Four-Piece Orchestra
	Children of the Ritz: Joyce Barbour

152   Words and Music

13. Ballets[24]

Three Sets
Announcer: Effie Atherton
(1) *Club*
Colonel (Acrobatic)
Page Boy
Waiter:
Four Bridge Players
Two Old Men (Newspapers)
Three Men with Glasses
(2) *Boarding House*
Old Lady: Ivy St. Helier
Proprietress: Ann Codrington
Tennis Girl: Norah Howard
Invalid: Joan Clarkson
Spinster: Millie Sim
Clergyman's Wife: Doris Hare
Skivvy: Joy Spring
Bank Clerk: John Mills
Clergyman: Gerald Nodin
Singer: Namara
(3) *Crèche*
Matron: Steffi Duna
Doctor: Romney Brent
Eight Nurses

14. Something to Do with Spring

Tabs One and Three
Joyce Barbour
John Mills
Twelve Girls
Twelve Men
Ivy St. Helier

15. Younger Generation

Set in Three
Mamma: Namara
Maid: Doris Hare
Moya Nugent
Phyllis Harding
Betty Hare

[24] One of his most highly acclaimed ballet productions, Léo Delibes' *Coppélia*, was staged in 1924 at the London Trocadero. After Cochran met Diaghilev and Igor Stravinsky in Seville, he hired Diaghilev for a 1921 season in London in which the Ballet Russe performed *Petrushka*, *The Firebird* and other works. The season also included flamenco dancers whom he met in Spain. He also fostered the career of several important dancers and choreographers, including American choreographer Agnes de Mille who created the dances for Cole Porter's *Nymph Errant* (1933) for Cochran. For more on this see *The Evening News*, 9 November 1924; also 'A Dainty Ballet: British Prima Ballerina's Success in *Coppélia*', *The Daily Chronicle*, 10 November 1924, and *Glasgow Bulletin*, 8 December 1924 (Cochran Collection Scrapbook 42, GB 71 TGM/97 misc. 1924–29).

	Pauline Barran	
	Twelve Men	
16. Wife of an Acrobat	Drop in One	
17. Midnight Matinée	Tabs in One. Set in Two. Tabs. Rostrum and Frame in Two	
	Septette	Ivy St. Helier
		Namara
		Joan Clarkson
		Millie Sim
		Joyce Barbour
		Norah Howard
		Effie Atheron
	Mrs Rowntree (*Organizer*)	Ivy St. Helier
	Visc. Hogan: Diane de Poitiers	Millie Sim
	Lady M. Hedley: Cleopatra	Namara
	March. of Lemworth: Nell Gwynn	Effie Atherton
	Hon. Mrs D. Draycott: Salome	Joyce Barbour
	Miss E. Ponting: Maria Antoinette	Ann Codrington
	Lady E. Sherrel: Court Lady	Joy Spring
	Miss R. Mosenthorpe: Court Lady	Sifa Treble
	Lady P. Gainton: Little Page	
	Hon. J. Porrage: Little Page	
	Miss Spence: Joan of Arc	Norah Howard
	Lady Westmorsham: Lady Blessington	Joan Clarkson
	Mrs F. N. J. Wilson: Lady Godiva	
	Stuart Ingleby (Announcer)	Romney Brent
	Lady Crouche: Angel	
	Mrs Philip Mere: Angel	
	Greek Chorus	Twelve Girls

Opening Chorus[25]

The scene is the Chorus dressing-room. It is circular with twelve dressing places and twelve mirrors. There is a stand in the middle upon which the dresses are hanging. Before the curtain rises the **Girls** *are heard singing. There are twelve of them seated on stools before each mirror, dressed in their underclothes and shoes and stockings.* **Maggie**, *a typical old theatrical dresser, is bustling about.*

---

25 Typical Cochran revues opened with a chorus line of beautiful dancing girls, similar in height, age and build, who were known in the West End as 'Cochran's Young Ladies'. Casting calls and images of these performers were regularly featured by the press. In this opening number, Coward plays with this convention by providing a provocative backstage view of their work that also highlights the division of labour in a London theatre.

The curtain rises.

Girls
    We shan't be on to-night
    We shan't be on to-night
    Because the overture is near
    We're paralysed with fear
    The opening chorus
    Is too complicated for us
    In this damned revue
    We've far too much to do
    We sing 'til our throats are aching
    Dance 'til our backs are breaking
    During the applause
    We rush and change our drawers
    Tearing at ribbons while our hands are
    Always getting dressed (*shaking*)
    We're worked to death
    Out of breath
    Nervous of every music cue
    Anxious the whole performance through
    Maggie!

1st 2nd
    Have you the scissors handy?

All
    Maggie!

3rd 4th
    We want a port-and-brandy

All
    Maggie!

5th 6th
    Our brassieres don't set right

All
    Maggie!

7th 8th
    We've upset all our wet-white

Maggie
    Oh my God don't hurry me
    You'll miss your entrance if you worry me
    Flurry me

All
    Maggie!

These aren't our first-act stockings
Maggie!
Our shoes are tight
Maggie! Maggie
Our trunks are far too baggy
We shan't be on to-night.

Maggie (*going to different girls*):
Now, Freda dear, you must
Do *something* with your bust
You'd best tie a knot, dear
You can't show them all you've got, dear
Dorothy my duck
Your eyelashes ain't stuck
Just like an Aberdeen dear[26]
Rosie 'old this pin
And keep your stomach in
And don't do a pratfall in your first routine dear
Nora, there's a smear
Of eye-black on your ear
You must look right
Every night
You know until the show is through
I have to take the blame for you.

All
Maggie!

9th 10th
We want an orange stick, dear

All
Maggie!

11th 12th
We're feeling rather sick, dear

All
Maggie!
Our mirrors need adjusting
Maggie!
Our make-ups look disgusting

Maggie
Oh, my God, don't hurry me
You'll miss your entrance if you worry me
Flurry me

---

26 This remark highlights the negative stereotypes of Aberdeen and Scotland in general that were prevalent in the 1930s.

All
> Maggie!
> Our shoulder-straps are slipping
> Maggie!
> There nothing right
> Maggie Maggie!
> They've made our wigs too shaggy
> We shan't be on to-night.
> Maggie Maggie Maggie Maggie!
> Maggie Maggie!
> Maggie Maggie Maggie Maggie!
> We shan't be on to-night.

The **Call Boy** *raps on the door.*

Call Boy
> Overture Beginners.

All
> La lalalalalalala
> Lalalalala la
> La lalalalalala
> Lalalalala la

The **Call Boy** *enters.*

Call Boy
> Overture Beginners.

Maggie
> All right all right.

Call Boy *exits.*

All
> La lalalala la la la
> La lalalala la la la
> La lalalala la la la
> La lalalala la la la
> We shan't be on to-night
> We shan't be on to-night.

They all struggle into their dress, and on a certain music cue march out of the room. **Maggie** *is left alone, fussing about and tidying up.*

Maggie (*reprise*)
> They must look right
> Every night
> Worked to death
> Out of breath
> I'll stay and tidy up a bit
> And pray the blasted show's a hit!

'The Lights Fade'

In front of tabs.

> Good evening, ladies and gentlemen,
> You'll be tickled to death
> To recognise the Chorus
> And as we're opening the show
> It's really comforting now and then
> To discover for once
> That you are here before us
> It may astonish you to know
> We're Mr Cochran's Young Invincibles[27]
> He much prefers us to the Principals
> For every scene he cuts out
> He says 'Just send the sluts out'
> And that's the reason why we have to work our guts out.
>
> Hallo!
> We're always on the trigger
> Hallo!
> Please note our girlish vigour
> Hallo!
> We have to hop and bustle
> Hallo!
> We're straining every muscle
> While we break our necks we feel
> That so much animation wrecks appeal
> Sex appeal
> Never
> Can show when there's too much
> Endeavour
> It lays it low
> We don't mind now
> We're really quite resigned now
> Hallo Hallo Hallo!

'Débutantes'[28]

(1)

> Four little débutantes are we
> Born of these restless, changing years

---

27 This is another term for Cochran's 'Young Ladies' who were typically between the ages of sixteen and twenty. Typical articles from the period describe them in gendered terms, such as a spread in *The Sketch* which called them 'a bunch of pretty buds.' (See Anonymous, *The Sketch*, Wednesday 11 April 1928.)

28 This number is a sharp satire on the British upper class, a common theme in Coward's works. There is also a striking similarity in tone to his lyrics for 'World Weary'.

Conscious of vague, unwilling fears
What is our Destiny to be?
Shall we escape the strange 'ennui'
Of civilised futility?
When we are old and wearied through
Shall we regret how wise we were?
Shall we at last have time to spare
Tears for the dreams we never knew?

'Children's Hour'[29]

The scene is a nursery.

Lilli, **Jane** *and* **Bobby** *are demurely playing with their yours, which consist of a rocking-horse, a doll's house, a clockwork train, etc. The two* **Mammas** *are watching them complacently.*

1st Mamma   They seem to be getting along splendidly.

2nd Mamma   It is more than good that my Lilli should have playmates of her own age. At home in Vienna her little friends are so formal, so *comme il faut*.[30] Here everything is more free and gay.

1st Mamma   I'm afraid that my two are terrible little tomboys sometimes, they play the naughtiest practical jokes, but I always say that it does children no harm to run wild occasionally.

2nd Mamma   You English are so sensible. It is wunderbar.[31]

1st Mamma   I think we might leave them now, don't you, so that they can really get to know one another?

2nd Mamma   Certainly. Be good, my Lilli.

Lilli   Yes, Mamma.

1st Mamma   Show Lilli your doll's house, Jane, and let her play with

Laura (*to* **2nd Mamma**)   That's her best doll, you know. I always encourage them to be unselfish.

Jane   Yes, Mamma.

---

29 An anonymous critic describes this sketch as Coward's opportunity to 'pour scorn upon those upon those who live useless lives in the big hotels'. (See Anonymous, *Nottingham Journal*, Saturday 17 September 1932).
30 Correct in etiquette and behaviour.
31 An anonymous critic notes that Coward 'pokes fun at the craze for German musical comedy'. (See Anonymous, *Nottingham Journal*, Saturday 17 September 1932, 7). Stereotypes of German culture were common leading up to the start of the Second World War in 1939. This type of satire regarding Germans appears in works such as James Laver's novel *Nymph Errant* which was adapted into Cole Porter's 1933 stage play for Charles B. Cochran.

1st Mamma Don't make too much noise.

Bobby No, Mamma.

The **Two Mothers** *go out.*

The **Three Children** *look at each other.*

Jane (*to* **Lilli**) Is it true about your friends in Vienna being so formal?

Lillie Quite true. Most of them are damned little prigs.

Bobby Environment, I expect, it's all a question of environment.

Jane We're better off here I think on the whole, we keep our presents in ignorance of the facts of life until the last possible moment.

Lilli (*laughing*) You English are so sensible. It's wunderbar.

Bobby I think the moment has come for you to show Lilli your doll's house, Jane.

Jane It's rather amusing really, we got the idea from the Shaneborough children, they had their's done when their mother was in Carlsbad.

She opens the doll's house and displays a perfectly little cocktail bar.

Lilli Absolutely charming – (*examining it*) – and a little machine for making ice as well.

Bobby We keep all the extras such as olives and salted almonds in a little drawer in the rocking-horse's behind. (*He demonstrates this.*)

Jane Chic, don't you think?

Lilli Quite, quite marvellous. I shall write to Fritzi and tell her all about it.

Jane Mix us a drink, Bobby. Who's Fritzi?

Lilli A friend of mine in Vienna, she's a bit passé now, over fifteen, but she gives very gay parties.

Bobby Martini?

Jane Yes, with a dash.

Bobby *proceeds to mix a cocktail.*

Lilli And not too sweet.

Jane Cigarette?

Lilli I'll smoke my own if you don't mind – your English cigarettes play hell with my throat.

She produces a small cigarette case which is hanging from a little gold chain inside her dress.

Bobby (*over his shoulder*) It's all a question of habit.

Jane   How is child life on the whole in Central Europe?

Lilli   We've been going through rather a bad suicide phase during the last year, all these stupid sex obsessions, you know.³²

Jane   It's high time people stopped making such a ridiculous fuss about sex – after all, what *can* it matter?

Lilli   Too much introspection, that's the trouble, really, far too much introspection.

Bobby   Freud started it of course, all that absurd dream nonsense.

(*He hands them cocktails.*) Here, try these.

Lilli (*sipping one*)   Very good.

Jane   A shade too much lemon, I think.

Bobby   The basis of most of the unrest nowadays is just simply lack of courage.

Lilli   Very true.

Bobby   Nobody seems to have the guts to look at themselves as they really are.

Jane   Or at Life as it really is.

Bobby   After all, we only have so many years and then phtt!

Lilli (*smiling*)   Why not enjoy them?

Bobby   Exactly.

Jane   Live every moment for what it's worth. Take every risk, every chance, live dangerously.

Trio: *'Let's Live Dangerously'*³³

Verse:

> Life won't fool us
> Because we're out to lick it
> We've got its ticket
> And we'll kick it
> In the pants
> Fate will never catch us asleep

---

32 Coward is poking fun at the craze for German psychoanalysis that peaked in the mid-1930s. See, for instance, Anonymous, 'Tributes to Sigmund Freud: Address by Leading Writers', *Aberdeen Press and Journal*, Tuesday 5 May 1936.

33 This is another musical number that highlights the Ritz Hotel and its association with London's upper crust. The suggestions of 'pill' and 'swill' refer to the use of drugs and alcohol among the upper classes. This barb at the upper crust would have been well understood by the society elites who attended the opening night of the production. The Cochran 'First Night' as it was known was a highlight of the social season. (See, for example, Anonymous, 'Greeting *Words and Music*', *The Tatler*, no. 1631, 28 September 1932, p. 32.)

We'll be ready to leap
When there's the slightest chance
Life won't rule us
Determined to subdue it
We'll give the raspberry to it
Do it in the eye
We believe in following through
All we're ready to do
Or die.

Refrain:

> Let's live dangerously dangerously dangerously
> Let's grab every opportunity we can
> Let's swill
> Each pill
> Destiny has in store
> Absorbing life at every pore
> We'll scream and yell for more
> Let's live turbulently turbulently turbulently
> Let's add something to the history of man
> Come what may
> We'll be spectacular
> and go 'Hey Hey'
> In the vernacular
> And so until we break beneath the strain
> In various ways
> We're going to be raising Cain.

Refrain 2:

> Let's live dangerously dangerously dangerously
> Let's all glory in the bludgeonings of chance
> Let's win
> Out in
> Spite of the angry crowd
> And if the simile's allowed
> Be bloody but unbowed
> Let's live boisterously boisterously boisterously
> Let's lead moralists the devil of a dance
> Let's succumb
> Completely to temptation
> Probe and plumb
> To find a new sensation
> Where we'll end up
> Nobody can tell
> So pardon the phrase
> We mean to be raising hell!

'Children of the Ritz'

Part One

Children of the Ritz
Children of the Ritz
Sleek and civilised
Fretfully surprised
Though Mr Molyneux has gowned us[34]
The world is tumbling around us
Without a sou[35]
What can we do?
We'll soon be begging for a crust
We can't survive
And keep alive
Without the darling Bankers Trust[36]
In the lovely gay
Years before the Crash[37]
Mr Cartier [38]
Never asked for cash
Now shops we patronised are serving us with writs
What's going to happen to the Children of the Ritz?

We owe Elizabeth Arden[39]
Several thousand pounds
Though we can't pay
We just blow in
If we're passing that way
While we're going
On our rounds
We'll persevere
Till our arteries harden
Then we shan't much care
Whether our chins
Have a crinkle in them
Whether our skins
Have a wrinkle here and there

---

34 Edward Molyneux (1891–1974) was a leading London fashion designer during Coward's day, who also provided fashion illustrations for *Smart Set* magazine.
35 A five-cent piece.
36 The Bankers Trust was an American financial institution based in New York City.
37 This refers to the Wall Street Crash of 1929 that led to the Great Depression.
38 Jacques-Théodule Cartier (1884–1941) was a leading jewellery designer whose brand is still well known.
39 Born Florence Nightingale Graham (1881–1966), Elizabeth Arden was a Canadian-American businesswoman who created one of the first global cosmetics brands, particularly popular with London elites.

We shan't much mind
For we shall then have left our dreary lives behind.

Children of the Ritz
Children of the Ritz
Vaguely debonair
Only half aware
That all we've counted on is breaking into bits
What shall we do
What's going to happen to
The foolish little Children of the Ritz?

'Mad Dogs and Englishmen'

The scene is a street in any tropical British colony. The set should be stylised and slightly burlesqued, with labels reading 'Government House', 'English Club', 'Anglo Anglo Bank', etc. The English Club is on the left with a small terrace on which are seated two Englishmen in white drill suits, sipping drinks at a table. On the right are two rickshaws with their owners squatting beside them. There are various natives wandering about and a few bank clerks, also a snake-charmer sitting on the ground wearing a fez and playing a reed pipe. There should be as much noise as possible with an undercurrent of music running through it. Every now and then there is suddenly a dead silence and the two Englishmen say respectively 'Have this one on me', 'No, have this one on me', whereupon they both clap their hands for the waiter, and the noise is resumed. A native policemen enters, walks to the centre of the stage and strikes a small triangle which he carries, at the same time lifting his leg casually and slowly above his head. Everyone immediately stops whatever they happen to be doing and sings.

Chorus:

> The Sun never sets on Government House[40]
> For English Might
> Selected the site
>
> No matter how much the Communists grouse[41]
> The Sun never sets on Government House
>
> The Sun never sets on Government House
> The Nation smiles

---

40 This refers to the government buildings throughout the British Commonwealth that housed governors-general, governors and lieutenant-governors of the British Empire. These were converted as the members of the Commonwealth assumed independence.

41 Coward's references to Communists here highlight the perpetual suspicions about the many socialists, many of whom were Jewish, who began to emigrate from Germany ahead of the Second World War. For more on this see Louise London, *Whitehall and the Jews, 1933–1948: British Immigration Policy, Jewish Refugees and the Holocaust* (Cambridge: Cambridge University Press, 2001).

O'er thousands of miles
No matter how much we sozzle and souse
The Sun never sets on Government House.

The street noises are all resumed, and to a very marked rhythm in the orchestra six planters' wives enter dressed in frilly garden party dresses and solar topis. Again the policemen strikes the triangle and lifts his leg. The planters' wives advance to the centre and sing.

'Planters' Wives'[42]

Our Husbands deal in Sugar and in Rubber
Our Husbands deal in Coffee and in Tea
Whenever we meet the Vicar's wife we snub her
To prove our vast superiority
We're usually sour and apathetic
In tropical heat
Nobody who's sweet, survives
We powder and primp
And try to be sympathetic
Oh dear
It's queer
That only with men
We're thoroughly energetic
We're Planters' Wives.

At the end of this the street noises are resumed for a moment, then everybody stands stock-still, and shouts 'The Governor', 'The Governor's Lady', 'The Governor', 'The Governor's Lady'. A very small native boy enters in uniform and announces: 'Sir Ronald Mullenty, Lady Mullenty' **Sir Ronald** *and* **Lady Mullenty** *enter in rickshaws. As they descend from them everybody sinks to the ground in a low curtsey.* **Sir Ronald** *bows courteously,* **Lady Mullenty** *waves her hand girlishly.* **Lady Mullenty** *and* **Sir Ronald** *sit down on special chairs just below the club. The native policeman approaches them and bows.*

Policeman   He has been sighted, Your Excellencies.

Sir Ronald   Who has been sighted, my man?

Policeman   The Lost Missionary, Your Excellency.

Lady Mullenty   That's the third we've lost since Whitsun.[43]

Sir Ronald   Who is he?

---

42 This number is a peculiar look at gendered colonial society. Coward references the government structure, the presence of the Church of England (e.g. the 'Vicar's wife') and trade, including coffee, rubber, sugar and tea.
43 The Christian feast of Pentecost, celebrated fifty days after Easter Sunday.

Policeman   The Reverend Inigo Banks. He has been lost for seventeen years in the very heart of the trackless jungle.

Lady Mullenty   We must ask him to lunch.

Amid a lot of cheering from the crowd, the **Reverend Inigo Banks** *enters in a rickshaw accompanied by twelve natives. He is wearing a tropical suit, very creased, a pepper-and-salt solar topi with a veil flowing from it and pince-nez. He carries an umbrella and a parrot in a cage. He also has three bearers with him carrying strange-looking luggage. He springs brightly from his rickshaw, bows low before* **Sir Ronald** *and* **Lady Mullenty** *and goes straight into his number:*

'Mad Dogs and Englishmen'[44]

In tropical climes there are certain times of day
When all the citizens retire
To tear their clothes off and perspire.
It's one of those rules that the greatest fools obey,
Because the sun is much too sultry
And one must avoid its ultry-violet ray.

Papalaka papalaka papalaka boo,
Papalaka papalaka papalaka boo,
Digariga digariga digariga doo,
Digariga digariga digariga doo,

The natives grieve when the white men leave their huts,
Because they're obviously definitely nuts!

Mad dogs and Englishmen
Go out in the midday sun.
The Japanese don't care to,
The Chinese wouldn't dare to,
Hindoos and Argentines sleep firmly from twelve to one.[45]
But Englishmen detest a siesta.
In the Philippines there are lovely screens
To protect you from the glare.
In the Malay States there are hats like plates
Which the Britishers won't wear.
At twelve noon the natives swoon

---

44 This list song is one of Coward's most popular numbers. Sheridan Morley argues that this number was meant to reflect on the status of the Empire in 1918, written during a period in which Britain thrived on the world stage. However, as he notes, the influence was far greater after the Second World War: 'Ironically, once the Empire collapsed under the financial, political and social strains of a Second World War and the seismic shift that followed the Labour government's 1945 landslide victory, the song came to be seen as a celebration of a vanished world and a dying breed of Englishman.' (See Sheridan Morley, *Noël Coward*, 54.)
45 This refers to the cultural practice of the siesta or midday rest.

And no further work is done.
But mad dogs and Englishmen
Go out in the midday sun.

It's such a surprise for the Eastern eyes to see,
That though the English are effete,
They're quite impervious to heat.
When the white man rides ev'ry native hides in glee,
Because the simple creatures hope he
Will impale his solar topee on a tree.

Bolyboly bolyboly bolyboly baa,
Bolyboly bolyboly bolyboly baa,
Habaninny habaninny habaninny haa,
Habaninny habaninny habaninny haa,

It seems such a shame when the English claim the earth
That they give rise to such hilarity and mirth.

Mad dogs and Englishmen
Go out in the midday sun.
The toughest Burmese bandit[46]
Can never understand it.
In Rangoon the heat of noon
Is just what the natives shun.
They put their Scotch or Rye down and lie down.
In a jungle town where the sun beats down
To the rage of man and beast.
The English garb of the English Sahib[47]
Merely gets a bit more creased.
In Bangkok at twelve o'clock
They foam at the mouth and run,
But mad dogs and Englishmen
Go out in the midday sun.

Mad dogs and Englishmen
Go out in the midday sun.
The smallest Malay rabbit
Deplores this stupid habit.
In Hong Kong they strike a gong
And fire off a noonday gun
To reprimand each inmate who's in late.
In the mangrove swamps where the python romps
There is peace from twelve till two.

---

46 Burma became Myanmar in 1948.
47 This term was typically associated with the presence of the English in Indian during colonial rule which lasted until 1947.

Even caribous lie around and snooze,
For there's nothing else to do.
In Bengal, to move at all
Is seldom, if ever done,
But mad dogs and Englishmen
Go out in the midday sun.

'Débutantes'

The gin is lasting out
No matter whose
We're merely casting out
The blues[48]
For gin, in cruel
Sober truth
Supplies the fuel
For flaming youth
A drink is known
To help a dream along
A saxophone[49]
Provides our theme song
Though we dishevel
Out girlish bloom
To the devil
With gloom!
The gin is lasting out
No matter whose
We're merely casting out
The blues
For gin, in cruel
Sober-truth
Supplies the fuel
For flaming youth
We can't refuse
The gin is lasting out
We're merely casting out
The blues!

---

48 This references the popular American form of the blues which was brought to Britain by Black performers at the end of the First World War. (See Jason Toynbee and Catherine Tackley, 'Black British Jazz: Routes, Ownership and Performance' and Thomas L. Riis,. 'The Experience and Impact of Black Entertainers in England, 1895–1920', *American Music* 4, no. 1 (1986), 50–8.
49 The saxophone was a symbol of the New Woman and the jazz era in the 1920s and 1930s.

'Let's Say Good-Bye'[50]

The scene is a terrace overlooking the sea. It is a moonlight night and across the bay there are lights twinkling. **Gina** *and* **Paul** *are seated at a little table upon which there is a shaded light. They have finished dinner and are drinking coffee and liqueurs.* **Gina** *is a well-dressed handsome woman in her thirties,* **Paul** *is about the same age. Somewhere, not very far away, music is playing softly.*

Gina Well, my dear, what are you thinking?

Paul You know perfectly well.

Gina The evening has been so gay and charming, we mustn't let it die into silence.

Paul How much do you mind me going away?

Gina What a foolish question!

Paul We're so near the end. I'm hating it bitterly.

Gina Not 'bitterly', please.

Paul Sadly, then.

Gina That's better. A little sadness, not too much, just enough to colour your memory.

Paul Are you so sure, so absolutely convinced that we are not causing ourselves unnecessary suffering?

Gina Quite sure. So are you, in your heart.

Paul No, I'm not, really I'm not. There's no real reason why you shouldn't come away with me, why we shouldn't be married.

Gina Every reason. We've loved each other for a little while, and it has been perfect, why spoil it?

Paul Why are you so certain that it would spoil it?

Gina Because – because – (*She sings.*)

'Let's Say Goodbye'

Verse:

> Now we've embarked on this love affair
> Don't let's destroy it with tears.

---

50 This became one of his most popular songs and bears a similarity in theme and style to 'Someday I'll Find You' from *Private Lives* (1934). He recorded this himself in 1932, and critics noted 'his singing has a style of its own, and every word is audience'. (See, for instance, Anonymous, 'Noël Coward Records His Own Songs', *Market Harborough Advertiser and Midland Mail*, Friday 18 November 1932.)

Once we begin
To let sentiment in
Happiness disappears.
Reason may sleep
For a moment in spring
But please let us keep
This a casual thing
Something that's sweet
To remember through the years

Refrain:

Let our affair be a gay thing
And when these hours have flown
Then, without forgetting
Happiness that has passed
There'll be no regretting
Fun that didn't quite last
Let's look on love as a plaything.
All these sweet moments we've known
Mustn't be degraded
When the thrill of them has faded
Let's say 'Good-bye' and leave it alone.

At the end of the song, the sound of a ship's siren is heard in the distance.

Gina   That was your ship, I expect.

Paul (*looking away*)   Yes. I expect it was.

Gina   It sails in an hour, doesn't it?

Paul   Yes.

Gina   Look at me.

Paul (*turning his head*)   Well?

Gina   We shall both of us suffer quite a lot during the next few weeks, and the colour will go out of everything for a bit, but when we do meet again, somewhere far away in the future, it will be gay and sweet and terribly exciting, because however many others we have loved in the meantime and however old and tired we may be, we shall have between us a perfect memory.

The siren sounds again.

Will you go now quickly, there's a dear, because you've never seen me cry either, and I don't want you to.

Paul   Darling – oh, darling . . .

Gina   Please – please . . .

Paul   I love you.

Gina   I love you.

He kisses her once and goes away.

She sings the refrain of the song very softly as the lights fade.

'The Hall of Fame'[51]

Announcement

Ladies and gentlemen
In this peculiar era
Communal unity
Is daily drawing nearer
We are indebted to the papers
For thus dispersing of the vapours
Which have hitherto concealed
A lot of simple lives that should have been revealed
Think what publicity
Means to the teaming masses
To all those lads and lasses
Who, but for being advertised,
Might have lived all their days unrecognised
So we and they together bless
The kindly efforts of the press.

'The Man Who Caught the Biggest Shrimp'

I'm the man who caught the biggest shrimp in the world
And the second biggest prawn as well
I live at Ryde[52]
And I take great pride
In the tale I have to tell.
The reporters flock
To examine every rock
And to explore each stretch of sand
Though why they choose
Me to figure in the news.
I shall never understand.

---

51 Coward's 'Hall of Fame' skewers the press by featuring stories of the unknown common Brit, ranging from a fisherman to a postmistress.
52 Located on the Isle of Wight.

'The Oldest Postmistress in England'[53]

I'm the very oldest postmistress in England
And probably the oldest on the Earth
I've been asked by all the papers for a statement
So I give you these few facts for what they're worth
My appetite is absolutely splendid,
There's nothing in the world I can't digest
I seldom feel uneasy or distended
And I'm never disagreeable or depressed
I still deliver all the letters daily
Though my memory is just as good as new
I've a hazy recollection of Disraeli[54]
And I lived in Bray in eighteen forty-two
I think the modern girl is very pretty
I've never smoked a single cigarette
I think all this divorcing is a pity
And I'm sorry that the nation is upset
I well recall in eighteen thirty-seven
My parents lived in Weston-super-Mare
I'm actually one hundred and eleven
But I cannot see why anyone should care!

'The Man Who Rowed Across Lake Windermere in an Indiarubber Bath'[55]

[Man]
For years and years and years and years
I've burned to satisfy
A passionate desire in me
To catch the public eye
When living in obscurity
In Station Road Penarth
I thought of crossing Windermere
In an indiarubber bath.

All
He rowed across Lake Windermere
In an indiarubber bath!

---

53 Interestingly, in 1910 the oldest living postmistress in Britain passed at the age of ninety-five. (See, for instance, Anonymous, 'Death of the Oldest Postmistress in Britain', *Aberdeen Press and Journal*, Monday 21 February 1910.
54 Benjamin Disraeli (1804–81) was the only Jewish prime minister and a Conservative Member of Parliament.
55 Lake Windermere is the largest lake in Britain.

[**Man**]
> The press responded to a man
> I'm known from coast to coast
> And eighty lonely women
> Have proposed to me by post
> I'm made a lifelong member
> Of a most exclusive club
> For I rowed across Lake Windermere
> In an indiarubber tub.

All
> He rowed across Lake Windermere
> In an indiarubber tub.

[**Man**]
> I'm grateful to the *Mirror*[56]
> And the *Sketch* for my success
> And also to the *Telegraph*
> The *Mail*, and the *Express*.
> It doesn't matter now to me
> What shadows cross my path
> For I rowed across Lake Windermere
> In an indiarubber bath!

All
> He rowed across Lake Windermere
> In an indiarubber bath!

'The Holiday Mermaid'

> I'm a typist from Putney, and once every year[57]
> I stay with my aunt at Torquay[58]
> And last time I went there, as no one was near
> I decided to bathe in the sea
> I'd put on me costume and folded me frock
> And was tying me 'air in a veil
> When two men nipped out from behind a big rock
> And gave me this kid with a pail
> Now me face wasn't powdered, me fringe wasn't curled.
> And me parents are properly wild
> 'Cos me photo's been published all over the world
> As a 'Holiday Mermaid with Child!'

---

56 Each of the newspapers listed here was known for biting theatrical critiques of theatrical works.
57 Coward's 'mermaid' is a Cockney figure from Putney in southwest London. The language here highlights the differences between class and station in 1930s London.
58 Torquay is a seaside town in Devon, England.

'The Clergyman Who's Never Been to London'

I'm the clergyman who's never been to London
I'm the clergyman who's never been to town
An enterprising journalist approached me
And every word I said he jotted down
I had to face a battery of cameras
And hold an extra service in the snow
And all because I've *never* been to London
And haven't got the *least* desire to go!

My Life Story[59]

I've been paid by kind Lord Rotherbrook
A very handsome sum
Though I'm stupid and illiterate
And practically dumb.
I cannot really count
How many choruses I've graced
But the story of my life
Is in the very best of taste
I was on the stage at seventeen
And off at twenty-three
And living with a business man
At Birchington-on-Sea[60]
My appendix caused me trouble
And in order to survive
I had it taken out three times
In nineteen twenty-five
In April nineteen twenty-eight
I married Lord St. Lyne
Divorcing him in January
Nineteen twenty-nine
I've been photographed for hundred times
On foot, and in my car
And that's the human story
Of how I became a star!

---

59 This life story centers on a chorus girl, similar to one of Cochran's Young Ladies, who uses her position in the theatre to capture the attention of several prominent men.
60 The likely star in mind for the 'boy' was either Valentino or Novarro (Morley, *Noël Coward*, 56). Sheridan Morley notes that this was dropped from the New York production due to concerns about it being sung by a well-dressed businessman instead of a young girl. (Morley, *Noël Coward*, 56). Film represented a legitimate threat to British theatre beginning with the first silent films in the 1920s.

Choral Finale

Long live the press[61]
Long live the press
We're grateful for its subtlety
Its power and its finesse
It's brought us from obscurity
To well-deserved success
Long live the daily press!

'Mad About the Boy'[62]

The first scene is outside of a cinema at night. There is a queue of people waiting to go in for the second performance; a man is playing a penny whistle while another man goes along with a hat. There are various noises of traffic blending in with the music, which supplies a continuous undercurrent. A variegated crowd of people come out of the cinema, mostly typists and working girls with their young men, among them a street-walker, a servant girl, a school-girl, and a smartly dressed woman in an evening gown and cloak. Suddenly the audience should become aware that everybody is whispering one phrase over and over again, 'Mad About the Boy'. The four principals step forward for a moment in order that they may be remembered later. The street-walker goes off by herself, the school-girl goes off with a seedy-looking young man, and the society woman with her woman friend steps down to hail a taxi. There is a blackout during which the music and whispering continue, then the lights go up on a smart flat in Mayfair. The society woman enters with her friend switching on the lights as she does so.

Woman   Want a drink?

Friend   I'd love one, darling.

Woman (*taking off her cloak*)   I'm breaking up, that's what I'm doing, breaking up.

Friend (*smiling*)   Never mind.

Woman   I mind violently. I feel deeply humiliated. That young man is common, dull, excessively stupid and far too short, I met him once and I know. And yet I wouldn't miss one of his pictures for anything in the world. I go and sit there slavering over him like a half-witted kitchen-maid. I've got a photograph of him in my bedroom. I solemnly kissed it last Tuesday all by myself. I'm crazy about him, I tell you, and it's undoubtedly the beginning of the end.

Friend   When did you meet him?

The woman sings the song.

---

61   This satirical finale skewers the press.
62   This number features four different women who represent a cross-section of the British public, ranging from a Cockney working girl, to a school girl, an upper-class lady and a street-walker.

At the end of the song the lights fade and the stage moves round disclosing a middle-class drawing-room with the school-girl doing her home-work at the table while her younger sister is practising at the piano. The school-girl is staring at a photograph propped up against a pile of books while she mumbles to herself 'J'aime, tu aimes, il aime' – etc.

She sings her verse and refrain and the lights fade. The stage moves round, disclosing a scullery with a sink and plate-rack, etc. The servant girl is busy washing and drying the crockery. There is the inevitable photograph propped up on the plate-rack. She sings her verse and refrain to it, at the end smashing a plate on the floor.

The lights fade and the scene changes to a bedroom in a cheap lodging-house. The street-walker comes in wearily, taking off her coat and hat, sits on the bed and lights a cigarette. She sings her verse and refrain of the song, at the end of which she comes out of the set in a spot-light; the other three join her also in spot-lights. All four of them sing the refrain, joined gradually by the whole chorus in the background, they are all again whispering to the music 'Mad About the Boy', working up into a crescendo.

When the climax is reached there is a blackout and an inset of the boy himself is show. He is sitting in an elaborate dressing-gown having his nails manicured. His feet are in a mustard bath and he obviously has a bad cold. He also wear pince-nez, as, off the screen, his eyes are weak. His secretary stands beside him with a pile of 'fan mail'. He tosses the letters casually aside merely saying gloomily, 'Send a photograph, send a photograph'.

Blackout.

Verse:

Society Woman
>I met him at a party just a couple of years ago
>He was rather over-hearty, and ridiculous
>But as I'd seen him on the screen
>He cast a certain spell.
>I basked in his attraction for a couple of hours or so
>His manners were a fraction too meticulous
>If he was real or not, I couldn't tell
>But like a silly fool, I fell.

Refrain:

>Mad about the boy
>I know it's stupid to be mad about the boy
>I'm so ashamed of it
>But must admit
>The sleepless nights I've had about the boy.
>On the silver screen
>He melts my foolish heart in every single scene
>Although I'm quite aware

That here and there
Are traces of the cad about the boy
Lord knows I'm not a fool girl
I really shouldn't care
Lord knows I'm not a school-girl

In the flurry of her first affair.
Will it ever cloy?
This odd diversity of misery and joy
I'm feeling quite insane
And young again
And all because I'm mad about the boy.

Verse:

School-girl
Home work, home work
Every night there's home work
While Elsie practises the gas goes pop
I wish, I wish she'd stop
Oh dear, oh dear,
Here it's always 'no, dear'.
You can't go out again you must stay home
You waste your money on that common picturedome[63]
Don't shirk – stay here and do your work
Yearning, yearning,
How my heart is burning.
I'll see him Saturday in 'Strong Man's Pain'
And then on Monday and on Friday week again
To me he is the sole man
Who can kiss as well as Colman,[64]
I could faint whenever there's a close-up of his lips
Tho' John Barrymore is larger[65]
When my hero's on his charger
Even Douglas Fairbanks Junior hasn't smaller hips[66]
If only he could know
That I adore him so.

---

63 A common name for a cinema in the 1920s and 1930s.
64 Ronald Charles Colman (1891–1958) was an English-born film actor, known for silent films as well as *Random Harvest* (1942) and others.
65 John Barrymore (1882–1942) was an American stage, screen and radio actor.
66 Douglas Elton Fairbanks (1883–1939) was an American actor, screenwriter, director and producer.

Refrain:

>Mad about the boy
>It's simply scrumptious to be mad about the boy,
>I know that quite sincerely
>Housman really
>Wrote *The Shropshire Lad* about the boy,[67]
>In my English prose
>I've done a tracing of his forehead and his nose
>And there is, honour bright
>A certain slight
>Effect of Galahad about the boy.[68]
>I've talked to Rosie Hooper
>She feels the same as me,
>She says that Gary Cooper[69]
>Doesn't thrill her to the same degree
>In 'Can Love Destroy?'
>When he meets Garbo[70] in a suit of corduroy,
>He gives a little frown
>and knocks her down
>Oh dear, oh dear, I'm mad about the boy.

'Cockney Verse'

Cockney
>Every Wednesday afternoon I get a little time off from three to eleven,
>Then I go to the picture house and taste a little of my particular heaven
>He appears in a little while, through a mist of tears I can see him smiling
>Above me.
>Every picture I see him in
>Every lover's caress
>Makes my wonderful dreams begin
>Makes me long to confess.
>That is ever he looked at me and thought perhaps it was worth the trouble to
>Love me.
>I'd give in and I wouldn't care however far from the path of virtue he'd
>Shove me,
>Just supposing our love was brief

---

67 *A Shropshire Lad* (1989) is a collection of sixty-three poems by English poet Alfred Edward Housman (1859–1936).
68 According to Arthurian legend, Sir Galahad was one of King Arthur's knights.
69 Born Frank James Cooper, Gary Cooper (1901–61) was an American film actor, whose many films included a 1933 adaptation of Coward's *Design for Living* (1932).
70 Greta Garbo was a Swedish-American actor best known for her work in *Grand Hotel* (1932) and *Ninotchka* (1939).

If he treated me rough
I'd be happy beyond belief
Once would be enough.

Refrain:

Mad about the boy
I know I'm potty but I'm mad about the boy.
He sets me 'eart on fire
With Love's desire
In fact I've got it bad about the boy.
When I do the rooms
I see 'is face in all the brushes and the brooms
Last week I strained me back
And got the sack.
And 'ad a row with Dad about the boy.
I'm finished with Novarro[71]
I'm tired of Richard Dix[72]
I'm pierced by Cupid's arrow
Every Wednesday from four till six.
'Ow I should enjoy
To let 'im treat me like a plaything or a toy
I'd give my all to him
And crawl to him
So 'elp me Gawd I'm mad about the boy.

Verse:

Tart

It seems a little silly
For a girl of my age and weight
To walk down Piccadilly
In a haze of love
It ought to take a good deal more to get a bad girl down
It should have been exempt, for
My particular kind of Fate
Has taught me such contempt for
Every phase of love,
And now I've been and spent my last half-crown
To weep about a painted clown.

---

71 Ramon Novarro (1899–1968) was a Mexican-American film actor best known for his silent films.
72 Born Ernst Carlton Brimmer, Richard Dix (1893–1949) was an American star of silent and sound films, best known for *Cimarron* (1931).

Refrain:

> Mad about the boy
> It's pretty funny but I'm mad about the boy
> He had a gay appeal
>
> That makes me feel
> There's something sad about the boy
> Walking down the street,
> His eyes look out at me from people that I meet
> I can't believe it's true
> But when I'm blue,
> In some strange way I'm glad about the boy.
> I'm hardly sentimental
> Love isn't so sublime
> I have to pay my rental
> And I can't afford to waste much time,
> If I could employ
> A little magic that would finally destroy
> This dream that pains me
> And enchains me,
> But I can't, because I'm mad about the boy.

'Journey's End'[73]

Announcement

Ladies and gentlemen
Forgive my strange appearance
Our kindly author has
With spending perseverance
Worked without stint for your enjoyment
And in this age of un-employment
He decided on a plan
To utilise as many aliens as he can
For, like Sir Oswald Stoll[74]
He feels an obligation
To do his level best
To help the German nation
and if Charell would condescend[75]

---

73 *Journey's End* is a 1928 play by British playwright R. C. Sherriff, set in the trenches of Aisne, France near the end of the First World War.
74 Sir Oswald Stoll (1866–1942) was an Australian-born British theatre producer who co-founded the Stoll Moss Group, which held a monopoly on British theatre until the 1960s. He also owned Stoll Pictures, one of the leading film companies in Britain.
75 Erik Charell (1894–1974) was a German theatre and film director who worked in Germany, London and New York, and was best known for revues and productions such as *The White Horse Inn* (1952).

To make a spectacle of 'Journey's End'
It is our author's little scheme
To show this strange 'Teutonic dream'![76]

Musical Version of 'Journey's End'

As Produced by Erik Charell

Characters in the order of their appearance:

Marie Françoise	Namara
Stanhope	Romney Brent
Trotter	
Raleigh	Steffi Duna
Frou-Frou	Ivy St. Helier
Harry Happy	John Mills
General	Gerald Nodin
The Emperor	

The first scene is a transparent painted curtain representing a French village. From the back of the theatre and down the centre gangway comes **Marie Françoise** *in national peasant costume singing a yodelling song, followed by six show-girls also in elaborate national costume carrying large baskets. They clamber up on to the stage by means of two small rostrums on either side of the proscenium and exit,* **Marie Françoise** *last, still yodelling. The interior of the dug-out gradually becomes apparent through the transparent curtain, which finally rises.* **Stanhope** *is discovered seated at a table upon which is a lace table-cloth, a silver bowl of fruit, a bottle of champagne and a glass, and an elaborate silver candelabra.*

Stanhope (*in a thick Spanish accent*)   Three years of this hell. Will it never end? God! I am tired. Only wine can keep me going. God! I am tired, tired, tired! (*He drinks a glass of champagne.*)

Enter **Trotter**.

Trotter   Lieutenant Raleigh, sir.

Stanhope   Leave me alone. We don't want any more snivelling subalterns. (*His voice rises to an hysterical scream.*) Leave me alone, I tell you! Leave me alone!

Trotter   Lieutenant Raleigh, sir.

Trotter *goes out right.*

Enter **Raleigh** *attired in a military overcoat and a tin hat.* **Stanhope** *starts to his feet.*

Stanhope   You!

---

[76] This references the German order of the Brothers of the German House of Saint Mary in Jerusalem, which from the nineteenth century conferred honorary Christian 'knighthoods'. Coward is no doubt referencing the Nazi regime, which borrowed these symbols and titles.

Raleigh   None other.

Stanhope   Why did you come? Why did you not stay in your so beautiful England where the grass is so green and there is peace, far away from this so terrible war?

Raleigh   I came to be near you, Mein Klein Pupchen.

She tears off her overcoat disclosing an evening dress made of khaki sequins. She sings a dashing song, 'Klein Pupchen', in course of which she steps out of the scene. The dug-out fades behind her. Two sets of trees (ground rows) are pushed on, one from each side of the stage, also two sign-posts with 'Herren' on one and 'Damen' on the other. A tank is pushed on from the prompt side (flat) which disgorges twelve chorus girls, also dressed in khaki sequins and wearing tin hats. The tank is pushed off again and at the end of the number **Raleigh** *and all the girls exit prompt side. As they go off a movable platform slides on opposite prompt side, upon which are six small narrow tables with a Diamond typewriter on each, six fantastically dressed typists with sequin eye-shades and cuffs, and, standing behind them, six staff officers. The officers dictate to music for a few seconds and then the platform slides back again, at the same moment as the tress are pushed off, disclosing the dug-out again.* **Stanhope** *is still sitting at the table.*

Stanhope   Three years of hell! Will it never end? God! I am tired. Only wine can keep me going. Wine and memories.

He produces a guitar from under the table, covered in American cloth with probably a few more sequins on it, and sings a Spanish serenade, during which six beautiful 'Senoritas' appear in elaborately stylised Spanish costume with mantillas, and dance round him, clicking castanets. They exit and **Trotter** *re-enters.*

Trotter   The German prisoners, sir.

Stanhope (*hysterically*)   Leave me alone! Leave me alone, I tell you! I don't want any German prisoners. Leave me alone!

Trotter (*inexorably*)   The German prisoners, sir.

Six German prisoners enter laughing merrily, in national costume. They execute a violent 'slapping' dance interspersed with loud whoops of pleasure, in course of which the dug-out fades behind them and in the tress are pushed on again. This time 'Hommes' and 'Dames' is painted on the sign-posts. As the German boys exit prompt side, the movable platform slides on again from opposite prompt side identically as before, and slides off again. A gondola is pushed on from the prompt side out of which step **Frou-Frou** *and* **Harry Happy**. **Harry Happy** *is a typical low comedian in comic Tyrolean costume, and* **Frou-Frou** *is the 'cute' variety of soubrette, with very large bows on her shoes and a very small hat. They sing a duet called 'A Gondola on the Somme', during which six saucily dressed nuns appear in a spotlight opposite prompt side and sing in harmony. At the end of the number they all exit, the tress disappear, and once more* **Stanhope** *is discovered sitting in the dug-out.*

Stanhope Three years of hell! Will it never end? God! I am tired. Only wine can keep me going. God! I am tired, tired, tired!

Trotter *enters.*

Trotter The General to see you, sir.

Stanhope (*frantically*) Leave me alone! Leave me alone, I tell you! I don't want the General. Leave me alone!

Trotter The General to see you, sir

Trotter *goes out right.*

The **General** *enters and goes straight into a spiritual number, 'Love and War'. He steps out of the dug-out which fades away. The movable platform slides on again from the opposite prompt side. The trees also reappear, this time with 'Caballeros' and 'Senoras' on the sign-posts.* **Trotter** *and* **Raleigh** *come on with a table (painted flat), also* **Frou-Frou** *and* **Harry** *with another one. All the chorus rush down from the back of the theatre, also with small painted tables which they plant in the aisles singing madly. At the end of the number they all disappear and once more the dug-out is disclosed.*

Stanhope Three years of this hell –

Trotter *enters.*

Trotter (*interrupting him*) The attack, sir!

The scene fades, there is a distant booming of guns. The trees come on again, this time there is Chinese writing on the sign-posts. A small boy in a surplice walks across the stage whistling. Four chorus rush across shouting 'The Emperor!' 'The Emperor!' The movable platform slides on, conveying, in addition to the conference, **Marie Françoise** *in still more elaborate national costume. At the same moment an illuminated dreadnought is pushed on from the prompt side, from which steps the* **Kaiser**.

Marie (*curtsying low*) Sire.

Kaiser (*in a strong Scotch accent*) My child!

Marie I am unhappy, sire.

Kaiser Happiness is ever-fleeting. Journeys end in lovers meeting.

Marie (*again curtsying*) Oh, sire.

She is whisked off backwards on the movable platform while the **Kaiser** *retires to his dreadnought. Suddenly from everywhere voices are heard shouting* 'Stanhope!' 'The attack!' 'Stanhope!' 'The attack!' *The trees go away, and through the transparent curtain which has been used for the* **Kaiser**'s *scene, the big attack is seen to be in progress. The transparent curtain rises as the stage behind begins to revolve. In the centre of the revolve is a small billocks with a ruined village on it. Below this, the stage is divided into four sections by illuminated barbed-wire entanglements, over which the chorus, representing the German and the British respectively, are leaping gaily and pelting each other with coloured-paper streamers. All the principals make a grand chain up and down the front of the stage, shooting puffs of powder out of* *diamanté rifles. From the orchestra, pit and the stage boxes, coloured balloons are flung onto the stage. The orchestra plays 'Deutschland Uber Alles'.*[77]

'Yodelling Song' (Marie Françoise)

Marie
    La dalaito
    La dalaito
    Swift mountain streams
    Play the music of dreams
    La dalaito
    La dalaito
    Morning sweet morning
    So happily gleams
    Morning sweet morning
    So happily gleams.

'Kleine Pupchen'

Kleine Pupchen
Boop oop adoop-chen
You are my own vis-à-vis
Kleine Pupchen
Boop oop adoop-chen
My sweetheart some day you'll be
So if you leave me
Don't go too far
Da da undahda
This is my firm protocol
Till my heart calls a bit
Display your charms a bit
There could be no harm in it
For you're my baby doll!

'Te Quiero'[78]

In an old Spanish garden I found you
The hibiscus was shining all round you
The guitars in the distance were playing
All the love songs I longed to be saying
'Neath the stars that were gleaming above you
I laid all my dreams at your feet
Tho' now I have lost you, I love you
'Te Quiero', my sweet Señorita.

---

77 Composed by Franz Joseph Haydn (1732–1809), 'Deutschland Uber Alles' has been part of the German anthem since 1922.
78 'I love you' in Spanish; Coward is referencing the many Spanish-themed songs and productions popular on the West End stage during this period.

Duet: *'A Gondola on the Rhine'*[79]

Both
> You and me in a gondola
> Just a gondola
> On the Rhine

She
> Gazing without ending
> In each other's eyes

He
> I shall catch you bending
> On your Bridge of Sighs

Both
> We'll tour all round the Mond-ola
> We'll abscond-ola
> Pom, pom!
> And maybe
> One day there will be three
> In our gondola on the Rhine.

'Love and War'

> Love and war
> Those are the games worth playing
> No man could ask any more
> When the bugles and trumpets bray
> Love and war
> Open adventure's door
> All that men sigh for
> Live, laugh and die for
> Love and war!

Part Two

'Housemaids' Knees'

Verse:

> Pretty little housemaids proper and sedate
> um um umum um um um
> We seldom go to bed too early and we rise extremely late.
> Pretty little housemaids eager to improve
> um um umum um um um
> Each shining hour, by slightly widening our small domestic groove.

---

[79] This comic Italian-themed number takes place on the Rhine River, which is the largest river in Germany.

We wish to help the nation
To forget its pence and pounds
Our little innovation
Is on patriotic grounds

Refrain:

Make England brighter
That's what we try to do
Our clothes are lighter
Our skirts are shorter too
When there's the slightest breeze
You see these
Housemaids' knees.
When there's a Crisis[80]
Forget it while you can
Our firm advice is
To every business man
Just take a look at these
Housemaids' knees.
In our domestic and our personal relationships
You must forgive us if our consciousness of 'station' slips
A little beauty
May stop you feeling blue
We feel our duty
Is to enable you
To gaze at skittish
Absolutely British
Housemaids' knees!

'Fairy Whispers'

The scene is the dining-room of a suburban villa.

Mr *and* **Mrs Harrison** *and* **Molly** *are seated round the table having just finished tea.* **Joan** *enters.*

Joan   Sorry I'm late all, but I've just got a new record. Vi gave it to me.

Mrs Harrison   I do hope it's not all Vo do deo dos like the last one she gave you.

Joan   It's called 'Fairy Whispers' and it's a twelve-inch.[81]

---

80 This is a reference to the global depression of the 1930s. By 1932 more than 3.5 million people were unemployed. See, for instance, Anonymous, 'Unemployment in 1932', *Aberdeen Press and Journal*, Friday 7 April 1933, p. 6.
81 The twelve-inch, single-side vinyl record which was introduced in 1902 but did not become popular until the rise of the household gramophone in the 1930s.

Mr Harrison Well, if we don't like it we can always send it to the hospital.

Molly Put it on, Joan, it ought to be lovely.

Mr Harrison You'd better try a new needle, we've used that one for seven months.

Joan (*putting the record on the gramophone*) Keep quiet because it says it's descriptive.

Mr Harrison I should think 'Fairy Whispers' would need to be a little descriptive.

Joan Here we go.

They all sit and listen to the record. At the end of it the lights fade and the scene changes to the interior of the gramophone studio. Four elderly women and two men are grouped round the microphone. In the background there is a four-piece orchestra consisting of two violins, one 'cello and a piano. None of the artists seem to care for one another very much, but nevertheless they proceed solemnly to make the record that we have just heard.

Narrator It is midnight, and the little silver clock in the nursery strikes 'Ding dong, ding dong' . . . Hush! Not another sound but the snoring of Rover in his kennel in the yard . . . ohoo, what's that? . . . It is little Betty waking up. . . .

Betty Oh dear – oh dear – quickly, Roger, quickly – it is midsummer night and there will be fairies on the lawn.

Roger I'm sleepy.

Betty Oh Roger, you pwomised.

Roger All right then, but I don't believe in fairies.

Betty Quickly, quickly, I'll wake Dotsie and Jane.

Narrator Dotsie and Jane, little sleepy heads just refuse to wake for ever and ever so long, finally, out of bed they hop helter-skelter.

Dotsie Fairies! Oh pease we would like to see the fairies.

Jane Woger! Woger! do hurry, oh Woger!

Narrator Tiptoe the madcaps scamper down the wide fumed-oak staircase and out on to the dew-drenched lawn – Hush hush or Rover will awake and kick up – Oh such a din!

Jane Oh Woger, aren't the fairies wonderful?

Dotsie It's all wonderful – too too wonderful!

Narrator See this dainty gossamer creature approaching – a bluebell come to life . . . a veritable flower.

Fairy I am the Fairy Queen.

Betty And I am the littlest girl.

Fairy Will you sing for us, littlest girl, although you are only a mortal we should enjoy it very much indeed.

Betty Ess I will (*She sings.*)

Fairy Now we'll all dance.

Gay dance music interspersed with childish laughter.

Narrator Hush! Rover is barking – quick, back to bed – Hurry – scamper – scurry – Ooo-Ooo if Nurse should awaken – but no, all is quiet again. Good-bye, fairies . . .

Fairies Sweet dreams, mortals.

Good night.

'Children of the Ritz'

Children of the Ritz
Children of the Ritz
Mentally congealed
Lilies of the field
We say just how we want our quails done,
And then we go and have our nails done,
Each single year
We all appear
At Monte Carlo or at Cannes.
We lie in flocks
Along the rocks
Because we have to get a tan.
Though we never work.
Though we always play,
Though we always shirk,
Things we ought to pay
Whatever crimes the proletariat commits[82]
It can't be beastly to the Children of the Ritz.

We all economise madly
Now in every way.
Only one car,
An Isotta,[83]
Though it doesn't go far
Still we potter

---

82 This refers to the controversial rise of the Communist Party in British politics and global society as a response to the economic downturn. See, for instance, Anonymous, 'Sacked for Political Views', *Todmorden Advertiser and Hebden Bridge Newsletter*, Friday 13 May 1932, which describes this party as a subsection of the Communist International.
83 Isotta Fraschini was an Italian luxury car manufacturer, popular in the 1920s and 1930s.

Through the day,
The times are changing –
We realise sadly
That we're near the brink.
Nothing to wear
We're in tatters,
And we honestly swear
That it shatters us to think,
It's really grim
To wonder just how long we're going to sink or swim
Children of the Ritz,
Children of the Ritz,
Though our day is past –
Gallant to the last –
Without the wherewithal to live upon our wits.
Please say a prayer
For all the frail and fair
And futile little Children of the Ritz.

Description of Ballets

1st ballet. The scene is a men's club smoking-room and the ballet is danced by four elderly members of the club. 2nd ballet. The scene is a boarding-house dining-room, the dancers are typical guests at a seaside boarding-house. 3rd ballet. This is danced by the doctor, matron and nurse of a crèche, the 'babies' being large rubber balls with faces painted on them. These are used in the routine of the ballet. Ballet music as in score.

Ballet Announcement

I.
Ladies and gentlemen,
The next scene needs explaining
And Mr Cochran hopes
You'll find it entertaining.
It is his firm determination
To make you use imagination
And to gather at a glance
The charm of ordinary life in terms of dance.
Think of an English Club[84]
On lines of Russian Ballet.[85]

---

84 This is a reference to the Ballet Club, which was formed by Dame Marie Rambert (1888–1982), who led the first ballet school in Britain.
85 Russian ballet was particularly popular in Britain, with several tours by figures such as Sergei Diaghilev and the Ballets Russes in the 1920s and 1930s.

Picture those dear old men
Cavorting musically;
What could be prettier to see
Than angry colonels in captivity,
Pointing the light fantastic toe
As through their daily lives they go!

II.
... See how the 'Dance' can bring to bloom
Even a boarding-house in Ilfracombe.[86]
The Ballet Spirit as portrayed
At number five Marine Parade.[87]

III.
... Now for the sake of our revue
You'll see a crèche of infants under two.
Note the effect of airy grace
In this clean sanitary place!

'Something to Do with Spring'[88]

Verse:

He
   The spring is here, dear
   Oh dear, Oh dear, dear
   Can't you see
   The simple agonising sheen
   On every angry little tree?

She
   I must admit it's rather fun
   To think that every single thing
   That Nature ever does is overdone.

He
   I know exactly what you mean.
   It all looks far too clean –
   A badly painted scene,
   The grass is far too green.

She
   Perhaps there's something we have missed.

---

86 Seaside resort on the north Devon coast in England.
87 The high street in Ilfracombe.
88 Although it was not a hit initially, this number was later recorded and referenced in British popular culture, including in an article on motorways. (See Anonymous, 'This "Miss Cinders" Isn't a Lonely Maid These Days!' *Daily Mirror*, Friday 20 September 1935.)

He
> I never could have kissed
> A sentimentalist.

She
> Still there's something in the atmosphere
> That makes me happy here.

He
> Don't make me giggle, dear.

Refrain 1:

She
> The sun is shining where could have been –

He
> Maybe it's something to do with spring

She
> I feel no older than seventeen –

He
> Maybe it's something to do with spring.

She
> A something I can't express,
> A sort of lilt in the air,
> A lyrical loveliness
> Seems everywhere.

He
> That sheep's behaviour is most obscene.

Both
> Maybe it's something to do with spring.

Refrain 2:

He
> The dewdrops glitter like diamond links –

She
> Maybe it's something to do with spring.

He
> They say that rabbits have minds like sinks –

She
> Maybe it's something to do with spring.

He
> The way that the sows behave
> May seem delightfully quaint,

But why should the cows behave
With *no* restraint?

She
I'd love to know what that stallion thinks –

Both
Maybe it's something to do with spring.

'The Wife of an Acrobat'[89]

Verse:

Always travelling to and fro, and always packing to go
Is apt to derange one.
I believe I should lose my head if once I slept in a bed
That wasn't a strange one.
Never topping the bill at all, in each variety hall[90]
We open or close them.
Apart from waving my hand about
When he's finished a trick
I do nothing but stand about
Feeling slightly sick.
Even if I had lovely legs I'm not the type of a girl
Who blatantly shows them.
When I look at the pair I've got it seems a little bit hard
To have to expose them.
People sat that a pride in tricks
Every animal feels.
I'd prefer to be one of six
Old performing seals.[91]

Refrain 1:

I'm the wife of an acrobat
And the world has passed me by.
I'm dressed in tights
To play 'Twice a Nights'
And only God knows why.
What a life!
For an acrobat

---

89 An anonymous critic wrote of Ivy St. Helier's performance: 'The pathos of Miss St. Helier's song as the wife of the elderly acrobat shows the depth of the author's feeling for the lesser lights of his profession. That, too, is revealed to some extent by the cast very few of whom come to the Adelphi as known stars . . .' (See Anonymous, *Nottingham Journal*, Saturday 17 September 1932.)
90 Variety hall is another term for music hall.
91 Animal acts were a common feature of the music hall from the eighteenth century onwards.

    As he flies from hoop to hoop
    I have a sort of feeling, when our souls have passed away
    When giving shows in Heaven, three performances a day,
    I'll say what all the angels are expecting me to say
    'Allez OOp – Allez OOp – Allez OOp!'[92]

Refrain 2:

    I'm the wife of an acrobat
    And our eldest boy's a scout.
    I hate the lad
    To come and see his dad
    Entirely inside out.
    Now the wives of the acrobats
    Form the most exclusive group
    You'll seldom see us riding 'Haute Ecole[93]' along the park
    And many of us look as if we'd come out of the Ark
    Our conversation meagerly consists of one remark
    'Allez OOp – Allez OOp – Allez OOp!'

Refrain 3:

    I'm the wife of an acrobat.
    When my old man don't feel well –
    To hold each prop
    And wonder if he'll drop
    Is my idea of Hell.
    What a life for an acrobat!
    When I watch him loop the loop
    I wonder what he's thinking upside down on the trapeze
    And is he's really happy with his head between his knees
    And then his face gets crimson and I know he's going to sneeze!
    'Allez OOp – Allez OOp – Allez OOp!'

Refrain 4.

    I'm the wife of an acrobat
    When our kids are in their cots
    It's kind of sad
    To realise their dad
    Is tying himself in knots.
    Now the wife of an acrobat
    Is the 'Dead Pan' of the troupe
    I've stood about for twenty years, my hair is turning grey
    I hear my old man gasping as I watch him swing and sway

---

92 From the French circus term said by an acrobat preparing to leap, '*Allez-hop!*'
93 This is the most elaborate and specialized form of horse riding, seen in the Vienna school of Lipizzaner horses.

And if he broke his bloody neck I know I'd only say
'Allez OOp – Allez OOp – Allez OOp!'

Close tabs.

'The Younger Generation'[94]

Scene: Mamma's bedroom.

Verse:

Girls
Mother, tell us, mother
Have you anything in your heart to tell the four of us
Are you perfectly sure of us.
We are eager to know?

Mamma
I trust you everywhere you go.

Girls
Mother, tell us, mother
If the dreams that you dreamed in springtime have come true for you,
What Love promised to do for you
Did it actually do?

Mamma
With Love the whole wide world seems new.

Girls
Teach us to understand this magic flame,
As you did when at first your lover came,
What did he bring to you?
What melodies did he sing to you?

Mamma
The same . . .
Melodies that lovers sing
Whenever the heart is gay with Spring
And Youth is there
I assure you the truth is there.
The years hurry for young love is brief
Tears follow with the fall of the leaf
Age may bring you sadly to grief
Unless you're wise and realise
That dignity is the greatest prize to guard.

---

94 This number references the social group known as the Bright Young things, according to several critics. (See Anonymous, 'Noel Coward as Censor Morum', *Truth*, Wednesday 28 September 1932.)

Girls
   We'll try so hard.

Mamma
   Once on a time I was young and fair like you

Girls
   We know.

Mamma
   Once on a time I was young and fair like you

Girls
   We know.

Mamma
   Happily dreaming my adolescence through

Girls
   Heigho

Mamma
   Then I married your father
   Gay and handsome and frank
   But it shattered me rather
   When I found he drank.

Girls
   Oh what a shock, that was really too bad

Mamma
   So sad
   Then I took stock of the assets that I had

Girls
   We're glad

Mamma
   Ten long years I had sly love
   Then I whispered to my love
   Get thee behind me
   Life has resigned me
   I'd never stoop to buy love.

Refrain:

Mamma
   Age calls the tune
   Youth's over soon
   That is the natural law.
   There's a younger generation
   Knock knock knocking at the door.
   Why sit and fret?

Vainly regret
Things that have gone before?
There's a younger generation
Knock knock knocking at the door
Though the world is well lost for love of dreams
There's wisdom above dreams
To compensate mothers and wives
This should last them
All their lives
I've had my fun
All that is done
Why should I sigh for more?
There's a younger generation
Knock knock knocking at the door.

Girls
Dear dear mamma
Your wise advice to us
Has made us see that the doubts in our hearts were vain.

Mamma
Love comes
But once or twice to us,
If it is wise love, the memory will remain
Through the years,
Have no more fears,
For age brings peace
Sweet release
From all
The fetters that have bound you,
Call
Your memories around you
All your troubled dreams will cease.

Spoken:

1st   Good night, Mamma.

2nd   Good night, Mamma.

3rd   Good night, Mamma.

4th   Good night, Mamma.

Mamma   Enjoy yourselves, my darlings.

1st   Are you sure that you won't be sad, left here all alone?

Mamma   Quite sure.

2nd   Have you got your spectacles?

Mamma   Yes, thank you.

3rd And your library book?

Mamma Yes, thank you.

4th And your hot-water bottle?

Mamma Yes, thank you.

1st Good night, Mamma.

2nd Good night, Mamma.

3rd Good night, Mamma.

4th Good night, Mamma.

Mamma Remember one thing, my darlings, I may be an old old woman but I am resigned to tranquility, and happy. Happy in my daughters and happy in my remembrance of things long past.

Girls (*together*) Yes, Mamma.

They all kiss her and file out of the room one by one.

When they have gone **Mamma**'s *gentle manner drops away from her, and with great animation she runs across to the bell-rope and tugs at it.*

Mamma (*singing*)
  Marie – Marie – MARIE!

Marie, *the maid, enters hurriedly.*

Mamma Don't keep me waiting
  Can't you see how very very late I am?

Marie
  May I venture to state, Madame,
  That I answered the bell.

Mamma (*speaking*) My dress quickly.

Marie *unhooks her dress and she steps out of it, wearing a white evening gown underneath. Singing:*

  So aggravating
  Can't you see in what a nervous state I am?

Marie (*singing*)
  It's a quarter to eight, Madame.

Mamma (*speaking*) Very well, very well. (*She looks at herself in the glass.*)

Marie (*speaking*) Your shoes, Madame.

Mamma (*speaking*) Yes, quickly.

She sits down in front of her mirror, **Marie** *hands her a shoe-horn and kneels at her feet to help her on with her white shoes.*

Mamma (*singing*)
> I waste a lot of time on those damned girls,
> I think I'll wear the rubies and the pearls.

Marie (*singing*)
> They're in the jewel case.
> But hadn't you better do your face
> And hair?

Mamma (*snatching off her white wig*)
> All right then, there!

She turns round and pats her hair into place in front of the mirror, singing to herself.

> La lala la la lalalala lala la
> Lalala lala lalala – lalala lala la

Marie (*singing*)
> This wig must be sent to be dressed,
> And could I be allowed to suggest
> That before retiring to rest
> You lock the door,
> And in this drawer
> Hide every garment that you wore
> From sight.

Mamma
> All right – all right.
> (*Singing.*)
> Who would suppose I was nearly forty-three
> Ah me!
> I can knock spots off those simpering
> 'Jeunes Filles'[95]
> You see
> Virgin charms don't allure men
> They need something beyond.
> All the wise and mature men
> Need a 'Femme du Monde'[96]
> I can be tender
> And wise and witty too
> It's true
> I don't surrender.
> Before surrender's due.
> A few –
> Lovers may have betrayed me

---

[95] An unmarried young woman.
[96] A sophisticated, worldly woman.

When my heart disobeyed me
But I've escaped now
I have them taped now
Life has indeed repaid me.

Marie *goes out.*

Mamma
Age can be gay
Age can betray
Destiny's foolish law
Though the younger generation's
Knock knock knocking at the door
Age is a joke
Planned to provoke
Dreams that the fools ignore
When the younger generation's
Knock knock knocking at the door
I shall still be gay and attractive
As long as I'm active
I'll savour each delicate sing
Not until my footsteps stagger
And I'm 'gaga'
I'll give in.
Give me a Moon
Give me a tune
Give me a dancing floor
There's a younger generation
Knock knock knocking at the door.

There is a loud knocking at the door, and as the lights fade an endless stream of **Young Men** *in evening dress march into the room.*

'Midnight Matinée'[97]

Opening Chorus

We're going to do a Midnight Matinée!
We're going to do a Midnight Show!
We're not *quite* sure
What charity it's for
But probably the press will know,
We're going to have a talk on Saturday
To make a list of friends who'll go.

---

97 This refers to the common practice of offering midnight theatre performances of revues for charitable causes.

The season's such a bore
We haven't had much excitement since the war
And so . . .
We'll do a Midnight Show.

Last year we did a 'Feather Parade'[98]
That was a great success.
But some got bent
And some would break
And a lot got sent
To Melton by mistake
At Easter we went mad I'm afraid
We really must confess
We gave a great –
Big 'Circus Ball'[99]
But forgot the date
So no one came at all.

We're going to do a Midnight Matinée!
We're going to do a Midnight Show!
A sort of 'Masque'[100]
Where everyone will ask
And nobody will *ever* know.
We're going to have a talk on Saturday
To make a list of friends who'll go
God knows how much we'll fetch
But we shall have all our pictures in the *Sketch*
And so –
We'll do a Midnight Show.

Characters[101]

Mrs Rowntree (*organiser*)
Viscountess Hogan   Diane de Poitiers
Lady Millicent Headley   Cleopatra
Marchioness of Lemworth   Nell Gwynn
Hon. Mrs Douglas Draycott   Salome
Miss Emse Ponting   Marie Antoinette

---

98 A reference to a carnival-like Mardi Gras celebration.
99 A themed society party.
100 A masquerade ball.
101 Each of the characters here is based on a historical reference, and the play-within-a-play format is that of a Victorian-style theatrical tableau – a common feature in Charles B. Cochran's revues – such as Cole Porter's *Wake Up and Dream* (1929), which was also produced by Cochran.

Lady Eleanour Sherrel	Court Lady
Miss Rebecca Mosenthorpe	Court Lady
Lady Patricia Gainton	Little Page
Hon. Julian Forrage	Little Page
Miss Spence	Joan of Arc
Lady Westmorsham	Lady Blessington
Mrs F. N. J. Wilson	Lady Godiva
Mr Stuart Ingleby (*announcer*)	

After the opening chorus, which is sung by **Six Ladies** *and* **Mrs Rowntree**, *the scene changes to a smart drawing-room in which the committee meeting is being held. Everyone present has a cocktail, except* **Mrs Rowntree**, *who has a pencil and paper. The* **Viscountess Hogan** *rises.*

Hogan   Darlings, I must fly – I've got to dress.

Mrs Rowntree   You *can't* go yet, we haven't settled *anything*!

Hogan   Diane de Poitiers – I shall be Diane de Poitiers, it's all arranged.

Mrs Rowntree (*miserably*)   I don't even know who she was.

Lemworth   Effie, how can you! She was Henry the something's little piece.

Westmorsham   She died in the most dreary agonies owing to having the wrong child at the wrong moment and having the wrong doctor as well and everything being awful.

Hogan   Anyhow she's the one I'm going to be. Pinkie will do me a dress, it will probably be nothing but oilcloth and isinglass – you know you he loves being a little different, but it's sure to look lovely in the lights. You *will* arrange about the lights properly this time, Effie. I don't want that Mona Lisa business all over again. Goodbye everybody. Come on, Millie . . .

She and **Lady Millicent Headley** *go out.*

Mrs Rowntree   I did so want her to be Mary Queen of Scots.

Mrs Wilson   The thing that worries me is, ought I to have a real horse or not?

Mrs Rowntree   Don't give it another thought, Mrs Wilson, it will be perfectly easy to get a horse.

Miss Spence   After all they had camels in *Chu Chin Chow*.[102]

Lemworth   And a bus in *Cavalcade*.[103]

Mrs Wilson   And I suppose I should have the hair sewn to the tights, just in certain places?

---

102   A 1916 musical comedy by Frederick Nortin and Oscar Asche, it was one of the most successful West End shows, running for 2,238 performances.
103   Cochran produced Coward's *Cavalcade* at Drury Lane in 1931.

Westmorsham You might have it sewn to the horse.

Miss Spence You do think it would be better to have her victorious, don't you, and not just a simple girl?

Mrs Rowntree Who?

Miss Spence Joan of Arc, of course.

Mrs Rowntree Don't give it another thought, Miss Spence. She must undoubtedly be completely victorious.

Mrs Draycott You will arrange for me to have a nice lot of space, won't you, Effie dear, and no obstructions, I haven't danced for years and I'm sure to be nervous.

Lemworth Do you cover *much* more ground when you're nervous, darling?

Mrs Draycott (*ignoring her*) And no tin tacks on the stage either because I shall have bare feet.

Mrs Rowntree Don't give it another thought, Mrs Draycott. Tin-tacks. (*She makes a note.*)

Lemworth I think I ought to have real oranges, don't you? Those papier-mâché ones look so un-appetising.

Westmorsham Certainly – it will be divine, we'll eat them all up at rehearsals.

Miss Ponting You know I am just the teeniest little bit worried about that ship.

Mrs Rowntree Which ship?

Miss Ponting The one Marie Antoinette had in her hair. There was a lot of talk about it at the time, I believe.

Lemworth Talk to Pinkie about it, darling. He'll probably give you a wreath of Aquitanias.[104]

Westmorsham If it's too small no one will be able to see the ship, and it it's too big no one will be able to see you, so I should leave it altogether if I were you.

Miss Spence (*discouraged*) Perhaps I'd better be Catherine the Great after all.

Lemworth She wasn't a Bygone Enchantress, she was just an angry old girl with idle fancies.

Westmorsham Do you know that for the last ten minutes I've been absolutely at war with myself?

Lemworth How very uncomfortable. Why?

Westmorsham Lady Blessington or Flora MacDonald, which shall I be?

---

104 The RMS *Aquitania*, which was built in 1913, was the only ship to be used during both of the World Wars. London's Theatre Royal, Drury Lane

Lemworth Neither.

Mrs Rowntree Not Flora MacDonald, dear Lady Westmorsham, she was really such a drab little thing, if you know what I mean, and so terribly difficult to *convey*. Unless you came on in a rowing boat I don't think anyone would know who you were, people are so dreadfully silly nowadays.

Westmorsham If I'm Lady Blessington I shall walk with a very high stick, imperiously, you know.

Lemworth Why?

Westmorsham Because I wish to, Violet.

Lemworth I don't believe Lady Blessington had a very high stick.

Westmorsham Darling, how could you possibly know? There's nothing in history to prove that she didn't have hundreds and hundreds of sticks and seventeen French poodles.

Lemworth I have no intention of appearing in the same programme with seventeen French poodles.

Westmorsham That, darling, wouldn't matter nearly as much as you think it would.

Mrs Rowntree (*peaceably*) Lady Westmorsham, please . . .

Mrs Wilson I must say I find this discussion very tedious.

Mrs Draycott It's always the way, nobody ever gets anything done . . .

Mrs Rowntree I don't see why you say that, Mrs Draycott; after all I'm sure I'm doing my best.

Miss Spence No one has told me yet where I am to go for my armour . . .

Lemworth These ridiculous arguments about sticks and poodles . . .

Suddenly the quarrel dies away as two flashlight photographers enter. Everybody smiles amiably. **Lady Westmorsham** *even goes so far as to lean girlishly over* **Lady Lemworth***'s shoulder.*

Blackout.

Twelve Girls *in Grecian costume walk on in front of the number one tabs, and arrange themselves in a group centre. They are all wearing very beautifully made masks, so the extremely witty introductory speech in verse which they recite in unison is rather lost on the audience.*

Girls
  Een arrarah ola brure
  Taala caana effalure
  Tar Apollo nuraling
  Jupiter abalaching

  Tanger weero avaloy
  Burel ammalee to Troy

Baara weether dolaser
Mount Olympus bolaser.

Een arrarah ola brure
Taala caana effalure
Tar Apollo nuraling
Jupiter abalaching

Hola jaaga ammo purtain
Borrodagh anula curtain.

Upon finishing this descriptive prelude They all walk off a trifle untidily.

Mr Stuart Ingleby *enters from the prompt side becomingly attired in Louis Quinze court dress, glittering with rhinestones and carrying a large sailor doll. He is greeted by a little desultory applause from the orchestra and is obviously exceedingly nervous.*

Mr Ingleby   Your Royal Highness, my lords, ladies and gentlemen. I – er – take – er – er very great pleasure – er in the – er – privilege of – er – having been asked – er – to appear before you in aide of this ABSOLUTELY SPLENDID charity – We all – er – as you know owe a very – er – deep debt to – er – absolutely ANYBODY who – er – has absolutely ANYTHING – to – er – do with the sea and – er – particularly in these trying times when everything seems so – so – um – INFINITELY – er – CHAOTIC, if you know what I mean – therefore this – er – particular cause, embracing as it undoubtedly does and stretching as it undoubtedly does to the – er – furthest corners of the far-flung – er EMPIRE – I feel – and I am sure you feel
too – that nothing we any of us do could every be – er – TOO MUCH so therefore I – er – have been asked by our brilliant organiser, MRS ROWNTREE –

Applause.

– who over so many years has done such SPLENDID work for every conceivable charity – who indeed could forget her Feather Fantasy of last year, and her Milky Way Ball of the year before, to say nothing of her 'Amants Inconnus' Raffle at the Palladium in 1929?[105] I have been asked by Mrs Rowntree to auction this beautiful doll, which has been personally made by the DUCHESS OF ENDLEBROOK, who as you know is almost completely an INVALID and seldom if ever leaves her very lovely house near WINDERMERE. I have already been offered twenty-five pounds by Lord Ackle – now then – who will offer me thirty? . . . Thirty pounds for this exquisitely wrought sailor – er doll – Come now – surely thirty pounds is not very much to as in such an admirable cause –

Dead silence.

– Any advance on twenty-five pounds? Look how ABSOLUTELY SPLENDIDLY it has been made, perfect to the last detail, accurate even to the LANYARD! Thirty pounds, please –

---

105   Built in 1910, the London Palladium is one of the largest theatres in Britain, and was the home of the variety shows, promenade concerts and aquatic performances.

Dead silence.

Mrs Rowntree *calls 'Thirty-five pounds' from the side of the stage.*

– Thank you, Mrs Rowntree – I have been bid thirty-five pounds by Mrs Rowntree – any advance on thirty-five pounds – ?

Dead silence.

Going – going – come now, forty pounds – will no one offer forty pounds?

Utter silence.

Going at thirty-five pounds – Going – Going – GONE.

Mrs Rowntree *enters from prompt side amid applause, attired in an elaborate evening dress with a large spray of orchids. She takes the doll from* **Mr Ingleby** *with a brief and angry little bow, and marches off again.*

Mr Ingleby   Now, Your Royal Highness, My Lords, Ladies and Gentlemen, we come to the Pageant of Bygone Enchantresses.

He nods to the musical director, who proceeds to play soft music. The curtains roll back, the prompt-side one sticks a little, but this is remedied by **Mrs Rowntree**, *who has been accidentally discovered behind them. She tugs at the curtain and finally coaxes it off all right. There is a frame at the back centre with a few steps leading up to it, and a terrace balustrade running along the top of the rostrum. The background of the frame is blue sky with fleecy clouds painted on it. The rest of the stage is masked in with black velvet.*

> Bygone Loves and bygone Lovers
> Live again in History's pages
> As one turns them one discovers
> Love's Romance across the Ages.

Diane de Poitiers – Viscountess Hogan

The music swells and the lights go out, a spotlight picks up the prompt-side corner of the rostrum and moves slowly along the terrace, down the steps and round the stage and off opposite prompt side, followed hurriedly by **Viscountess Hogan** *as Diane de Poitiers, who is unfortunately unable to catch up with it and is therefore practically indiscernible.*

> Queen of every fascination
> This Enchantress lives again
> Siren of the Restoration
> Mistress Gywnn of Drury Lane[106]

---

106 Eleanor Gwynn (1650–87) was a notable celebrity of the Restoration period, known for her comic performances at London's Theatre Royal, Drury Lane and elsewhere and her role as the longtime mistress of King Charles II. Here she is given the title of Marchioness or a woman who holds the rank of marquess.

Nell Gywnn – Marchioness of Lemworth

This time it is really the **Marchioness of Lemworth** *as Nell Gywnn. She comes dancing on girlishly, determined not to be put out by the violently Eastern Cleopatra music which is being played by the orchestra. She carries a large basket of oranges, and just as she reaches the foot of the steps, the bottom of the basket falls out and all the oranges roll about the stage. She gives a gay, if rather false little laugh, and dances merrily off the stage.*

> Eastern Stars your light grows less
> Oh Eastern Moon your beauty pales
> Before this sinister Princess,
> Salome of the Seven Veils.

Salome – Honourable Mrs Douglas Draycott

The lights change to blue, and **Mrs Draycott** *enters to a suitable music as Salome. She steals sinuously along the terrace, scantily dressed and carrying a large head on a charger. On reaching the foot of the steps she suddenly realises that she has never rehearsed with the head on the charger and will be unable to dance with it, so with great sang-froid she hands it to* **Mr Ingleby***, who reluctantly accepts it, and stands holding it, looking extremely uncomfortable while* **Mrs Draycott** *endeavours to dance effectively without treading on any of the oranges.*

Finally she goes off looking faintly disagreeable before her music is quite finished. **Mr Ingleby***, supremely embarrassed by the head on the charger, looks miserably after her in the vain hope that she many come back and fetch it. Then, still holding it, he begins his next speech, stops short, and places the charger on the stage behind him.*

> Tragic Queen of Tragic Story
> Memory that haunts us yet
> Here we see you in your glory
> Lovely Marie Antoinette.[107]

Marie Antoinette – Miss Esme Ponting. Court Ladies – Lady Eleanour Sherrel and Miss Rebecca Mosenthorpe. Pages – Lady Patricia Gainton and the Honourable Julian Forrage.

Miss Ponting*, as Marie Antoinette, with the* **Court Ladies** *and* **Pages** *enter briskly together, and owing to the width of their hoop skirts become jammed on the steps and have to retreat and come down sideways. Having succeeded in manipulating the steps they go off with a great air of eighteenth-century dignity which is slightly marred by* **Julian Forrage***, the smallest page, wailing miserably throughout.*

---

107 The last queen of France before the French Revolution, Marie Antoinette (1755–93) captured the public imagination in Britain from the eighteenth century onward.

Mr Ingleby *is about to embark upon his next announcement when he hears a strange clicking just behind him. He is obviously puzzled but doesn't look round for fear of looking awkward. The clicking is caused by* **Mrs Rowntree**, *who is endeavouring to hook the charger off the stage with a walking-stick. Finally she gives it up and comes on bravely and carries it off.*

> Battle Queen of History
> Gallant Memory, Brave Romance
> Welcome, Welcome, Hail to Thee
> Joan of Arc. The Maid of France![108]

Joan of Arc – Miss Spence

Miss Spence *enters as Joan of Arc. The orchestra plays an appropriate trumpet call. She is attired in shining armour with a very long blue cloak flowing behind her. She comes to an abrupt halt at the foot of the steps and is nearly strangled owing to her cloak catching in the balustrade at the top of the steps. She stands stock-still in a brave effort not to betray that anything is wrong.* **Mr Ingleby** *goes up to her and falling on one knee repeats the last two lines of his verse.* 'Welcome, Welcome, Hail to Thee, Joan of Arc, the Maid of France.' *She shoots an agonised look at him which he doesn't understand and so he goes back to his place at the side of the stage. The orchestra plays her music through again. At last* **Mrs Rowntree** *is seen crawling along the terrace on her hands and knees. She unhitches the cloak and crawls back again.* **Miss Spence** *marches off very quickly.*

> Beauty rare, and stately calm
> England holds your memory dear
> Queen of Fashion, Queen of Charm
> Lady Blessington[109] is here.

Lady Blessington – Lady Westmorsham

Lady Westmorsham, *as Lady Blessington, walks on with great dignity and a very high stick. Nothing goes amiss with her until she is just about to go off, when her stick catches in a hole in the stage and she has to go back for it. Apart from this her appearance is a triumphant success.*

> Lady sweet beyond compare
> Strange the legend, strange the deed
> Shielded by your flowing hair
> Riding on your snow-white steed.

---

108 Joan of Arc (?–1431), or the 'Maid of Orléans', played a heroic role in the Hundred Years' War and was canonized as a saint after she was burned at the stake.
109 Marguerite Gardiner (1789–1849), Countess of Blessington, was an Irish novelist and journalist, best known for her relationship with the English poet Lord Byron (1788–1824).

Lady Godiva – Mrs F. N. J. Wilson

Nothing happens at all. **Mr Ingleby** *looks anxiously behind him and repeats the verse again. Still nothing happens. A lot of whispering and scuffling is heard off-stage, interspersed with the clip-clopping of horses' hooves and an occasional neigh.* **Mrs Rowntree** *is heard to give a little shriek and say in audible tones: 'There – look what it's done now!' Finally* **Mrs Wilson** *stumps along the terrace down the steps, and off on foot, looking very cross indeed. The music changes and all the Bygone Enchantresses come on together, some from the terrace at the top and some from downstage. With only a very slight muddle they take up their positions on the steps for the Grand Tableau.* **Lady Blessington**, *who enters from the terrace rather late, trips on the top step and falls headlong, knocking Marie Antoinette's wig a little on one side. The Others do their best to conceal this mishap from the audience by crowding round her prone figures, so that until the end she remains completely hidden from view. Two angels on wires slide on at the back, about six feet above the assembled company. They bump into each other in mid-air and remain hunched together in not quite the attitude that had been rehearsed. The orchestra plays a very loud chord and the lights fade.*

'Débutantes'

Prelude to Finale[110]

Four little débutantes, so tired.
Yearning to seek our virgin beds
Longing to rest our aching heads
Weary of all that we desired
When in the morning we awake
Shall we be glad to undertake
Further exhausting hours among
Pleasures and joys so carefully planned
Shall we continued to withstand
The heavy task of being young?

'Three White Feathers'

Both are seated in a motor-car. He a guardsman. She a débutante.

She   We haven't moved for an hour and three-quarters.

He   I know.

She   I suppose there's no chance of us slipping out and nipping in the back way?

He   I don't believe there is a back way.

She   There must be, they couldn't take the groceries past those sentries.

He   I can't understand you being so nervous.

---

110 This short musical prelude pokes fun at the débutantes of the Bright Young Things.

She   Nervous! I'm petrified. I'd rather face a Monday night audience at the Bolton Hippodrome.

He   Relax, my dear, just relax.

She   How can I relax with all those rubber necks gaping at me?

He   You ought to be used to people looking at you. You've been on the stage since you were four.

She   I wish I'd never married you. I do really.

He   Darling.

She   Not that I don't love you, I do, but I wish to God you were a nice comfortable comedian.

He   It'll soon be over.

She (*looking out of the window*)   That woman in the red hat's laughing at me.

He   Pay no attention.

She   Saucy cat. (*Out of the window.*) Go on, have another look and enjoy yourself.

He   Darling, please.

She   I'm sorry, but you'd think they'd have something better to do.

He   You really must be a little more dignified.

She   Dignified with three feathers perched on my head. I feel like one of the horses in *Cinderella*.[111]

He   Keep calm.

She   It's all very fine for you, you're used to it. Here am I, a dancing soubrette for fifteen years suddenly shoved on in the Palace scene without a rehearsal.

He   Why don't you try to forget the theatre for a little?

She   It's all I have to remember, that and father's pawnshop. This isn't my cup of tea and I believe they all know it.

He   Nonsense, darling – you look lovely and I'm very proud of you.

She (*patting his hand*)   Sweet, I won't let you down, honestly I won't. I'll be serene and dignified and everything you want me to be. (*She looks out of the window and waves violently.*) Oo-oo-oo –

He (*pulling her back*)   Dearest, don't for heaven's sake.

She   Don't be silly – that's Mum:

---

111   *Cinderella* was a popular theme for the many Christmas pantomimes performed at the Theatre Royal, Drury Lane in the first half of the twentieth century.

Verse 1:

> I can't help feeling
> Fate's made a fool of me rather,
> It placed me where I shouldn't be
> And really couldn't be by rights;
> We lived at Ealing,
> Me and me Mother and Father,
> I've scaled the social ladder
> And I've never had a head for heights;
> We had a pawnshop on the corner of the street,
> And Father did a roaring trade.
> I used to think those rings and necklaces were sweet,
> Though now I wouldn't give them to my maid.

Refrain:

> I've travelled a long, long way
> And the journey hasn't been all jam;
> I must admit
> The Rolls in which I sit[112]
> Is one up on the dear old tram,
> I say to myself each day,
> In definitely Marble Halls.[113]
> To-day it may be three white feathers,
> But yesterday it was three brass balls.

Verse 2:

> By easy stages
> Though my beginnings were humble
> I've studied each small movement
> Of my self-improvement
> From the start;
> I've toured for ages,
> I'll never falter or stumble;
> I'll give an air of breeding
> And a first-rate reading
> Of the part
> You must forgive me if I kid myself a bit,
> In me tiara and me gown,
> And though my accent may not altogether fit,
> Don't be afraid I'll let you down.

---

112 Rolls-Royce, a popular luxury vehicle manufactured in Britain since 1904.
113 This phrase appeared in many popular works, including Michael William Balfe's 1843 opera *The Bohemian Girl*.

Refrain 2:

> I've travelled a long long way,
> And had a lot of jolts and bumps,
> I'll concentrate
> And be ahead of fate,
> Whichever way the old cat jumps;
> I'll wink as I slyly drink
> To the ancestors who line our halls,
> To-day it may be three white feathers.
> But yesterday it was three brass balls.

Refrain 3:

> I've travelled a long long way,
> And now I've found the man I love;
> I'll do my share, so long as he is there,
> To help me with a gentle shove . . . (*She stops singing.*)

She We're moving

She winks, but they assume a dignified attitude as the lights fade.

Close white tabs.

Finale

'The Party's Over Now'[114]

(1) *Scene in One.*

(2) *Full Set.*

Characters

(1)
Four Débutantes
Policeman　　　　　　　　　　Gerald Nodin
1st Street Cleaner
2nd Street Cleaner
Lamp-Lighter

---

114 Sheridan Morley calls this 'the end of a happy evening enjoyed by the 1930s version of Bright Young Things . . .' referring to Coward's associations with the young, sensual, intellectual group of young artists, musicians, playwrights and aristocrats who aspired to a bohemian life, including Evelyn Waugh and others, who were so-named by the British press (Morley, *Noël Coward*, 55). For more see D. J. Taylor, *Bright Young People: The Lost Generation of London's Jazz Age* (1st American edn, New York: Farrar, Straus and Giroux, 2009).

(2)
Young Girl	Doris Hare
Young Man	John Mills
Hostess	Joyce Barbour
Leonara	Steffi Duna
Lady Skeffington	Ivy St. Helier
Lord Skeffington	Romney Brent

Full Company

At the end of the prelude sung by the **Four Débutantes***, the light fades out, and in the darkness two lighted windows appear, dimly at first and then, as they grow brighter, the party music is heard and the silhouettes of the dancers are thrown on to the blinds. The scene appears dimly in a blue light and it is seen to be the outside of a house, with a lamp over the front door and the painted steps leading to it.*

A **Policeman** *walks on from the side and meets the* **Two Street Cleaners** *with their barrow and hose.*

1st Street Cleaner   Party goin' on?

Policeman   What did you think it was – a tennis tournament?

1st Street Cleaner   All right, all right.

2nd Street Cleaner   You'd never think there was a Crisis, that's wot I say – you'd never think it, not for a moment you wouldn't.[115]

Policeman   No 'arm in enjoying yourself even if there is.

2nd Street Cleaner   Funny way to enjoy yourself, staying up all night when you don't 'ave to.

1st Street Cleaner   Cheer up, Frank, the Season's nearly over.

2nd Street Cleaner   And wot a Season it 'as been! My ol' woman's been fairly rushed orf'er feet, I give you my word. Winkle parties and fried fish cabarets every night, just a ceaseless round of social activities.

The **Lamp-Lighter** *comes on from right and puts the lamp out above the front door of the house. The lights all fade, and in the darkness the front scene goes up, and the same house is seen again at the back, but this time it is built and the steps are solid.*

The door of the house opens and a **Young Girl** *and a* **Young Man** *come down the steps.*

Young Girl   We can get a taxi at the corner of the Square.

---

115   A reference to the economic crisis of 1929.

Young Man All right – darling.

He tries to kiss her.

Young Girl No, dear, not now.

Young Man Why not?

Young Girl It's over.

Young Man What's over?

Young Girl The party, silly, all that was part of the party, now we're tired. It's no use going on with things when you're tired and spoiling them.

Young Man Not just once?

Young Girl (*smiling*) If you must.

He takes her in his arms and kisses her passionately.

Young Girl (*escaping from him*) No more, my sweet – the party's over now.

They sing 'The Party's Over Now', and after a short dance they go off.

The front door opens again and the **Hostess** *comes out on to the steps with* **Leonara**.

Hostess Are you sure you won't let me telephone for a taxi for you?

Leonara There's a rank at the corner. I can see it from here.

Hostess It was so sweet of you to come, and dance for us so beautifully. I'm tremendously grateful.

Leonara I've had a lovely time and enjoyed every minute of it, thank you so much.

Hostess I'll send you your cheque in the morning.

Leonara I really haven't earned it.

Hostess Yes, you have. Good night, my dear.

Leonara Good night.

The **Hostess** *goes in again and* **Leonara** *comes down the steps.*

The music swells from inside the house and she begins to dance a graceful little waltz by herself. When she has gone, the door opens again and **Lord** *and* **Lady Skeffington** *come out.*

Lady Skeffington (*disagreeably*) Why isn't the car here?

Lord Skeffington I sent it home.

Lady Skeffington Quite typical of you and extremely irritating.

Lord Skeffington You've been excessively disagreeable all the evening. It would be properly consistent to keep it up all the way home.

Lady Skeffington   You know, dear, you'd spoil a good party for anyone, let alone a dreary one like that.

Lord Skeffington   I do hope you haven't been drinking, my love.

Lady Skeffington   That is one thing you can be perfectly sure of. I haven't touched a drop of Millicent's champagne for seventeen years.

Lord Skeffington   A bad principle; it might at least make you more amiable or kill you.

They sing the second half of the refrain:

> Though we hate
> Abominate
> Each party we're invited to
> To stay out
> And dance about
> Because we've nothing else to do.
> Though every night
> We start out bright
> And finish with a row
> We've been so bored
> Thank the Lord
> That the party's over now!

*They go off, and out of the house comes the **Hostess** followed by all the **Guests**, singing a full refrain.*

Verse:

> Night is over, dawn is breaking
> Everywhere the Town is waking,
> Just as we are on our way to sleep.
> Lovers meet and dance a little,
> Snatching from romance a little
> Souvenir of happiness to keep.
> The music of an hour ago
> Was just a sort of 'Let's pretend'
> The melodies that charmed us so
> At last are ended.

Refrain:

> The party's over now
> The dawn is drawing very nigh
> The candles gutter, the starlight leaves the sky
> It's time for little boys and girls
> To hurry home to bed
> For there's a new day waiting just ahead.
> Life is sweet

But time is fleet
Beneath the magic of the moon
Dancing time
May seem subline
But it is ended all too soon.
The thrill has gone
To linger on
Would spoil it anyhow
Let's creep away from the day
For the party's over now.

End.

PART II
Post-war Musical Plays

Pacific 1860

Critics' Notes

The critical response to *Pacific 1860* was mixed, and reflected the attitudes towards both American stars in the post-war period and the contradictory responses to Coward's return to Britain. The show bore special significance as the first to reopen the Theatre Royal, Drury Lane, which had been the unofficial national theatre since the eighteenth century. *The Tatler* noted the disrepair of the theatre, stating: 'the reopening of "the Lane" is a notable event in post-war stage history ... Much hard work had to be put in to clear away the debris and repair it for the first night of the new operetta.'[1] The opening night was a grand event, and as the *Yorkshire Post and Leeds Intelligencer* noted: 'The war years seemed to fall completely away when the fine stage was occupied by one of the "Lane's" traditional scenic effects – the departure of a full-sized steamer from the harbour of a picturesque Pacific Island. Mr Coward is in a gently sentimental mood and keeps his famous cynicism firmly in check.'[2] Similarly, an anonymous critic recalled:

> In the old Drury Lane, of course, the ship would have blown up or have been riven apart by lightning, while the man she left behind her would at least have plunged into the harbour to swim after his love. But the idea was on the right lines, and in itself it showed how seriously the author had applied himself to the task of satisfying the expectations of Drury Lane audiences.[3]

Mary Martin's performance was the highlight of the show. Cecil Wilson and others later drew comparisons between Mary Martin's performance in *Pacific 1860* and her success in *South Pacific*.[4] Martin, the 'Texas-born red-haired America stage and screen star' who played opera singer Elena Salvador, was introduced to Coward after her performance of Cole Porter's 'My Heart Belongs to Daddy', also a popular London hit.[5] Despite high hopes for the performance, the work stayed open a mere three weeks. The *Daily Herald* noted a considerable loss of around £31,000 for Drury Lane, of which £28,000 was from *Pacific 1860*.[6] The failure of *Pacific 1860* only exacerbated concerns about the presence of Americans in London, and the large worries about the health of the theatre industry.[7]

---

1. Anonymous, 'Mary Martin, of *Pacific 1860*: An American Star at Drury Lane', *The Tatler*, Wednesday 25 December 1946.
2. Anonymous, 'Drury Lane Premiere', *Yorkshire Post and Leeds Intelligencer*, Friday 20 December 1946.
3. Anonymous, 'Drury Lane: *Pacific 1860*', *The Stage*, Thursday 26 December 1946.
4. David Lewin, 'But the Backstage Party Was Ecstatic', *Daily Express*, 2 November 1951 (see the *South Pacific*, Drury Lane, 1951 press clippings files, Victoria and Albert Theatre Museum Archive).
5. Anonymous, 'Noël Coward's new lead – Mary Martin', *The Sketch*, Wednesday 11 December 1946.
6. Anonymous, 'Coward Show Lost', *Daily Herald*, Wednesday 17 September 1947.
7. Anonymous, 'Aid for Songwriters: Leslie Boosey at P.R.S. Lunch', *The Stage*, Thursday 2 July 1953.

Original Cast

Elena Salvador, *a diva*
Rosa Cariatanza, *her duenna*
Felix Kammer, *her manager*
Mr Stirling
Mrs Stirling
Louise & Caroline, *their daughters*
Kerry Stirling, *their son*
Rollo Stirling, *his elder brother*
Penelope, *a friend of the girls*

His Excellency Sir Lewis Grayshott, *Governor General of Samola*
William Revanescar & James Culross, *ADC in Government House*

Narrator

Musical Numbers

'Family Grace'	Mr Stirling
'If I Were a Man'	Louise & Caroline
'Uncle Harry' (*insertion by Barry Day*)	Kerry & Rollo
'Letter Song'	
'Dear Madame Salvador'	Kerry
'My Horse Has Cast a Shoe'	Elena & Kerry
'I Wish I Wasn't Quite Such a Big Girl'	Penelope & Girls
'Bright Was the Day'	Elena & Kerry
'Invitation to the Waltz'	Louise, Caroline, William & James
'His Excellency Regrets'	Grayshott, Louise, Caroline, William & James
'The Party's Going with a Swing'	Rollo, Penelope & Kerry
'Dear Friends, Forgive Me, Pray'	Mr Stirling
'Alice Is at It Again'	Elena
'Make Way for His Excellency'	Full Company
'One, Two, Three'	Elena
'This Is a Night for Lovers'	Rosa
'I Never Knew'	Elena & Kerry
'This Is a Changing World'	Rosa
'Come Back to the Island'	Full Company
'Gypsy Melody'	Rosa & Elena
'My Horse Has Cast a Shoe'	
'This Is a Changing World'	Elena
'Mother's Lament'	Mrs Stirling
'Pretty Little Bridesmaids'	Louise & Caroline
'I Saw No Shadow on the Sea'	Elena
'Wedding Chorus'	Full Company
'Bright Was the Day' Reprise	Elena & Kerry

Act One

We see a man sitting in a club armchair. He is obscured by the copy of The Times *he is reading. From the snorting and muttering going on behind it, it seems clear that he is dozing. He wakes with a start, removes the paper and sees the audience for the first time.*

Grayshott   Oh, I do beg your pardon. Must have dozed off for a moment. Not surprising . . . Never anything in the damn paper these days, except the country's going to the dogs (*again*) or somebody's threatening to declare war on somebody else over something or other . . . Except there was something that caught my eye. What was it, now?

His eye finds something at the bottom of the fold and he holds it up and away from his face and begins to read aloud . . .

Oh, yes – 'Samola . . . British possession in the South Seas, a part of the British Empire since 185 5 . . .' Hm – can't even get the date right. It was 1856. I should know, because that was the year they sent me out as the first Governor General.

He lapses into reminiscence . . .

Those were the days. Eh? Well, pre-history now, of course, but I can still see it as clearly as if it were this morning.

He puts the paper down in his lap and speaks directly to the audience. It's obvious that the memories are beginning to flood back over the years.

Ah, Samolo . . . a world of its own, when I was there. And, of course, there were the Stirlings . . . a sort of first family. If anyone upheld the old Victorian family values, they did . . . well, most of them did . . . Let me see . . .

He consults his fob watch.

It would be breakfast time there now and the whole tribe of them would have to show up for that. A stickler for tradition was old John Stirling . . .

As he mentions them by name, the members of the family enter carrying chairs which they place as though they were sitting round an invisible table. The first to arrive is **John Stirling**, *a stern but pleasant man. Next is his wife,* **Elizabeth**, *a still pretty but faded lady . . .*

Grayshott   And his wife, Elizabeth, was definitely not one to argue with him . . . Well, I don't suppose she had the energy left after giving him two girls and two boys! They were quite a brood. I can see them now round that breakfast table out on the terrace . . . Louise, the eldest of the girls – and she was the prim one of the family . . .

Louise *enters and takes her place.*

Grayshott   Then Caroline. She had the sense of humour . . .

Caroline *does the same.*

Grayshott Then there were the boys. Rollo was the eldest.

Rollo *enters.*

Grayshott A chip off his father's block was Rollo. Steady, conservative – what we used to call a 'safe pair of hands'.

Kerry *enters.*

Grayshott Kerry, now, *he* was quite different. You see, Kerry was a 'Romantic' – his parents never quite knew what to *make* of him!

He consults his watch again.

Grayshott If I'm not mistaken, Mr Stirling would be just about to say grace to mark the end of the meal and the start of a new day. How do I *know* all this, when I wasn't even there? Senior British statesmen know EVERYTHING – that's why they're senior British statesmen!

He takes his chair to the side of the stage and exits. The family now begin to chatter to each other. Up to now they have been standing around an imaginary table miming conversation to each other. **Mr Stirling** *now rises to his feet and looks around the group to ensure they're paying attention. A deferential silence falls over the assembly.*

'Family Grace'

Mr Stirling
    For what we have received
    May the Lord fill our hearts with gratitude
    And through the coming day
    We humbly pray
    With appetites relieved
    In this remote, most eccentric latitude
    That He, with tolerance of small mistakes
    May walk beside us
    And, in his understanding, guide us.
    For what we have received
    Accept, O Lord, in your serene beatitude
    Today and all our days
    Our thankful praise
    For tropic fruits
    And bamboo shoots
    For tender roots – incredible
    And fortunately edible
    And also for the boon
    Of most delicious fish from the lagoon.
    This morning prayer
    Represents our attitude
    Please fill our hearts,

Instil our hearts
With gratitude.
Amen

All
Amen.

At the end of this, when everyone has respectfully sung 'Amen', **Mrs Stirling** *moves away from the table.*

Mrs Stirling   Well, well, well – another day begins.

Mr Stirling   At about this time, my love, it usually does.

Mr Stirling *goes into the house, accompanied by* **Mrs Stirling**.

Rollo   I hope you ladies don't have any complicated social plans, as I shall be using the wagonette this evening.

Kerry   What do you want the wagonette for?

Rollo   I have to go into the town to see Wilks about the dance music for the party. I also have to have my hair cut.

Louise   I wish I were a man and could drive the wagonette into town whenever I wanted to and gallop around the plantation and give people orders and have my hair cut –

Caroline   If I were a man I'd do more interesting things. It's horrid being a girl – men have much more fun.

Kerry   As the Almighty has already settled the issue in advance, I cannot see that this argument is leading us anywhere.

Song

'If I Were a Man'

Louise
  If I were a man I would marry a wife
  Who would help me to lead an exemplary life,
  And the house that I'd build
  Would be pleasantly filled
  With children belonging to me
  It would also command
  Several acres of land
  And an excellent view of the sea,
  A most excellent view of the sea.

Caroline   Oh, Louise – that doesn't sound very exciting. If I were a man, I'd be an adventurer. I'd search for treasure and travel all over the world, and when I was very old I'd return to my true love.

Kerry What should she be doing while you were away?

Caroline Just staying at home and having babies.
 If I were a man I would sail away
 To the uttermost ends of the earth,
 And I would return a millionaire
 With jewels of fabulous worth.
 Diamonds and rubies beyond compare
 Ropes of pearls for my true love's hair
 And I'd guarantee on that happy day
 That, unlike us, she need never say
 That she hadn't a thing to wear!

Louise I fear, Caroline, that your day-dreams are a thought mercenary. I trust that you have not been reading anything you shouldn't.

Caroline
 We can't all be noble and good, Louise,
 And I'm not at all sure that we should, Louise,
 For think of your miserable plight, Louise,
 If everyone else were as right, Louise,
 And true, Louise,
 As you, Louise!

Rollo Nicely put, Caroline. Louise's virtuousness is sometimes oppressive.

Louise Just because I happen to have set my heart on higher things, you scoff at me.

Rollo Higher than what?

Louise
 If I were a man I would make up my mind
 To be wise, understanding and gentle and kind,
 I wouldn't catch fish and I wouldn't kill birds,
 I wouldn't shoot poor defenceless rabbits
 Nor would I use inelegant words
 And I'd try to control my annoying habits.
 I wouldn't play jokes and make apple-pie beds,
 Get drunk and stagger upstairs,
 Nor steal people's pencils and break off the leads,
 And leave grease on the backs of the chair.
 I wouldn't be sly and get money from Mother,
 If I were a man,
 If I were a man.
 I would not be my brother!
 So there!

Kerry That disposes of you, Rollo. But after all, I am Louise's brother, too – I'm hurt.

Caroline There now – you've upset Kerry – you know how sensitive he is!

Kerry (*putting his arm round her*)   Never mind, baby – you needn't defend me.

Caroline   If I were a man, I'd want to be like you.

Louise   Oh, Caroline, don't be such a little goose! If you go through life adoring Kerry so much you'll never have room to love anyone else.

Caroline   Oh yes, I shall. But I'll always love him best.
  If I were a man I'd go out in the dawn
  And I'd gave at the curve of the bay
  And I'd write in a book
  How the mountains look
  At the very beginning of day.
  If I were a man
  I should wish to be born
  With a dream that would set me apart
  And I'd search the world over
  To find my true lover
  And give her my passionate heart.
  I'd search the world over
  To find my true lover
  And give her my passionate heart!

Louise   Caroline! You're far too young to think of such things.

Kerry (*turning away*)   No, no – she's right.

Rollo   Well, well – so you're prepared to give some lucky lady *your* passionate heart, are you?

Kerry   We'll see – should that day ever come to pass!

Caroline & Louise
  If I were a man I'd be dashing and bold
  And exceedingly witty and cruel.
  My heart would be warm but my eyes would be cold,
  And the legend for hundreds of years would be told
  How I died for the honour I'd lived to uphold,
  In the Bois de Boulogne[8] –

All
  Why the Bois de Boulogne?

Caroline & Louise (*firmly*)
  In the Bois de Boulogne – in a duel!

They all laugh at this.

Caroline   Oh, I *do* wish the Stirling family wasn't quite so prim and proper! We're so upright and predictable.

---

8   The Bois de Boulogne is a public park in Paris.

Louise Even *I* wish we were descended from buccaneers instead of boring missionaries!

Rollo (*looking meaningfully at* **Kerry**) Well, you know, there are missionaries – and *missionaries.*

Kerry You mean – Uncle Harry?

Rollo Uncle Harry.

Song

'Uncle Harry'

Kerry & Rollo
  Our family has traditions,
  We've heard them a thousand times,
  Our ancestors were unequivocally right.
  They frequently went on missions
  To very peculiar climes
  To lead the wretched heathen to the light.
  Though some of them got beaten up
  And some of them stampeded,
  Though quite a lot were eaten up,
  A few of them succeeded,
  On one of those expeditions
  An uncle we'd thought a bore
  Turned out to be more spirited than ever he'd been before . . .

  Poor Uncle Harry
  Wanted to be a missionary
  So he took a ship and sailed away.
  This visionary,
  Hotly pursued by dear Aunt Mary,
  Found a South Sea Isle on which to stay
  The natives greeted them kindly and invited them to dine
  On yams and clams and human hams and vintage coconut wine
  The taste of which was filthy but the after-effects divine.

  Poor Uncle Harry
  Got a bit gay and longed to tarry,
  This Aunt Mary couldn't quite allow.
  She lectured him severely on a number of church affairs
  But when she'd gone to bed he made a get-away down the stairs,
  For he longed to find the answer to a few of the maiden's prayers.
  Uncle Harry's not a missionary now.

  Now Uncle was just a 'seeker'
  A 'dreamer' sincerely blest,

Of this there couldn't be a shadow of doubt.
The fact that his flesh was weaker
Than even Aunt Mary guessed
Took even her some time to figure out.
In all those languid latitudes
The atmosphere's exotic,
To take up moral attitudes
Would be too idiotic,
Though nobody could be meeker
Than Uncle had been before
I bet today he's giving way
At practically every pore!

Poor Uncle Harry
Having become a missionary
Found the natives' morals rather crude
He and Aunt Mary
Quickly imposed an arbitrary
Ban upon them shopping in the nude
They all considered this silly and they didn't take it well,
They burnt his boots and several suits and
Wrecked the mission hotel,
They also burnt his mackintosh, which made a disgusting smell.
Poor Uncle Harry
After some words with dear Aunt Mary
Called upon the chiefs for a pow-wow.
They didn't brandish knives at him, they really were awfully sweet,
They made concerted dives at him and offered him things to eat,
But when they threw their wives at him, he had to admit defeat.
Uncle Harry's not a missionary now.
Uncle Harry, Uncle Harry, Uncle Harry, Uncle Harry –
Uncle Harry's not a missionary now!

Applause.

Encore.

Kerry
Poor dear Aunt Mary,
Though it were revolutionary,
Thought *her* time had come to take a bow.
Poor Uncle Harry looked at her, in whom he had placed his trust,
His very last illusion broke and crumbled away to dust

Rollo
For she'd placed a flower behind her ear and frankly exposed her bust.

Both
Uncle Harry's not a missionary now.

He's left the island
But he's certainly not a missionary now.
Uncle Harry, Uncle Harry, Uncle Harry, Uncle Harry –
Uncle Harry's not a missionary now!

Louise I'm longing to the party on Saturday – it's *always* the nicest event of the year.

Caroline I still feel uncomfortable about that poor Madame Salvador – with all the island coming it seems so unkind to leave her out.

Rollo We don't know her – we've never even seen her.

Louise Penelope has – she saw her a week ago in the evening riding along Naruchi Beach. She was wearing white riding breeches – *men's*! Obviously we couldn't possibly invite *her*.

Kerry I don't suppose she'd come to the party in breeches, even if she were invited.

Caroline What did Mama say?

Louise Well, you know what Mama is – she looked vague and rather distressed and said that Father would have to decide.

Caroline *Has* he decided?

Kerry He hasn't said a word, but I'm going to tackle him. I agree with Carline, it's inhospitable and rude not to invite her, and after all she is a stranger to the island.

Louise Don't be so silly, Kerry. We don't know what sort of person she is –

Kerry We know that she is a famous singer and that she has been ill and that she is here for a rest and is probably lonely.

Lousie If she's a famous singer she is probably both fast and immoral.

Caroline Jenny Lind[9] isn't fast and immoral. She sings oratorios and knows the Bishop of Norwich.

Louise Madame Salvador is *not* Jenny Lind.

Rollo And jolly good job too – I hate oratories.

Louise I don't see how she *can* be so lonely with all those awful foreigners round her.

Kerry How do you know they're awful?

Louise Mama's point is that as she hasn't been asked to Government House –

Kerry She may have been asked for all we know – maybe she didn't want to go.

Louise Miss Scobie says –

---

9 Jenny Lind (1820–87) was an opera singer known as 'the Swedish Nightingale'.

Kerry (*heatedly*) Who cares what Miss Scobie says! Miss Scobie is a silly gossiping old maid; all she can do is make drop scones and tear people's characters to shreds. I think it's rude and unkind of us not to invite her. It's different for His Excellency and Lady Grayshott, they're official and they have to be high and mighty from time to time, but we're not official. We're a large comfortable family and we're giving our annual comfortable party and here we have a poor lady living only a couple of miles away and we are afraid to ask her – a) because she is a singer; b) because she hasn't been to Government House; and c) because she has been seen wearing riding-breeches.

Caroline I agree with Kerry.

Rollo Bravo, Sir Galahad![10]

Mr *and* **Mrs Stirling** *come out of the house*

Mrs Stirling Kerry – what are you shouting about?

Rollo Kerry's worked himself up into a chivalrous stew about Madame Salvador.

Mr Stirling Madame Salvador?

Kerry I think we ought to invite her to the party.

Mrs Stirling We can't possibly, dear.

Kerry Why not?

Mrs Stirling Your father does not wish it.

Kerry What is wrong with her, Papa?

Mr Stirling That is one of the things I have no intention of discovering.

Kerry But Papa –

Mr Stirling Nor do I wish the subject referred to again.

Kerry It's unfair to condemn someone's character when you haven't even seen them – unfair and unkind.

Mr Stirling I was not privileged to meet Jezebel personally, my boy; none the less, I am quite content to condemn her on hearsay.

Kerry What has Jezebel to do with Madame Salvador?

Mr Stirling That is something that I hope *you* will never have the opportunity of discovering.

Mr Stirling *offers his arm to* **Mrs Stirling** *and leads her off towards the gate. They are followed by* **Rollo** *and* **Louise**. **Caroline** *and* **Kerry** *hang back.*

Caroline Don't be upset, Kerry – it doesn't really matter.

---

10 A knight of the legendary King Arthur's Round Table.

Kerry It's a question of principle and good manners, and I think it does.

Caroline She might quite possibly be – well, not very nice, you know.

Kerry Mama should have called upon her ages ago, but Papa wouldn't let her – I supposed he'd been talking to Miss Scobie.

Caroline I'm on your side, really – I long to see for myself what she's like.

Kerry We'll go and call one day –

Caroline Oh, Kerry – if only we dared!

Kerry We dare!

Kerry and Caroline go off in the direction of the gate. The stage is empty for a moment or two. **Penelope** *enters.* **Penelope** *is a sweet-looking, jolly, rather plump girl in her early twenties.*

Servant (*offstage*) The family will be back soon, Miss Penelope. May I fetch you something? A cool drink, perhaps?

Penelope No, thank you. I'm fine. I think I can hear them now.

The girls come flying on, followed more sedately by **Mr** *and* **Mrs Stirling**, **Rollo**, *and* **Kerry**. *Everyone welcomes* **Penelope** *with enthusiasm. The following few lines are spoken more or less simultaneously.*

Caroline Oh, Penny – you're just in time. We're going right out beyond Narouchi for a picnic –

Louise Caroline wants to go to Cobb's Cove, but I think it's too far –

Caroline The sand there is so much whiter and nicer than Narouchi –

Mr Stirling (*silencing the babel with a lordly wave of the hand*) And how is your dear mother, Penelope?

Penelope Very well, thank you, Mr Stirling.

Mrs Stirling (*kissing her*) Welcome, my dear! What a pretty bonnet! The girls will be ready to start quite soon.

Penelope (*greeting* **Rollo**) Hello, Rollo!

Rollo Welcome, Penny.

Kerry (*greeting her*) Mama is quite right – it is a pretty bonnet.

Penelope Oh, indeed I am so glad you like it; I trimmed it myself. Mama helped me, of course, but the idea was mine.

Louise Come indoors and take it off at once – you can't waste a new bonnet like that on an ordinary girls' picnic. I'll lend you my straw.

Kerry (*shouting, as they all troop indoors*) I don't think you ought to wear bonnets at all at a picnic – you ought to wear riding-breeches!

Louise (*over her shoulder*) Don't be silly, Kerry.

They all go in, laughing and chattering. **Kerry** *and* **Rollo** *are left alone.*

Rollo Cheer up, Galahad!

Kerry You ought to marry soon, you know, Rollo – your sense of humour is wasted at home.

Rollo Why did you get into such a frizz about Madame Salvador?

Kerry It was nothing to do with Madame Salvador. I've never even set eyes on her. It was that I hate to think of my own family behaving without grace.

Rollo Well, she's not invited, so that's that. You'd better write to her and tell her how sorry you are –

Kerry I've a jolly good mind to.

Rollo Don't forget to apologise for being a snobbish little colonial.

Rollo *goes off.* **Grayshott** *reappears and stands in the wings, while* **Kerry** *exits, so that he can return with pen and paper if needed.*

Grayshott (*to audience*) Don't you find that there are points in life when you do some small thing that makes all the difference later on – but at the time you don't realize it? For instance, if Kerry hadn't made up his mind to write that letter . . . well, there wouldn't have been a story. And I'd be out of a job . . . But he *did* write it . . .

He exits as **Kerry** *starts to sing.*

Letter Song

'Dear Madame Salvador'

Kerry (*singing as he writes*)
Dear Madame Salvador,
Although this note may seem absurd to you,
I feel impelled to run the risk of your disdain.
In writing thus a warning word to you,
My one desire is but to spare your pain.
Poor Madame Salvador –
Poor Madame Salvador,
I do not know if you're aware or not
Of the malicious, foolish things that people say.
I gravely doubt whether you care or not
But all the same – in quite a humble way,
Dear Madame Salvador,

Your name and reputation I am eager to defend,
So count on me, I beg of you, sincerely as your friend.

Elena Salvador *comes quietly on from the direction of the gate. She is a lovely young woman in her early thirties. Her clothes are exquisite and have an unmistakable chic. She stands looking appraisingly at* **Kerry** *with her head a little on one side. He – quite unaware of her presence – continues to sing.*

Kerry   There – if I should send it,

Would she just tear it angrily in half
Or would she know – how very deeply I intend it
To be of service to her – or would she laugh?

Elena   She wouldn't laugh – nor would she be angry. She would be touched and very grateful.

Kerry   Oh!

Elena   Forgive me for eavesdropping. I would not have done so had I not heard my name. It *was* to me that you were writing?

Kerry   Yes – that is – I didn't really mean – I don't think I should ever have had the courage to send it.

Elena   Why not?

Kerry   I am a complete stranger to you – you would have considered me most presumptuous.

Elena   May I see?

Kerry (*handing her the letter rather reluctantly*)   It's very badly written.

Elena (*reading it*)   So they have been gossiping about me, have they?

Kerry   It is only because you are so apart, so far away from them, that they cannot quite . . .

He breaks off.

Elena   And you – why should you take such a different view?

Kerry   I don't know, except that – except that –

Elena   Please don't try to explain – I would hate to repay your kindness and consideration by embarrassing you. In any case – I think I understand.

Kerry   Do you?

Elena (*smiling*)   Yes – you are a Romantic.

Kerry   I suppose I must be.

Elena   And who could blame you – living here in this lovely house with this lovely garden, on this lovely, lovely, island? You do live here?

Kerry Yes. This is my father's plantation. I was born here. So was he. His name is John Stirling.

Elena And yours?

Kerry Kerry. Short for Kerrymuir. We have much pride in our Scots blood.

Elena I will not introduce myself, as it seems that we are already old friends.

Kerry You make me very happy. I beg of you to come indoors – the sun is so hot – I will call my mother.

Elena No, no, please – I love the sun – and I would be ashamed to inconvenience your mother by appearing at this hour in the most unconventional manner. Perhaps she would be so kind as to receive me later on? I really must explain – I am not in the habit of walking unannounced into people's gardens – but you see – a little accident has occurred.

Kerry An accident?

Elena Nothing in the least serious. My horse has cast a shoe. Please don't look so startled – I was not riding him in these clothes, I always wear breeches for riding.

Kerry Yes I know.

Elena (*raising her eyebrows*) You *know*?

Kerry The whole *island* knows.

Elena Oh dear! – and I did take care to go out only in the late evening – and they are my late husband's breeches. Does that make it any better?

Kerry (*shaking his head*). Worse. I didn't know you were a widow.

Elena It wasn't my fault – he died a natural death – several years ago – in Geneva.

Kerry (*at a slight loss*) Geneva?

Elena Such a pretty town – you know it?

Kerry No – I have never been away from this island.

Elena Well, whenever you do, you must make a point of going to Geneva. Now let us talk about something quite different . . .

She notices his puzzled expression.

Have I shocked you?

Kerry No – of course not – not in the least.

Elena (*gently*) I didn't care for my husband very much, although I nursed him devotedly – it was a '*marriage de convenance*' – they nearly always are in Europe. He was of Spanish descent, and you know what the Spanish are.

Kerry I'm afraid I don't.

Elena He was also rather peppery, and on the small side.

Kerry I see.

Elena I don't see how you can really, those sort of things are so difficult to explain. I have tied my horse and trap to your gatepost. Do you think you could possible help me to get back to my house? It is not very far, but I have been a little ill . . . and to walk at this time of day . . .

Kerry Of course – of course – forgive me, I beg of you!

He claps his hands and calls.

Oh, Travers!

Servant (*off*) Yes, Master Kerry?

Keery Will you get the trap ready, please. I'm giving Madame Salvador a ride home.

Servant (*off*) Certainly, sir.

The music which has been playing softly suddenly brightens. **Elena** *begins to sing.*

Song

'My Horse Has Cast a Shoe'

Elena
   My horse has cast a shoe,
   A careless thing to do.
   Although he has apologised
   And shown that he is most upset
   For conduct so uncivilised
   I cannot quite forgive him – yet.

Kerry
   Of course – of course,
   There is nothing so incautious as horse.

Elena
   My horse has cast a shoe,
   So I appeal to you
   I meet you by a happy chance
   In this untimely circumstance
   Pray tell me what to do.

Kerry
   To be able to assist Madame Salvador
   Is an honour that I shan't forget.
   I will drive you safely home
   In my father's wagonette.

Elena
   You are so kind
   I'll be ever in your debt

For your chivalry combined
With your father's wagonette.
Who could foretell
That a most obliging fate
Would arrange for what befell
To befall me just exactly by your gate!
Who knows
What magic power guides the hearts
Of those
Who drive about in little carts?

Kerry
Often in dreams
I have known about this meeting
And awakened to the beating
Of my too romantic heart,
Although it seems
Too ridiculous to mention
My intolerable tensions
Have been lightened by a little horse and cart.

Elena
I know

Kerry
My dreams are fated to come true,

Elena
And so

Kerry & Elena
My/your horse discreetly cast a shoe.

Kerry   Forgive me for being rude but I can't quite make out your accent. What was your first language?

Elena   English – or rather American. My father was American, but he died when I was five years old, and my mother – who was French – took me to Paris.

Kerry   Is she there now?

Elena   No, she died too – when I was thirteen – I keep on telling you about people dying – I do hope I'm not depressing you?

Kerry   No, I love to hear – all about you.

Elena   That would take too long – but I can sketch in the essentials. I was brought up in a convent near St. Cloud – the Mother Superior had a heavy moustache but was, on the whole, kind. My Aunt Mathilde arranged my marriage for me when I was eighteen. My husband, Esteban Salvador, was an operatic tenor. He sang very loudly, particularly in *Norma*. I think that was what finished him.

Kerry Did he leave you penniless?

Elena Alas, no – he had saved an immense amount of money – and then there was his mother's jewellery, which was quite hideous – vulgar settings, you now – but useful.

Kerry Why did you become a professional singer?

Elena Because I was bored. You'll never know how boring it is to be a widow at twenty and just sit about.

Kerry No, I don't suppose I shall.

Elena Also, of course, I was able to pay for my own concerts, to start with – that irritated everybody very much.

Kerry Were they successful, those first concerts?

Elena Deadly!

Kerry Oh!

Elena I made the initial mistake of singing very sad songs very slowly. I'm told I looked exquisite – pathetic and appealing, you know – but it wasn't enough. I'd had my voice trained too, which was fatal.

Kerry Why?

Elena I was perpetually fussing in my mind as to whether I was singing head notes, chest notes, or diaphragm notes – the result was a harassed expression which was mot unbecoming. One day I burst out laughing in the middle of a song about a girl drowning herself in a brook. From that moment onwards my success was assured.

Kerry (*gently*)   You know I don't believe one word of all this, don't you?

Elena Oh, what a pity! I was trying so hard to be convincing!

Kerry Tell me one thing truly. Why did you come to Samolo?

Elena Really and truly?

Kerry Yes, please.

Elena (*taking a deep breath*)   Well – I've been over-working for two years. I did three long concert tours in Europe – including Scandinavia, which was particularly exhausting because of it being daylight for such a long time. Then I went to America and sang in New York and Boston and Philadelphia and all over. Then, more dead than alive, I had to go to Mexico to sing for the Emperor Maximilian – they seemed to think that it would cheer him up.

Kerry   And did it?

Elena   Not really, I'm afraid. He gave me a medal in rather a vague way and the Empress Charlotte gave me a hot-water bottle. I must say they both seemed very depressed.

Kerry   And then?

Elena   I broke down. I was very ill in a hospital for a month – then a French doctor with a large wart ordered a sea voyage, and so I drove in a rattling old coach down to Acapulco and went on board a dear little ship which wandered about until it finally arrived here. I came ashore, looked at the island and burst into tears.

Kerry   Why did you burst into tears?

Elena   Because I fell in love.

Kerry   In love?

Elena   With the island. I always cry when I'm in love.

Kerry   Have you been in love much?

Elena   Not very much.

Kerry (*turning away*)   Neither have I.

Elena (*resting her hand sympathetically on his arm*)   Never mind.

Kerry   Perhaps you were right about me being a Romantic. That would explain why no one in my life has ever touched my heart – until now.

Elena (*withdrawing her hand*)   What is that mauve tree – over there?

Kerry   A jacaranda.

Elena   And the one next to it – with the strange leaves?

Kerry (*looking at her*)   The natives call it Alani-Tali. Because the leaves are shaped like stars – Alani is the word for stars.

Elena   How clever of you know which one I meant without looking.

Music starts softly.

Kerry   I know this garden by heart.

Elena   And you love it?

Kerry   Yes.

Elena (*rising*)   Show me a little more of it before I go.

Kerry   How very strange it is . . . (*He also rises.*)

Elena What is so strange?

Kerry I feel as though I'd known you before – for many years.

Elena It is always charming to meet an old friend – for the first time.

Both
Who could have known
We should feel this lovely glow?
We were strangers and alone
Such a little while ago.
Fate set the course,
And decided to unbend
By arranging that my horse
Should have led me to the finding of a friend.
Who knows
What magic power guides the hearts
Of those
Who drive about in little carts?

The music continues to play under as they exit. **Louise**, **Caroline** *and* **Penelope** *come out. They are all chattering like magpies.*

Louise I told Elisha to have the carriage at the lower gate – it saves us going all round. Caroline – Caroline – did you see about the lunch?

Caroline Don't fuss, Louise – that was all done hours ago.

Louise Now you're not to worry about your figure today, Penny – I absolutely forbid it. We're going to enjoy ourselves.

Penelope I always worry about my figure – so would you if you got fatter with every mouthful you ate!

Louise You exaggerate. You look exactly the same as you did at Christmas – and the Christmas before that.

Penelope That's just it – I don't *want* to look exactly the same as I did at Christmas. I want to be thin and pale and interesting.

Caroline It's not all that interesting to be pale – look at Louise.

Louise Caroline! It's all a question of attitude of mind, Penny. If you have the right attitude of mind you can be any size you like.

Penelope You're wrong. I've tried and tried. I've even mentioned it in my *prayers* – but it's no good.

Caroline (*laughing*) Oh, Penny – poor Penny! I do sympathise, truly I do – but it *is* a little funny, isn't it?

Penelope Not for me, it isn't.

Song

'I Wish I Wasn't Quite Such a Big Girl'

Penelope
> I was told
> When not very old,
> That if my will were strong enough,
> And if I tried for long enough,
> The wish that I wished would come true.

Girls
> Penny, dear,
> We're pining to hear
> Just how, and when and where you built
> Those castle in the air you built
> And whether or not they vanished – or if they grew.

Penelope
> Sad to relate,
> A cruel fate
> Disdained my plea
> And mocked at me
> For the only wish I ever made
> Was doomed, biologically, to fade.

Girls
> Tell us, please, we're all on fire
> To hear of this frustrated heart's desire!

Penelope
> I wish I wasn't quite such a big girl,
> It's not a very nice thing to be.
> I've prayed to be more delicate and suffer from migraines,
> But even with a temperature my appetite remains.
> I wish I wasn't sturdy and healthy
> To such an unromantic degree.
> Nobody even in joke
> Would ever lay down his cloak
> For a big girl – like me.

Girls
> Penny dear,
> No really sincere
> True love would ever mind a bit
> If you stuck out behind a bit
> Provided your heart was for him.

Penelope
> That, dear friends.
> Entirely depends

On snatching opportunity
And in this small community
The chances of finding true love – are rather dim.

Girls

That may be so,
But still you know,
You'll never win
If you give in.
The only thing for you to do
Is take a more optimistic view.

Penelope

I know you're right, but come what may
I must continue wistfully to say:

Girls

Well?

Girls

She wishes she wasn't quite such a big girl!

Penelope

It's such a very dull thing to be.
I fell into the water once when playing on the
Brink,
But no one paid attention for they knew
I couldn't sink.
I never really eat all I want to,
But still I seem to grow like a tree.
Nobody quite understands
The strange irresolute glands
Of a big girl – like me.

Girls

'I wish . . .'

Penelope

I wish I wasn't quite such a big girl
I wish I could be more '*petite fille*' –
I'm rather good at guessing games because I'm not a dunce,
But if I'm playing hide-and-seek I'm always
Found at once!
When Papa used to come to the nursery
He'd never let me sit on his knee –
The stars may blaze above
But no one ever makes love
To a big girl – like me.

At the end of the song, **Penelope** *and the* **Girls** *all go off. We hear the sound of native singing off stage, as* **Kerry** *and* **Elena** *return.*

Elena All the natives on this island sing, don't they?

Kerry Without ceasing.

Elena They're as bad as the Austrians.

Kerry I should love to go to Austria.

Elena It's agreeable at first, but after a little time it gets on your nerves – they are sweet people, but over-musical.

Speaks in rhyme:
   When you wake in the morning the very first things
   That the Austrians do is to sing and to sing:
   And when death overtakes them, in Heaven or Hell
   I'm perfectly certain they yodel as well!

They both laugh.

Elena I wrote that myself in an ornate little chalet near Salzburg. It made everyone very cross.

Kerry I wish this morning would never come to an end.

Elena That's a very charming thing to say. It will, however, so you must brace yourself.

Kerry I have a favour to ask you.

Elena What is it?

Kerry Will you come to our party?

Elena Party?

Kerry (*hurriedly*) Yes – we give a party every year. My mother and father and I and all of us would be so very, very honoured if you would come.

Elena You would be pleased to see me, perhaps, but are you so sure they would be?

Kerry But of course – why shouldn't they be?

Elena Your tone lacked conviction when you said that. I suspect you are being a naughty boy.

Kerry (*turning away*) It was only that I want so very much to see you again.

Elena (*gently*) Come and call on me – I will give you tea and little cakes.

Kerry May I – may I really?

Elena I want you to.

Kerry   Oh.

Elena   What is it?

Kerry   If you only spoke the truth, I should feel so much more secure.

Elena   That was the truth. Security is dull anyway – but that *was* the truth – please believe me.

Kerry (*looking at her*)   I believe you.

Elena (*after they have gazed into each other's eyes for a moment*)   I have a dismal suspicion that I am behaving badly.

Kerry   You are so lovely . . .

Elena (*looking down*)   Please don't . . .

Song

'Bright Was the Day'

Kerry

This morning when I woke, the light was clear in
The sky,
A sweet wind murmured through the trees.
A singing bird was singing very near in the sky,
And in the breeze
Which drove the clouds so gaily by
I thought I heard a different note – a little sigh
Which seemed to say . . .
This is your day,
Be careful, please,
Be careful, please!
Don't let this light enchantment fade away,
This is your day.

Elena

This morning when I woke I seemed to know in my
Heart
That some new happiness was near.
I waited for this unexpected glow in my heart
To disappear.
But strange to say it would not go
And as the moments hurried by, it seemed to grow
If, as you say,
This is your day,
Kind cavalier,
Kind cavalier,
We'll try to let this brief enchantment stay

Just for today –
　　　This is your day.

Kerry
　　　Though we may never meet again,
　　　There'll never be a day so sweet again,
　　　Deep in my heart, no matter what the troubled
　　　Years may bring,
　　　A secret voice – will ever sing.

　　　Bright was the day when you came to me,
　　　Someone had whispered your name to me.
　　　Someone had told me how fair you were,
　　　Then at last – there you were!
　　　Light was the music that played for me,
　　　You were the song destiny had made for me.
　　　I heard the melody start
　　　Delicately – delicately – in my heart.

Elena
　　　Here in the sunshine I came to you,
　　　Someone had whispered my name to you,
　　　Some potent magic impelled me here,
　　　Touched my heart – held me here!
　　　Dreams long forgotten revive again,
　　　Suddenly life sees to be alive again,
　　　I heard the melody too –
　　　Beckoning me – beckoning me – here to you!

The music continues. They stand there gazing at each other. We now hear off-stage voices humming the melody. This continues under dialogue.

Elena (*she now feels relaxed enough with* **Kerry** *to joke with him*)　　The natives pick up melody very quickly, don't they?

Kerry　　They're as bad as the Austrians.

Elena　　*Worse* than the Austrians.

Elena *and* **Kerry**
　　　Light was the music that played for me,
　　　You were the song destiny had made for me
　　　I heard the melody start –
　　　Delicately – delicately – in my heart.

At that moment **Rosa Cariatanza** *enters, looking flustered. Seeing* **Elena** *safe and sound, she breathes an obvious sigh of relief.* **Rosa** *is her chaperone, a majestic lady of middle years who was a reasonably successful opera singer herself in her day.*

Rosa　　Oh, Elena, forgive me but I was so worried when you did not return on time.

(*To* **Kerry**.) She has not been well, you know, and she will not be told. Such a headstrong . . .

Kerry *smiles and bows to* **Rosa**.

Elena (*cuts her short but in a kindly way*)   This is Rosa. She does everything for me. Without her I could manage nothing. Rosa, this is Mr Stirling the younger, who is also my savior. My horse inconveniently cast a shoe – conveniently at Mr Stirling's door and he has kindly consented to drive us home in comfort and safety.

Kerry (*looking off*)   I can see the wagonette is ready for us at the gate. Ladies, shall we?

He holds out an arm to **Elena** *who takes it immediately.* **Rosa** *looks a little suspiciously, then followed them as they exit. As they walk off, the native voices swell louder.*

Grayshott *enters. He is now wearing his official uniform jacket as Governor General, since he will appear in character later in this scene.*

Grayshott   Well, the night of the Stirlings' party came round – as they have a habit of doing. I can't say they're my favourite occasions. All that noise and all those names and faces are just a blur to me and everyone expects the Governor to remember them. I usually manage to remember the *ladies* – especially if they're pretty! But those young fellows who follow them around like young puppy dogs. I'm always afraid I'm going to be trampled underfoot. Ah, well – I was probably the same myself once. Now, *there's* a sobering thought! These two particular young puppies are my aides, William Something-or-Other and James Whatever-his-Name-Is.

As he speaks the **Stirling** *girls have entered –* **Louise** *and* **Caroline**. *Now two young men,* **William** *and* **James**, *enter and approach them. They sing 'Invitation to the Ball'.* **Grayshott** *exits as the groups converge . . .*

Song

'Invitation to the Ball'

Girls
This is the high –
Light of the year for us
Dressed to the nine,
Up to our chins,
Stars in the sky
Moonlight is clear for us
Candlelight shines
And the music begins.

Men
Social event
Reeking with quality

Gentlemen bow
Ladies advance
We represent
Stately frivolity
Youth's at the prow
And so on with the dance.
When we say 'how good the floor is –
Providential
Circumstance.'

Girls
We shall blush
And reply
'What a crush!
Really we'll swoon
If they play one more tune!'

Men
'Music' We'll say 'furthermore is
So essential
To romance!'

Girls
What seems a terrible bore is
That you'd far rather talk than dance!

This is the high-
Light of the year for us.

Men
Gentlemen bow
Ladies advance.

All
Stars in the sky
Moonlight is clear for us
Youth's at the prow
And so on with the dance.

Men
Ladies – dear ladies – beguiling and sweet

Girls
Gentlemen – gentlemen – please try to be discreet.

Men
Ladies – dear ladies – be kind to our –
Blind to our –
Faults.

    One waltz
    Need not sweep you off your feet.

Girl
    Tra-la!

Men
    Though we may gasp at your beauty,
    Sense of duty
    Will prevail
    We represent
    To a large extent
    The purely domestic male.
    Strong emotions and desires
    Training has taught us to check.

Girls
    What if you unbanked the fires?

Men
    God forbid. We'd get it in the neck!
    Ladies – dear ladies – how charming you are.

Girls
    Gentlemen – gentlemen – don't think us too bizarre
    Though we're prepared to be kind to your –
    Blind to your
    Faults
    One waltz
    Will *not* get us very far!

Caroline   You dance with such verve – I declare I am quite breathless.

William   It's part of his training, you know. The Foreign Office considers it essential for Comptrollers of the Household to be fleet of foot.

Louise   How grand that sounds – Comptroller of the Household.

William   He rose from the ranks – he was originally only a common A.D.C.

James   Morally it is a most shocking profession, I assure you. Day in day out our duties compel us to lie unblushingly on the least provocation.

Song

'His Excellency Regrets'

Girls
    Oh, tell us please – entirely confidentially
    How A.D.C.s are trained in social grace.
    It's awfully brave – daily to be called upon to

    Save
    His Excellency's face!

Men

    Any explanations – of the duties of an A.D.C.
    Prove the complications
    That are rife at Government House
    Certain situations
    We could never let a lady see
    There are strange vibrations
    In the life at Government House
    Truth is often sacrificed for reasons of
    Diplomacy.

Girls

    That, of course, we understand –
    But all the same it must be grand –
    To be so suave, so calm, so dignified!

Men

    If you knew what all that signified – we –
    Who break the ninth commandment every day
    Would hang our heads in shame and say
    Forgive – we have to live
    Officially on feet of clay.
    Every minute
    We're made to sin
    It is really very depraved
    But to hell with the lies we tell
    His Excellency's honour must be saved.

The **Men** *speak in unison.*

Oh, you should *hear* some of the things he makes us say!

As they do so, **Grayshott** *enters and stands to one side of the group. They appear to be unaware of him.*

Grayshott

    His Excellency regrets
    That owing to an attack of gout
    He really dare not venture out
    On Saturday to dine.
    His Excellency regrets
    That owing to doctor's orders he
    Cannot attend the mission tea
    And also must decline
    Your kind invitation
    For Wednesday week.
    A slight operation

And poor circulation
Combined with a weedy physique
Has made him unable to speak.
All this in addition to what
The doctor's describe as a 'clot'
Which may disappear
By the end of the year
But may, very possibly, not!
His Excellency regrets
That owing to his exalted state
He can no more associate
With amiable brunettes.

Men
So now we know
About the diplomatic corps
How it can so
Corrupt the soul of youth.
What happens if
Some day you gave the waiting world a whiff
Of plain, unvarnished truth?

Girls
So now we know – about the diplomatic corps
How it can so – corrupt the soul of youth.
What happens if – some day you gave the waiting world a whiff
Of plain, unvarnished truth?

Men (*shocked*) Public morale would crumble right away!

Grayshott
His Excellency regrets
That, failing a better alibi,
He must admit he'd rather die
Than open your bazaar.
His Excellency regrets
Tha, lacking enough official scope,
He can't disband the band of hope,
No matter where they are.
He frankly despises
The people he rules
He gorge also rises
When giving the prizes
At co-educational schools
To rows of illiterate fools.
And if you should write in the book
He'll give you a murderous look.
For it ruins his day

To be taken away
From his rod and his line and his hook!
His Excellency regrets
He hasn't enough to run the house
Or pay the staff – or feed a mouse
Upon the pay he gets
Heigho-heigho – he's up to his ears in debts
But that's one of the least of the things
That's one of the least of the things . . .
That's one of the least of the things . . .
His Excellency regrets!

The **Girls**, **Grayshott** *and* **Young Men** *exit.* **Rollo** *and* **Penelope** *enter from the other side of the stage.*

Penelope   No, Rollo, I mustn't – really, I mustn't. I'll stay here.

Rollo   Let me bring you something then.

Penelope   I don't trust you – you'll bring me Tipsy-cake covered in cream, or Chocolate Mould and I shan't be able to resist it –

Rollo (*gallantly*)   Some gentlemen *prefer* ladies to be on the plump side, you know.

Penelope   Do *you*?

Rollo   I don't know – I've never really thought about it. All I know is that if you suddenly became skinny and pale you wouldn't be you any more.

Penelope (*gratefully*)   Oh Rollo – you *do* say the sweetest things.

Kerry *and* **Caroline** *now enter.*

Kerry   Uncle Samuel's looking for you, Rollo. He's with Mr Kettling and they're on the war path about the church fête. I think he wants to talk to you about organising a gymkhana or something.

Rollo   Oh, God!

Caroline   Rollo – that's blasphemous.

Kerry   Not at all – he was thinking of the church fête.

Rollo   It's hard enough to get all our relations through this party without bloodshed, let alone a church fête.

Penelope   Everything's going well so far – all except Aunt Laura and Mr Fowler.

Kerry   What happened?

Penelope   They were having a little argument about whist in the dining-room and suddenly Aunt Laura slapped him with her fan and knocked his pince-nez into the trifle.

Kerry   Mrs Trenchard cut Mrs Watts dead on the verandah.

Rollo   Uncle Francis found Father's whisky in the library. He's spoiling for a fight.

Kerry   The party's going with a swing all right.

Song
'The Party's Going with a Swing'

There's something about a family rout
That thrills us
We like to observe our elders on the sly.
We have to repress the urge to laugh which
Nearly kills us
But nevertheless we try.
Observing every action
And recording every clue,
We notice with satisfaction
What some claret cup can do.
The party's going with a swing, with a swing
Gay abandon seems to be the thing
We can say sincerely that it's really really
Really
Very pretty to see our elders have an
Adolescent fling
Dear old Mrs Giles,
Having driven thirty miles
Has an appetite that wouldn't shame a horse.
Having tucked away
Nearly all the cold buffet,
She shows every indication that she's going to stay the course.
We're all so glad that Cousin Maud
(Thank the Lord,)
Hasn't yet been prevailed upon to sing
Tho' Dear Miss Scobie's principles forbid her to
Carouse,
She's apt to get flirtatious when the atmosphere
Allows
But it's hard to be seductive when there's junket on your blouse –

The party's going with a swing
The state advance
Of uncles and aunts in dozens
Is something to be remembered till we die
It's often a strain to be polite to all our cousins –
But nevertheless we try.
When gossiping and scandal has the party in its
Grip

The only way to handle is just to let it rip.
The party's going with a swing, with a swing
Mrs Drew quite took away our breath
She remarked with candour
Sitting out on the verandah
That, as far as she knew, old Mr Drew had drunk
Himself to death.
Pretty Mrs Bowles,
Having had five sausage rolls,
Was compelled to leave the ball room at a
Bound.
Also Colonel Blake,
Rather gay on tipsy cake,
Emitted first a hiccup then a more peculiar
Sound.
We can't say what the vicar did,
(God forbid,)
But we can blame the moonlight and the spring
With heart joviality he started playing 'bears'
He pounced on Mrs Frobisher and took her
Unawares,
We had to cut her laces at the bottom of the
Stairs –
The party's going with a swing

The party's going with a swing, with a swing
All the old folks hand in hand with youth.
Mrs John Macmallard
Bit an almond in the salad,
Which completely removed the stopping from
Her one remaining tooth.
Dear old Mrs Spears, who's been mad for several years
And believes she has the gift of second sight,
Went into a trance
Just before the supper dance
And let loose a flood of language which was
Highly impolite.
We're glad Aunt May who's deaf and dumb
Couldn't come
For she does put a blight on everything
Mrs Rogers did some conjuring which held us
All in thrall
She cleverly produced a lot of rabbits from her
Shawl
But after that the rabbits did the neatest trick
Of all –
The party's going with a swing.

Rollo *and* **Penelope** *exit.*

Caroline   You haven't told anybody?

Kerry   No.

Caroline   I wonder if she really *will* come?

Kerry (*agitated*)   Oh, don't! I shall feel awful if she does, and probably worse if she doesn't.

Caroline   Is she so *very* lovely?

Kerry   Lovelier than anyone I've ever seen – ever *thought* of seeing.

Caroline   Oh, Kerry.

Kerry   Let's go out on to the verandah where we can see the drive . . .

Grabbing her hand.

Come on . . .

They exit. **Louise** *enters with* **William**.

Louise   But Penelope saw her with her own eyes – they were white riding breeches – *men's*! I told her she should have looked away. Mama was in two minds whether to invite her to this part or not – but *that* settled it!

William   She *is* a very famous person, you know.

Louise   In that case, what on earth is she doing on this island? If you ask me, there's something very fishy about it.

Mr *and* **Mrs Stirling** *enter.*

Mrs Stirling   Good evening, William – I do hope you and the other young men are enjoying yourselves.

William   But immensely, Mrs Stirling – I do declare the room looks even prettier than it did last year – And the flowers – so charmingly arranged – a veritable bower.

Mrs Stirling   We have the girls to thank for that – they both have a delightful touch with flowers.

Louise   We have just been discussing the mysterious Madame Salvador. Alice Kettling heard on excellent authority that she had come here secretly to have a *baby*!

Mr Stirling   An eccentric spot to choose –

Mrs Stirling   Yes – *I've* always felt that.

Mr Stirling   Elizabeth – *please*!

William   I understood that she's been presented to the Queen at Windsor and sung for her privately –

Mr Stirling   Pure gossip – you know well how people exaggerate.

Mrs Stirling   Come, John dear – it is time for you to make your usual speech.

Mr Stirling   One would imagine, my love, from your unfortunate choice of the word 'usual' that I made exactly the same speech every year.

Mrs Stirling   Forgive me, my dear – your speeches are always charming.

Mr Stirling   That implies monotony.

Mrs Stirling (*in some confusion*)   Travers! Strike the gong!

She makes a sign into the wings and we hear the sound of a gong. The introductory music chimes in with it and the guests and family gather around. **Penelope**, **Rollo** *and* **Kerry** *come in last and stand down stage.* **Mr Stirling** *arranges himself and clears his throat. Everyone applauds.*

Song

'Dear Friends, Forgive Me, Pray'

Mr Stirling
Dear friends, forgive me, pray
If as your host
I should seem importunate
But my paternal pride
Can't be denied.
My daughter's natal day
Demands a toast,
Which is very fortunate,
For though the lemonade and cup's all right,
No wine has flowed yet –
I haven't heard a cork explode yet.

All
How charming – how appropriate – what perfect rectitude!
Dear Mr Stirling never says a word that might
Be misconstrued.

Mr Stirling
Allow me to express
My cheerful mind
In this refined community
And say with what delight
I see tonight –
Our friend the Dean
And Mrs Green
Accompanied by Oliver
And dear Miss Ruxton-Bolliver.
I also must extend
To Canon Banks

My ardent thanks
For bringing Jane and Harriet
And also Mr Marryot
Our ever faithful friend
Who never leaves a party 'til the end.

So now, my dearest girl.
Pray the most
Of this opportunity
This evening you may frolic with impunity
In faith be strong,
Refrain from wrong,
And may your life be both enjoyable and long.

When the toast is over and everyone is laughing and chattering, we hear the **Servant***'s voice off-stage.*

Servant (*off, announcing*)   Madame Elena Salvador.

The talking dies down and there is dead silence as **Elena Salvador** *sweeps in. She is dressed magnificently, if a trifle extravagantly.* **Elena** *looks about and sees* **Kerry**. *She smiles.* **Kerry** *goes forward, kisses her hand and leads her to* **Mrs Stirling** *and* **Mr Stirling** *who are standing transfixed.*

Kerry   Mama – Papa – this is – this is my friend – Madame Salvador.

Mrs Stirling (*frigidly*)   How do you do.

Mr Stirling (*unsmiling*)   I welcome you to our house, madam.

Elena (*curtsying*)   It was most gracious of you to invite me.

There is a long silence.

Kerry (*in a gallant attempt to save the situation*)   Madame Salvador has been ill, Mama. She has been living in complete seclusion. I think it is most charming of her to honour us with her presence here tonight.

Mrs Stirling   We are all very flattered.

She smiles distantly.

Kerry I feel sure that you would like to take your friends into the dining-room and offer them some refreshment.

She turns away.

Ah, my dear Penelope – there are you – I had not forgotten my promises to show you those new Tahali lilies that you were so interested in. They are in the conservatory – John is overwhelmingly proud of them and we both expect you to be green with envy. Come, John – Penelope –

She sweeps out followed by **Mr Stirling** *and a reluctant* **Penelope**. **Elena** *stands stock still, rigid with anger, then, with a great effort, she smiles gaily.*

Elena What an enchanting house. I knew from the outside that it was certain to be charming inside, but I had no idea it would be like this – such elegant proportions –

Caroline (*coming forward*) I do hope that you admire the way we arranged the flowers. We've been slaving over them all the afternoon – haven't we, Louise?

Elena They are quite exquisite.

Kerry (*introducing*) This is my sister Caroline. And this is Louise.

Louise *and* **Caroline** *curtsey* – **Caroline** *enthusiastically,* **Louise** *perfunctorily.*

Louise (*coldly*) Please forgive me, Madame Salvador, but we have promised Mama to see about the fairy lights in the garden.

Louise *goes out. The others stay.*

Kerry It is in honour of Caroline's birthday that we are giving the party. Rollo –

Rollo *comes forward.*

Kerry This is my brother, Rollo –

Rollo (*bowing politely*) How do you do.

Caroline (*excitedly – rising from her curtsey*) This is the most exciting thing that ever happened, Madame Salvador – we have heard so much about you.

Elena I am sure you have. I think the situation needs clarifying a little –

Kerry (*wretchedly*) Madame Salvador – please –

Elena This is very interesting, as a social manifestation of the British colonial system – I have never encountered it before – very interesting indeed.

Kerry (*miserably*) Can you ever forgive me?

Elena Nonsense – nonsense – there is nothing to forgive.

(*To* **Caroline**.) You have been most charming to me – I see that there has obviously been some sort of misunderstanding – however, what I cannot see is that it should in any way prevent us from enjoying ourselves. Mr Kerry – your dear mother suggested with the greatest consideration that I might like a little refreshment. Over that she was quite right. I should. Also if we stay here any longer most of the ladies present will be forced into the garden where they will possibly catch the most appalling colds –

(*Pointing off-stage.*) Is that where the refreshments are?

Kerry Yes.

Elena Lead the way, then – my throat is absolutely parched.

She takes **Kerry**'s *arm and, laughing and talking, exits followed by* **Caroline** *and* **Rollo**.

Caroline I don't care – I'm *glad* she came – I think she's lovely.

Mr *and* **Mrs Stirling** *return. At the same moment* **Louise***. They all converge in the centre.*

Mrs Stirling (*with decision*) Where is Rollo?

Louise I imagine he's in the dining-room with Kerry and – the others –

Mrs Stirling Would you mind fetching him, dear? I wish to speak to him immediately.

Louise Yes, Mama. Poor Mama. How trying this must be for you.

Mrs Stirling Thank you, Louise. It is.

Louise Shall I fetch your smelling salts at the same time?

Mrs Stirling No, thank you, Louise – I have no intention of fainting until the end of the evening.

Louise *exits.*

Mrs Stirling It's outrageous, it really is –

Louise *returns with* **Rollo***.*

Rollo You wanted me, Mama?

Mrs Stirling His Excellency must be warned – he's probably already started out – if he arrives and finds this – this *creature* here we shall never be able to hold our heads up again. You must intercept him – Take Vulcan and ride out and meet him – take the plantation road, it will be quicker.

Rollo But, Mama – what can I possibly say? We have nothing against Madame Salvador – she is behaving with the utmost decorum.

Mr Stirling Do not argue, my boy. Your mother is obsessed by the dramatic values of the situation. Give the horse her head.

Mrs Stirling Really, John, that was unkind of you – I am at my wits' end.

Mr Stirling That is only too apparent, my love – however, so be it.

Mrs Stirling Go, Rollo – I implore you not to waste a moment – Go!

There is a burst of laughter from off-stage. **Mrs Stirling** *shudders and puts her hand to her head.* **Rollo** *goes.*

Mr Stirling Come, Elizabeth – you must shepherd your resources. We will go into the library – we shall be safe from intrusion there. You had better get the smelling-salts just in case, Louise.

Mrs Stirling*, tottering slightly under the stress of her emotion, is led off by* **Mr Stirling***.* **Louise** *goes off.*

There is another burst of laughter off-stage. **Elena** *comes in together with* **Kerry**, **William**, **James** *and* **Caroline**. *They are all quite obviously enjoying themselves immensely.*

Elena   But I *assure* you it is perfectly true! She achieved fame and fortune – which only goes to prove that virtue doesn't always pay! –

James (*laughing delightedly*)   Scandalous – upon my word – scandalous!

Elena   Of course, her fame was questionable and her fortune occasionally rather precarious – but still one can't have everything.

William   I'd like to see our Mr Kettling's face if he heard that story.

Elena   Who is 'our Mr Kettling'?

James   The vicar of this parish – a most formidable character – do you mean to say that he hasn't called upon you?

Elena   Alas, no – but you see I have been very ill and living in the greatest seclusion. When one is convalescent, formidable characters are dreadfully exhausting.

William   Do you know any more stories, Madame Salvador?

Elena (*smiling*)   Heaps – but you are far too young to hear them.

James   I'm dying to hear more about that 'Alice' you were talking about just now in the dining room.

All   Yes, tell about Alice . . .

Elena (*hesitates, then laughs. She is enjoying herself, too*)   Oh, very well. It's practically a moral tract, anyway . . .

Song

'Alice Is at It Again'

Elena
   In a dear little village remote and obscure
   A beautiful maiden resided,
   As to whether or not her intentions were pure
   Opinion was sharply divided.
   She loved to lie out 'neath the darkening sky
   And allow the soft breeze to entrance her.
   She whispered her dreams to the birds flying by
   But seldom received any answer.

   Over the field and along the lane
   Gentle Alice would love to stray,
   When it came to the end of the day,

She would wander away unheeding,
Dreaming her innocent dreams, she strolled,
Quite unaffected by hear or cold,
Frequently freckled or soaked with rain,
Alice was out in the lane.
Whom she met there
Every day there
Was a question answered by none,
But she'd get there
And she'd stay there,
Till whatever she did was undoubtedly done.
Over the field and along the lane
When her parents had called in vain,
Sadly, sorrowfully, they'd complain,
'Alice is at it again.'

Though that dear little village
Surrounded by trees
Had neither a school nor a college,
Gentle Alice acquired from the birds and the bees
Some exceedingly practical knowledge.
The curious secrets that nature revealed
She refused to allow to upset her
But she thought when observing the beasts of
The field
That things might have been organised better.

Over the field and along the lane
Gentle Alice one summer's day
Met a man who was driving a dray
And he whisked her away to London
Then, after many a year had passed,
Alice returned to her home at last,
Wearing some pearls and a velvet train,
Bearing a case of champagne
They received her
Fairly coldly
But when the wine had lifted the blight
They believed her
When she boldly
Said the Salvation Army had shown her the
Light.
When she had left by the evening train,
Both her parents in grief and in pain
Murmured brokenly, 'more champagne –
Alice is at is again!'

As she ends the song, everyone laughs and applauds.

Elena Now, I have monopolized you all enough – think of all the charming young ladies who are pining to dance with you –

James We'd rather talk to you than dance any day of the week – you're the most tremendous event that has struck this island since the earthquake of eighteen thirty-seven.

As they chatter away to **Elena** . . . **Grayshott** *enters and stands in the wings.*

Grayshott And now we officially meet the most important character in our story . . . ME!

William *and* **James** *have spotted him and have to warn the others.*

William He's here! His Excellency is here!

Song

'Make Way for His Excellency'

All
>   Make way for His Excellency!
>   Make way for His Excellency!
>   Make way for His Excellency!
>   Kindly step aside,
>   He is a symbol representing
>   Sceptre and crown and mighty race
>   Gently but firmly ornamenting
>   This remote but pleasant place –
>   Over the ocean's far horizon
>   Proudly the ruler of the state
>   Keeps her astute and watchful eyes on
>   Every wandering delegate.
>   Hail to the diplomatic service
>   Which, so discreetly, sent him here.
>   Make way for His Excellency!
>   Make way for His Excellency!
>   Make way for His Excellency!
>   Welcome him with pride.

Servant (*off-stage. Announcing in stentorian tones*) His Excellency the Governor General.

Everybody forms a large semi-circle. **Grayshott** *comes majestically forward.* **Mr** *and* **Mrs Stirling** *advance to receive them.* **Mr Stirling** *bows correctly;* **Mrs Stirling** *curtsies.*

Grayshott Charming, my dear Mrs Stirling – the room looks perfectly charming. And how prettily the flowers are arranged – a veritable bower. Ah, Mr Stirling. How nice to see you. No more of those tiresome rheumatics, I hope. Penelope – *what* a big girl you're getting –

He pauses in front of **Louise** *and* **Caroline**.

Grayshott   Now which is which? I always get so muddled. I know it's *someone's birthday*. But sill, never mind – Many happy returns – er, to *whichever* of you it is.

During this parade **Grayshott** *is wandering down the line of people murmuring pleasantries. He arrives at* **Kerry** *who is standing next to* **Elena**.

Grayshott   Good evening, Kerry – my dear boy, how flushed you look – I do trust you are not feverish!

He now sees **Elena**. *He stops in his tracks, which the others take for disapproval. Then he smiles broadly and slaps his thigh. He is obviously more pleased to see her than any of the rest.* **Elena** *curtsies, then* **Grayshott** *kisses her on both cheeks.*

Grayshott   My dear Elena – I am so delighted to see that you have finally decided to emerge from your tiresome seclusion – *Doesn't* she look well, Mrs Stirling?

As **Elena** *curtsies.*

Grayshott   You *do* look *triumphantly* well. I congratulate you on your recovery, my dear.

To **Mrs Stirling** *who is thunderstruck.*

Grayshott   Madame Salvador and I are old friends. She and Lady Grayshott were in a convent together in France. Though not for very long. She stayed with us in England just before Mary and I came out here – I was at the Foreign Office then – what a day season *that* was, wasn't it?

Elena   I have seldom been so happy.

Grayshott   The dear girl's laid up today with a touch of something-or-other but she can't wait to see you. Now that you are once more in circulation you must come to Government House – we'll have a quiet evening – just ourselves. I'll send William or James to call on you tomorrow.

Mrs Stirling (*almost hysterically*)   Madame Salvador – I do so hope that my son has been looking after you properly.

Elena   Thank you very much. Both of your sons and your daughter have been the soul of courtesy.

Mr Stirling (*with an effort*)   We are a small colony, madam – secure in our traditons, but not, alas, quite secure enough in our behaviour – I must ask you to pardon us.

Elena   That was most gracefully said, Mr Stirling. I will *consider* it.

Caroline   Won't you sing something for us, Madame Salvador? It would make me *so* happy!

Kerry   Caroline!

Elena (*she turns to the room*)　How could I possible refuse such a charming invitation? As you may know, I have been ill and my voice is more than a little rusty. However, as Mr and Mrs Stirling have been kind enough to receive me here tonight with such unparalleled warmth and hospitality, I *would* like to sing for my supper. I nearly always do. Your Excellency, have I your permission?

Grayshott *nods and smiles.*

Grayshott　Yes, of course. Certainly!

Elena　Thank you. I will sing something gay – the occasion demands it. Your Excellency – ladies and gentlemen – I do not wish to alarm you but there has been another revolution in France – the entire country has been invaded and conquered –

She pauses and there is a buzz of anxious conversation. We hear **Grayshott** *say to the* **Stirlings***, 'I should have received another telegram.'* **Elena** *holds up her hand and silences it.*

Elena　By a hop, skip and a jump!

Song

'One Two Three'

Elena
  A brand new dance
  Invaded France
  In April eighteen forty
  Through every street
  The rhythm beat
  It swept beyond
  The demi-monde
  And though some people hissed it
  They couldn't long resist it.
  The Right Bank fell
  The Left Bank fell
  And though the court was haughty,
  They took the floor
  When some old bore
  Declared the dance was naughty.
  Sur le pont d'Avignon – people cried '*c'est bon*'
  As they twirled in the magic of the moon
  All the world and his wife
  Seemed to take new life
  From that absurd – hurdy-gurdy little tune.

  There is nothing so beguiling as one-two-three,
  A one-two-three – and a hop
  The music sets you buzzing like a bumble bee,

Oh dear me!
You dance until you drop.
Old folks can't abide the one-two-three,
The reason's easy to see
Every beat for them
Spells defeat for them –
One – two-three.
But of course for flaming youth
It's quite a different affair,
They maintain with perfect truth
That nothing can compare
With the fascinating rhythm of the one-two-
Three,
It makes them shining and free
Point your toe,
Off you go –
One-two-three.

There is nothing so exciting as a one-two-three,
A one-two-three – and a hop
It definitely *épaters* the bourgeoisie
Oh dear me!
Their eyes begin to pop.
Missionaries frown upon the one-two-three,
Deacons dither with fear.
Grave anxiety
Racks society
When they hear
Those scandalous audacious strains
They give a terrible cry
They fear that such flirtatious strains
Are bound to lead to – My! My! My!
So when anybody shudders at the one-two-three
We just say 'fiddlededee!'
Arms out straight
Tête-a-tête
One-two-three!

The music continues and **Kerry** *and* **Elena** *now dance. One by one the other young couples pair off and join in. The elderly people are shocked and horrified. There is a tremendous shaking of heads and tapping of fans.* **Mrs Stirling** *taps* **Penelope** *on the shoulder. She and* **Rollo** *stop dancing. The other two couples –* **Louise** *and* **William**, **Caroline** *and* **James** *– also take the hint and stop dancing.*

Now only **Kerry** *and* **Elena** *are still dancing.*

They are aware of what is going on but continue with utmost sangfroid until the music ends. There is now total silence.

Then they stand looking at each other, smiling a little breathlessly, as though they were alone in the world. Suddenly, as though impelled by some force over which she had no control, **Elena** *leans forward and kisses him on the mouth. There is a gasp from everybody and the rest of the cast freeze. Then an ominous silence.*

Elena, *realising that she has gone much too far, runs impetuously off-stage.* **Kerry** *pauses a moment, then runs after her. The room is now abuzz with chatter, everyone reacting to the scandalous behavior in their own way. Only* **Grayshott** *remains.*

Grayshott   Well, *that* kept tongues wagging, I can tell you. Nobody could remember more scandalous goings-on. Bridges had been crossed, boats burned but two people at least were too happy to care. Though there *were* other people who – knowing perhaps a little more of the world – cared for *them* . . . and wondered what would happen next. As I'm sure you're wondering, too. Well, we'll be back to tell you in just a few minutes.

End of Act One.

Act Two

Grayshott *enters.*

Grayshott (*to audience*)   Now, where were we? Ah yes –

Running through the plot in his mind.

Madame Salvador . . . comes to Samolo . . . meets young Kerry Stirling . . . she's older . . . they fall in love with each other . . . Victorian society . . . a definite no-no . . . big scandal at the Stirlings' party . . . she kisses him in public . . . shock, horror . . . Elena and Kerry leave in a hurry . . . *Meanwhile* – as they say in all the best Victorian novels – up at the house Elena is renting, her loyal companion Rosa is waiting for her return. She's never known Elena so happy but she knows that Life (*with a capital 'L'*) is all too fond of handing you a gold coin – which turns out to be brass. But, then, it *is* a wonderful evening. You might even say – it's a night for lovers. Now, if *that* isn't a cue . . .

Song

'This Is a Night for Lovers'

Rosa
>The clouds are following the moon,
>The night will be over soon.
>The silver pathway fades from sight
>Across the still lagoon,
>The mountains stand against the sky
>Watching the little clouds pass by,
>Watching the shadows grow
>On the sleeping world below.
>
>This is a night for lovers
>A night to be set apart
>For ever in somebody's heart.
>This is a moment for ever and above,
>This is a night for love.
>Soon when the dawn discovers
>Secrets the night conceals,
>There'll be bright new hills and a coloured sea
>Instead of the delicate mystery
>The moon only half reveals.
>When dawn is lighting up the sky,
>The air will be shrill with birds,
>The magic of love will gently die
>Along with its foolish words.
>The mountains stand against the sky

Watching the clouds pass by,
Watching the shadows grow
On the sleeping world below.

This is a night for lovers
Set between yesterday's fears
And tomorrow's most probably tears,
This is a moment for ever and above,
This is a night for love.

Grayshott *enters as narrator.*

Grayshott Rosa, of course, could understand and sympathise with Elena's feelings – but she was worried where the romance was leading. Elena's impresario, Felix Kammer, had just arrived on the island to escort her back to Europe to resume her career – and was less than pleased to discover that, in his absence, Elena had developed other priorities . . .

Grayshott *exits as* **Felix** *enters.*

Felix I heard the sound of carriage wheels on the lower road.

Rosa They're coming back.

Felix It's after midnight and we have no time to waste. We have to sail first thing in the morning.

Rosa Felix – I've tried all I can. She refuses to leave the island.

Felix I will change her mind tonight. I must – for *all* our sakes.

Rosa Elena is in love – and you know how obstinate she can be?

Felix After all these years, Rosa, you and I know her all too well. But I must try. I shall be on the other patio – let me know when she is alone.

He goes out swiftly.

Rosa *sighs. There is the sound of voices outside.* **Elena** *and* **Kerry** *comes in. They are laughing gaily and obviously haven't a care in the world.* **Elena** *flings her arms around* **Rosa**.

Elena I knew it – the dragon waiting in the cave – snorting fire and brimstone! Look, Kerry – are you frightened as you should be?

Rosa You should be ashamed, Elena.

Kerry It was all my fault – we drove up to the Lailanu Pass – it was so lovely that we couldn't tear ourselves away –

Elena We watched the moon come up, Rosa. You know what happens when the moon comes up over the sea and the shadows on the mountains suddenly become sharp and black as though they had been painted. You know what happens when you're with someone –

She pauses and looks at **Kerry**.

Elena Someone who is very sweet – and you're high up looking out over the world – and there's nothing between you and the stars – or have you forgotten all those moons and stars and dawns of your wicked, unregenerate past?

Rosa No – I haven't forgotten.

Elena Dearest Rosa – don't be angry and disapproving – we are so very, very happy.

Kerry Elena – I must go – it's dreadfully late and if you want to drive to the other side of the island tomorrow, we shall have to start early –

Elena Rosa – take pity on us – the moon is still high – and we want to say goodnight!

Rosa (*unsmiling*) Good-night, Mr Stirling.

Kerry (*bowing*) Good-night.

Rosa This is a dangerous island.

Rosa *goes out.* **Elena** *and* **Kerry** *fly into each other's arms.*

Kerry (*softly*) Elena!

Elena I want you to believe something, my darling – this has never happened to me before – never like this – I swear it – I do so very much want you to believe that.

Kerry I believe it.

Elena I never knew it could be possible – this feeling I have for you – in all the years I've lived – I never knew –

Song

'I Never Knew'

Elena
   I never knew
   That love could be so sweet before,
   I never knew
   That life was incomplete before.
   I never knew – this tremulous ecstasy
   That seems like a dream to me
   Could yet be true.
   How could I guess, dearest, that within my heart,
   All other loves apart,
   There would be you?
   How could I know
   That I should love you so
   I never knew – I never knew.

Kerry
    The dearest love I ever knew,
    To hold for ever and for ever
    Though this moment sweet
    May with its magic fade away
    It is complete for us
    For ever and a day.
    No more – no more
    Our hearts will beat alone
    No more asleep or waking
    This is our own
    This happiness we've known
    This lovely moment is our own
    All other loves forsaking
    I never knew,
    I never knew you could love me –
    I never knew.

Elena
    Dear love, let this be true
    Dear love to last for ever
    Though the magic of tonight
    May fade away
    We'll remember it
    For ever and a day.
    No more we'll be alone
    No more asleep or waking
    This is out own
    This loveliness our hearts have
    Never known
    This is our own
    All other loves forsaking
    Dear love, I never knew
    Dear – could be so true
    Love – I never knew.

Both
    I never knew
    Such happiness could be – before.
    I never knew
    Such colours in the sea – before.
    I never knew those mountains were dear to me
    Until you were near to me
    And made it true.
    I feel that now every bird that sings to me
    Will lend its wings to me
    To bear me through
    Each weary day
    That I'm away from you
    I never knew –
    I never knew.

When the song is over he takes her in his arms again and kisses her. The music is still playing.

Kerry   Good-night, my love – until tomorrow.

Elena   Good-night, my love – until tomorrow.

He kisses her hand and goes. She stands at the door for a moment looking after him. **Rosa** *re-enters.*

Elena   Don't wait up for me, dear Rosa – I couldn't sleep yet – I know I couldn't.

Rosa   He seems a very charming young man.

Elena   Who – Kerry?

Rosa Yes. A little naïve, perhaps.

Elena Why do you say that?

Rosa I'm not blaming him – you couldn't expect him to be anything else, could you? Living all his life in a dead and alive place like this –

Elena I thought you liked Samolo.

Rosa It's all right for a little while – a holiday – but it's too hot here – hot and sleepy – I feel homesick for Europe – for all the familiar things that we've been brought up with – the smell of Paris on a May morning with all the chestnuts out – Vienna in winter, when there's a sprinkling of snow on the ground and you can have steaming hot chocolate in that little café on the Ringstrasse – then Stockholm – do you remember?

Elena What are you up to, Rosa? What are you trying to say?

Rosa I'm not up to anything – I'm just saying what I feel. I'm getting. A little restless, you know. We want to get back to work – play is all very fine for a while – but in the long run it's work that makes life exciting.

Elena Why are you treading so warily, Rosa – what is it?

Rosa (*altering her tone*) Oh, my dear – I'm *worried*.

Elena About me?

Rosa Yes.

Elena Because I'm happier than I have ever been in my life?

Rosa Because you are no longer *wise*.

Elena (*softly*) I am in love – deeply in love – is that so foolish?

Rosa Young love may be very charming – but it passes –

Elena You keep talking about Kerry as though he were an adolescent. He's not a boy – he's a grown man – he's only a year or so younger than I.

Rosa A *little* more than that . . .

Elena Well, what does that matter?

Rosa He's a stranger – he knows nothing of you or your world or your life –

Elena He can learn.

Rosa (*with vehemence*) *You* can learn, too – but it may be a bitterly painful lesson.

Elena Rosa!

Rosa Listen, my dear. Love is neither reliable nor permanent – everything passes and the world changes. Years ago, when my career seemed practically assured, I gave up everything for love – I sang no more and I worked no more – and my love failed me – I might well have become a famous prima donna – I might well have had the love and admiration of hundreds of thousands of people to warm me through my older years – but I gave it all up for the love of one man – and he went away and I was alone – I am reasonably content and I have few regrets until I see someone like you – with everything at your feet – on the verge of making the same stupid mistake that I did –

Elena Wasn't it worth it – while it lasted?

Rosa (*emphatically*) No.

Elena Perhaps you – neither of you loved each other enough.

Rosa Love is a traitor, Elena – beware of it – it changes its face and its heart too often – enjoy it if you must – but enjoy it lightly.

Song

'This Is a Changing World'

Rosa

    The world was young
    So many, many years ago
    The passage of time must who
    Some traces of change,
    Love songs once sung,
    Much laughter, many tears
    Have echo'd down the years,
    The past is old and strange.
    Each waning moon,
    All dawns that rise, all suns that set,
    Change like the tides that flow across the
    Sands.
    Each little tune
    That fills our hearts with vague regret,
    Each little love duet
    Fades in our hands.
    Don't stray among the moments that have fled,
    New days are just ahead,
    New worlds are still unsaid.

    This is a changing world, my dear,
    New songs are sung – new stars appear.
    Though we grow older year by year,
    Our hearts can still be gay.
    Young love at best is a passing phase,
    Charming and foolish and blind.
    There may be happier, wiser days
    When youth is far behind.

Where are the snows of yesteryear?
When winter's done – and spring is here
No regrets are worth a tear,
We're living in a changing world my dear
This is a changing world, my dear,
New dreams are dreamed,
New dawns appear.
Passion's a feckless cavalier
Who loves and rides away.
Time will persuade you to laugh at grief,
Time is your tenderest friend.
Life may be lonely and joy be brief
But everything must end.
Love is a charming souvenir,
When day is done and night draws near.
No regrets are worth a tear –
We're living in a changing world, my dear.

At the end of the song **Rosa** *exits and* **Felix** *enters.*

Felix Good evening, Elena – or perhaps it would be more accurate to say 'Good morning'.

Elena Felix – what are *you* doing here?

Felix Guarding my interests, my dear – and yours.

Elena Felix, my mind is made up. I thought you understood that.

Felix And I thought by now you might have come to your senses. We have a commitment to begin your next tour in Leipzig on May the first . . .

Elena May the first is a long way off . . .

Felix So is Leipzig. It is now November and we have far to travel.

Elena You insisted that I should not leave here until I had completely recovered.

Felix You *have* completely recovered. Our ship sails at dawn. There will not be another one for three months.

Elena No, Felix. I am not going.

Felix Well, I *am*, and so is Rosa.

Elena Rosa would *never* leave me –

Felix Her bags are already packed. See for yourself. She is in complete agreement with me that the only way to safeguard both your career and your reputation is for all three of us to leave this island at once.

Elena Please do not speak to me like that.

Felix Are you so lost to all common-sense and reason that you can't see what a disastrous mistake you are making?

Elena Is it such a disastrous mistake to love and be loved? Through all these years I thought you were a wise man and my friend. Now I discover that you are merely a *shrewd* man and my impresario.

Felix (*turning away*) That, my dear, was both cruel and inaccurate. If ever I have proved myself your friend it is by speaking to you as I am speaking now. You may, as you say, love and be loved. You may, under the spell of your infatuation, consider your world, and the world of those who belong to you and depend on you, well lost for it. I do not. I am outside the magic. I can see the fantastic folly you are committing.

Elena How can you be so sure?

Felix Listen my dear. I beg you, I implore you to listen, without anger, but with courage and honesty –

Elena (*beginning to break a little*) Don't speak like that, Felix – please don't.

Felix I must – believe me – I *must*. For your sake. For the sake of all those people who love and admire you, not only for your talent, but for the quality, the unassailable dignity of your personal life. No other light singer in all the history of the profession has ever been honoured. And now, in the course of only a few days, you are prepared to sacrifice everything that all those hard years have brought you.

Elena Why should everything be sacrificed? Why have I not the right to accept true love when it comes to me?

Felix In the first place you have yet to be sure that it *is* true love and time alone can prove that. You have only known the young man in question for a few days; and he is a very *young* man. He knows nothing about you and you know nothing about him. He is unsophisticated and impressionable. How long will it be before you realise that you have nothing in common and that you have exchanged a brilliant career for life as a Samolan housewife?

Elena (*almost in tears*) Felix, don't – please don't.

Felix (*inflexibly*) In the *second* place, you have created a situation in this small colony that cannot fail to have scandalous repercussions. I have been making enquiries. It was not difficult. The whole island is in an uproar. The boy's father regards you – in common with everyone else – as a scarlet woman. If you were high-handed enough to marry his son without his consent, he would cut him off without a shilling and never see or speak to him again.

Elena Why should money enter into it? I have enough for the both of us.

Felix To live as social outcasts on this tiny island? Would you really drag him down to such a level? The prospect is intolerable. You know this is all madness – impulsive wilful madness. If your stubbornness won't let you see that, I can't help you – and I won't stay here to see the consequences of your behaviour. Nor will Rosa. We could not bear it.

Elena Oh, Felix, I don't know what to do!

Felix Yes, you do. Come with us. Resume your career. Spare him ruin. Give him a chance to forget you – or at least keep a beautiful memory, untarnished by reality. Give him back his *life*.

Elena (*sobbing hopelessly*) But I *can't* – I can't – I can't go like this – without seeing him again – without saying goodbye.

Felix Write to him.

Elena No – no – no –

Felix You can't drive to the Stirling plantation in the middle of the night and demand to see him. That would make the scandal worse than ever. Write to him – tell him you'll come back – tell him anything you like.

Elena (*controlling herself*) No, Felix – I can't do this to him.

Felix You must. And in your deep heart you know that I am right.

Elena If I write the letter – will you promise me on your honour that he gets it tonight – in time to come to the ship – to say good-bye –

Felix But Elena –

Elena Is it too much to ask?

Felix Very well – write it now – I will see that he gets it in time.

Elena (*dully*) Thank you.

Felix I'm sorry – believe me I am deeply sorry to cause you so much pain. Try not to think too harshly of me for telling you what is true. I can only beseech you to be honest with yourself and, with your courage, that I have never known to fail, do what is wise and what is right.

Felix *rests his hand for a moment on her shoulder and goes out quietly.*

Elena (*brokenly*) Oh, Kerry!

She exits opposite. **Grayshott** *enters.*

Grayshott I saw what happened next with my own eyes. In many ways, I wish I hadn't. I was down at the harbour the next morning. I was seeing a visiting diplomat off and the quay was crowded . . . I saw Elena and her party go aboard . . . But I thought it best not to be seen.

We hear off-stage native voices singing 'Come Back to the Island'.

Grayshott The Samolans were singing their traditional song of farewell, as the ship weighed anchor and drew away from the dock. Just then Kerry appeared, distraught and shouting helplessly after the departing vessel. But, of course, she couldn't hear him.

On cue **Kerry** *rushes on and goes to the opposite side of the stage, from which the ship is obviously sailing.*

Song

'Come Back to the Island'

Samolans
    Come back to the island,
    Please leave your heart behind you.
    Heartache
    Is a keepsake
    That you will haunt you and remind you.
    Keep faith – and remember
    Keep faith – and we'll find you
    Come back to the island,
    Come back to your heart.

    Soon – the shore will fade,
    The pounding surf you will not hear,
    The mountain tops will disappear
    And be a memory
    Beyond the empty sea.
    Here – the sun and shade,
    The green lagoons, the gleaming sand
    Of this benign and loving land
    Still will be
    Your certainty.

    Come back to the island,
    Please leave your heart behind you.
    Heartache is a keepsake
    That will haunt you and remind you.
    Keep faith – and remember
    Keep faith – and we'll find you
    Come back to the island,
    Come back to your heart.

Grayshott   Time passed. Elena Salvador sailed away and resumed her career. Her popularity was greater than ever and thousands of hearts were hers – all except one. Her own. It is now a year later, practically to the day. Rosa and Felix had been wrong. She *had* left it in Samolo and now she'd return to reclaim her heart – and her love. We're back at Elena's house and this time the ladies are *un*packing. Rosa enters and starts busying herself. As she mimes unpacking and hanging up clothes, she sings to herself.

Elena *enters and overhears her. She is clearly delighted to find* **Rosa** *so happy. She comes up behind her and puts her hands on* **Rosa**'s *shoulders.* **Rosa** *is startled but also pleased to find* **Elena** *happy, too.*

Elena   Oh, Rosa, I love it when I hear you singing one of those gypsy songs. No, please – another for me. *Please . . .*

Rosa *pretends to demur but is clearly pleased to be asked and soon continues the song. At a point* **Elena** *joins in and turns the ending into a duet* . . .

Song

'Gipsy Melody'

Rosa
I'll sing a song to you, both sad and true . . .
About a highly born Hungarian,
Although the husband she was married to
Was far removed from a barbarian
She loved a proletarian.

Rosa   My dear, I won't croak any more – there must be something in the air today – I feel it, too – I expect it is your foolish irrational heart's desire – at last coming true –

Elena   He was writing to me, you know – on that first day I saw him – writing me a little note, out of the sweetness of his heart, to warn me that people were saying unkind things about me – it was just chance – the whole thing was just chance –

Elena
My horse had cast a shoe
A careless thing to do
Then Kerry smiled and sympathised
And said that all could be arranged
And suddenly I realised
That everything in life had changed.

Rosa
Of course, of course
I could *murder* that annoying little horse!

Elena   Oh, Rosa, how can you be so unkind!

Rosa   Look at the trouble he's caused us all – trailing back and forth across the seven seas . . .

Elena   He's the dearest horse that ever lived. A lyrical Olympian horse, the only horse I have ever loved.

Elena
Then when Kerry whispered 'dear Madame Salvador'
I discovered that my eyes were wet
And he drove me safely home in his father's
Wagonette.
How could I know
What incalculable force
Could impel that rather slow
But beguiling little horse?

>   How can I wait
>   Till the evening shadows fall
>   To go through that little gate
>   And to find, in him, that answer to it all?
>   That cart led me to him and now I know
>   My heart will never, never let him go.

Rosa   Oh, my dear –

Elena   Rosa – what *is* the matter with you?

Rosa   I don't know – perhaps I'm envious.

Elena
>   This is a changing world, my dear
>   The clouds have gone – the skies are clear
>   What is there in the atmosphere
>   That lifts my heart away?
>   Can you not hear it, that lovely tune,
>   Urgent, entrancing and sweet
>   Telling me clearly how soon,
>   How soon, my love and I will meet?
>   This that I feel will always be,
>   This voice that calls is destiny
>   Can't you hear it – can't you see
>   That love has changed the changing world for me?

At the end of the song, **Felix** *comes in.*

Elena   Felix – at last!

Felix (*quite expressionless*)   I made all the enquiries you asked me to make.

Elena (*sensing something in his tone*)   Yes – well –

Felix (*gently*)   You must be brave, my dear – I have bad news for you.

Elena   No, Felix, there must be a mistake.

Felix   You have come back too late, Elena.

Elena   He's gone away? You mean he is no longer on the island – that doesn't matter – I can be brave about that – I'll find him wherever he is.

Felix   He has not gone away – he is still here.

Elena   What are you trying to tell me, Felix – what has happened?

Felix   It is a great day on this damned island, Elena – a very festive occasion – the whole town is agog with excitement – young Master Stirling is being married today – this afternoon – people are talking of nothing else. There is to be a big reception and dance this evening. There will also be a procession of natives with torches. They are to escort the happy couple to the new house by the sea that Papa Stirling has kindly had built for them. There will also be . . .

Elena (*quietly*)   No, Felix – don't say any more.

Rosa (*going to her*)   Elena –

Elena (*moving away*)   No, Rosa, dear – please don't come near me – I'm quite calm, really I am.

Felix   Forgive me for being the bearer of such wretched, contemptible tidings –

Elena   You couldn't possibly be mistaken?

Felix   No doubt anywhere.

Elena (*sitting down*)   It's odd, isn't it? I don't feel anything at all – will the pain begin soon? There will be no need to unpack any more, Rosa – we shall be leaving very shortly.

(*To* **Felix**.)   Does the ship we came in sail tomorrow or the day after?

Felix   The day after.

Elena   I must ask you both, most humbly, to forgive me.

Felix   Don't be absurd, Elena –

Elena   I mean it – there is much to forgive – I have been intolerably stupid.

Felix   You have followed your heart across the world, my dear. That is not stupid. Your love may have betrayed you but at least *you* have not betrayed your *love.*

Elena   That was most gracefully put, Felix, but very sentimental – I am surprised at you –

Rosa   Elena –

Elena   It was also, I am afraid – inaccurate. I have not followed my heart across the world, nor has my love betrayed me. One cannot be betrayed by something that doesn't exist and my love doesn't exist – it never existed really, I supposed – except in my own highly romantic imagination. That is why I apologised to you both just now for being intolerably stupid. There is nothing more stupid than sacrificing the substance for the shadow. I know that what I have done is in the finest tradition of Grand Opera heroics, but then I was never cut out for Grand Opera. I am – as you have pointed out many times before, Felix – a light singer of light songs. I should have remembered that before, shouldn't I? For the life of me I cannot understand why are you standing there looking so dismal. Why aren't you laughing as I am laughing?

She begins to laugh.

The situation is funny enough – it's *more* than funny – it's grotesque. Please laugh. We had better laugh while we can and make the most of this moment because I am dreadfully afraid that I shall never, never see him again.

Suddenly she runs off. **Felix** *and* **Rosa** *pause, looking after her. They exchange concerned looks, then exit.* **Grayshott** *enters as she rushes past. He looks back at her sympathetically.*

Grayshott   Over at the Stirling home, as you can imagine, the mood was very different. The garden festooned with lights that must have taken hours to put up. All the usual suspects are there . . . Try keeping them away!

As he speaks the friends of the **Stirling** *family that we met earlier come on, chattering to one another – in fact, all of the cast – except* **Elena**'s *party – apart from those who need to make a subsequent entrance. They all now sing. . .*

Song

'Opening Chorus'

This is a night
Made for posterity.
Here on this isle
Weddings are rare
We can, with slight
Lack of sincerity,
Greet with a smile
This most fortunate pair.
Here without doubt
Nature can grin again
Men can be slow,
Men can be sly.
Girls who come out
Have to go in again,
Principally owing to lack of supply.

Please do not think we are jealous
Or disgruntled, or aggrieved.
We can sigh,
We can coo,
We can cry
'Really it's too –
Too too good to be true!'
All social instincts compel us
To be joyful and relieved
Still we'd like someone to tell us
How this marriage has been achieved.

This sublime and Christian rite
Aims to replenish the stock
But of course the bridal night
Frequently – is something of a shock!

Life we believe
Really requires some
Sine qua non
Neatly defined,
Owing to Eve
Having been tiresome,
Man must go on
Reproducing mankind.

When this is over **Mrs Stirling** *enters with* **Grayshott**.

Grayshott   What a *transformation*, my dear Mrs Stirling – the garden looks as pretty as a picture – and the coloured lights too – quite enchanting –

Mrs Stirling   I am so glad you think so – the girls took a great deal of trouble.

James   This must be a great day for you, Mrs Stirling?

Mrs Stirling   It is a great day for us all.

Grayshott   In that case, dear lady, explain to me something a mere man can never hope to understand – why do mothers always *weep* at weddings?

Mrs Stirling (*more cheerful than we have seen her so far*)   Now that I've had a sherry, Your Excellency, I will share the secret of the ages with you. It isn't only the thought of the young chick leaving the home nest – it's the monotony of the home nest.

Grayshott (*as if he had overlooked something*)   But you *do* have your husband . . .

Mrs Stirling (*sharply*)   That is *precisely* what I meant.

Grayshott *is clearly somewhat taken aback.*

Mrs Stirling   I suppose a mother's lot cannot be described as being wholly agreeable – so much fuss and fume at the beginning, and such an anti-climax at the end – Ah me!

Song

'Mother's Lament'

Mrs Stirling
Here in the twilight of our days,
From all maternal bondage free'd,
We've earned this sweet repose, no doubt,
But still it's dull to sit about
And watch the sand of time run out
With such indecent speed.

Now, as our eyes begin to glaze,
We peer from our domestic cage.

Here in the sere and yellow leaf
Our task is done, our time is brief,
We know that we should feel relief
But all we feel is rage.

Being at last put out to graze,
Like cows that are too old to breed,
We know that by maternal pride
Our spirits should be fortified
But all the same we're mortified –
And very cross indeed.

She ends as **Mr Stirling** *enters hurriedly.*

Mr Stirling   Elizabeth, there you are – I have been searching for you everywhere.

Mrs Stirling   What is the matter, my love?

Mr Stirling   I fear that old Mr Marryot is getting out of hand again. He has just drunk three glasses of claret-cup in quick succession and is making the most inflammatory remarks about Mr Gladstone.

Mrs Stirling   Good heavens! So soon? As a rule he never gets on to Mr Gladstone until the end of the evening.

Grayshott   It sounds as though a little gunboat of diplomacy is called for.

Mrs Stirling *and* **Mr Stirling** *and* **Grayshott** *exit right.*

Louise *and* **Caroline** *enter from the left.*

Louise   This is a great day but oh, how I wish it were over.

Caroline   My shoes are too tight and I'm exhausted.

Louise   We're all tired.

Caroline   I'll never be a bridesmaid again – it's hateful.

Louise   I suppose one day it will happen to us – being married, I mean – If it doesn't, I shall go straight into a convent.

Caroline   It's all our relatives that are so depressing. I should like to be married in a cave with a lot of robbers and pirates and exciting people toasting my bright eyes in rich Madeira –

Louise   I should find that most embarrassing.

Caroline   It would be different at any rate. I'm tired of all this simpering and smiling and these wretched little posies – I'm sick of standing about in groups and wishing other people happiness – I want to enjoy myself.

Louise   We all want the same thing really, I suppose.

Song

'Pretty Little Bridesmaids'

Both

    We humbly and devoutly pray
    That some kind gentleman some fine day
    Will fling all gnawing doubts away
    And cordially invite us
    To stroll along some shady path
    And there to offer us home and hearth,
    Remarking, as an aftermath,
    That the church should first unite us.

Caroline

    We long to bear the heavy weight
    Of the matrimonial halter,
    We're tired of following friends we hate
    Sedately to the altar.

Both

    We're sick of being pretty little bridesmaids,
    We're weary of the fussing and the fume
    We dread the awful destiny that guides maids
    Unwanted and unmarried to the tomb.

Caroline

    We long to lose our purity
    And plump for the security
    A wedding-ring undoubtedly provides.

Both

    We're sick to death of being pretty little bridesmaids
    Instead of pretty little brides.

Louise

    We're bored with all those brooches made of seed pearls,
    We hate each insignificant bouquet.
    We'd like to feel that, should we ever need pearls,
    We could earn them in a more attractive way.

Caroline

    We'd face with equanimity
    The intimate proximity
    Of someone snoring loudly by our sides,

Both

    For we're sick to death of being pretty little bridesmaids
    Instead of pretty little brides.

Caroline
>We shudder every time we see the vicar,
>We shrink from orange blossom and champagne.

Louise
>It's such a very acid-making liquor
>No sooner down than up it comes again.
>There's nothing very nice about
>Relations throwing rice about
>But that we'd bear and other things besides,
>If just for once, instead of pretty little bridesmaids,

Both
>We might be being pretty little brides.

Louise
>We can't enjoy those roguish implications
>Concerning the approaching bridal night
>Nor share the strange, vicarious sensations
>In which our elder relatives delight.

Caroline
>If ever we are married off,
>We pray that we'll be carried off
>To where no eager family presides,

Both
>For we'd loathe to think of all our beastly little bridesmaids
>Imagining us pretty little brides!

When the girls finish their number they both exit. The stage remains deserted for a moment. **Elena** *comes quietly on with* **Felix**.

Elena   They're all indoors.

Felix   Someone might come out at any money.

Elena   They're dancing a waltz – I wonder if *he* is dancing –

Felix   Elena – my dear – please come away – you will achieve nothing by this foolishness.

Elena   I only want to see him – just once – I'll keep my promise – really I will. He won't see me – he won't even be thinking of me. I swear I'll be discreet and allow no one to know I am here. I'll stand there in the shadows behind the tree.

Felix   But Elena – suppose by some chance he should find out that you were here – watching him from behind trees – it would be so shameful for you and so – so cruel to him. Even if he has tried to put you out of his mind, he cannot entirely have succeeded. To be suddenly confronted with you again might break up everything for him and make everyone concerned bitterly unhappy – please come away – please –

Elena (*putting her hand on his arm*)   I know you are right, Felix, but I have travelled the width of the world to see this man that I love and who, I believe, loved me. I know that it is all over and that there is neither reason nor dignity in what I am doing – but I must do it – I must see his face, see his smile, even if he is smiling at someone else. Just for one fleeting second – I must – I must see my love –

Her voice breaks but she controls herself.

Leave me now, as you promised – wait for me by the lower gate – even if you have to wait a long time – forgive me and understand.

Felix   Very well, my dear.

He kisses her hand gently and goes away. **Elena***, left alone, sings*

Song

'I Saw No Shadow on the Sea'

Elena
>I saw no shadow on the sea,
>No warning star appeared,
>The skies were free
>No vagrant gypsy told me
>Of a fascinating stranger,
>Gave no hint of where the danger
>Might be.
>
>Then came that strange, disturbing day
>That love I so desired,
>The sun and the moon conspired
>Above me
>Now like a ghost I watch my happiness depart,
>The light of love has cast a shadow on my heart.
>
>All through my life I have wandered,
>Ambition my compass and my chart
>Moments I heedlessly squandered
>Now return to haunt me – mocking at my heart.
>Love, with its lovely illusions,
>I neatly, discreetly set aside
>Fear kept me safe from confusion,
>Leaving me with only
>Loneliness and pride.
>Cold was the starlight above me,
>Time in its passing was slow.
>I had no need of a lover to love me
>But oh –
>That was long ago.

I saw no shadow on the sea,
No voices called to me,
My life was free
How could I open wide my arms
To the paradise around me
When no love had ever found me
The key?
And then I dreamed some foolish dreams
And, leaving my world behind,
I gaily set out to find
My lover
Now, in a moment, all those dreams are torn apart,
The light of love has cast a shadow on my heart.

When the song is over **Elena** *moves to the back of the stage. Everybody rushes on.*

Caroline   It's time for the procession to begin –

Louise   Mama, Mama – are we to drive back or walk?

Mrs Stirling   We are all coming back in the wagonette.

Grayshott *enters with great dignity.*

Grayshott   The whole thing – most charmingly organised, Mrs Stirling – quite an event – quite an event – and the coloured lights – a veritable fairy land.

Caroline   Aren't we going to drink to the bride and groom before we start?

Mrs Stirling   Control yourself, Caroline – I'm ashamed of you.

Grayshott   Oh, a capital idea – 'The bride and groom' – 'The bride and groom'.

Many voices take up the cry. In a moment or two all the guests step to one side in order to make way for the bride and groom. They both come slowly out and stand shyly together. It is not, as perhaps some members of the audiences have suspected, but **Rollo** *and* **Penelope**. *Everyone cheers and claps. There is music playing and a general buzz of delighted conversation.*

Grayshott (*to* **Mr Stirling**)   Are you going to propose one of your delightful toasts, Stirling?

Mr Stirling   No, Your Excellency – *that* is the duty of the best man.

Grayshott   The best man – where *is* he – where *is* the best man?

Everyone takes up the cry. In a moment **Kerry** *comes out. He is apparently cheerful and smiling but anyone who knows him well would detect a strain in his manner.*

Caroline   They want you to do the toast, Kerry.

Silence falls on the assembled company. **Kerry** *stands for a moment. The music starts softly in the orchestra. He begins to speak – a trifle haltingly at first.*

Song

'Wedding Toast'

Kerry
Your Excellency – ladies and gentlemen –
Dear friends – in this sweet circumstance
When all the air around us and above
Is charged with tenderness and early love
And that enchantment which is called romance,
I beg of you to lift your glasses up
And drink to those we love – a loving cup.

Grayshott   The dear boy – so gracefully put.

Kerry *gives them a fleeting smile and continues to sing.*

Kerry
No one can vouch for love – none can be sure
How long its ardent magic may endure.
No one can order love – all we can do
Is, in our deepest hearts, to keep it true.

Caroline (*softly to her mother*)   Oh, poor Kerry – his hand is trembling.

Mrs Stirling (*whose hand and voice are shaking, too*)   Hush, my dear.

Kerry (*lifting his imaginary glass*)
To you we love – to you we hold so dear
I drink to here and now and every after.
May every tear you shed dissolve in laughter,
May joy be yours through every changing year.
I drink to you with certainty and know
That destiny could never part
Two lovers when they love each other so

His voice breaks.

And oh, I envy you with all my heart.

Everyone applauds and raises imaginary glasses. **Penelope** *runs to* **Kerry** *and flings her arms around him.* **Rollo** *rings his hand. The music grows louder.* **Penelope** *takes* **Rollo**'s *arm and they move to the front of the stage. The two girls form up behind them and the* **Stirlings** *behind them. The procession begins and they all exit. Everyone is chattering and when they have all gone their voices are heard in the distance.* **Kerry** *stands there.* **Caroline** *comes running back.*

Caroline   Kerry. Aren't you coming?

Kerry   No, not for a moment –

He turns away.

I can't – really I can't –

Caroline Are you still so unhappy – so *dreadfully* unhappy?

Kerry Yes. I think I always shall be. She'll be in my heart always – until the day I die.

Caroline *looks at him sadly but there is nothing she can do to help him. She kisses him lightly and runs off. He stands looking after her for a moment and then turns back to face the audience.*

Kerry
Though we may never meet again,
There'll never be a day so sweet again.
No matter what the troubled years may bring,
A secret voice – will ever sing . . .

Elena *moves out of the shadows and downstage towards* **Kerry**. *She stops centre stage, still looking at him. As she moves, she begins to sing softly* . . .

Elena
Bright was the day when you came to me,
Shyly you whispered your name to me
I knew the theme of your song before
Far away – long before.

Kerry *turns at the sound and see her. For a moment he is transfixed, unbelieving. Then he moves slowly towards her and they meet centre stage.*

As they move together, **Grayshott** *appears at the side of the stage. He carries the newspaper he had in the beginning.*

Grayshott Oh, yes – it was a happy ending, all right. What makes me so sure? Well, I did give the bride away . . . and I am the godfather of their oldest boy – who I see is to be prime minister.

He indicates The Times.

Why didn't I tell you all this in the first place? Well, that would have spoiled the story, wouldn't it? It's what we call – diplomacy.

He gives a little salute and exits.

Elena & Kerry
Sweet was the music that played for me,
Part of a dream that can never fade for me
I heard the melody start . . .

Voices off: passionately – passionately . . .

Elena & Kerry   . . . in my heart

They walk into each other's arms and kiss.

Go to black, bows, entire cast enters.

Reprise
'Bright Was the Day'

Entire Cast
    Bright was the day when you came to me
    Shyly you whispered your name to me
    I knew the theme of your song before
    Far away – long before.
    I heard the melody, too –
    Beckoning me – beckoning me – here to you!

The End.

Ace of Clubs

Critics' Notes

Critics held conflicting views on *Ace of Clubs*, unaccustomed to Coward's version of gangster life, and attempted to define it against his commentaries on high society, such as *Private Lives* (1930). *The Stage* argued: 'Mr Coward here gets well away from the glossy world to which he was in the habit of introducing us in his pre-war revues. Patrons of the "Ace of Clubs" – the howling cads – do not even wear evening clothes. But the play is more than a cynical commentary on the days in which we live. Almost inevitably, considering the authorship, the club scenes are much more identified with cabaret than crookery.'[1] The critic draws parallels between the late Herbert Farjeon, and reminds us that Coward retains his ability to craft provocative lyrics that encapsulated the political and cultural moment.

Similarly, an anonymous critic noted: 'To jingling tunes, which have an exhilarating if faintly reminiscent air, Noel Coward's romance, "Ace of Clubs", at the Cambridge Theatre, is set mainly within a Soho night club, and exploits in a mixture of sentimental comedy and tough drama the adventures of a queer and not entirely likeable set of characters.'[2] This critic notes that the characters speak almost entirely in Cockney accents, and wonders if he intends this as a compliment to his native city, stating, 'But it is a dubious compliment, for so many of the creatures of this nocturnal underworld are of shady repute', again highlighting Coward's departure from his expected style of writing.

While the critics largely enjoyed the work, certain audience members felt differently. A review in the *Birmingham Daily Gazette* raised concerns about Coward's representation of a criminal underworld and its possible influence on British youth culture. This review noted: 'While his three spiv-shouldered "juvenile delinquents" strutted and boasted across the Birmingham Theatre Royal stage last night, Noel Coward, author of "Ace of Clubs", condemned critics of his taste in mocking the delinquency problem.'[3] They further note that a Birmingham magistrate attempted to get the song deleted from the script. 'Among those who laughed most heartily at the trio was Mrs Kate McKie, Chief Inspector to the Birmingham Licensing Committee who censors plays for the committee.' Regardless of public opinions from the era, it is clear that Coward was still very much an influential cultural figure in the 1950s.

1 Anonymous, 'The Cambridge: *Ace of Clubs*', *The Stage*, Thursday 13 July 1950.
2 Anonymous, 'The London Theatres: Noel Coward's "Ace of Clubs"', *The Scotsman*, Monday 10 July 1950.
3 Anonymous, 'Coward explains – it's only satire', *Birmingham Daily Gazette*, Friday 30 June 1950.

Original Cast

Manchester and Cambridge Theatre:

Elaine	Bubbly Rogers[4]
Rita Marbury	Sylvia Cecil[5]
Benny Lucas	Raymond Young[6]
Sammy Blake	Robb Stewart[7]
Fleix Felton	Myles Eason[8]

Ace of Clubs Girls:

Dawn O'Hara	Sylvia Verney[9]
Dorren Harvey	Margaret Miles[10]
Ruby Fowler	June Whitfield[11]
Greta Hughes	Pamela Devis[12]
Betty Clements	Lorna Drewes[13]
Mimi Joshua	Vivien Merchant[14]
June April	Lisbeth Kearns[15]
Baby Belgrave	Jean Carson[16]
Hercules Brothers	Victor Harman[17]
	Ronald Francis[18]
	Stanley Howlett[19]

---

4   'Bubbly' Rogers appeared in a number of London revues beginning in the 1940s, including *Black Vanities* (1941).
5   Sylvia Cecil (1898–1983) was an English stage actor and singer who began her career with the D'Oyly Carte Opera Company.
6   Raymond Young (1918–2011) was born Raimondo Jaquarello in London and was a stage, television and film actor.
7   Robb Stewart (?) was a London stage actor. Other stage credits include *Chrysanthemum* (1956).
8   Myles Eason (1915–77) was an Australian stage actor.
9   Sylvia Verney (?) was a London stage actor.
10 Margaret Miles (?) was a London stage actor.
11 Dame June Rosemary Whitfield (1925–2018) was an English radio, television, stage and film actress. Other credits include *Absolutely Fabulous* (1992–2012).
12 Pamela Devis (1926/28–2004) was a West End stage and film actor and choreographer, whose credits include the film *Ivanhoe* (1950).
13 Lorna Drewes (?) a London stage actor.
14 Vivien Merchant (1929–82) was born Ada Brand Thomson and was an English stage actor. She was known for her work with Harold Pinter, to whom she was married from 1956 to 1980.
15 Lisbeth Kearns (1930–2010) was a stage and film actor also known as Lisa Daniels. Film credits include voice work in Disney's *101 Dalmatians* (1961). Lisbeth Kearns (?) was a London stage actor. Other shows include *Meet Mr Callaghan* (1953).
16 Jean Carson (1923–2005) was an American stage and television actor. Other credits include *The Andy Griffith Show* (1960–8).
17 Victor Harman (?) was a London stage actor, whose other credits included the ensemble in *South Pacific* (1949).
18 Ronald Francis (?) was a London stage actor.
19 Stanley Howlett was a London stage actor. Other credits include *King Henry V* (1928).

Joseph Snyder   Elwyn Brook-Jones[20]
Gus   Patrick Westwood[21]
Pinkie Leroy   Pat Kirkwood[22]
Harry Hornby   Graham Payn[23]
Clarice   Eileen Tatler[24]
Eva   Renée Hill[25]
Yvonne Hall   Jean Inglis[26]
Mavis Dean   Gail Kendall[27]
Detective-Inspector Warrilove   Jack Lambert[28]
Policeman   Michael Darbyshire[29]
Mr Price   Philip Rose[30]
Mrs Price   Stella White[31]
Juvenile Delinquents   Peter Tuddenham[32]
                            Colin Kemball[33]
                            Normal Warwick[34]
First Plain-Clothes Man Manfred Priestley[35]
Second Plain-Clothes Man Christopher Calthrop[36]
Drummer   Don Fitz Stanford[37]
Waiters   George Selfe[38]
                            Richard Gill[39]
                            Jacques Gautier[40]

---

20 Elwyn Brook-Jones (1911–62) was a London stage and film actor. Other credits include *Odd Man Out* (1947).
21 Patrick Westwood (1924–2017) was an English stage and television actor. Other credits include *The Crime of the Century* (1956–7).
22 Pat Kirkwood (1921–2007) was a British stage actor, singer and dancer, and was the first woman on British television to have her own show, *The Pat Kirkwood Show*.
23 Graham Payn (1918–2005) was a South African-born English actor who was Coward's longtime romantic partner.
24 Eileen Tatler (1925–2007) was an English stage actor who began her stage debut as a pantomime performer.
25 Renée Hill was a London stage actor; other credits include Coward's *Relative Values* (1952).
26 Jean Inglis was a British stage actor, also known for her appearances in pantomime.
27 Gail Kendall was a London stage actor.
28 Jack Lambert (1899–1976) was a London stage actor; other credits include *Count Me In* (1942).
29 Michael Darbyshire (1917–79) was an English stage, film and television actor. Other credits include the 1968 film *Chitty Chitty Bang Bang*.
30 Philip Rose (?) was a London actor.
31 Stella White (?) was a London actor.
32 Peter Tuddenham was an English television and stage actor; other credits include the TV programme *Blake's 7*.
33 Colin Kemball (1928–2008) was an English stage actor whose credits included *The Rainbow Jacket* (1954) and *Oh! What a Lovely War!* (1965).
34 Normal Warwick (1924–89) was an English actor, best known for films including *Superman* (1978).
35 Manfred Priestley was a Shakespearean actor in the 1940s and 1950s, known for such works as *Hamlet*.
36 Christopher Calthrop (?) was an English character actor.
37 Don Fitz Stanford (?) was an English character actor.
38 George Selfe (?) was an English character actor.
39 Richard Gill (?) was a London actor.
40 Jacques Gautier (?) was a French stage actor.

Night Club Habitués and Visitors   Nina Alvis[41]
Irene Derek[42]
Hilda Fayre[43]
Julia Hand[44]
Diana Houlston[45]
Lorna Kilner[46]
Melanie Paul[47]
Claire Pollock[48]
Barbara Dalby Smith[49]
Susan Swinford[50]
Dorothy Thomas[51]
Madge White[52]
Stella White[53]
Pater Armsten[54]
Charles Blechier[55]
Peter Fairaine[56]
George Humphries[57]
Tony Hilton[58]
Vernon Kelso[59]
Carl Lacey[60]
Herbert Lister[61]

41 Nina Alvis (?) was a London stage actor.
42 Irene Derek (?) was a London stage actor.
43 Hilda Fayre (?) was a London stage actor.
44 Julia Hand (1931–) is an English stage and television actor.
45 Diana Houlston was a London stage actor. Other credits include *The Lady from the Sea* (1945).
46 Lorna Kilner is a British stage and television actor. Other credits include *Shoulder to Shoulder* (1974).
47 Melanie Paul (?) was a London stage actor.
48 Claire Pollock (1924–2001) was an English stage, film and television actor. Other credits include *The Pickwick Papers* (1952–3).
49 Barbara Dalby Smith (?) was a London stage actor.
50 Susan Swinford is an actor and writer. Other credits include *Sons and Daughters* (1982).
51 Dorothy Thomas (?) was a London stage actor.
52 Madge White (1892–1978) was an English stage and film actor. Other credits include *The Eleventh Hour* (1922).
53 Stella White (?) was a London stage actor.
54 Pater Armsten (?) was a London stage actor.
55 Charles Blechier (1925–68) was a London stage, film and television actor. Other credits include *A Night to Remember* (1958).
56 Peter Fairaine (?) was a London stage actor. Other credits include *See How They Run* (1949).
57 George Humphries (?) was a London stage actor.
58 Tony Hilton (1928–84) was an English actor and writer, known for works including *One for the Pot* (1968).
59 Vernon Kelso (1893–1958) was an English actor, known for such works as *Once in a New Moon* (1934).
60 Carl Lacey (1909–62) was an English stage actor. Other credits include *Probation Officer* (1959).
61 Herbert Lister (1908–95) was an actor, stage manager, dresser and chauffeur, whom Coward nicknamed 'Nanny'.

	Michael Mellinger[62]
	Arthur Norman[63]
	Stuart Pearce[64]
	John Raymonde[65]
	Philip Rose[66]
	Frank Singuineau[67]
	Bernard Verney[68]
Producer	Noël Coward
Orchestral Direction	Mantovani[69]
Designer	G. E. Calthrop[70]
Orchestration	Ronald Binge & Mantovani[71]

Scenes

Act One

Scene One	The Club	1 a.m.
Scene Two	The Office	A few minutes later
Scene Three	The Club	A few minutes later
Scene Four	Soho Square	A minute later
Scene Five	The Club	A few minutes later
Scene Six	The Club	5.30 the next afternoon
Scene Seven	Soho Square	10.30 p.m.
Scene Eight	The Club	Midnight
Scene Nine	The Office	About 1 a.m.
Scene Ten	The Club	A few minutes later

Act Two

Scene One	The Club	About two minutes later
Scene Two	Soho Square	The same time
Scene Three	The Office	A few minutes later
Scene Four	The Club	The next afternoon

62 Michael Mellinger (1929–2004) was a German film and stage actor. Other credits include the film *Goldfinger* (1964).
63 Arthur Norman (?) was a London stage actor.
64 Stuart Pearce (?) was a London stage actor.
65 John Raymonde (?) was a London stage actor.
66 Philip Rose (?) was a London stage actor.
67 Francis 'Frank' Ethelbert Dominic Singuineau (1913–92) was a Trinidadian actor whose other credits include work with the Unity Theatre company.
68 Bernard Verney (1915–70) was an English stage and film actor. Other credits include *Curse of the Mummy*.
69 Annunzio Paolo Mantovani (1905–80) was an Anglo-Italian conductor and composer.
70 Gladys Edith Mabel Calthrop (1894–1980) was a visual artist and set and costume designer who worked with Coward extensively and designed the sets and costumes for many of his productions.
71 Ronald Binge (1910–79) was a British composer and arranger who worked closely with Mantovani.

Scene Five	Soho Square	About 7 p.m.
Scene Six	The Office	Just after midnight
Scene Seven	The Club	A little later
Scene Eight	The Office	A little later
Scene Nine	The Club	A littler later

Time: The Present

Musical Numbers

Act One

1. 'Top of the Morning'	Baby & Ace of Clubs Girls
2. 'My Kind of Man'	Pinkie
3. 'This Could Be True'	Pinkie & Harry
4. 'Nothing Can Last for Ever'	Rita
5. 'Something About a Sailor'	Harry
(*Dance arranged by* Freddie Carpenter)	
6. 'I'd Never, Never, Know'	Pinkie
7. *'Three Juvenile Delinquents'	Colin, Peter, Norman
8. 'Sail Away'	Harry
9. 'Josephine'	Pinkie
10. Reprise: 'My Kind of Man'	Pinkie
11. 'Would You Like to Stick a Pin in My Ballon?'	Club Girls

Act Two

1. 'In a Boat, on a Lake, with My Darling'	Baby & Felix
2. 'I Like America'	Harry & Ace of Club Girls
(*Dance arranged by* Freddie Carpenter)	
3. 'Why Does Love Get in the Way?'	Pinkie
4. *'Three Juvenile Delinquents'	Colin, Peter, Norman
5. 'Evening in Summer'	Rita
6. Reprise: 'Sail Away'	Harry
7. 'Time for a Baby's Bottle'	Baby, Yvonne, Mavis
8. 'Chase Me Charlie'	Pinkie
9. Reprise: 'Nothing Can Last for Ever'	Rita
10. Reprise: 'My Kind of Man'	Pinkie

* 'Three Juvenile Delinquents' may not be performed in any production of *Ace of Clubs*.[72]

---

[72] This particular number raised the ire of local law-enforcement officials and was removed after the Birmingham try-out.

Act One

Scene One

The club. About 1 a.m.

The Ace of Clubs is a night-club in the Soho district of London. It is owned and financed by **Rita Marbury**, *and run by* **Benny Lucas**. **Rita** *is an ex-musical comedy actress who left the stage to marry a rich manufacturer who died and left her fairly well-off. She is a shrewd woman somewhere between forty and fifty. Her clothes are good, if a little flash, her hair is a trifle redder than nature intended it to be.* **Benny Lucas** *is a man of about thirty-five. He is smooth and good-looking, with a thin line of black moustache and patent-leather hair. The club is successful and specialises in a floor show, the star of which is* **Pinkie Leroy**, *a tough, ambitious girl of about twenty-eight.* **Pinkie** *has a good voice, a great deal of hard professional assurance and a sense of humour. In addition to these assets, she has good character.* **Felix Felton**, *the leading man, dance arranger and compère*[73] *of the floor show, sings and dances adequately, has overwhelming vitality and an unqualified belief in his own charm and ability. He is quite amiable but inclined to be temperamental.*

Baby Belgrave, *the 'soubrette' of the show, whose cradle was a property basket in the King's Theatre, Southsea during the pantomime season, is an experienced little 'pro' who can put over numbers with technical efficiency. There is no trick of the trade that she doesn't know and she is a good-hearted girl easily moved to transports of theatrical sentimentality. The floor show, extracts from which we are privileged to enjoy during the evening, is entitled 'London Frolics'.*

The characters concerned with the story, but unconnected professionally with the club, are:

Harry Hornby, *a cheerful young sailor who is on seven days' leave while his ship is refitting at Chatham;*

Joseph Snyder *('Smiling'* **Snyder**), *a middle-aged and fairly successful racketeer;*

Gus, *his attendant thug;*

Detective-Inspector Warrlove, *a pleasant-looking typical police inspector who is sympathetically disposed towards* **Rita**, *but both suspicious and disapproving of* **Benny**.

Minor characters of the story will be described in order of their appearance.

The main set is the interior of the club. There is a small stage at the back with a proscenium and workable tab curtains made of white velvet with two large black aces of clubs emblazoned upon them.

From the stage three wide, shallow steps lead down on to the dance floor. On the audience's left of the stage and on the same level is a small rostrum for the band. The band need not number more than five or six pieces including a small upright piano

---

73 Host of a variety show.

and drums. The members of the band are dressed in rather grubby white suits with the inevitable aces of clubs stitched on their breast pockets. Downstage on the left is a door marked 'Office'. Above this can be seen an illuminated sign 'Gentlemen's Cloak Room'. On the right of the stage there are three similar pillars and a sign reading 'Ladies' Cloak Room'. Below this, downstage, is the entrance to the bar. This entrance is curtained so as not to interfere with the lighting effects of the floor show. During the floor show it must be possible for the chorus to enter and exit from the back, round the band rostrum on the left and from the back of the stage on the right.

In the night scenes when the club is functioning, little can be seen between and behind the artificial pillars as all light is concentrated on the dance floor and the stage. In the daylight scenes the walls can be seen shabbily draped in red. There is a window – fairly large – in the right-hand wall which is curtained by night and exposed by day. The foyer and entrance to the club is offstage on the left. The dance floor in the centre is fringed with tables. In the daylight scenes these are piled up on top of each other. The predominant colour, apart from black and white, is bright red.

When the curtain rises on the first scene, it is about 1 a.m. and the dance floor is crowded with people doing a samba. The band is making as much noise as possible and resolving coloured lights are playing on the dancers. The dance comes to an end, there is a spatter of applause and the customers return to their table.

Pepi *and* **Vic**, *two waiters, bustle about with drinks, and* **Elaine**, *a languid blonde with large bosoms, saunters from table to table with a tray of cigarettes.*

There is a general babel of conversation.

Rita *comes out of the bar and is seen talking for a moment at one of the tables. As she moves away she meets* **Benny**, *who is coming from the foyer offstage left. They talk for a moment.* **Rita** *goes offstage back.* **Benny** *nods to* **Sammy Blake**, *the pianist.* **Sammy** *plays a chord. There is a drum roll, the lights go down, a white spotlight plays on the centre of the stage curtains. The general chatter dies away.* **Felix** *bounds through the curtain. He is wearing a white dinner-jacket with padded shoulders and an artificial red carnation in his buttonhole.*

Felix (*with flashing charm*)   Friends, Romans, countrymen – here we go again, as the actress said to the bishop – which only goes to prove that everything's all right if you only know how to handle it! Wait for laugh – no laugh – rise above it and press on! Here I am – Felix Felton in person, the talented laddie with too many teeth – which reminds me of a filthy story I told to my old grandmother only last Tuesday – nobody here is old enough to understand it.

Felix *claps his hands, points first to the band and then to the curtains, and bounds down the steps and off behind the stage on the right.*

The music begins and the curtains part disclosing a backcloth representing Covent Garden Market.[74] *The eight Ace of Clubs* **Girls**, *dressed as Cockney flower girls in 'pearly' brassieres and trunks and large feathered hats, come vivaciously down the steps,*

---

74 Large indoor market in London since 1845.

doing an untidy but determined dance routine. This is mercifully brief, and at the end of it they arrange themselves, four a side, on the dance floor and points towards the stage.

Baby Belgrave *comes on, dressed as a Covent Garden porter, in blue satin dungarees, a white open-necked shirt and a blue velvet cap. She sings:*

'Top of the Morning'

Verse:

> On my way
> Walking along the street
> Noticing the expressions
> Of the people that I meet
> I seem to feel a sort of gay beginning
> To a brand new lovely summer day beginning
> Come what may
> Winter is on the wing
> I can't prevent myself from singing –

Refrain:

> Top of the morning to you!
> Top of the morning to you!
> The sun is high,
> The summer sky
> Is clear and gay
> And I've just heard from the BBC.
> There won't be rain today.
> London is shining and free
> That is, as free as Democracy can be.
> Though your cares distract you
> Though your boss has sacked you,
> Though your dad has cracked you
> On the jaw –
> Yesterday's
> As hazy as a far-off shore
> Top of the morning
> After the night before!

At the end of the number the **Girls** *and* **Baby Belgrave** *make an exit through the tables at each side and disappear backstage.*

Felix *bounces through the curtains, which have closed during the latter part of the number.*

Felix   And now, ladies and gentlemen – particularly the ladies – you are going to have the greatest thrill since Eugen Sandow[75] exposed his torso and ate nut cutlets. The Hercules Brothers!

---

75 Eugen Sandow (1867–1925) was a Prussian bodybuilder and showman.

Felix *stands aside. There is a drum roll. The* **Hercules Brothers** *come through the tabs. They are enormous men wearing white diamanté trunks decorated with jet aces of clubs. The band plays their signature tune which is probably the 'Skater's Waltz',*[76] *and they move majestically down the steps and take up a preparatory position in the centre of the dance floor.*

The lights fade.

Scene Two

The office. A few minutes later.

The office is quite small. There is a curtained window in the back wall. Under this there is an old leather couch.

On the left is a desk with a swivel chair. Behind this is a door leading to a passage which leads to the foyer.

Above the desk and next to the window is a small safe let into the wall.

On the right is a door leading into the club.

When the lights go up on the scene, **Snyder** *is seated in the swivel chair,* **Gus** *is smoking a cigarette on the couch and* **Benny** *is standing in front of the desk.*

Benny I don't like it, Snyder – I don't like any of it.

Snyder You wouldn't like Uncle Joe to lose his temper, now would you, Benny boy? Uncle Joe cam be very, very nasty when he loses his temper.

Benny It's Rita. If she finds out, she'll raise hell.

Snyder Then it's up to you to see that she doesn't find out.

Benny She's been suspicious ever since we nearly got caught out with that nylon business.

Snyder That was your fault, Benny boy. You were indiscreet. I hope it taught you a lesson.

Benny (*pleading*) But Joe – can't you do it some other way – somewhere else?

Snyder Of course I can, but I don't intend to. This is the way I've planned it, and this is the way it's going to be. I've told you you'll get your rake-off, so what are you bellyaching about? There isn't any danger, it's all cut and dried.

Benny What's in the package?

Snyder Ask no questions, Benny boy, and you won't hear no lies.

---

76 'The Skater's Waltz' or 'Der Schlittschuhläufer-Walzer' op. 183 was composed by Emile Waldteufel in 1882.

Benny You've got to tell me what's in it, or I won't have anything to do with it.

Snyder (*firmly*) Don't take that line with me, Benny – you'll do as I tell you, because you know damn well what sort of trouble you'll be in if you don't.

Benny That's blackmail.

Snyder That's right, Benny boy – that's just exactly what it is – blackmail. You're in quite deep with me one way or another. There are lots of things Rita doesn't know about, aren't there?

Benny Joe . . . look here . . .

Snyder (*with sudden violence*) Shut up! Don't waste any more of my time! Have you got it clear?

Benny (*giving in*) Yes – I suppose so.

Snyder (*sharply*) Supposing isn't enough. Give it back to me and I'll check.

Benny (*resigned*) A man called Alf Martin arrives with a mackintosh and the package is in the left-hand pocket of it . . .

Snyder It doesn't matter which pocket it's in . . . go on . . .

Benny You said the left-hand pocket.

Snyder Go on.

Benny Martin checks the mackintosh in the cloakroom, comes up to me by the entrance to the bar and gives me the ticket – then he scarpers.

Snyder Right.

Benny While the show's on I go to the cloakroom and collect the mac, telling Eva that it belongs to one of the customers who wants it – I'll have to do that, otherwise she'll wonder what the hell I'm up to.

Snyder All right. Then –?

Benny Then I take the package out of the pocket and put it in the safe here, and give it to you after the show . . .

Snyder Okay.

Benny Then I return the mac to the cloakroom – get the ticket again – and give it to Gus in the bar. Gus collects the mac after the show when the crowd's on the way out.

Snyder Brilliant! You're a clever boy, Benny – it's a pity you haven't got more guts.

Benny Won't you tell me what's in it – just in case anything goes wrong?

Snyder (*rising*) If anything goes wrong, Benny boy – you'll be in such bad trouble that you won't care what's in the God-damned package! Come on, Gus –

Gus *rises and follows* **Snyder** *out as the lights fade.*

Scene Three

The club. A little while later.

When the lights go up on the scene the **Hercules Brothers** *have just finished their act and are taking their calls. They spring up the steps and through the curtains and then spring back again, shaking their hands above their heads and bowing.*

When they have nearly exhausted their applause they finally disappear – and **Felix** *comes through the curtains. He runs down the steps, shakes his hands above his head just as they have done, and gets a laugh.*

Felix And now, ladies and gentlemen, girl friends and boy friends, waiters and whatnots – we present to you the Ace of the Ace of Clubs – the one and only – Pinkie Leroy!

He signals to the band, runs down the steps and disappears behind the stage.

The band plays some introductory chords and **Pinkie** *comes through the curtains. She is wearing a glittering dress and her entrance is greeted with loud applause. She comes slowly down the steps and begins her first song:*

'I Want to Find My Kind of Man'

Verse:

> In me you see a lonely girl
> Though certainly not the only girl
> Whose love-life is as cold as driven snow
> I can't explain why passion chills me so,
> I only know –

Refrain 1:

> I want to find my kind of man,
> My heart has designed my kind of man
> He may be – a gay hussar,[77]
> A movie star,
> A gentleman of renown,
> But when we meet I'll never let him down,
> And I shall do the best I can
> Tom, Dick or Harry,
> Till I find my kind of man.

Refrain 2:

> I want to find my kind of man,
> I've never defined my kind of man,
> He may be – a copper's nark,
> A City clerk,

---

77 A member of the calvary in Eastern European armies from the seventeenth to eighteenth centuries.

Or even a gigolo –
But when we meet I'll never let him go.
I want to find my kind of man,
And I shall do the best I can
Not to fall for any stinker
Hook line and sinker
Till I find my kind of man.

Refrain 3:

I want to find my kind of man
My dreams have designed my kind of man
He may be a country type
With tweeds and pipe
Or merely a London spiv[78] –
But when we meet, I'll give and give and give.
Until I find my kind of man,
I'll keep my heart so spick and span,
All decked out in love's apparel
Lock, stock and barrel,
When I find my kind of man.
When I find my kind of man,
We'll start a five-year – jive-year plan,
Maybe tinker – maybe tailor,
Soldier – or sailor,
But I'll find my kind of man.

Pinkie *sings the verse of the song on the steps, and then moves down on to the dance floor. She goes from table to table with the spotlight following her. She first of all stops at a table at which a bald old gentleman is sitting with a made-up young woman who might be his daughter but isn't. He looks slightly self-conscious while* **Pinkie** *sings to him; the young woman assumes an air of remote detachment.*

Pinkie *moves on to another table; the spotlight falls upon it and discovers* **Harry Hornby**, *who is sitting along with a bunch of roses lying on the table before him. When* **Pinkie** *sings to him, he stands up and gives her the roses. There is laughter and applause; she accepts them lightly with a little smile, and moves way across the floor.*

The spotlight falls on **Snyder**'s *table. He is sitting with* **Clarice**, *a weary-looking blonde, obviously the partner of some of his lesser enterprises.* **Pinkie**, *recognising him, moves quickly away to another table at which are sitting a young couple holding hands. They both giggle steadily as she sings to them. She then moves back again across the floor to* **Harry**'s *table, sings a special couplet to him and gives him one of the roses from the bunch he has just given her. There is more applause at this.*

As she is moving back again, she passes near **Snyder**'s *table. He jumps up and grabs her. She tries to push him away. Obviously irritated by the way she evaded his table*

---

78 Petty criminal who deals in black-market goods.

the first time, he tightens his grip on her, twists her arm behind her so that she gives a little cry of pain and kisses her forcibly. **Harry** *jumps up like a flash, runs swiftly across the floor and knocks him down. There is a general murmur from the audience.* **Snyder**, *livid with rage, staggers to his feet and pulls a gun.* **Pinkie** *sees him do it and jerks his arm up as he fires.*

There is an immediate uproar when the shots are fired. **Harry** *gives* **Snyder** *a hook on the jaw which knocks him out. He bangs his head against the leg of the table as he falls.* **Clarice** *screams. Other women scream too.*

Pinkie *grabs* **Harry** *by the hand and drags him out in the direction of the gentlemen's cloak room.*

The lights fade.

Scene Four

Soho Square. A minute later.

The scene is a 'scrim' front cloth of Soho Square. There are trees with dark buildings showing behind them. On the left centre there is a seat and, a little further to the left of the seat, a street lamp.

Pinkie *and* **Harry** *come running on from the right.* **Pinkie** *has a mackintosh hung round her shoulders.*

Pinkie   Let's sit down a minute while I get my breath.

Harry   (*anxiously – as they sit*)   You're all right, aren't you? He didn't hurt you?

Pinkie   You know, sailor, you'll get yourself into serious trouble if you go about knocking people down like that.

Harry   If serious trouble means getting you all to myself – I'll settle for it.

Pinkie   Romantic, hey?

Harry   All sailors are romantic – we're trained to it. Fighting the elements, you know – saving innocent maidens from worse than death – doing a good deed every day.

Pinkie   I thought that was Boy Scouts.

Harry   The same spirit, only more developed.

Pinkie   You're lucky not to be lying in hospital with a bullet inside you.

Harry   (*looking at her*)   I'm lucky all right, always have been. Here we are – you and me alone on a seat in the moonlight. What could be luckier than that?

Pinkie   Stop that silly sort of talk, and listen to me for a minute. You may be lucky and trained to fight the elements, but you're not trained to fight gangsters in nightclubs. They're liable to be a bit too quick for you. Snyder's a dangerous man, and unless you've killed him – which I doubt – you'll find yourself in a dark alley with your head bashed in.

Harry It would be worth it!

Pinkie Now look here – what's your name?

Harry Hornby – Harry Hornby – born of respectable parents near Guildford – intentions strictly honourable –

Pinkie Never mind about that now – I've got to get back to the club and see what's going on. You'd better beat it. (*She rises.*)

Harry (*earnestly – pulling her down again*) Please don't go – not for a minute –

Pinkie (*with not very sincere impatience*) What *is* all this?

Harry I've got seven days' leave because my ship's refitting at Chatham. Three of them have already gone. I've been to the club three nights running to see you – that's why I bought you the roses –

Pinkie I never said thank you for them, did I?

Harry You looked as though you liked them – that was enough for me.

Pinkie I did – but I'm afraid they got lost in the scuffle.

Harry May I bring you some more to-morrow?

Pinkie I wonder who this mackintosh belongs to? I just snatched it up as we nipped through the gents.

Harry May I –?

Pinkie (*with her head down, examining the mackintosh*) I'd rather you didn't come to the club again – really I would. You might get hurt.

Harry Would you mind?

Pinkie Don't be silly – of course I should I should feel sort of responsible.

Harry You are – you're responsible for more than you know.

Pinkie (*methodically taking things out of the mackintosh pockets*) One glove – one box of – (*she shakes it*) empty – two bus tickets – one brown paper parcel – (*shakes that too*) it doesn't rattle, so it can't be the missing diamonds – one handkerchief – on the dirty side –

Harry (*taking her hand*) I think you're wonderful – honest I do. I thought so in the club when you were singing your songs and wearing those lovely dresses – but I think you're more wonderful than ever now – sitting out here with me – quite ordinary – wearing someone else's mac –

Pinkie I must go back – really I must! They'll be wondering what's happened to me.

Harry (*looking into her eyes*) I'm wondering what's happened to me.

Pinkie Thanks ever so much for the roses, and for going for that son of a bitch when he tried to maul me. I wish you hadn't really, but in a way I'm glad you did . . .

There is a long pause, then she rams the things back into the mackintosh pocket and stands up.

I must go now. Good-night, Harry.

The package falls by the seat unperceived.

Harry (*also rising and taking her hand again*) Can't I see you again?

Pinkie It would be better if you didn't – truly it would.

Harry Why?

Pinkie Oh, I don't know – there are lots of reasons really.

Harry Give me one – one real one – and I won't say another word . . .

The music begins, and they sing.

Duet
'This Could Be True'

Verse:

> Chance brought us both together
> In a strange, unconventional way
> Here in the starlight with the night all round us
> Destiny seems to have caught and bound us.

Refrain 1:

> This could be true,
> This could be true.
> Let's both be terribly careful
> What we say or do.
> We may find – shadows on the stairway
> When we try to climb too high,
> We may find – hazards on the fairway
> N***** in the woodpile,
> Daring us to try – but –
> This could be right
> Love at first sight
> Let's take particular pains
> To keep the flame alight
> Let's face the fact
> That wonderful – wonderful moments in life are few,
> Let's defy those n****** in the woodpile, darling,
> This could be true.

Refrain 2:

> This could be true

This could be true
Maybe the ultimate goal
Our lives were leading to
Let's take care – people may resent us
Laugh at us and call us fools
Let's beware – time is only lent us
Stick to regulations
Follow all the rules – for
This could be sweet
Gay and discreet
If you will give me your hand
The future's at out feet.
This is the most –
Incredible, magical moment we ever knew
So to hell with rules and regulations, darling
This must be true!

At the end of the number **Harry** *takes* **Pinkie** *in his arms and kisses her.*

The music continues to play softly.

Harry To-morrow?

Pinkie All right – but don't come to the show – promise you won't! Snyder and his gang will be gunning for you – I'm certain they will!

Harry I can take care of myself.

Pinkie Don't be too sure of that.

Harry I've got to go down to Guildford to-morrow to see my mum, but I'll be back in the afternoon. What about having a bit of dinner with me before the show?

Pinkie Okay. Pick me up at the club after rehearsal, at about five-thirty. It'll be quite safe then in the broad daylight.

Harry I'll bring a couple of police dogs.

Pinkie Police constables would be better.

Harry Yes, but not so affectionate.

Pinkie (*kissing him lightly*) Good-night, sailor.

Harry Good-night, Pinkie.

Pinkie *goes off.*

Harry *looks after her for a moment, then, smiling happily, sings a reprise of the song. He catches sight of the package lying by the seat, picks it up, wonders for a moment whether or not to take it back to the club, decides not to and saunters off with it as the lights fade.*

Scene Five

The club. A minute or two later.

The club is empty, and unattractively lit by a working light. The band has packed up, the stage curtain is up, disclosing the bare back wall.

Benny *is sitting at one of the empty tables.* **Eva**, *the cloak-room girl, is standing in front of him in tear.*

Gus *is sitting on one of the other tables, smoking a cigarette.*

Benny Somebody must have taken it – who was it?

Eva I've told you – I don't know! It was hanging on a peg by the door – I found the ticket on the floor just by where it was hanging – it must have dropped off.

Benny You must have seen whoever it was take it – they'd have to climb over the counter under your silly nose to get at it!

Eva It must have been when I ran out – when the shots were fired. Crowds of people came at me with a rush – I didn't know where I was . . .

Benny You had no right to run out. You ought to have stayed where you were, whatever happened.

Eva (*with spirit*) It's no use shouting at me, Mr Lucas – I've told you all I know, and that's that, and if you don't like it you know what you can do with it!

Benny Get out! You're fired!

Eva (*losing her temper*) That's fine with me – but the next time there's a shooting up in this crooked lousy joint – do me a favour and get in front of the gun.

Eva *stamps out.*

Gus (*laughs unpleasantly*) The boss'll be pleased to hear about this when he comes round, and no error.

Benny Shut up!

Gus He'll die laughing, I shouldn't wonder.

Benny I wish to God he would.

Gus That's not a nice way to talk, Benny boy – not nice at all. The boss wouldn't like it.

Pinkie *comes quietly on at the back, wearing the mackintosh. Upon seeing* **Benny** *and* **Gus**, *she stops.*

Benny What the hell am I to do?

Gus Just find that mac, and quick – that's all you've got to do.

Benny You're enjoying yourself, aren't you?

Gus You could always advertise in *The Times*, of course. 'Mackintosh missing from smart West End Club – contains valuable package – kindly return and oblige. Handsome reward offered – Drinks on the house, and one night of love with Pinkie Leroy'!

Benny You leave Pinkie out of this! If Snyder hadn't made one of his dirty passes at her we wouldn't be in this jam now.

Pinkie, *upon hearing the package mentioned, puts her hand in the pocket of the mackintosh to see if it is there all right. She discovers that it isn't, quickly searches the other pockets, puts her hand up to her mouth in panic, and then begins to tip-toe away.* **Benny** *turns and caches sight of her.*

Pinkie Where the hell have you been?

Pinkie (*turning – deciding to brazen it out*) Who are you shouting at?

Benny Where have you been?

Pinkie Out. I don't stand about dreaming while your refined upper-class patrons start firing guns off in my ear.

Benny That mac! Where did you get that mac?

Pinkie I took it off a peg in the gents on my way through the side door. What are you going to do about it? Have me up for stealing?

Benny (*snatching it off her shoulders*) Give it here!

Pinkie Where's the fire?

Benny (*going through the pockets frantically*) It's not there!

Pinkie What's not where?

Benny There was a package in it – where is it?

Pinkie How should I know? I don't go about rifling other people's pockets!

Rita *comes out of the office.*

Rita What's all the shouting about?

Pinkie Just Benny going out of his mind, that's all.

Benny (*calming down*) Pinkie happened to grab one of the customer's macs when she ran out – he's making a scene about it.

Rita What customer? What's his name?

Benny I – er – I didn't catch his name.

Rita How are you going to get it back to him, then?

Benny He said he'd call round to-morrow evening.

Rita (*to* **Gus**) Are you mixed up with this?

Benny (*quickly*)   No – it's nothing to do with Gus.

Gus   I just popped in to have a little chat with Benny.

Rita   Well, you can pop out again – the club's closed.

Gus   Now see here, Rita . . .

Rita   And don't 'Rita' me, either. I don't like you, or your friends – so get out and stay out.

Gus (*unpleasantly*)   I don't think Joe Snyder would like to hear you ordering me about like that.

Rita   What Mr Snyder likes or doesn't like is a matter of supreme indifference to me.

Gus   You may find out that it matters a lot.

Rita   Don't you threaten me, you slimy little rat!

Gus   If you're afraid your precious Benny's going to get into trouble, you're right – he's in trouble now – bad trouble. Good-night, all – nice to have known you!

Gus *goes out.*

Rita (*to* **Benny**)   What did he mean by that? What trouble are you in?

Benny   Nothing. He was talking cobblers – trying to frighten you.

Rita   What were all those lies you were telling me about a mackintosh?

Pinkie   It's nothing, Rita – really it isn't. I grabbed up somebody's mac as I ran out with the sailor, and . . .

Benny (*quickly*)   Where did you go?

Pinkie   Only just round the corner into the square.

Benny (*grabbing her by the hand*)   Come with me – I want to see exactly where you were.

Rita   The good name of this club is my business. This is something to do with Snyder, isn't it? It must be, otherwise Gus wouldn't have been hanging about. Tell me, Benny – you must tell me.

Benny (*shouting*)   Lay off me, I tell you, and mind your own business!

Rita   I got you out of one jam with Snyder, and you promised you'd have nothing more to do with him. For God's sake be sensible, and use your loaf. I might be able to get you out of this if only you'll tell me what's going on. (*She puts her hand on his arm.*) Please, Benny . . .

Benny (*shaking her off violently*)   Stop pawing me about!

Rita (*crying out*)   Benny –!

Benny (*losing control*) I'm sick to death of you – is that clear? Sick to death of you! I'm sick of being bossed about and being told what to do and what not to do. There was a time – when we were both of us a bit younger, dear – when you weren't so damned interested in the good name of the club and being respectable – but all the good times we had together are over and done with since you decided to run the bloody joint like a church social. I wouldn't be in this jam now if you weren't so mingy with the money your old man left you!

Rita (*quietly*) You're no good, Benny – I suppose I've always known it, really. Go on, Pinkie – go and help him to find whatever it is he's looking for. I'll remember what you said, Benny. Good-night.

Benny (*ashamed*) Rita – I'm sorry – I didn't mean –

Rita We'll talk it all over to-morrow – if you're not in gaol!

Benny Rita . . .

Rita Get out, Benny. You damned fool!

Benny *goes out, dragging* **Pinkie** *with him.* **Rita**, *left alone, sinks down at one of the tables. She rests her head in her hands for a moment, then pulls herself together and fumbles in her bag for a cigarette. She finds one, lights it, and sings.*

'Nothing Can Last for Ever'

Verse:

>Why should I mind?
>Why should I weep for him?
>Love as frail as ours could never last.
>A little time will pass
>And everything we've said and done
>Will lie forgotten in the past.
>Yesterday
>Swiftly fades away
>Now it is over there's nothing to say
>Early or late
>Guided by Fate
>Passion will lie to you
>And when that moment comes
>It's wise to face the truth,
>The best of it belongs to Youth.
>Why should I mind?
>My heart will keep for him
>Some of the love he left behind.

Refrain:

>Nothing can last for ever,
>Love is a lost endeavour,

Foolishly I
Would plan and scheme,
Foolishly try
To hold my dream
Dreading the hour of waking
Dreading the moment of breaking
Now it is dead
And buried in the past,
Nothing can ever last.

At end of number the lights fade.

Scene Six

The club. 5.30 the next afternoon.

Felix, *wearing a coloured open-neck shirt and grey flannel trousers, is rehearsing the* **Girls** *in a new dance routine.*

The **Girl**, **June April**, **Betty Clements**, **Ruby Fowler**, **Sunny Claire**, **Dorren Harvey**, **Greta Hughes**, **Mimi Joshua** *and* **Dawn O'Hara**, *are in practice dress, which consists of abbreviated shorts and blouses or tight-fitting jerseys.*

At a table downstage are seated **Baby Belgrave**, **Yvonne Hall** *and* **Mavis Dean**. *These three are not in practice dress.* **Baby** *and* **Yvonne** *are looking at a movie magazine;* **Mavis** *is knitting.*

Sammy Blake, *a pale, rather unhealthy-looking young man, is playing the piano. He has a cigarette hanging from his under-lip and a cup of tea on top of the piano.*

When the lights go up on the scene, the number is in full swing. The **Girls** *are in line on the dance floor with their arms round each other's shoulders, doing right leg high kicks. At a given moment in the number they separate, do a few turns interspersed with taps, and skip in concerted formation up the steps towards the stage.* **June April** *trips and falls.*

Felix Sweet God! You've done it again!

June It's getting on to the step after the turn.

Felix I'll tell you something else it is – it's not thinking what you're doing. Back again.

The **Girls** *re-form their line.* **Felix** *stamps his foot twice and shouts,* 'One – two!' *The routine is repeated. This time* **June** *manages not to fall, and the number continues until just before the end, when the eight* **Girls** *are required to dance lightly up and down the steps three times and exit. The others do it all right, but* **June** *lose count, and, while the others are going off, turns and scampers up the steps alone.* **Felix**, *with a groan of despair, claps his hands and stops the music.*

Felix Wherever it is you're going, dear, drop us a postcard to say you've arrived safely.

June Sorry – I lost count.

Felix Oh, that's what it was? I thought you were just tired of it all.

June As a matter of fact, I am. I didn't get to bed fill five this morning.

Felix You must be slipping. Back again! One – two –

The **Girls** *re-form their line and start again.* **Baby** *whispers something to* **Yvonne***, and they both go off into gales of laughter.* **Felix** *turns on them in a fury.*

Felix Will you *keep quiet*? How the hell can I rehearse with you squawking like bloody parrots?

Baby (*to* **Yvonne**) Did you hear anything, dear?

Yvonne Just the wind in the willows.

Baby I thought it was mice.

Felix If you were as funny on the stage as you are off, you'd get a percentage.

Baby Save all that flashing humour for the show, dear – it's wasted on us.

Felix The trouble with this lousy set-up is that there's no discipline.

Baby (*rising*) Listen, my fine-feathered friend – don't you talk to us about discipline. Just remember that you were with ENSA,[79] not the Commandos.

Felix And what was wrong with ENSA?

Baby Come and sit down, dear, while I explain – it'll only take three and a half hours.

At this moment the number comes to an end. The **Girls***, having made their exit, come clattering back.*

Yvonne See what happens when you leave 'em alone? They get it right!

Felix Break rehearsal for a quarter of an hour – I can't stand any more of this – (*with a baleful look at* **Baby**) – beating my brains out over a lot of giggling amateurs!

Felix *stamps off.*

The **Girls** *relax – some of them sit down on the steps.* **Harry** *comes on, carrying a bunch of roses.*

Baby Hold on to everything, girls, the fleet's in.

Harry Is Miss Leroy here?

Baby She's round the corner at the dressmaker's, having a fitting – she won't be long.

Yvonne You're the one who was here last night, aren't you?

Harry That's right.

Yvonne Pleased to meet you, I'm sure. We all got home an hour earlier on account of your little dust-up with Snyder.

---

[79] The Entertainments National Service (ENSA) was a Second World War performance organization that was established in 1939 by Basil Dean and Leslie Henson that sent British performers around the globe.

June It was wonderful what you did – I said to my friend Mr Lazarus afterwards – that's a sailor all over, I said.

Harry He asked for it, and he got it.

Baby Come over to the Moo-Cow and have a cup of coffee with us while you're waiting for Pinkie. We'll leave word where you are.

Harry (*grinning*) Thanks – I'd like to.

Dawn Where's your ship?

Harry I left it tied up under Charing Cross Bridge.

Doreen Were you in the war?

Harry Of course I was.

Sunny Sink any submarines?

Harry Hundreds of 'em!

Betty Turn it up!

Harry Well, seventeen all told, including one that got hysterical and scuttled itself before we could get to it.

June My auntie knew a sailor once, but he went away.

Harry That's the trouble with sailors – here today and gone to-morrow.

June Wil you be gone to-morrow?

Harry Maybe – but I'll come back.

June That's what *he* said to my auntie.

Harry *sings.*

'Something About a Sailor'

Verse 1:

> The songs they sing of the rollicking deep
> Are rather out of key
> But one thing you'll agree – is true
> That men who work for the women who weep
> Acquire a roving eye
> Nobody in their senses would deny.

Refrain 1:

> There's always something about a sailor
> Nobody's ever able to define
> There's a gay, salty sort of tang about
> His devil-may-care
> His nautical air

> Of brawn and brine
> When wives and sweethearts are told the fleet's in
> Most of them have a perm and tuck the sheets in
> Girls in Gosport[80] hit an all-time high,
> Wives in Weymouth[81] have a spree
> Brides in bridal veils
> Will vault the altar rails
> To follow – the fellow who follows the sea.

Verse 2:

> The course is set for original sin
> On every man-of-war
> As everyone ashore – well knows.
> Yo-ho, my lads, and a bottle of gin
> Inspires the happy thought
> Of somebody else's wife in every port.

Refrain 2:

> There's always something about a sailor
> Every time he sets his foot ashore
> All the pubs do a roaring trade until
> Each swaggering Jack
> Goes staggering back
> To sea once more.
> So hang the flags out and throw confetti
> Liberty boats are heading for the jetty,
> Tarts are tearful when the anchor's weighted,
> Geishas grumble on the quay,
> Every courtesan
> From Tyne[82] to Turkestan[83]
> Will follow – the fellow who follows the sea.

At the end of the number, **Harry** *and the* **Girls** *dance off.*

The stage is empty for a moment. **Rita**, **Benny** *and* **Detective-Inspector Warrilove** *come out of the office.*

Benny   Would you like a little drink before you go?

Warrilove   No, thanks – it's a bit early for me.

Rita   It was nice of you to come and see us in a friendly way, Inspector – we appreciate it.

---

80 A town in Hampshire, England.
81 A seaside town in Dorset, England.
82 The River Tyne is located in north-east England.
83 Also spelled Turkistan, it is a historical region in Central Asia.

Warrilove   I don't want to have to close you down, you know, but any more brawling and shooting, and you've had it.

Rita   There won't be any more, I promise. It wasn't really out fault last night. This man made a pass at Pinkie Leroy while she was singing her first number and the sailor jumped up and went for him. It was all over before we could do anything.

Warrilove   And you don't know who the man was?

Benny   No. There was a bit of an uproar when the shots where fired, and a lot of people made a bee line for the street. His friends must have got him away in the crowd.

Warrilove   And you don't know the sailor's name, either?

Benny   I'd know him if I saw him. He's been here a couple of nights running – but he disappeared too.

Warrilove   You know a man called Snyder, don't you?

Benny (*after a slight hesitation*)   Yes – he's been here once or twice.

Warrilove   It wasn't by any chance him that started the row last night and fired the shots?

Benny   Of course not. (*With a quick look at* **Rita**.) I know him by sight – so does Rita. Don't you, Rita?

Rita   Yes – I know him by sight all right.

Warrilove   He wasn't here last night at all?

Benny   Not to my knowledge. Did you see him, Rita?

Rita (*looking* **Warrilove** *in the eye*)   No.

Warrilove (*with a slight smile*)   Very well, Mrs Marbury. I think I understand. I suspect that you know as well as I do that Snyder has a bad record, and that he has got his fingers in a whole lot of dirty little rackets all over town. If you want to keep your club open and above board, you'd be well advised to keep him and his friends out of it.

Rita   Yes, Inspector.

Warrilove   He is also on the suspect list over the Sunningdale jewel robbery. We shall get him eventually all right, and when we do, you'd better see that your noses are clean. I thought I'd just warn you. Good-bye. (*He shakes hands with* **Rita**.)

Rita   Good-bye, Inspector. Thank you again.

Benny *takes* **Warrilove** *out.*

Rita *walks about thoughtfully for a moment.* **Benny** *comes back.*

Benny (*with forced cheerfulness*)   Whew! That was a bit tricky. You were wonderful, Rita! So help me, I've never seen anything like the way you handled him – it was –

Rita (*cutting him short*)   I don't like having to lie, Benny – for you or anyone else.

Rita *goes back into the office and slams the door.*

Benny *irritably snatches the cigarette out of his mouth, throws it on the floor and stamps on it.* **Pinkie** *comes on from behind the stage. She is wearing street clothes.*

Pinkie   What's happened to the rehearsal? Where's everybody gone?

Benny (*irritably*)   How the hell do I know?

Pinkie   What's the matter with you, anyway?

Benny   Sign off the quiz programme, there's a good girl.

Pinkie   More trouble?

Benny   We've had the police here nosing around – asking damn-fool questions – all on account of that upstanding, four-square sailor of yours.

Pinkie   He isn't mine.

Benny   Well, whoever he is, you'd better tell him to stay away from this club, or it will be the worse for him.

Pinkie   Tell him yourself, and see what you get! And while we're on the subject of general reform, I'd like to explain something to you, and it's this – the next time anybody starts any monkey business when I'm singing that number, I'll walk out on you once and for all, and you can get someone else to go tarting round the tables getting herself groped by your dirty crook friends!

Benny   Snyder didn't mean nay harm. Why didn't you pass it off with a laugh, instead of screaming like a scalded cat?

Pinkie   Listen here, Benny. I'm the star of this show – such as it is – and I'm not paid to be mauled about by any greasy racketeer you happen to be caught up with.

Benny   What do you mean by that?

Pinkie   Exactly what I say.

Benny (*conciliatorily*)   You've got it all wrong, Pinkie. Snyder doesn't mean anything to me – he's just a paying customer, that's all.

Pinkie   Like hell he is!

Benny   Look here, Pink –

Pinkie   I'm looking. I've been looking for a long time. Why don't you use your loaf and run this place on the level? It's doing well enough, isn't it, without you having to go behind Rita's back and do a lot of under-the-counter finagling?

Benny   Mind your own business.

Pinkie   It is my business. I've got to make a career for myself, and I don't want to have it bitched by bad publicity.

Benny (*with charm*) Don't you worry about your career, sweetheart. You're all set. There's nobody can put over a number like you can – you're going places.

Pinkie Yes, but not in a police van!

Benny I appreciate your talking to me frankly like this, Pinkie – truly I do – and I'm sorry for what happened last night.

Pinkie Cut out the smooge, Benny, and keep that breathless charm for those who can't see through it.

Benny (*with a smile*) Where's your sailor boy? Have you got him locked in the lulu?

Pinkie He isn't my sailor boy – and how should I know where he is, anyway?

Benny All right, all right, I only wondered – seeing the roses and putting two and two together.

Pinkie (*quickly*) What roses!

Benny (*pointing to the roses* **Harry** *has left on the table*) There.

Pinkie (*running to them*) Oh!

Benny Where's his ship?

Pinkie (*smelling the roses*) Chatham.

Benny It's a long journey to Chatham, old girl – you'll need all your courage.

Pinkie Stop being so witty – my ribs are aching!

Benny Cross my palm with silver, lady, and I'll tell your fortune.

Pinkie He shouldn't have wasted his money . . . (*She sniffs the roses again.*) They smell lovely.

Benny (*dreamily*) I see a dark stranger – something to do with the wide open spaces – I see a tatty little house in Chatham – by the window there sits a faded woman who was once beautiful – she is waiting – waiting – her hands that were once white are now red and calloused from ceaseless housework . . .

Pinkie Shut up!

Benny There is a child in her arms . . . two more at her knee . . . and another at Borstal . . .

Pinkie Do me a favour and cut the comedy, Benny – it's getting me down.

Benny Just as you say, lady! (*As he goes.*) Love's certainly a beautiful thing, but you won't forget about that career of yours, will you?

He goes.

Pinkie (*calling after him*) Go to hell!

Pinkie *sits down at the table with the roses in her lap. She looks at them and smiles, then she gives a sigh. The music plays softly. She sings:*

'I'd Never Know'

Verse:

> I met a boy – an ordinary character
> A little shy, a bit reserved
> Until that day – my heart had known no trespasser
> I put my trust in Fate
> I knew my path was straight
> But now my path has swerved
> And I'm alone in time and space
> Now the whole world is quite a different place.

Refrain 1:

> Why is the summer giving
> London this lovely glow?
> What is this joy of living?
> Without him – I'd never, never know –
> I'd never, never know.
> Why do I feel excited
> Each time he says 'Hallo'
> Why do the streets seem lighted?
> Without him – I'd never, never know –
> I'd never, never know.
> He wouldn't please the highbows
> Or drive Alan Ladd[84] from the screen,
> But when he lifts his eyebrows
> I blush like a girl of fifteen.
> Soon it will all be over
> He'll say good-bye and go –
> I love him so –
> But will he ever know?
> Will he ever, ever know?

Refrain 2:

> Why do I like 'torch numbers'
> Crooned on the radio?
> Why do they haunt my slumbers?
> Without him – I'd never, never know –
> I'd never, never know.
> Why do I sing quite loudly
> Hurrying through Soho?
> Why do I walk so proudly?

---

[84] Alan Ladd (1913-1964) was an American film actor and producer, particularly known for Westerns.

Without him – I'd never, never know,
I'd never, never know.
I'd never quite surrender
I wasn't cut out for a slave,
But when his voice goes tender,
My heart has a permanent wave.
When he's 'in front' I tremble,
Can't hardly play the show,
I love him so – but will he ever know?
Will he ever, ever know?

At end of number the lights fade.

The lights come up again on:

'Three Juvenile Delinquents'

Verse 1:

>Three juvenile delinquents
>Juvenile delinquents
>Happy as can be – We
>Waste no time
>On the wherefores and whys of it;
>We like crime
>And that's about the size of it.
>People say that films demoralise us
>Psycho-analyse us
>Blimey what a game!
>They don't know how to treat us,
>For if they should beat us
>That would never do.
>When they say 'Go steady!'
>We've the answer ready:
>———— And the same to you!

Verse 2:

>Three juvenile delinquents
>Juvenile delinquents
>Happy as can be – We
>Hit and run
>For the thrill and the sport of it;
>Nice clean fun
>And that's the long and short of it.
>Dear old ladies often get the vapours
>When we meet them after dark – whoo!
>Then next day we read about our capers
>In the daily papers,

Blimey what a lark!
We thrill the Sunday readers,
But the silly bleeders
Haven't got a clue.
When the Judge says 'Chokey'[85]
We say 'Okey-dokey'
———— And the same to you!

Verse 3:

Three juvenile delinquents
Juvenile delinquents
Happy as can be – We
Lick our chops
When we read what they write of us.
All the cops
Hate the bloody sight of us.
Once we pinched a Cadillac and drove her
From the Marble Arch to Kew;
Hit a fat old geezer in a Rover
Fairly bowled her over,
Blimey what a do!
We said 'You mustn't fuss, dear,
There's a lovely bus, dear,
Number twenty-two.
If we've bruised your bonnet,
Stick a plaster on it',
————And the same to you!

Scene Seven

Soho Square. About 10.30 p.m.

When the lights go up on the scene, **Pinkie** *and* **Harry** *are sitting on the seat locked in each other's arms.*

Pinkie (*breaking away*)   Oh, Harry!

Harry (*looking into her eyes*)   Oh, Pinkie! I can hardly believe it – really I can't!

Pinkie   Neither can I.

Harry   You do mean it, don't you? I mean, you're not just being kind?

Pinkie   No – I'm not just being kind – I think I'm being a damn fool, though.

Harry   Why do you say that?

Pinkie   Oh, I don't know. I'm probably laying up a nice little dose of misery for myself.

85 Chokey is British slang for prison.

Harry I love you.

Pinkie I know.

Harry Does that make you miserable?

Pinkie You'll be going away in a couple of days –

Harry Only to Chatham. You promised you'd come down one day. You will, won't you?

Pinkie I'll need all my courage. (*She laughs suddenly.*)

Harry Why are laughing?

Pinkie Something Benny said.

Harry Benny?

Pinkie He was teasing me about you.

Harry I'll clock him!

Pinkie You've clocked quite enough people to be going on with.

Harry You're fond of him, aren't you?

Pinkie Yes – I suppose I am in a sort of way.

Harry Was he ever – I mean – did you ever –?

Pinkie No, Harry. He wasn't ever, and we didn't ever. We're just friends. I like him because he's good-hearted under all that 'madam' he puts on, and I'm worried about him because he's weak and easily led and thinks he's much smarter than he is. Rita does her best to keep him under control. She's been crazy about him for years. But he keeps bad company and I'm afraid he'll land himself in a jug if he's not careful.

Harry Black market?

Pinkie Yes – in a small way – you know, nylons and French perfume and what not. There's something going on between him and Snyder now, and that's liable to be dangerous. You should have seen the fuss that went on about me taking that mackintosh last night! You'd think I'd pinched the crown jewels!

Harry That parcel – I forgot to tell you –

Pinkie What about it?

Harry I picked it up – after you'd gone – it had fallen down by the seat.

Pinkie Where is it now?

Harry In my locker at the YMCA.

Pinkie Oh dear!

Harry What shall I do with it? Give it to the police?

Pinkie No. Leave it where it is and bring it to me to-morrow.

Harry Oughtn't we to open it?

Pinkie No. It's nothing to do with us, and the less we know about it the better. I'll give it back to Benny – he was working himself into a lather over it last night . . .

Harry Maybe it's something we ought to hand over to the police.

Pinkie I don't care what is it – you and me aren't going to know anything about it. Promise me you won't open it.

Harry All right, I promise.

Pinkie And you'll bring it to me after to-morrow's rehearsal?

Harry It's as good an excuse as any – to see you again.

Pinkie You don't need any excuse now. (*She gets up hurriedly.*) I must go. I shall be off. The first show starts in a half an hour.

Harry (*also rising*) I'll be there.

Pinkie Why are you so stubborn? I've told you I'd rather you didn't come to the club after dark – I'll meet you anywhere you say afterwards – I swear I will!

Harry I can take care of myself.

Pinkie That's what you think.

Harry Besides, I want to hear you sing again. Even if I can't have you to myself, it's better than nothing.

Pinkie I really would rather you didn't.

Harry Don't worry – I'll keep my eyes skinned. If I see anything that looks like trouble, I'll scarper – I always do.

Pinkie (*kissing him*) Oh, Harry!

Harry (*with his arms round her*) What's the matter? You're trembling.

Pinkie (*in a muffled voice*) So you always run away from trouble, do you?

Harry He who fights and runs away lives to fight another day.

Pinkie What about this? Are you going to run away from this?

Harry (*laughing*) This isn't a fight – yet!

Pinkie (*kissing him again quickly*) So long, sailor – see you later.

Harry Okay!

Pinkie *runs off.*

Harry *stands looking after her for a moment. The music starts, and he sings:*

'*Sail Away*'

Verse 1:

> When a sailor goes to sea
> Though he leaves his love behind

Time and tide will set him free
From the grief inside him.
Sea and sky will ease his heart
Regulate his troubled mind,
Every sailor has a chart
And a star to guide him – home.

Refrain 1:

When the storm clouds are riding through a winter sky –
Sail away – sail way.
When the love-light is fading in your sweetheart's eye
Sail away – sail away.
When you feel your song is orchestrated wrong
Why should you prolong
Your stay?
When the wind and the weather blow your dreams sky-high
Sail away – sail away!

Verse 2:

Love is meant to make us glad
Love can make the world go round,
Love can drive you raving mad
Torment and upset you.
Love can give your heart a jolt
But philosophers have found
That it's wise to do a bolt
When it starts to get you – down.

Refrain 2:

When your life seems too difficult to rise above,
Sail away – sail away.

When your heart feels as dreary as a worn-out glove,
Sail away – sail away.
But when soon or late
You recognise your fate,
That will be your great, great day
On the wings of the morning with your own true love,
Sail away – sail away – sail away!

At the end of the song the lights fade.

Scene Eight

The club. About midnight. During the first show.

When the lights go up on the scene, the show is in full swing. The audience is applauding while **Baby Belgrave**, **Yvonne Hall** *and* **Mavis Dean** *are taking a call. They are dressed* *as little girls with large bows in their hair and all three are holding toffee apples on sticks. When they finally disappear* **Felix** *comes through the curtains.*

Felix   And now, lasses and lads – boys and girls – Swan and Edgars and Fortnum and Masons – we come to one of the high spots of this glittering, colossal and overdressed entertainment. Our one and only Pinkie Leroy portraying one of the most glamorous lovers that history has ever known. A little girl who started in a small way and finished in a big way – if you all know what I mean – and I am afraid you do. Ladies and gentlemen – allow me to present to you – the Toast of Paris – Boney's Baby – the Empress Josephine![86]

Felix *claps his hands. There is a fanfare from the drum and saxophone.*

He bounds down the steps and disappears.

The curtains part, disclosing a painted act drop of the Palace of Fontainebleau. The eight **Girls**, *dressed as Directoire beauties and gallants respectively, mince uneasily down the steps.*

June   La! But her Imperial Majesty is in good form this evening!

Dawn (*a gallant*)   Has she not every reason to be, with His Majesty her husband away at the wars?

Sunny   Fie, Monsieur Le Dook! You have been listening to idle gossips, I'll be bound.

Doreen   Hist! She approaches!

Pinkie *enters, dressed as the Empress Josephine. She is wearing a white dress, a long blue velvet cloak and a glittering crown of diamonds. She comes down the steps with great dignity, and sings:*

'Josephine'

Verse 1:

> The lady was beautiful – the lady was dark,
> She wasn't too dutiful – but still left her mark
> On volumes of history – and thousands of cheques
> And all through the mystery – of 'Ole Debbil Sex'!

Refrain 1:

> Josephine – Josephine
> From the first was rather chic,
> As a tot she would trot
> Through the island of Martinique
> Her fortune was told by an aged crone
> Who prophesied fame and romance,
> And who hissed in her ear – the outrageous idea
> That she'd also be Empress of France!

---

86 Joséphine Bonaparte, born Marie Josèphe Rose Taschar de La Pagerie (1763–1814), was the Empress of France and first wife of Emperor Napoleon I.

Josephine – Josephine
Had, with men, a set routine,
And the people who thought
Her technique was self-taught
Didn't know – Josephine.

Verse 2:

Whatever she nearly did – from five to fifteen
We know that she really did – begin the Beguine.
On first meeting Bonaparte[87] – she murmured 'Hell's bells!'
You let down the tone, apart – from everything else!

Refrain 2:

Josephine – Josephine
Very seldom lost control
Though her wit – was a bit
Over-seasoned with 'Sauce Creole'.[88]
She very soon married this short young man
Who talked about soldiers all day
But who wasn't above – making passionate love
In a coarse, rather Corsican way.
Josephine – wasn't keen
And she made an ugly scene,
Until Bonaparte said 'We must rumple the bed!
Just for show – Josephine!'

Refrain 3:

Josephine – Josephine
Though a Queen remained at home
While her lord was abroad
Sending post-cards, in code, from Rome.
He often appeared, with a three-day beard
From Austria, Poland or Spain,
And one dreadful night, he arrived, rather tight
Having balled up the Russian campaign.
Josephine – turning green –
Cried 'Whatever does this mean?'
Then Napoleon said 'Whoops!
I have lost all my troops
In the snow, Josie –
Oh, Josie
Snow – Josephine!'

As the number finishes the lights fade.

---

87 Reference to Napoleon Bonaparte.
88 Reference to Creole cuisine, popular in the Southern United States, particularly New Orleans.

Scene Nine

The office. About 1 a.m.

Gus *is by the window.* **Snyder,** *with a grubby bandage round his head, is standing by the door that leads into the club. He is holding the door a crack open and peering through it.*

Snyder   It's all right – he's here.

Gus   Fine.

Snyder   He's just come out of the bar.

Gus   Alone?

Snyder   Yes. He's got his God-damned roses with him, too.

Gus   He'll wish they were arum lilies by the time I've finished with him.

Snyder   Window all right?

Gus   Window okay.

Snyder   Where's Benny?

Gus   Moxie's taking care of him in the bar.

Snyder   Rita got the phone message all right?

Gus   I saw her go – Bert got her a taxi.

Snyder   Detective-Inspector Bloody Warrilove will get a nice surprise when that painted old meat-axe wakes him up in the middle of the night!

Gus   Has he sat down yet?

Snyder   Yes. He's sipping his beer.

Gus   Fancy ordering beer at a place like this! You'd think he'd know better, wouldn't you?

Snyder   The show's starting – better have the lights out.

Gus   Right. (*He switches out the lights.*)

Snyder   Let's have it. I'll check.

Gus   Wallop – straight through here – out of the window – down the fire escape – car at the corner of the square.

Snyder   He's all set – sitting as innocent as a newborn babe – just a yard away from this door. We can relax now. She won't be on for a few minutes.

Gus   Okay.

The lights fade.

Scene Ten

The lights go up on the scene as **Pinkie** *comes on to her applause.*

She starts singing 'I Want to Find My Kind of Man'.

The stage is dark except for the spotlight which follows her from table to table. After she has gone to two tables she crosses over and arrives at **Harry**'s *table for the end of the first refrain. She smiles and winks at him. He makes a movement to give her the roses, but she motions him to wait. She moves away across the room again, singing the second refrain. She stops at a table at which there is a man sitting with two women, possibly his mother-in-law and wife.* **Pinkie** *sings to him, takes up his glass and takes a sip.*

There is the sound of a scuffle and a strangled cry on the other side of the stage. **Pinkie** *doesn't hear it, and moves to another table at which there is a party of five, three men and two girls. They all seem to be pretty drunk, so she leaves them quickly and moves back across the floor to* **Harry**'s *table. The spotlight falls on it.* **Harry** *has disappeared. His cap, a glass of beer and the bunch of roses are on the table. His chair is overturned.* **Pinkie**, *with a look of horror, falters, pulls herself together, sings the last phrase of the song, and runs quickly up the steps and vanishes through the curtains.*

Felix, *who is standing by the band, realises there is something wrong, and claps his hands. The band strikes up the 'Balloon' number. The* **Girls** *enter from each side of the stage carrying coloured balloons and singing shrilly:*

'Would You Like to Stick a Pin in My Balloon?'

Would you like to stick a pink in my balloon, Daddy?
Would you like to stick a pin in my balloon?
Just make a grab
When you hear the melody stop
One little jab
And you'll hear a beautiful pop
If you'll only suit the action to the tune, Daddy
You'll be bound to get the hang of it soon
All the boys I know can do the trick
So Daddy, Daddy, won't you stick
A pin in my balloon?

The curtain falls.

Act Two

Scene One

The club. About two minutes later.

When the curtain rises the **Girls** *are finishing the 'Balloon' number. They exit to rather tepid applause.*

Felix *comes through the curtains with* **Baby Belgrave**. *On their appearance the band plays some introductory chords.* **Felix** *is wearing a coloured blazer, white flannels and a straw hat.* **Baby** *is in a gay summer frock. They come down the steps and sing:*

'On a Boat, on a Lake, with My Darling'

Verse:

> In my dreams I often get a
> Vision that's divine
> Of a very still lagoon
> With you in white
> And me in blue
> Alone in quite
> A safe canoe.
> Failing this what could be better
> Than the Serpentine
> On an afternoon
> In love – in June?

Refrain:

> In a boat, on a lake, with my darling
> In the heat of a sweet summer day
> There's the sound of the breeze
> In the green willow trees
> And the noise of the town fades away
> Letting time flutter by like a starling
> As we gaze into
> The infinite blue
> Above
> Hand in hand
> Heart to heart
> Just a moment apart
> In a boat, on a lake, with my love.

In the course of the second refrain the **Girls** *reappear in summer frocks and wander about singing languidly. Finally the curtains part, disclosing a backcloth of the Serpentine, in front of which* **Felix** *and* **Baby**, *who have made an unobtrusive exit while the* **Girls** *were singing, are discovered reclining in a canvas boat and singing the last eight bars of the number.*

As the number finishes the lights fade.

Scene Two

Soho Square. The same time as the preceding scene.

Gus *and* **Snyder** *come on from the right dragging the inert body of* **Harry** *between them. Just as they get to the seat they stop.*

Gus Look out! – Copper!

They quickly sit on the seat and prop **Harry** *up between them. A* **Policeman** *comes on from the left. He stops and looks at them suspiciously.*

Snyder (*affably*) Good evening, officer.

Policeman What's going on?

Snyder Nothing – why?

Policeman (*looking at* **Harry**) What's the matter with him?

Snyder Brandy on top of beer. It's my young cousin. He passed out cold – you know what sailors are!

Gus He's got to be on board his ship first thing in the morning. We brought him out here to get a breath of fresh air before putting him in the train.

Policeman Where is his ship?

Snyder Portsmouth. You wouldn't make any trouble for him, would you, officer? It's the last night of his leave. We'll get him round all right and take him to Waterloo and see him into his train and nobody'll be any the wiser.

Policeman He'd better have some black coffee.

Snyder Thanks, officer – when he's got a bit of fresh air into his lungs we'll take him back to the club and give him some.

Gus Lucky we was with him really – don't know what might have happened to him if he'd been on his own.

Policeman Okay – good-night.

Snyder Good-night, officer.

The **Policeman** *goes off right.*

During the above scene **Harry**, *unnoticed by the others, comes to. He slowly lifts his head, realises where he is, then drops it again.*

Snyder (*looking off left after the* **Policeman**) Wait until he's got round the corner by the pillar-box, then nip over and get the car – bring it right here.

Gus Right.

Snyder Wait a minute

There is a pause.

328   Ace of Clubs

Now –

Gus *gets up and runs off.*

Snyder *leans* **Harry** *back on the seat. He lights a cigarette.* **Harry** *gives him a sidelong glance and then, with one swift movement, gives him a mighty jab in the stomach with his left elbow and a sharp hook under the chin with his right fist.* **Snyder** *gives a grunt and collapses.* **Harry** *staggers to his feet and runs unsteadily off right.*

Snyder *rolls off the seat on to the ground and the lights fade.*

Scene Three

The office. A few minutes later.

Rita *is sitting at the desk.* **Detective-Inspector Warrilove** *is sitting on the couch under the window. There is a tray of drinks on the desk.* **Warrilove** *is sipping a whisky and soda.*

Warrilove   And you couldn't recognise the voice on the telephone?

Rita   No – but it must have been Snyder – or one of his lot.

Warrilove   And you're certain he hasn't been here tonight?

Rita   You heard what Benny said. He'd have seen him if he'd been in.

Warrilove   I don't always believe what Benny says.

Rita   Benny's a fool, Inspector. He likes showing off and thinking he's smart. I'm not saying he isn't capable of lying – he most certainly is – but you frightened him this afternoon and I'd be willing to swear he hasn't seen Snyder to-night.

Warrilove   Somebody must have wanted to get you out of the way for some reason or other.

Rita   Well, nothing out of the ordinary has happened as far as I can see. The show's going on as usual. I can't understand it.

Warrilove   I think I'd better let you in on a little secret, Mrs Marbury.

Rita   I'd rather you didn't. I don't want to know anything.

Warrilove   All the same you want to keep Benny out of trouble, don't you?

Rita   Yes.

Warrilove   Then you'd better know what's in the wind and help me all you can, hadn't you?

Rita   I don't seem to have much choice, do I?

Warrilove   You remember that I mentioned the Sunningdale jewel robbery this afternoon?

Rita Yes.

Warrilove We've managed to recover most of the stuff but there's still something missing. It's an emerald and pearl necklace, with earrings to match, an heirloom, worth about twenty thousand pounds.

Rita I haven't got it, Inspector.

Warrilove (*with a smile*) I didn't think you had. But somebody has, and what's more it's been in this club. It may be here now, for all I know.

Rita What do you mean?

Warrilove We picked up a miserable little runt called Alf Martin to-day. He confessed, after a little persuasion, that he had brought a small parcel here last night and checked it in the cloakroom in the pocket of a mackintosh.

Rita (*without expression*) A mackintosh?

Warrilove It was to be collected by Snyder – but it disappeared and he never got it.

Rita I don't know anything about it.

Warrilove Maybe not – but Benny does.

Rita Then you'd better ask him, hadn't you?

Warrilove I'm after Snyder, not Benny. I've been trying to nail him for a long time. His idea is to smuggle this necklace out of the country and sell it abroad. It's too easily traceable here.

Rita I don't know what you expect me to do about it?

Warrilove Keep your eyes open, Mrs Marbury, and tell me the truth when I ask you questions.

Rita I always do.

Warrilove You didn't this afternoon.

Rita Listen, Inspector, I –

Warrilove Snyder *was* here last night, wasn't he?

Rita Yes, Inspector.

Warrilove And it was he who pulled the gun and fired the shots and caused all the trouble, wasn't it?

Rita Yes.

Warrilove (*rising*) That's all I want to know for the moment –

Rita (*also rising and going to him*) Please, Inspector – Benny only lied because he was frightened – Snyder's got something on him – he's blackmailing him. I'm sure he doesn't now what's in that parcel – in the first place I don't think Snyder would trust him enough to tell him. Please believe me.

Warrilove All right, Mrs Marbury. But you'll tell me the truth next time, won't you?

Rita Yes – Yes, I will.

Warrilove Right – Thanks for the drink – I think I'll go and have a look at the show.

Rita *and* **Warrilove** *go out.*

There is a moment's pause. **Harry** *comes cautiously through the window curtains. He is about to tip-toe out through the left-hand door leading to the foyer, when he hears someone coming and dives down behind the desk.* **Benny** *and* **Pinkie** *come on from the left-hand door.* **Pinkie** *is in a wrapper. She has obviously been crying but is now grimly determined.*

Pinkie – I mean it, Benny.

Benny But have a heart, Pinkie – you can't walk out in the middle of the show –

Pinkie I can and I will – unless you find out where he is and what's happened to him.

Benny How the hell can I?

Pinkie Snyder's got him. I know it. They've either taken him back to Snyder's flat to beat him up there – or they've left him in an alley somewhere. You've got to find out. If you don't, so help me God I'm going to the police now and tell them everything. Not only about Harry, but about the blasted mackintosh and the missing package.

Benny But, Pinkie –

Pinkie I'll give you twenty minutes to go to Snyder's flat and find out what's happened. I'll wait here for you – Baby can work 'Josephine', she's done it before.

Benny What did the bloody young fool want to come here again for anyway?

Pinkie Never mind about that – are you going or aren't you?

Benny You're being hysterical.

Pinkie So you won't go?

Benny What would be the use? I'd be too late anyway. If they've beaten him up they've beaten him up, and serve him damn well right.

Pinkie (*grimly*) If you don't go as I say, Benny, that package will be with the police tomorrow.

Benny (*startled*) What do you mean?

Pinkie I happen to know where it is.

Benny (*gripping her by the shoulders*) What! Where is it? – Have you got it?

Pinkie Leave go of me.

Benny (*shaking her*) Where is it?

Pinkie (*giving him a ringing slap on the face*) Now will you do as I tell you?

Benny (*staggering back*)   You little bitch!

Pinkie   Never mind the fancy dialogue – get out – and if you're not back inside of twenty minutes you'll find me at Scotland Yard.

Benny   You're lying!

Pinkie   If you go now I'll give you that package to-morrow. I swear it.

Benny (*pleadingly*)   Pinkie –

Pinkie (*inexorably*)   Go on – get cracking.

Benny *goes out through the door on the left.*

Pinkie, *let alone, collapses on the couch and bursts into tears.* **Harry** *comes quietly out from behind the desk and gently puts his arms round her. She gives a little cry.*

Harry   It's all right – the Navy's here!

Blackout.

Scene Four

The club. The next afternoon.

When the lights go up on the scene **Felix** *is rehearsing the* **Girls** *in a new production number. The number is entitled 'Time for a Baby's Bottle' and* **Felix** *is singing it himself with the* **Girls** *in a row behind him. They are in practice dress and he is wearing flannel trousers and an open shirt. He is working hard and is very hot.*

Felix (*singing rather breathlessly*)
  Oh, it's time for Baby's bottle
  Baby's bottle of scent.
  Sweet perfume
  Leads to love in bloom
  So that's – money well spent.
  You can fill her Christmas stocking
  Full of emeralds and pearls
  But some Schiaparelli 'Shocking'[89]
  Is the way to get the girls.
  When it's time for Baby's bottle
  Give her a bottle of scent!

Felix *proceeds to do a fairly corny dance routine – shouting orders to the* **Girls** *as he does so. They finally get themselves on to the stage and* **Felix** *finishes centre on the dance floor. He stops, breathing heavily, bows to imaginary applause – shouts* 'One Two' *to* **Sammy Blake** *at the piano.* **Sammy** *changes the tempo of the number into waltz time and the girls, one by one, come down the steps again.* **Felix** *gasps out the*

---

89   A perfume released in 1937 by French perfumer Jean Carles (1892–1966).

names of the perfumes that they represent as they pass him. (For names of scents see **Felix**'s song on pp. 350–1.) The wretched **June April** loses count as usual and, instead of descending the steps like the others, remains uncertainly at the top. **Felix**, enraged, claps his hands and stops the music.

Felix   Listen, you flat-chested dumbcluck – that's the fifth time we've done the number and you haven't got it right yet.

June (*with spirit*)   You leave my chest alone.

If Mr Lazarus heard you talking to me like that he'd have a fit.

Felix   I'm surprised he hasn't had one before now.

June (*furiously*)   You're always picking on me and I'm sick of it, so there!

Felix   You may be God's gift to the tired business man but you're a pain in the next to me.

June   Who do you think you are anyway? – Talking about ladies' chests in public – it's not decent.

Felix   Listen, sweetie-pie – I don't give a hoot in hell whether you're flat-chested, double-breasted or duck-bottomed! All I care about is whether you can count up to four beats – and you can't.

June   Don't shout at me, because I won't stand it.

Felix   Oh, put a sock in it!

June   You ought to know what Mr Lazarus thinks about you – what all nice men think about you – all teeth and eyelashes and an off-white dinner-jacket!

The **Girls** *titter at this.*

Felix   Shut up – all of you!

Dawn   Shut up yourself – and stop blowing yourself up like a balloon – you'll burst a blood vessel.

Felix   Mind your own business!

Dawn   This is a night-club, this is not Gestapo Headquarters. We're all sick to death of you tearing yourself to shreds every five minutes and yelling the place down. Go outside and cool off.

Felix   Rehearsal dismissed!

He stamps off.

Doreen   Well – that's something gained. (*She sits down on the steps.*)

June   I've never been so insulted. I haven't really. It's my birthday to-morrow too.

Dawn   All right, dear, we know – you've told us every day for a week – we've all clubbed together to buy you a metronome.

June Mr Lazarus has got something lovely for me.

Dawn He doesn't look as if he had.

June Don't make any cracks about Mr Lazarus now, Dawn. He may not be much to look at but he's been more than a father to me.

Dawn I'll bet the hell he has!

June I'm sure I don't know what you mean.

Dawn Listen, Little Eva – you've known the facts of life since you were a frog in 'Where the Rainbow Ends'.[90]

June Miss Conti wanted me to be a frog but my auntie wouldn't let me – so I was a dragon-fly.

Dawn Well, buzz off, you're breaking my heart.

June *flounces off in the direction of the dressing-rooms.*

The **Girls** *giggle.* **Baby Belgrave**, **Yvonne Hall** *and* **Mavis Dean** *come on from the street.*

Baby Where's June?

Dawn In the dressing-room – she's had another upper and downer with Felix the cat.

Baby I've got them – in the shop you told me.

Dawn Let's have a look.

The **Girls** *cluster round while* **Baby** *undoes a small parcel.*

Baby Keep a look-out somebody in case she comes back.

Doreen All right.

Doreen *stands a little apart from the others and keeps watch while* **Baby** *produces from the parcel a pair of elaborately decorated false bosoms. She holds them up in triumph.*

Baby There! They're called 'Fancy Falsies'.

Dawn (*in fits of laughter*) What a surprise for Mr Lazarus!

Baby Write on the card, Yvonne, while I do them up again.

Yvonne Okay. (*She takes a card from her bag and a small pen and sits at a table.*)

Dawn When is she going to get them?

Baby (*busy doing up the parcel again*) We thought between the shows – it'll be about midnight – just the right time.

Dawn That'll teach her to ram her damned birthday down all our throats.

---

90 A 1911 children's play written by Clifford Mills and John Ramsey.

Yvonne Listen – is this all right? 'Many happy returns and may you carry all before you in your twenty-first year.'

Dawn If that girl ever sees twenty-six again I'll take down the veil.

Yvonne I've signed it 'From all in number three dressing-room'.

Baby *finishes doing up the parcel and puts it down on the table with her handbag and hat.*

Harry *comes in from the street. He is carrying the usual bunch of roses and the package.*

Baby Why, look who's here! Popeye the Sailor.[91]

Yvonne We missed you last night – what happened to you?

Harry (*cheerfully*) Plenty. I got taken for a ride.

Baby Now then – now then – none of that film talk, Humphrey Bogart.[92]

Harry It's true – they slugged me.

Mavis Who did?

Harry Snyder and his friends. I was sitting having a beer at that table over there and they crept up behind me in the dark, knocked me out and dragged me through the office window and down the fire escape.

Baby Then I supposed they tied you up in a lonely cellar by the river with the tide rising – rising –

Harry They probably would have if I hadn't come round unexpected-like and taken them by surprise.

Mavis How many were there?

Harry (*nonchalantly*) Five all told – including a weedy little chap who drove the car.

Baby Oh – so they took you in a car, did they? To a lonely farmhouse, I suppose?

Harry They would have if I'd let 'em.

Baby We know that farmhouse, don't we, girls? It's on a moor miles away from anywhere, wrapped in a thick fog summer and winter, with a whacking great bloodhound baying its guts out.

Yvonne You mean Boris Karloff's[93] little place?

Mavis Don't interrupt. (*To* **Harry**.) Go on.

Baby Don't hurry him – give him time to work on the script.

Yvonne How did you get away?

Harry (*defiantly*) I'll show you.

---

91 A fictional cartoon character created in 1929 by Elzie Crisler Segar.
92 Humphrey DeForest Bogart (1899–1957) was an American film and stage actor, known for such films as *Casablanca* (1942).
93 Born William Henry Pratt, Boris Karloff (1887–1969) was an English actor known for roles in horror films.

He puts the package and the roses on the table next to **Baby***'s parcel and handbag.*

Baby   This had better be good – we're a tough audience.

Harry   They dragged me to the square, see, and just as they was about to shove me into the car, a policeman came by –

Yvonne   Why didn't you ask him the time?

Harry   I was unconscious.

Mavis   How did you know it was a policeman, then? It might have been Harry Roy.

Harry (*with slight irritation*)   I came to.

Baby   In the nick of time?

Harry (*firmly*)   Yes – in the nick of time.

Baby   You took in the situation at a glance – feigned unconsciousness – waited until they were quarrelling amongst themselves – then suddenly sprang to your feet – swung from the nearest lamp-post – kicked them all in the teeth – leapt into the car – and drove off at breakneck speed on the wrong side of the road!

Harry (*giving in*)   All right, all right – have it your own way. Here I am anyhow. Where's Pinkie?

Yvonne   You tell him, girls – I can't face that dumb, hurt look in his eyes.

Harry   What are you talking about?

Baby   Don't think too hardly of her, Harry boy – she had given you up for lost.

Harry   Stop fooling a minute – where is she?

Baby   She was married quietly this morning in Westminster Abbey to the Early of Stufitup.

The **Girls** *giggle.*

Harry   Okay – joke over – where is she?

Mavis   In her dressing-room changing – she won't be a minute.

Baby   Got any idea for entertaining us while you're waiting? What about an old sea shanty?

Harry   Don't know any.

Mavis   A little travel talk, then. You must have been places. Tell us about the naughty night life in Rio de Janeiro.

Harr   Too noisy – you can't hear yourself speak.

Baby   Any truth in that rumour about the little Japanese ladies?

Yvonne   And those donkeys in Port Said!

Baby   Come on, sailor – give! Tell us about the great big world outside.

Mavis   The nearest we've ever got to foreign parts is Golders Green!⁹⁴

The **Girls** *and* **Harry** *sing.*

'I Like America'

Girls
   Tell us, sailor,
   Tell us please
   For we're terribly keen to know
   What's it like to be fancy free
   Footloose on the rolling sea?
   China girl chop-chop
   Gay Maltese
   Hot Mommas from Mexico –

Harry
   If you'll forgive a crude remark
   And don't resent a rude remark
   I'll let you into a secret –

Girls
   Well?

Harry
   They're all alike in the dark!

Girls
   There must have been
   Some place you've seen
   Superior to the rest?

Harry
   As a matter of fact
   With political tact
   I like America best.

Girls
   There's a good time a-comin on de ole plantation
   For a jolly Jack Tar⁹⁵
   Has just confessed
   That he likes American best!

Harry
   I don't care for China
   Japan's far too small

---

94 This is a slang term used to refer to seamen of the Merchant or Royal Navy.
95 Originally referred to seafarers of the merchant marine and the Royal Navy during the time of the British Empire.

I've rumbled the Rio Grande
I hate Asia Minor
I can't bear Bengal
And I shudder to think
Of the awful stink
On the road to Samarkand.[96]

Girls

The heat and smell
Must be sheer hell
On the road to Samarkand.

Harry

I like America
I have played around
Every slappy-happy hunting ground
But I find America – okay.
I've been about a bit
But I must admit
That I didn't know the half of it
Till I hit the USA
No likely lass
In Boston Mass:
From passion will recoil
In Dallas Tex:
They talk of sex
But only think of oil
New Jersey dames
Go up in flames
If someone mentions – bed
In Chicago Illinois
Any girl who meets a boy
Giggles and shoots him dead!
But I like America
Its society
Offers infinite variety
And come what may
I shall return some day
To the good old USA.

Verse 2:

I've loathed every acre
From Cannes to Canton
I also deplore Bombay
I've jeered at Jamaica

---

96 A city in Uzbekistan along the Silk Road.

    And seen through Ceylon
    And exploded the myth
    Of those Flying Fith
    On the Road to Mandalay.

Girls
    We'll never mith
    Those blasted fith
    On the Road to Mandalay.

Harry
    But I like America
    I have travelled far
    From Northumberland to Zanzibar
    And I find America – okay.
    I've roamed the Spanish Main
    Eaten sugar-cane
    But I never tasted cellophane
    Till I struck the USA
    All delegates – from Southern States
    Are nervy and distraught
    In New Orleans – the wrought-iron screens
    Are dreadfully overwrought
    Beneath each tree – in Tennessee
    Erotic books are read
    And when alligators thud
    Through the Mississippi mud
    Sex rears its ugly head.
    But – I like America
    All the sentimental crap of it
    And come what may
    Give me a holiday
    In the good old USA.

At the end of the number the **Girls** *all dance off.* **Baby** *snatches up her hat, handbag and the package as she goes.*

The parcel containing **June***'s birthday present is left on the tables with* **Harry***'s roses.* **Harry** *sits down on the steps and fans himself with his hat.* **Pinkie** *comes on from backstage.*

Pinkie   Harry! No one told me you were here.

Harry (*kissing her and then holding her away from him*)   You look wonderful!

Pinkie   I try to please.

Harry (*taking the roses from the table and giving them to her*)   Here – these are with my love.

Pinkie I know they are. But you mustn't buy me any more – really you mustn't – I can hardly get into the flat as it is. (*She buries her face in them.*) They're gorgeous.

Harry (*glancing at his wrist-watch*)   Think of it – we've got four whole hours – before you have to go to work – what shall we do with them?

Pinkie Have you got it?

Harry The package of course.

Harry Yes – (*Nodding towards the table.*) It's there.

Pinkie (*moving towards it*)   I'll give it to Benny.

Harry (*stopping her*)   Pinkie – I've been thinking seriously about it – we ought to hand it over to the police.

Pinkie We can't do that. You know we can't.

Harry Why not?

Pinkie It might get Benny into trouble.

Harry And so what? If Benny's doing a lot of black marketeering he deserves to get into trouble.

Pinkie He's a friend of mine, Harry – I couldn't do anything that might hurt him.

Harry We don't know what's in that package – it might be dope, stolen jewellery, anything. It's our duty to turn it in.

Pinkie Oh, dear! Smiling the boy fell dead!

Harry There is a difference between right and wrong you know, and it wouldn't do your friend Benny any harm to realise it.

Pinkie We will now sing hymn one hundred and forty-six.

Harry Look here, Pinkie –

Pinkie Give me the package and don't be silly.

Harry I'd rather not.

Pinkie It's none of your business anyway. I found it in the first place. It's nothing to do with either of us really.

Harry I don't care who it's got to do with – we ought to give it to the police – and if your precious Benny's so keen on breaking the law with his dirty little rackets, it's high time he took the rap for it.

Pinkie He's not 'my precious Benny' and you're not the Archbishop of Canterbury – so come off your high horse and be yourself.

Harry I suppose you were crazy about him once, weren't you?

Pinkie Who? – The Archbishop of Canterbury?

Harry   You know what I'm talking about.

Pinkie   Yes I do – and I don't like any of it.

Harry (*bitterly*)   After all we've only just met really – we don't know much about each other.

Pinkie   We seem to be learning.

Harry   You and Benny were lovers, weren't you? That's why you're so keen on keeping him out of the clink.

Pinkie (*losing her temper*)   Listen to me for a minute, will you? If Benny and I had been lovers fifty times over it's none of your damned business. Is that clear?

Harry (*triumphantly*)   Then you were!

Pinkie (*furiously*)   That's all I wanted to know. It's been swell while it lasted – Here – take your bloody package.

Harry, *livid with rage, snatches the parcel up from the table and throws it on the floor at* **Pinkie**'s *feet.*

Then he stamps out.

Pinkie *looks after him, makes a movement to call him back, then bends down and slowly picks up the parcel.*

She looks at it thoughtfully for a moment, biting her lip.

She is just about to open it when **Benny** *comes out of the office.*

Benny (*anxiously*)   Have you got it?

Pinkie (*gloomily*)   I've had it!

Benny   What are you talking about?

Pinkie   I'll tell you if you're interested. I'm sick of you and this club and everything to do with it. If it hadn't been for you and your cheap 'spiv-ing' I wouldn't be standing here now feeling as if I had been hit by a truck. And the next time you let your lousy blackmailing friends get their hooks into you don't expect any help from me. Here – take your bloody package!

She throws it at his feet. He mutters, 'Thank God!', grabs it and rushes back into the office.

The music begins. **Pinkie** *sings.*

'Why Does Love Get in the Way So?'

Verse:

>   Suddenly my world has altered
>   Suddenly my step has faltered
>   Common sense has flown
>   Here I am alone

Coping with these new sensations
Dark despairs and wild elations
Eros with his bow – has laid me low.

Refrain 1:

Why does love get in the way so?
What have I done – that the son-of-a-gun should pick on me?
A little while ago my heart was serene and bright
Everything seemed all right
Now I've been struck by a charge of dynamite
Why does love lead one astray so?
Tell me why – I want to laugh – I want to cry?
I was gay as a sparrow
Till Cupid's arrow
Punctured this perfect day
Why does love – get in the way?

Verse 2:

Everything is blown to blazes
Ordinary familiar phrases
Seem to mean much more
Than they did before.
Colours look a great deal brighter
Black is blacker, white is whiter
Every sight and sound
Has changed around.

Refrain 2:

Why does love get in the way so?
Why should it fret
And completely upset
My peace of mind?
A little while ago my heart was serene and gay
Everything seemed okay
And now I suddenly find – I've lost my way.
Why does love lead one astray so?
Why the hell – should I be caught within its spell?
Life was quite un-enchanted
All that I wanted
Now it's a Passion Play![97]
Why does love get in the way?
Why does love get in the way?

At the end of the song the lights fade.

The lights come up again on:

---

97 A dramatic representation in the Christian faith of the death of Jesus Christ.

'Three Juvenile Delinquents'

Verse 4:

> Three juvenile delinquents
> Juvenile delinquents.
> Every now and then – when
> Kind old cranks
> Mention angels of light to us
> We say 'Thanks'
> Don't forget to write to us.
> Now-a-days the younger generation
> Never has to face brute force.
> Some old judge, instead of flagellation,
> Puts us on pronation!
> Bilmey what a sauce!
> Last night we got an earful
> From a rather tearful
> Clergyman we knew.
> When he turned the sobs on
> We replied 'With knobs on'
> – And the same to you!

Verse 5:

> Three juvenile delinquents
> Juvenile delinquents.
> Happy as can be – We
> Break our backs
> To achieve popularity;
> Three sharp whacks
> Faith, Hope and Charity.
> Once we knocked a pair of silly sluts out
> Just behind the 'Horse and Plough',
> Dragged them round to where the railing juts out,
> Bellowing their guts out,
> Blimey what a row!
> We had to cosh 'em proper
> Then we saw a copper
> Starting to pursue.
> So we cried vibrato
> 'How's your old tomato?'
> – And the same to you!

Scene Five

Soho Square. A little later.

Rita *is sitting on the seat smoking a cigarette. A* **Policeman** *comes on from the left.*

Policeman Good evening, Mrs Marbury.

Rita Good evening, officer.

Policeman Taking a little time off?

Rita It's nice and cool out here.

Policeman It's certainly been a scorcher to-day all right. Makes one wish one was in the country.

Rita I don't like the country – too lonely. London's good enough for me. I like the feel of people being near – sort of cosy.

Policeman I should have thought you would have had enough of 'em in that club of yours.

Rita I don't mean that sort of people. I mean ordinary people who go to offices and work all day and then go home and sit in the garden.

Policeman Like my dad – he loves his garden – potters away in it for hours on end.

There is a slight pause.

Well, I'll be moving along.

Rita Good-night, officer.

Policeman Good-night, Mrs Marbury.

*The **Policeman** goes off right.*

Rita *drops her cigarette on the ground, stubs it out with her foot. She sings:*

'Evening in Summer'

Verse:

    After the heat of the day is done
    Everyone
    Who has a garden like to sit in it and dream
    Or read the paper – while the noises of the distant traffic seem
    Remote and gentle
    Sentimental variations on a theme
    That comes and goes
    Only London knows
    This sweet repose.

Refrain:

    Evening in summer
    London in June
    Sparrows from roof-tops calling
    Two streets away
    You hear a barrel-organ tune

    Night will very very soon
    Be falling
    Ships on the river
    Londoners hear
    Suddenly near
    Sweet to the ear
    Twilight is fading
    Stars shining down
    Evening in summer
    Evening in summer
    Summer in London Town.

At the end of the number she strolls off.

After a little pause **Harry** *comes on and sits down gloomily on the seat. He pushed his cap back, sighs and lights a cigarette.* **June April** *comes on from the left.*

June (*brightly*)   Halloo! Fancy meeting you.

Harry (*laconically*)   Hallo.

June (*sitting down next to him*)   Waiting for Pinkie?

Harry   No.

June   She's wonderful, isn't she? Everybody's crazy about her.

Harry   I'm sure they are.

June   Benny gave a birthday party for her in April – it was lovely – He made a speech and gave her a bracelet and we all cried. It's my birthday tomorrow. I shall be twenty-one – imagine!

Harry   I'll try.

June   Mr Lazarus has got a present for me but he won't say what it is. He wants it to be a surprise.

Harry   Let's hope it is. (*After a slight pause.*) I suppose this Benny what's-his-name is pretty keen on Pinkie, isn't he?

June   Of course he is. We all are. She's so vital.

Harry   I suppose living the same sort of life and having the same sort of jokes is bound to bring people together.

June   How funny. Do you know, I was saying just that to Mr Lazarus only the other day. (*She glances at an expensive watch on her wrist.*) My goodness, he'll be waiting. (*She gets up.*) He can't bear me to be a minute late. Isn't that sweet? Bye-bye.

Harry   Cheerio.

June *minces off.*

Harry, *left alone, sings a reprise of 'Sail Away' and walks off as the lights fade.*

Scene Six

The office. Just after midnight.

Baby Belgrave, **Yvonne Hall**, **Mavis Dean** *and all the* **Girls** *except* **June April** *are waiting for* **Benny** *to pay them their weekly salaries. They all are in wrappers.*

Dawn   If he keeps us waiting much longer we shall be off.

Doreen   That's the whole difference between the theatre and this night-club racket. After all, even on tour the business manager comes to the dressing-room and hands you your dough in a little envelope – it's much more classy. All this queuing up's so degrading.

Dawn (*derisively*)   La-di-bloody-da!

June *bursts in from the door on the left. She is radiant.*

June   Oh, girls!

Girls (*singing untidily*)   Happy birthday tew yew – Happy birthday tew yew –

June   I don't know how to thank you – I don't really.

Dawn   Sing us a song!

June   I've just opened your present – it's gorgeous! Just what I wanted.

Baby   You're telling us.

June   Wait 'til I show them to Mr Lazarus – he'll have a fit!

Mavis   Why aren't you wearing them?

June   I'm saving them for the perfume number. Of course I know they're only props but they look absolutely genuine – I'm thrilled. Mr Lazarus will be thrilled too.

Baby   Maybe they'll discourage him – after all he's used to you as you are.

June   He'll love them. He's ever so artistic. I hope he doesn't dip them in vinegar to see if they're real!

Baby   Sometimes, dear, you go too far!

Benny *comes in hurriedly from the left. He is followed by* **Snyder** *and* **Gus**.

Benny   Sorry, girls – I'll fix you after the show – I've got some important business to discuss. Scram.

Dawn   I knew there was a catch in it.

Benny   Go on – hop it – all of you.

Baby   Come on, girls – break up the bread line.

Benny *bustles them all off, grumbling as they go.*

When they have gone he shuts the door after them.

He goes to the safe and unlocks it.

Benny   Before I give it to you, Snyder, I want one thing clearly understood – this is the last time, see? – I can't stand the nerve strain.

Snyder   All's well that ends well, Benny boy.

Benny   Rita's been at me – Pinkie's been at me – I've had hell all round.

Snyder (*cheerfully*)   No stamina – that's always been your trouble – too sensitive – isn't he, Gus?

Gus   Come on – give him his gazuma – take the doings, and let's beat it. There's no sense in hanging about, it's too risky.

Snyder   Keep calm, Gus – everything's under control.

Benny (*giving* **Snyder** *the parcel which he has taken from the safe*)   Here you are.

Snyder   Thanks, Benny Boy – and this is for you.

(*He takes an envelope out of his pocket and gives it to* **Benny**.) You'd better count it.

Benny (*quickly slitting open the envelope and taking out a large wad of pound notes*)   Whew! What's in that package anyway – the Koh-i-noor diamond?[98]

Snyder (*complacently*)   Fair's fair, Benny – your Uncle Joseph always plays straight – you ought to know by this time.

Gus (*impatiently*)   Come on, guv'nor – what's the use of mucking about!

Snyder (*suavely*)   Why, you're nervous, Gus – I've never seen you nervous before – it must be catching.

Benny (*agitated*)   Listen, Snyder – you must tell me what's in that package – I've got to know.

Snyder (*slipping the package into his pocket*)   You haven't got to know anything, Benny boy – in fact the less you know the better – you're none too good at keeping your trap shut at the best of times.

Rita *comes in from the door on the right. She stops dead on seeing* **Snyder** *and* **Gus**.

Rita   What does this mean?

Snyder (*affably*)   That's a smashing dress, Rita – I congratulate you.

Rita   What are you doing here?

Snyder   We just dropped in to have a little chat with Benny.

Rita   What about?

Snyder   Just a private matter, Rita – nothing to do with you at all.

---

98 The Koh-i-Noor Diamond, also spelled Kohinoor, is one of the largest cut diamonds in the world, weighing 105.6 carats.

Rita Get out.

Snyder You'd better not use that tone to me, Rita – you might regret it.

Rita Get out – and stay out.

Gus Come on, guv'nor – there's no sense in arguing with the silly cow – let's go.

Snyder (*dangerously*) We've got as much right in this club as anyone else – we're not only paying customers – we're members! And if you want things to go smoothly and well with the club – and your Benny included – you'd better stop ordering me about and mend your manners. (*To* **Gus**.) Come on.

Snyder *and* **Gus** *go out.*

Rita What did they want?

Benny Now look here, Rita –

Rita You didn't give them anything, did you?

Benny Don't be silly – what could I have given them?

Rita You might have given them a pearl and emerald necklace worth twenty thousand pounds!

Benny (*thrown off his guard*) What!

Rita Did you – did you? –

Benny I haven't the faintest idea what you're gabbing about.

Rita The package! – You found the package and gave it to them!

Benny Rita –

Rita (*sinking on the couch*) Oh, my God! You've done for yourself this time!

The lights fade.

Scene Seven

The club. A little while later.

As the lights go up on the scene there is a drum roll and **Felix**, *distinctively attired in a bright blue tail suit, comes through the curtains and sings:*

'When It's Time for Baby's Bottle'

My lady's boudoir, satin, silk
And foamy laces cast aside
A pair of shoulders white as milk
A woman's glory and her pride
A tendril here, a dimple there
The flutter of a painted fan
Can catch a fellow unaware

Can make a fool of any man.
Yet, lovely ladies, if by chance
To challenge you I should presume
I vow the essence of romance
Lies in the magic of perfume.

Refrain 1:

When it's time for Baby's bottle
Give her a bottle of scent
Fragrant perfume
Leads to love in bloom
And that's money well spent.
You can fill her Christmas stocking
With emeralds and pearls
But Schiaparelli Shocking[99]
Will always get the girls
When it's time for Baby's bottle
Give her a bottle of scent.

Refrain 2:

When it's time for Baby's bottle
Give her a bottle of scent
Soir de Paris[100]
Makes her say 'Oui oui'
Without father's consent
She may cone a social cropper
And really go to far
If you'll just pull out the stopper
Of Chypre[101] or Shalimar[102]
When it's time for Baby's bottle
Give her a bottle of scent.

At night to greet the Eastern Star
My lady's drenched in Shalimar

Another spring has come to pass (Wait for it)
Full of fragrance of Blue Grass[103]

When evening breeze the branches stirs
My heart responds to Quelques Fleurs[104]

---

99 'Shocking' is an Amber perfume by Schiaparelli, which debuted in 1937.
100 A French perfume from 1928.
101 A family of woody, citrus perfumes. Also references in Aldous Huxley's *Brave New World* (1932).
102 Perfume created by Guerlain in 1925.
103 A perfume by Elizabeth Arden.
104 A French perfume from 1912.

A water nymph beside the Loire[105]
Her melody is Narcisse Noir[106]

A shaded light a kiss unseen
A night of love and Crepe de Chine[107]
Two throbbing hearts 'neath passion's sway
Ladies beware it's Indiscret.[108]

The Seine Montmartre and you chérie
Toujours, l'amour Soir de Paris[109]

Two roguish eyes serenely mocking
A whispered promise – that is Shocking

Any wolf who's any good
Pounces on Red Riding Hood
But to-day – he will not get away with it
Modern maids are mellowed in the wood
If you find that cheek to cheek
Dinner dances twice a week
Don't get quick results
You'll get slick results
With my new technique . . .

The **Girls***, dressed in brief shorts and brassieres, support him. At a given moment in the number they disappear through the curtains and reappear a little later, having put on transparent cellophane crinolines and headdresses made in the shape of bottle stoppers.*

They come languidly down the steps while **Felix***, from the side, shouts out the names of the perfumes they represent.*

June April *comes last as 'Shocking'. In addition to her cellophane costume made vaguely in the shape of a 'Shocking' bottle, she is wearing a dazzling necklace and earrings of pearls and emeralds. She walks slowly down after the others and, like them, passes along by the tables.*

The spotlight falls for a moment on a ringside table at which is sitting **Detective-Inspector Warrilove***.*

He is accompanied by two quietly dressed and quite obvious plain-clothes men. He suddenly sees the necklace round **June***'s neck and half rises from his chair.*

---

105 French perfume.
106 Perfume created in 1911.
107 Perfume by Millot that debuted in 1925.
108 A perfume by Lucien Lelong that launched in 1936.
109 Perfume by Bourjois that launched in 1928.

June, *noticing the interest she has caused, gives a ravishing smile, fingers the necklace complacently, and passes on.*

As the number finished and she goes off behind **Felix** *and the other girls,* **Warrilove** *and the two plain-clothes men get up and follow her backstage.*

Felix, *rather breathless, appears through the curtains again.*

Felix   And now, what you've been waiting for – what I've been waiting for – what the whole world has been waiting for. Our own Pinkie Leroy singing – 'Chase Me, Charlie!'.

He signals to the band, which strikes up the introductory chords, and stands aside.

Pinkie *comes through the curtains to applause. She is wearing a little girl's nursery dress made of coloured sequins. She has bobby-socks and shoes with large sequin bows. In her hair is an enormous sequin bow. She carries a vast toy black cat with a red ribbon round its neck. She runs down the steps, sits the cat down on the bottom step and sings:*

'Chase Me, Charlie'

Verse 1:

> When it's late
> And the world is sleeping
> Our little black cat
> No bigger than that
> Has a date
> Which she's keen on keeping
> No use dissuading her
> She's serenading her – beau
> In the garden below
> She sings 'Oh, won't you –

Refrain 1:

> Chase me, Charlie
> Chase me, Charlie
> Over the garden wall?
> I'd like to wander for miles and miles
> Wreathed in smiles
> Out on the tiles with you
> Chase me, Charlie
> Chase me, Charlie
> Don't be afraid to fall
> Love in the moonlight can be sublime
> Now's the time
> Charlie I'm
> Bound to give in if you'll only climb
> Over the garden wall.'

Verse 2:

>   Every night
>   At about eleven
>   Our little black cat knows
>   Our little black cat goes
>   Quick as light
>   To her private heaven
>   No use restraining her
>   She's set on gaining her – prize
>   With her amorous cries
>   Hypnotising him.

Refrain 2:

>   Chase me, Charlie
>   Chase me, Charlie
>   Over the garden wall.
>   Who gives a damn if the neighbours yell?
>   Let's rebel
>   Just for the hell of it.
>   Chase me, Charlie
>   Chase me, Charlie
>   Maybe I'll give my all!
>   Won't you come out and be gay with me
>   Play with me
>   Stay with me?
>   Just try a roll in the hay with me
>   Over the garden wall.

Refrain 3:

>   Chase me, Charlie
>   Chase me, Charlie
>   Over the garden wall.
>   Why not give in to the joys of spring
>   Have a fling
>   Why are you lingering?
>   Chase me, Charlie
>   Chase me, Charlie
>   This is my final call.
>   Pussy-cat pussy-cat don't be shy
>   This is my
>   Alibi
>   Nature intends us to multiply
>   Over the garden wall.

At the end of the number –

Scene Eight

The office. A little later.

Benny *is sitting at the desk checking over the salary list. The door on the left bursts open and* **Snyder** *and* **Gus** *come in.* **Snyder** *is obviously livid.*

Benny (*rising to his feet*)   What is it – what's happened?

Snyder   You know what's happened all right – you stinking, double-crossing little rat!

Benny   But, Snyder –

Snyder (*flinging the pair of false bosoms on the desk*)   That's what's the matter!

Benny (*looking at them and then back again at* **Snyder**)   I don't know what you're talking about –

Snyder   Where is it?

Benny   I don't understand – I swear I don't.

Snyder   What have you done with the necklace and earrings?

Benny   What necklace and earrings?

Snyder (*seizing him by the coat and shaking him*)   Don't lie to me – where are they?

Benny   Stop shouting – people will hear –

Snyder (*menacingly*)   You ought to know better than to play tricks on me, Benny boy. If you don't tell me what you've done with that stuff right here and now – you're in for a very unpleasant time indeed – get his arms, Gus.

Gus (*seizing* **Benny** *and putting his arms behind him*)   Right.

Benny (*terrified*)   Let me go – I don't know what you're talking about – I swear I don't –

Gus *gives his arms a sharp twist.*

Benny   Ouch –

Warrilove *comes quietly out from behind the curtains. He holds a gun in his right hand, with which he covers* **Snyder** *and* **Gus**. *In his left hand he is dangling the necklace.*

Warrilove   Is this what you were looking for, Snyder?

Gus (*letting* **Benny** *go*)   Oh, God!

He and **Snyder** *put up their hands.*

Warrilove (*shouting*)   Right!

The two plain-clothes men come quickly through the door on the left, they go straight to **Snyder** *and* **Gus** *and snap handcuffs on to them.* **Benny** *backs up against the wall.*

Snyder (*to* **Benny**)   I'll fix you for this if it's the last thing I do.

Warrilove   You'll have to wait quite a long while, Snyder. Come on – get going –

Rita *comes in through the door leading to the club.*

Rita   Benny – are you all right?

Warrilove   Benny isn't here, Mrs Marbury. I don't even know who he is – I wouldn't recognise him if I met him in the street.

Rita (*with a catch in her voice*)   Thank you, Inspector – thank you very very much.

The plain-clothes men bustle **Snyder** *and* **Gus** *out of the door on the left.*

Warrilove   You'd better keep your nose clean in the future, Benny Lucas. You won't find me quite so easy next time.

Detective-Inspector Warrilove *goes out, closing the door behind him.*

Benny *sinks down at the desk and puts his head in his hands.* **Rita** *goes over to him.*

Rita (*putting her hand on his shoulder*)   Benny – oh, Benny –

Rita *sings a reprise of the waltz she sang in the first act, very softly and the lights fade.*

Scene Nine

The club. A little later.

The finale of the floor show is going on. The audience is applauding. The **Girls** *come running through the curtains – they kiss their hands to the public and then arrange themselves on the steps.*

The **Hercules Brothers** *come on – the applause rises. They also retire to each side of the stage.*

Felix *bounds on and receives his due of applause. He takes a stand at the bottom of the steps and points towards the stage.*

Pinkie *comes through the curtains. The band strikes up 'I Want to Find My Kind of Man'.*

She comes slowly down the steps singing it.

The spotlight falls on **Harry** *sitting alone at his usual table with a bunch of roses on the table in front of him.* **Pinkie** *gives a little gasp of relief and surprise, falters in her song. He rises to his feet and presents her with the roses.*

Everyone applauds.

She takes them and as she does so he takes her in his arms.

The stage band stops playing and the theatre orchestra plays softly the last part of 'Sail Away'.

Pinkie and **Harry** (*singing together*)

   On the wings of the morning
   With your own true love
   Sail away – Sail away – Sail away!

Curtain.

PART III
Broadway Plays of the 1960s

Sail Away

Critics' Notes

Sail Away had a complicated critical reception, unsurprising given the shrewd critical eye that was cast on Coward's American return. Critic Harold Taubman of the *New York Times* noted:

> As a book writer, composer, lyricist and director Noel Coward is an old pro. He has summoned all – well, nearly all – his gifts into assembling *Sail Away* . . . [it] is a big, handsome, rakish vessel of a musical. It carries a cargo of shrewdly observed people, swift funny lines, full-length comic scenes, gay production numbers and a sentimental love story. Its tunes cover a wide cruise repertory – from the styles of old lace and valentines to rock n' roll . . . Remember, however, that the knowing, sharp-tongued Mr Coward is your captain.[1]

Taubman's concerns about the work centred on the lack of original humour in the work, or what he claims are stale jokes that Coward would have avoided in his earlier day.

However, as Taubman notes, Coward's work provides the sharp-witted critique of Western life through its presentation of American, Italian and British upper classes who must meet and mingle with the rest of the world on a sea voyage. Yet it was not a hit in New York and Coward lamented: 'It is perfectly possible that I *am* out of touch with the times. Have I really . . . reached the crucial moment when I should retire from the fray and spend my remaining years sorting out my memories and sentimentalizing the past at my expense.'[2] Despite both Coward's and the critics' concerns, the work displays many aspects of Coward's style, including his quintessential wit and comedic timing, his sense of romantic longing (as seen in the love affair that was later cut from the show) and his deep understanding of human relationships. Coupled with the large-scale form of the 1960s Broadway musical, this work remains an iconic representation of Coward's late style.

---

1 Howard Taubman, 'Theatre: Noel Coward at the Helm: His "Sail Away" Opens at the Broadhurst,' *New York Times (1923-Current file)*, Oct 04, 1961.
2 Philip Hoare, *Noël Coward: A Biography* (Chicago: University of Chicago Press, 1998), 472.

Characters[3]

Mimi Paragon	Elaine Stritch[4]
Verity Craig	(Cut after try-out)
Johnny Van Mier	James Hurst[5]
Nancy Foyle	Patricia Harty[6]
Barnaby Slade	Grover Dale[7]
Joe Coleridge, *the ship's Purser*	Charles Braswell[8]
Mrs Van Mier, *Johnny's mother*	Margalo Gillmore[9]
Elinor Spencer-Bollard, *Nancy's aunt*	Alice Pearce[10]
Lawford Craig, *Verity's husband*	(Cut after try-out)
Mrs Lush	Evelyn Russell[11]
Alvin Lush, *her son*	Paul O'Keefe[12]
Shuttleworth, *Chief Steward*	Keith Prentice[13]
Sir Gerard Nutfield	C. Stafford Dickens[14]
Lady Nutfield	Margaret Mower[15]
Mr Sweeny	John Richards[16]
Mrs Sweeny	Paula Bauersmith[17]

3 Bonard Productions, Inc., 10 July 1961. This is the first performance script, before Coward reworked it for the New York opening. Additions from Stewart Nicholls' 2000 reconstruction have been noted throughout.
4 Elaine Stritch (1925–2014) was an American actor and singer known for her cabaret performances and work on Broadway and in television sitcoms including *30 Rock* (2007–13).
5 James Hurst (1922–2013) was an American stage and television actor, known for his role in the television programme *77 Sunset Strip* (1958–64).
6 Patricia Harty (b. 1941) is an American stage and screen actor known for her work in Broadway shows such as *Fiorello!* (1959) and television programmes including *Blondie* (1968–9).
7 Grover Dale (b. 1935) is an American actor, dancer, choreographer, theatre director and publisher, best known for his work in films such as *The Unsinkable Molly Brown* (1964) and *Half a Sixpence* (1967).
8 Charles Braswell (1924–74) was an American stage actor whose credits included *Wildcat* (1960), *Mame* (1966) and *Company* (1970).
9 Margalo Gillmore (1897–1986) was an American stage and film actor whose credits included the televised production of *Peter Pan* (1954) with Mary Martin and *High Society* (1958).
10 Alice Pearce (1917–66) was an American actor best known for her character work, including Gladys Kravitz in the television sitcom *Bewitched* (1964–6).
11 Evelyn Russell was an American stage actor who was married to choreographer Joe Layton. Other work included a revival of *On the Town*.
12 Paul O'Keefe (b. 1951) is an American actor known for his work in *The Patty Duke Show* (1963–6).
13 Keith Prentice (1940–92) was an American stage actor best known for his work in *The Boys in the Band* (1968).
14 Charles Stafford Dickens (1888–1967) was a British actor, screen and film director. Credits include *Dead Men Tell No Tales* (1938) and *The Idol of Paris* (1948).
15 Margaret Mower (dates unknown) was primarily known for her silent film work including *The First Man* (1922) and *Lady of the Rose* (1925).
16 John Richards (1938–2003) was an American actor known for *The Lieutenant* (1964) and *Scream of the Butterfly* (1965).
17 Paula Bauersmith was an American actor who appeared in Broadway works including *Breakfast at Tiffany's* (1966).

Clara Brassey, *a Stewardess*	(Cut after try-out)
Skid Paragon	(Cut after try-out)
Ali, *an Arab Guide*	Charles Braswell
Elmer Candijack	Henry Lawrence[18]
Maime Candijack, *his wife*	Betty Jane Watson[19]
Glen Candijack, *their son*	Alan Helm[20]
Shirley Candijack, *their daughter*	Patti Mariano[21]
Mr Rawlings, *a drunk*	James Pritchett[22]
Marybelle Fisher	(Cut after try-out)
Lillie Dukes	(Cut after try-out)
Cassidy, *a little boy (girl in Broadway run)*	Ann Fraser[23]
Man from American Express	Richard Wood[24]

The Little Ones:
Bobby Allen, Paul Gross, Bridget Knapp, Mary Ellen O'Keefe, Dennis Scott, Christopher Votos

Passengers, Stewards, Arabs and Italians:
Jere Admire, Don Atkinson, Gary Crabbe, David Evans, Pat Ferrier, Dorothy Frank, James Frasher, Gene Gavin, Curtis Hood, Wish Mart Hunt, Cheryl Kilgren, Nancy Lynch, Patti Mariano, Alan Peterson, Alice Shanahan, Dan Siretta, Gloria Stevens

Production Team

Musical Numbers and Dances	Joe Layton[25]
Book, Music, Lyrics and Direction	Noël Coward
Orchestrations	Irwin Kostal[26]
Vocal Arrangements	Fred Werner[27]
Assistant Choreographer	Buddy Schwab[28]
Production Design	Oliver Smith[29]

18 Unknown.
19 Elizabeth Jane Watson (1921–2016) was an American stage actor, known for originating the role of Laurey in the London production of *Oklahoma!* (1947).
20 Alan Helm (b. 1938) is an American actor, known for such films as *We, the Accused* (1980).
21 Patricia Mariano (b. 1945) is an American actor known for films including *Charlie's Angels* (1976).
22 James Turner Pritchett Jr. (1922–2011) was an American actor known for his role in the soap opera *The Doctors* (1963–82).
23 Unknown.
24 Richard Wood (1923–2001) was an American actor known for his work in the television series *Dark Shadows* (1966–71).
25 Joe Layton (1931–94) was an American choreographer and director.
26 Irwin Kostal (1911–94) was an American arranger for films and orchestrator of Broadway musicals.
27 Fred Werner (birth date unknown) is an American composer and arranger known for his work on such shows as Noël Coward's *High Spirits* (1964) and *Sweet Charity* (1986).
28 Buddy Schwab (1930–92) was an American choreographer known for his work in *Thoroughly Modern Millie* (1967) and *Camelot* (1967).
29 Oliver Smith (1918–94) was an American scenic designer known for works such as *My Fair Lady* (1956) and *West Side Story* (1957).

Costume Design	Helene Pons & Oliver Smith[30]
Lighting	Peggy Clark[31]
Musical Direction and Dance Arrangements	Peter Matz[32]

* indicates number was cut from first performance

Act One *Musical Numbers*

1. Opening Music	Full Company
2. 'Come to Me'	Mimi & Chorus
* 3. 'I Am No Good at Love'	Verity
4. 'Sail Away'	Johnny
5. Reprise: 'Sail Away'	Full Company
6. Reprise: 'Come to Me'	Mimi
7. 'Where Shall I Find Him?'	Nancy
8. 'Beatnik Love Affair'	Barnaby & Nancy
9. 'Later than Spring'	Johnny
10. 'The Passenger's Always Right'	Joe & Stewards
11. Reprise: 'Sail Away'	Johnny
12. Reprise: 'Where Shall I Find Her'	Barnaby
13. 'Useful Phrases'	Mimi
* 14. 'This Is a Night for Lovers' (Replaced with 'Go Slow, Johnny')	Verity & Johnny
15. You're a Long Long way from America (*Finale*)	Mimi & Full Company

Act Two

Scene One	A Square in Tangiers (Noon)
Scene Two	The Ship's Nursery (Afternoon. A few days later)
Scene Three	The Sun Deck (The Bay of Naples. Early evening. A few days later)
Scene Four	A Street in Taormina (Early afternoon. A few days later)
Scene Five	The Pathenon (Noon. A few days later)
Scene Six	The Parthenon (Moonlight. Later that night)
Scene Seven	The Promenade Deck (An hour or so later)
Scene Eight	The Sun Deck (Villefranche. Some days later. Late afternoon)
Scene Nine	The Promenade Deck (A few evenings later)
Scene Ten	Another Part of the Deck (The next evening)
Scene Eleven	The Main Hall (Morning)

---

30 Helene Pons (1898–1990) was a costume designer whose credits include *Gay Divorce* (1932) and *Porgy and Bess* (1935).
31 Peggy Clark (1915–96) was an American lighting, set and costume designer whose credits include *Bells Are Ringing* (1956) and *Bye Bye Birdie* (1960).
32 Peter Matz (1928–2002) was an American composer, arranger and conductor who worked with several stars including Marlene Dietrich and Barbra Streisand.

Musical Numbers

1. 'The Customer's Always Right — Ali & Chorus
2. 'Something Very Strange' — Verity
3. 'The Little One's ABC' — Mimi & Children
4. 'You and I' — Verity & Johnny
*5. 'Tourist Ballet'
(Replaced with 'Don't Turn Away from Love') — Company
6. 'When You Want Me' — Barnaby & Nancy
7. 'Why Do the Wrong People Travel?' — Mimi
*8. 'This is a Changing World' — Verity
9. 'Bronxville Darby and Joan' — Mr & Mrs Sweeny
(Added for the London production)
10. Reprise: 'Later than Spring' — Mimi
*11. Reprise: 'This Is a Changing World' — Verity
*12. 'Bad Times' — Nancy, Barnaby, Candijack Family & Elinor
13. Reprise: 'When You Want Me' — Barnaby & Nancy
14. Finale — Full Company

Act One

Scene One

The main hall of the SS Carolina.

At the end of the overture there is the booming blast of the ship's siren.

As the lights fade in on the scene there is no music but the deafening sounds of a great many people talking at once. Presently, under the noise of voices, the music creeps in again and the general bustle and movement takes on a certain rhythm and style.

Neatly uniformed **Stewards** *are waiting at the entrance to the gangway to collect the passengers' hand baggage as they come on board. There are one or two* **Ship's Officers** *keeping an eye on things and* **Joe Colleridge**, *the Purser, occasionally emerges from his office to confer with* **Shuttlesworth**, *the Chief Steward.*

Singly and in groups the passengers come on board. The order of their appearances must be left to the discretion of the choreographer and the director. The principal characters not in the order of their appearance but in the order of their importance are as follows:

Verity Craig, *a handsome, beautifully dressed woman in her late thirties accompanied by her husband,* **Lawford Craig**, *a good-looking man of about forty-five, come on together and are claimed by a* **Steward**. *She looks irritable and strained and he has a harassed expression. He says something to her to which she replies sharply and with a shrug of annoyance. Owing to the general din it is impossible to hear what they say. She follows the* **Steward** *off while he lags a little behind looking disconsolate.*

Nancy Foyle, *a simply dressed, pretty young girl, comes on with her aunt,* **Mrs Spencer Bollard**. **Elinor Spencer-Bollard** *is a famous American novelist. She is a well-disposed megalomaniac and the ideal of Women's Clubs from San Francisco to Portland, Maine. As they are being led to their cabin a press photographer steps forward.* **Elinor** *graciously pauses to allow him to take a photograph before they go off.*

John Van Mier, *a tall, handsome young man in his twenties comes on accompanied by his mother,* **Mrs Van Mier**, *a faded, once pretty woman with a steely eye and the authoritative air of a prominent Bostonian matron. She approaches* **Joe**, *the Purser, produces her ticket from her bag and proceeds to argue. It is obvious that she is complaining about something.* **Johnny**, *with an expression of some impatience, finally takes her arm and leads her away. He shrugs his shoulders resignedly and gives* **Joe** *an understanding wink as they go.*

Barnaby Slade, *an eager young man with crew-cut and horn-rimmed glasses, emerges from the gangway as though he had been propelled from a gun. He is laden with cameras, a pile of books tied up with string and several packages. He immediately trips over a stray suitcase and falls down. The packages and books fly in all directions and are retrieved by the* **Stewards**. **Joe** *helps him to his feet, waits,* *while he fumbles for his ticket and finally puts him in charge of a* **Steward** *who leads him away to his cabin.*

Sir Gerard *and* **Lady Nutfield** *come on. He is tall and distinguished and is an ex-British colonial governor, so exquisitely true to type that one feels he should wear a monocle.* **Lady Nutfield** *is pale and wispy and has obviously been exposed far too long to tropic suns.* **Joe** *and* **Shuttleworth** *greet them with a certain deference and* **Shuttleworth** *personally conducts them off to their cabin.*

Mrs Lush *comes on with her fattish ten years old son* **Alvin***. She is a small, sharp little woman with overdone blueish hair and a hat that looks as though it might shoot off her head from sheer exuberance. A* **Steward** *steps forward and tries to take from* **Alvin** *a large package that he is carrying.* **Alvin** *wrestles with him, shrieks loudly and kicks him on the shin.* **Mrs Lush** *smiles indulgently, wags a cheerfully admonishing finger at her little darling as They follow the scowling* **Steward** *to their cabin.*

Mr *and* **Mrs Sweeny** *appear from the gangway. They are an elderly couple. She is expensively dressed and wears a large mauve orchid attached to the collar of her coat which tickles her chin. She smiles at everyone with overpowering sweetness as she and her husband are led away.*

The **Candijack** *family emerge, talking vociferously, from the gangway. They also are loaded down with cameras, boxes of candy and various packages.* **Elmer** *and* **Maime** *are young middle-aged. Their son and daughter,* **Glen** *and* **Shirley***, are in their late teens or early twenties. All four of them are noisy, slightly common and filled with good will. Chattering like magpies they are led off to their cabin.*

By the time all these characters have made their entrances the general hubbub has abated slightly. There is still a great deal of movement but this too dies away with the music.

Shuttleworth *and* **Joe** *move down stage.* **Shuttleworth** *looks worried.*

Shuttleworth (*glancing at his wrist watch*)   She's late.

Joe   Mimi's been late for every cruise – she's a last-minute girl – don't worry, it's still a half hour before sailing time.

Shuttleworth (*calling one of the* **Stewards**)   Pop down onto the dock, Hoskins, and see if you can find Mrs Paragon.

Hoskins   Aye aye, sir.

He turns to go down the gangway

At this moment **Mimi Paragon** *bursts enthusiastically from the gangway. She is carrying several boxes, a string of colored balloons, an azalea in a pot and a small pug under her arm.* **Stewards** *rush forward and relieve her of the balloons, the boxes and the azalea.* **Mimi** *is chic and well-dressed but everything about her is a trifle exaggerated. Her vitality is inexhaustible and her humour sharp.*

Mimi   Sweet God I've made it!

Joe   Only just.

Mimi   Don't look disapproving, Joe. It will make deep deep furrows down your lovely sunburned cheeks and sad, defeated bags under your eyes. What sort of an assignment have we got this trip? Any drunks, junkies or women of light reputation?

Joe   It's too early to tell yet.

Mimi   (*beckoning a* **Steward**)   Brewster, be an angel right from heaven and take Adlai to the tip topmost deck and give him a tiny walk. He's over-excited and hasn't had a moment.

She hands him the pug

Joe   You know he ought to go straight to the kennels.

Mimi   Nonsense, dear. We've been through all that before. If Adlai sleeps in a kennel I sleep in a kennel and that would be death to prestige. If you are forbidding, unapproachable and un-operative, Joe darling, mother will lock herself in her diving inside cabin and you'll have to run those damned bingo tournaments on your own.

She stretches out her arms wide

How glorious to be home again after those dreary sun-drenched days on West Seventy-third street.

She looks up at all the **Stewards** *smiling down on her from the upper decks*

Boys, you look wonderful!

Stewards (*in unison*)   So do you, Baby.

Mimi   That's the sort of welcome that warms my old heart. It makes me feel like Queen Victoria.

The **Stewards** *start to sing the lead-in to 'Come to Me'*

'Mimi's Entrance'

Boys
   Thank the Lord
   Mimi Paragon's on board
   She can organise the horde
   Of morons – we said morons
   That we take abroad
   She will see that they're occupied every moment of the day
   Keep the fatheads out of our way
   Hurray Hurray Hurray!
   Give a cheer
   Mimi Paragon is here
   She will firmly commandeer
   the dumb-clucks – we said dumb-clucks

Till they're on their ear
She will ride 'em till they qualify for the psychopathic ward
Hallelujah – Thank the Lord
Mimi Paragon's on board.

Mimi

They christened me 'Mimi'
My tiny heart is frozen
But heaven forbid that I should shirk
The work – that I have chosen
To be a professional pepper-upper
Isn't anyone's cuppa tea
But I've wit and guile
And a big false smile
And the tourists rely on me.

Boys

That's quite true
They always do
They're crazy about Mimi.

Mimi

On the very first dreadful day
I stand them in line –

Boys

She keeps them in line

Mimi

I stand them in line – and say

Refrain:

If you're mad keen to be cultural
I'm the gal
With whom you should roam
I can show you every ruin from Jerusalem to Greece
Also quite a few between Antibes and Nice
If you can't live without antique pots
I'll find lots for you to take home
If you long to take bad photographs of classical debris
Come to me – Come to me
If you want to crouch in churches till you've water on the knee
Come to me – poor fools – Come to me.

Boys

She's terribly energetic
She's so full of vim and zip
If we hit a gale
and the turbines fail

She can easily drive the ship.

Refrain 2:

Mimi
    If to play games is what you call fun
    I'm the only one
    To keep you in form
    I can organise a 'treasure hunt' or even clockwork trains
    Anything to occupy your poor, dim brains
    We've some fine backgammon boards on board
    If the Lord
    Should sense us a storm
    If 'canasta', 'bridge' or 'bingo' are your kind of jamboree
    Come to me – come to me
    If you want to play 'strip-poker' with the girls in cabin B
    Come to me – dear boys – Come to me.

Scene Two

Verity's *cabin.*

Verity *comes in followed by* **Lawford**. *She looks strained and unhappy. She puts the small make-up case She is carrying on the dressing-table, sits on the bed, takes off her hat and lights a cigarette.*

Verity   I wish you hadn't come. I should have been perfectly all right by myself. You know I hate being seen off.

Lawford   I couldn't have let you come on board all alone.

Verity   I don't see why not. You've left alone quite a lot during the last year.

Lawford (*unhappily*)   I suppose I asked for that.

Verity (*with a little laugh*)   I'm not blaming you. I'm merely stating a fact. Your attentions have been – shall we say – otherwise engaged?

Lawford (*wearily*)   I've already promised you that I am not going to see her any more.

Verity   I didn't ask you to promise anything. You volunteered it.

Lawford   Does it really interest you whether I do or not?

Verity (*hopelessly*)   No it doesn't – it doesn't.

She bursts into tears

Clara Brassey, *the* **Stewardess**, *enters.*

Clara   Good morning, Mrs Craig.

Verity (*pulling herself together*) Good morning.

Clara I am your stewardess. Your luggage will be up in a few minutes. If there is anything you require, just press that little green button by the bed.

Verity Thank you.

Clara I see you have some flowers. Would you like me to put them in water?

Verity (*surprised*) Flowers?

She sees a large package in the corner.

Oh yes – do – that would be very kind.

Clara *picks up the package and detaches the card.*

Clara The card, madam.

Verity (*taking it*) Thank you – thank you very much.

Clara At your service, madam.

She smiles and goes out with the package.

Verity (*slitting open the envelope and looking at the card*) Oh! – They're from you.

Lawford Yes, they're from me. They're yellow roses. You always liked yellow roses.

Verity It was kind of you to remember, Lawford. Thank you.

She turns her head away.

Lawford (*hesitantly*) Verity –

Verity (*still looking away*) I really think you'd better go now. They'll be banging that gong in a minute. It's nearly sailing time.

Lawford You're sure you are not making a mistake?

Verity Quite sure.

She turns to him.

I'm sorry I was disagreeable. I didn't sleep much last night. I feel strained.

Lawford There's still time for you to change your mind.

Verity I'm not going to change my mind, Lawford – I just – can't.

Lawford Is what I did so – so very unforgivable?

Verity You know it isn't only that.

Lawford I wish I knew what happened to us – what really went wrong.

Verity So do I, Lawford – so do I. That's why I'm forcing myself to go on this cruise. To give myself time to think – time to find out.

Lawford Are you still set on divorce?

Verity (*edgily*) I don't know. All I do know is that we're not happy together. We haven't been happy together for quite a time. Whether it was your fault or my fault is beside the point. We fell out of love.

Lawford Are you so sure?

Verity It isn't very fair of you to choose this particular moment to become sentimental.

Lawford Has it ever occurred to you that you ask too much of life, and demand too much of love?

Verity For God's sake don't let's start bickering again. Please go now.

Lawford (*bitterly*) Of course the situation is more familiar to you than it is to me. You have been married before. This is my first attempt. I seem to have messed it up a bit.

Verity Well, let's hope that your next try will be more successful.

Lawford Verity!

Verity Go away – please go away – I can't bear any more.

Lawford (*quietly*) Very well.

He goes to her.

Good-bye.

He kisses her on the cheek.

Verity (*in a muffled voice*) Good-bye.

Lawford Take care of yourself. Try to relax. Have a good trip.

Verity Yes, Lawford, I'll try. I really will try.

He looks at her indecisively for a moment and then goes out, shutting the door behind him. She rises involuntarily to call him back and then sits down miserably on the bed again.

'*I Am No Good at Love*'

I am no good at love
I try and I try in vain
To capture the magic I know is there
But never quite attain
For something within me breaks the spell
And I am alone again.

I cannot ever quite believe
That love can be
Really happening to me
My jealous mind seems to keep my heart
From being free
A strange uncertainty
Destroys the dream for me
Will I never never know?
Will I never discover why
The dream must die?

I am no good at love
I betray it with little sins
I see the unhappiness of the end
The moment it begins
And the bitterness of the last good-bye
Is the bitterness that wins
Is the bitterness that wins.

Scene Three

Johnny Van Mier's *cabin.*

Mrs Van Mier *is sitting in a small arm-chair by the dressing table.* **Johnny** *has hoisted one of his suitcases onto the bed and is unpacking it.*

Johnny – Don't let's go on about it any more, mother. You were right and I was wrong. Let's leave it at that.

Mrs Van Mier I knew she was no good the first moment I set eyes on her. When you brought her out for that dreadful week-end last September.

Johnny Nonsense, mother. You liked her very much, so did everybody else. And it wasn't a dreadful week-end at all.

Mrs Van Mier She had a hard mouth, dear, and a calculating expression. Of course you were too besotted about her to notice.

Johnny (*patiently*) I wasn't particularly besotted about her then. It was later that I fell in love with her.

Mrs Van Mier Are you still?

Johnny (*irritably*) Still what?

Mrs Van Mier In love with her?

Johnny One can't fall out of love all in a minute. I'm doing my best.

Mrs Van Mier (*rising and going to him*) I can't bear you to be unhappy, Johnny. You're all I've got you know.

Johnny Yes, Mother, of course I know. But you mustn't worry about me so much. I'll be all right I promise I will. My heart isn't all that that broken you know, just bruised. But bruises are painful, so just be a dear and stop prodding about them. They'll heal themselves in time.

Mrs Van Mier I know you're secretly blaming me for all this.

Johnny (*wearily*) I'm not blaming anyone – except myself.

Mrs Van Mier I know you've resented some of the things I've said. It's no use denying it. A mother's instincts are seldom wrong.

Johnny A mother's instincts are very often wrong when she starts meddling with her son's love affairs.

Mrs Van Mier You see I *was* right. You *do* blame me.

Johnny (*almost losing his temper*) Once and for all, Mother, will you stop going on like this!

Mrs Van Mier There's no need to shout dear.

Johnny (*going to her and putting his hands on her shoulders*) Now listen, Mother. We're setting off on this cruise together. You for my sake, me for your sake. I am to get over my troubles, while you forget about being ill and get well and strong again. Let's for God's sake start off on the right foot. Now just be a darling and go to your cabin and help your stewardess to unpack. I *don't* want to walk any more.

Mrs Van Mier You certainly do remind me of your poor father sometimes.

She goes out wrapped in hurt dignity and shuts the door sharply behind her.

Johnny*, left alone, hurls a bundle of socks he is holding onto the floor.*

Johnny God damn it! God damn everything!

He laughs ruefully, stops down to pick up the socks and begins to sing.

Sail Away

Refrain 1:

> When the storm clouds are riding through a winter sky
> Sail away – Sail away
> When the love-light is fading in your sweetheart's eye
> Sail away – Sail away
> When you feel your song is orchestrated wrong
> Why should you prolong
> Your stay?
> When the wind and the weather blow your dreams sky high
> Sail away – Sail away – Sail away.

> A different sky
> New worlds to gaze upon

The strange excitement of an unfamiliar shore
One more goodbye
One more illusion gone
Just cut your losses
And begin once more.

Refrain 2:

When you can't bear the clamour of the noisy town
Sail away – Sail away
When the friend that you counted on has let you down
Sail away – Sail away
But when soon or late
You recognise your fate
That will be your great,
Great day
On the wings of the morning with your own true love
Sail away – Sail away – Sail away.

Scene Four

The sun deck.

In the darkness before the lights fade in on the scene there is a tremendous clamour. The ship's siren booms loudly and the noise of gongs being banged echoes through the ship together with the sound of **Stewards**' *voices shouting: 'All visitors ashore please.'*

When the lights fade in, the rails are lined with passengers all shouting and talking at once as in Act One, Scene One. There is a further blast from the ship's siren and everyone bursts into a reprise of 'Sail Away'. At the end of this there is more shouting and waving and it is obvious that the ship is beginning to move slowly out into the Hudson River.

Gradually the crowd thins a little. A **Steward** *in a white coat strides along the deck strides along the deck striking a small chiming gong to announce lunch.*

The **Candijack** *family, on the left side, are hanging over the rail and shrieking with excitement.*

Glen   I can still see Aunt Trudi.

Shirley   Where – where –?

Glen   There. Just behind the woman in the red hat.

He shouts.

Hi – Aunt Trudi!

Elmer (*cupping his hands and yelling*)   Don't forget to get the cat fixed. you'll never have any peace until you do.

Maime   Stop it, Elmer. You're always ribbing poor Trudi about that cat, and she did come all the way in from White Plains to see us off.

Elmer   She can't hear anyway. She's deaf as a post.

On the other side of the deck, **Alvin Lush**, *held on to tightly by* **Mrs Lush**, *is hanging over the rail alternately screaming and blowing a whistle.* **Sir Gerard** *and* **Lady Nutfield**, *who are standing beside them, register extreme distaste.*

Mrs Lush   Keep still, Alvin. You don't want to fall into the water, do you?

Alvin (*shrilly*)   I'm a sea-gull – I'm a sea-gull –

He squawks loudly and blows a piercing blast on his whistle.

Sir Gerard   Is it quite necessary for your little boy to go on blowing that whistle? There's enough noise as it is.

Mrs Lush   The child's only enjoying himself.

She lifts **Alvin** *down.*

Mrs Lush   Give mother that whistle, Alvin, you're upsetting this poor old gentleman.

She snatches the whistle from **Alvin**'s *hand and blows a defiant blast on it.*

Mrs Lush   I'm enjoying myself, too.

Alvin *puts his tongue out at* **Sir Gerard** *as* **Mrs Lush** *drags him away, protesting loudly.*

Sir Gerard   Really, these Americans! They're savages, all of them.

Barnaby (*who is standing next to them and overhears this*)   That's our tallest wigwam, sir. We call it the Empire State Building.

The **Nutfields** *give him a look of supercilious scorn and move away.* **Barnaby** *lifts a camera to his eyes and takes a swift shot of the view.* **Mrs Van Mier** *comes on from the left and meets the* **Nutfields** *face to face.*

Mrs Van Mier   Sir Gerard! What a pleasant surprise. I had no idea you were on board. I am Mrs Van Mier. We met in Washington with the dear Cunninghams. Don't you remember?

Sir Geard   Ah yes – of course.

He turns to his wife.

Mildred, you remember Mrs Van Mier?

Lady Nutfield (*shaking hands*)   Indeed yes.

Mrs Van Mier   I had a letter from Hester Cunningham only last week. Her eldest girl is getting married at last.

Sir Gerard   Is that the noisy one or the quiet one?

Mrs Van Mier   Oh, the quiet one. The noisy one became a nun.

At this moment, **Mimi** *comes from behind the bar. She has a passenger list in her hand. She sees the* **Nutfields***, glances at her list and approaches them.*

Mimi   You are Sir Gerard Nutfield?

Sir Gerard (*stiffly*)   That is correct.

Mimi   I knew it. Just from the way you were standing. Nobody but the British can achieve quite that air of casual distinction. I am your cruise hostess, Mimi Paragon.

Sir Gerard (*without enthusiasm*)   Indeed?

Mimi   It is my duty and pleasure to see that you enjoy every fascinating moment of this great, glamorous, gorgeous adventure. Do you care for Bingo?

Sir Gerard   Who is Bingo?

Mimi (*laughing delightedly*)   Isn't that wonderful? And they say the British have no sense of humour. I do hope you will all do me the honour of coming to my 'Get Together' cocktail party at six-o'clock this evening in the Winter Garden Lounge.

Sir Gerard   'Get Together' cocktail party.

He shudders.

Heaven forbid.

Mimi   Don't say another word. The idea nauseates you. I can see it in your eye. I was a mad, crazy fool ever to think of it. I implore you to wipe the whole sordid suggestion from your mind. If there is any teeny weeny thing I can do to make your voyage carefree, irresponsible and sheer heaven, just let me know. I can supply anything from a fourth at bridge to an alcohol rub. Arrivederci for the momento.

She kisses her hand gaily to them and goes off along the deck.

Sir Gerard   The woman's quite obviously a lunatic.

Lady Nutfield   Oh dear. I was afraid this sort of thing might happen.

(*To* **Mrs Van Mier**.) My husband and I were planning to have a little sherry in the smoking-room before luncheon. Perhaps you would care to join us?

Mrs Van Mier   That would be delightful.

They go off through the centre door. **Mimi** *goes over and stands next to* **Barnaby***, who is still busily taking photographs.*

Mimi   I've never seen New Jersey look lovelier, have you?

Barnaby   Actually, I've never seen New Jersey at all. I come from Milwaukee.

Mimi   We must wipe the past from our minds and concentrate on the future. Are you travelling alone?

Barnaby Yes.

Mimi Thank God! I had a dreadful feeling that you might be one of a honeymoon couple. Honeymoon couples are disaster on a cruise. They only think of one thing and it isn't shuffleboard. Are you the retiring type or are you willing to open wide your arms to adventure and savour life to the full?

Barnaby I don't know, ma'am. I've never thought about it.

Mimi Don't be alarmed. I'm your cruise hostess, Mimi Paragon. Unattached young men are my natural prey. What's your name?

Barnaby Barnaby – Barnaby Slade.

Mimi Come and have a drink, pal. Mother can use you.

Barnaby (*grinning*) That's okay by me.

Mimi *sings a reprise of one refrain of 'Come to Me' and she and* **Barnaby** *go off arm in arm.*

Reprise 'Come to Me'

Mimi
 If you feel lonely and need a pal
 I'm the gal
 To take you in tow
 If you're pining for affection and a sympathetic friend
 I've a large collection I can recommend
 If you want something discreetly planned
 On this grand
 And gracious bateau
 If you're basically frustrated and a martyr to ennui
 Come to me – Come to me
 If you need a 'Marijuana' or a quiet cup of tea
 Come to me – lost lamb – Come to me.

Verity *comes through the centre door and strolls over to the rail on the right. She leans on the rail and stares out at the view.* **Mr** *and* **Mrs Sweeny**, *who have been silent since the beginning of the scene, sidle along nearer to her.*

Mrs Sweeny (*conversationally*) Aren't those little tugs the cutest things you ever saw?

Verity (*vaguely*) Yes – yes, they are.

Mrs Sweeny I am Mrs Sweeny. This is my husband, Mr Sweeny. This is the first time we've ever been on a trio together and we've been married over fifty years – Haven't we, Edgar?

Mr Sweeny Yes, sweetheart.

Mrs Sweeny (*persevering*) You'd never think that those tiny boats could turn a great big ship like this right round, would you?

Verity (*without expression*)   No – I don't suppose you would.

Mrs Sweeny (*giving up the struggle*)   Well – Bye-bye for now.

Verity (*forcing a smile*)   Bye-bye.

The **Sweenys** *wander off.* **Johnny** *comes on from the right and leans on the rail a little way from* **Verity**. *The orchestra begins to play 'Sail Away' very softly. A group of people pass along the deck talking and laughing, followed by a* **Steward** *banging the lunch gong.* **Verity**, *with a sigh, produces her cigarette case from her bag, takes a cigarette out and is searching for her lighter when* **Johnny** *moves along towards her.*

Johnny (*politely*)   Allow me.

He takes a cigarette from his own case and lights it. They both stand in silence looking at the New York skyline slipping by. The music continues to play softly.

Johnny (*breaking the silence*)   It's impressive isn't it? – The skyline I mean.

Verity   Yes – very.

Johnny (*with a smile*)   If you'll forgive me for saying so, you don't look as if you cared whether it was impressive or not.

Verity   You're quite right – I don't.

Johnny   Personally, I'll be glad to see the last of New York – for a while anyway.

Verity   So shall I.

Johnny   We obviously have a great deal in common. I hope we meet again.

Verity   It would be a remarkable coincidence if we didn't.

Johnny *bows smilingly. She smiles back. He strolls off down the deck while she, still smiling, looks after him.*

The music swells in the orchestra and the lights fade on the scene.

Scene Five

Mrs Spencer-Bollard's *cabin.*

When the lights fade in on the scene, **Elinor Spencer-Bollard** *is lying on the bed propped up against three pillows reading aloud from a volume of poetry.*

Nancy Foyle *is on her knees on the floor unpacking a suitcase.*

Elinor (*reading*)

   'When I have fears that I may cease to be

   Before my pen has gleaned my teeming brain'

She breaks off.

The handkerchiefs can go with the stockings in the top drawer.

Nancy   Yes, Aunt Elinor.

Elinor (*resuming Keats*)

'Before high piled books in characterery

Hold like full garners, the full garners, the full ripen'd grain'

Throwing the book down.

That was Keats, dear.

Nancy   Yes, Aunt Elinor.

Elinor (*discoursively*)   You see, he was afraid he was going to die before he could write all there was in him to write. I sometimes feel like that myself. – A sort of impotent rage against the impermanence of life. Where are my heart pills?

Nancy   I put them in the drawer by your bed.

Elinor   It was so kind of the Scarsdale Book of the Month Club to send me all that fruit. I don't know what we're going to do with it. You'd better put the typewriter on that little table.

Nancy (*rising and doing so*)   Yes, Aunt Elinor.

Elinor   We shall have to go through all those telegrams later. Are you a good sailor?

Nancy   I don't know . . . I've never been on a ship before.

Elinor   Well – we must hope for the best. Sea-sickness is largely mental you know. Are all my notes together?

Nancy   Yes. In the brief-case.

Elinor   Veronica always used coloured rubber bands, a different colour for each country. She was very methodical.

Nancy   Yes, Aunt Elinor, you told me. I've done the same.

Elinor   Good girl. I'm sure we shall get on famously. It's all a tremendous adventure, isn't it?

Nancy   Yes. I'm thrilled. I can hardly believe it.

Elinor (*rising rapidly from the bed and flinging out her arms*)   Heig-ho! I'm going to take a little trot round the deck while you finish unpacking. Health comes first.

She picks up the poetry book and reads.

'The world is too much with us; late and soon,

Getting and spending, we lay waste our powers'

She flings the book down again:

I've never wasted a moment since the day I was born. What nonsense Wordsworth wrote sometimes, didn't he?

Nancy   I don't know. I've never read him.

Elinor (*appalled*)   Never read your Wordsworth? What a little ignoramus we are to be sure.

(*She embraces her warmly.*) We must remedy all that during the voyage mustn't we? –

'The rainbow comes and goes – and lovely is the rose'.

Don't forget to tell the steward about my hot-water bottle.

She goes swiftly from the cabin. **Nancy**, *left alone, sinks back onto her heels and murmurs 'Oh dear!' rather despondently. The music starts.*

Where Shall I Find Him

Nancy (*singing*)
>   Oh darling mother this
>   Was a mistake. I can never do the job
>   I never should have come
>   I'm far too dumb.
>   I know she's going to miss
>   That other girl, for at least she knew the job.
>   Can you imagine how she'd rage at me
>   Should she discover
>   I'm really searching for a lover?

(*Speaking.*) I mustn't think of that – I really mustn't. It's disloyal to Aunt Elinor. She's paying all my expenses. I must do all I can to help her. I can touch-type. My shorthand's all right, as long as I don't get into a fluster and lose my head. I must keep calm.

(*Singing*)
>   I'll lose her notes
>   and misquote 'quotes'
>   She's bound to take a hate to me
>   And if she should dictate to me
>   I'll either turn and flee
>   Or fling myself, head first, into the sea!
>   (*Spoken.*) Damn!

Verse:
>   I just can't keep out of my mind
>   What my heart is longing to find
>   All I do is wait and hope
>   And wait just a little bit more.
>   Shall I find my personal dream
>   On some distant shore?
>   Or will he appear
>   Suddenly – right here?

Refrain:

> Where shall I find him?
> Where shall he be?
> Where shall I find him
> The one for me?
>
> Suddenly – suddenly – maybe we'll meet
> On an ordinary day – on some ordinary street.
> How shall I know him?
> What will he wear?
> How shall I show him
> How tenderly I care?
> How shall I prove to him
> Make him clearly see
> That he's the only love for me.

Scene Six

The sun deck.

The ship has been at sea now for several days and the atmosphere on board is no longer strained with unfamiliarity and the excitement of leaving. Most of the passengers know each other, at least by sight: cliques have been formed; incipient romances among the young have begun; people have adapted themselves gradually to a daily shipboard routine; the sea is calm and the sky is blue.

The open part of the deck is dotted with steamer chairs in which various passengers are relaxing and taking advantage of the weather. On the left, with wide doors opening on to the deck, can be seen the portion of a cocktail lounge in which a few people are perched on high stools at a semi-circular bar enjoying their pre-luncheon aperitifs. Just below this a few tables are visible. At one of these, four people are playing bridge; at another a man and a woman are engrossed in gin rummy with a friend sitting near them keeping the score.

Above the bar the portion of an upper deck can be seen. This is connected to the sun deck by a small outside companion way. This upper deck adjoins the swimming pool which is out of sight and on it certain of the younger passengers can be observed wearing bikinis or bathing trunks and sunning themselves.

On the right of the sun deck **Elinor Spencer-Bollard**, *wearing a large hat, is seated in a steamer chair. Perched on the foot of it is* **Nancy** *with a note-book on her knees.*

More in the centre **Verity** *is seated, reading a book. She is wearing a beautifully tailored sports suit and dark sun-glasses.*

A little way away from her the **Candijacks** *are busily and noisily occupied in photographing each other.* **Glen** *is in bathing trunks and* **Shirley** *is wearing a bikini* *with a towel over her shoulders.* **Maime** *and* **Elmer** *are attired in fairly unsuitable sports clothes.*

When the lights fade in on the scene there is a good deal of movement. Various people pass to and fro along the deck and through the var. One young man in running shorts appears and disappears at a brisk canter throughout the scene.

Mr *and* **Mrs Sweeny** *stroll on arm in arm. They stop by* **Verity**'*s chair.*

Mrs Sweeny   It's a beautiful day, isn't it?

Verity (*looking up*)   Yes – yes it is.

Mrs Sweeny   Early this morning, Mr Sweeny looked out of the port-hole and saw a whole school of porpoises. Didn't you, Edgar?

Mr Sweeny   Yes, sweetheart.

Mrs Sweeny   At least the steward said they were porpoises.

Verity   Stewards always know.

Mrs Sweeny   He told us that we shall be passing Gibraltar sometime tomorrow night. That will be our first glimpse of Europe. We've never been away from the States before.

Verity (*with a rather weary smile*)   Yes, I know. You told me on the first day out.

Mrs Sweeny   It's wonderful, just wonderful at our age to be seeing the world together.

Verity (*with a certain finality*)   I'm sure I hope it comes up to your expectations – the world I mean. Fortunately there's quite a lot of it.

Mrs Sweeny (*after a slight pause*)   Well. We'll leave you to your book.

Verity (*politely, but with slight irony*)   Thank you – Thank you so much.

The **Sweenys** *go off.* **Verity** *gets up and wanders to the bar.* **Glen** *and* **Shirley Candijack** *leave their parents and run, whooping, up the companion-way to the pool.* **Elmer** *and* **Maime** *go into the bar and order gin fizzes rather loudly. The young man in running shorts trots on and off again*

The lights concentrate on **Mrs Spencer Bollard** *and* **Nancy** *on the right of the deck.*

Elinor (*dictating*)   – 'He helped her to dismount then, suddenly obeying an instinct too strong to be resisted, he crushed her to him. She gave a strangled cry and battered his sun-tanned chest impotently with her fists, but his arms were like steel bands around her quivering body' – I'm not quite sure about 'quivering body'.

Nancy   They have them in Trinidad, don't they?

Elinor   What are you talking about?

Nancy   Steel bands. I've heard the records.

Elinor   You must *not* interrupt, Nancy. It breaks the flow.

Mrs Van Mier *comes on from the right.*

Mrs Van Mier   Good morning.

Elinor (*with a professional smile*)   Good morning.

Mrs Van Mier   Forgive me for disturbing you but I just cannot resist the opportunity of telling you how much I have enjoyed all your delightful books.

Elinor   Thank you – thank you – how very kind.

Mrs Van Mier   I am Mrs Van Mier. My mother was at school with Edith Wharton,[33] you know.

Elinor   No, I didn't know.

Mrs Van Mier   They used to get up to all sorts of mischief together. And my elder sister knew Pearl Buck[34] intimately in Hong Kong – or was it Edna Ferber?[35]

Elinor   If it was Hong Kong it was Pearl Buck.

Mrs Van Mier   Perhaps you would join my son and me for luncheon one day?

Elinor   I'm afraid I never eat luncheon. Just a baked potato and a glass of white wine.

Mrs Van Mier   How sensible.

She bows.

Au revoir for the moment.

She goes.

Elinor   Make a note, Nancy, 'Mrs Van Mier' celebrity snob – literary pretensions – hard as nails – where were we?

Nancy (*looking at her notes.*)   Quivering body.

Mrs Lush *comes through the bar and on to the deck leading* **Alvin** *by the hand.* **He** *is sucking a candy-stick. He drags back as they pass* **Mrs Spencer-Bollard***'s chair.*

Alvin (*indicating* **Mrs Spencer-Bollard** *with his candy-stick*)   Mom – why is that lady wearing a funny hat?

Mrs Lush (*pulling at him*)   How often has mother told you that it's rude to point.

Alvin (*as he is dragged off*)   She looks like a horse.

---

33 Edith Wharton, who was born Edith Newbold Jones (1862–1937) was an American writer and designer.
34 Pearl Sydenstricker Buck (1892–1973) was an American writer who spent much of her life living in and writing about China.
35 Edna Ferber (1885–1968) was an American novelist and playwright, best-known for such works as *Show Boat* (1926).

They disappear.

Elinor That child should be kept in a cage. Change 'quivering body' to 'shrinking form'.

Nancy Yes, Aunt Elinor.

Mimi, *having worked her way vivaciously through the bar, emerges on to the deck and spots* **Mrs Spencer-Bollard**.

Mimi Ah, Mrs Spencer-Bollard – working away as usual! You're indefatigable. I don't know how you do it.

Elinor I must admit I'm finding it increasingly difficult.

Mimi I was wondering if I could persuade you to give a little talk one evening in the Winter Garden Lounge? I can assure you it would be deeply appreciated.

Elinor Really, Mrs Paragon, I'm afraid –

Mimi (*exuberantly*) I implore you not to let that ghastly word 'No' fall from your lips, Mrs Spencer-Bollard. We *need* you. I have had deputation after deputation begging me on their bended knees to ask you this great great favour.

Elinor My dear Mrs Paragon – I –

Mimi (*mowing her down*) Don't say anything now. Just consider it. Mull it over in your brilliant mind. Brood on it. You are a great woman, Mrs Spencer-Bollard. You are loved and revered from the Rocky Mountains to the Mexican border. I suppose it's no use trying to interest you in the shuffleboard tournament?

Elinor It most certainly is not.

Mimi You're so right. A woman of your intellectual calibre shoving away at those gruesome little disks. Quelle fantasie! I was insane even to think of it. Now I must run like a little hunted hare and tot up the Bingo scores. Auf Wiedersehen.

She rushes off.

Elinor Make a note, Nancy. 'Professional hostess – synthetic vivacity – lonely as a cloud – no man in her life – will probably end up as a drunkard!'

Nancy I rather like her. It must be a terrible job having to cope with everybody and keep them amused.

Elinor (*rising*) I am going to the cabin. My inspiration has withered on the bough. Type out that chapter and come to me at two-thirty sharp.

Nancy (*also rising*) Yes, Aunt Elinor.

Mrs Spencer-Bollard *collects her bag, flings her cashmere shawl over her arm and strides off along the deck.* **Nancy**, *left alone, glances through her notes with a sigh and puts them in a brief-case.* **Barnaby** *appears from the right.*

Barnaby At last we are alone!

Nancy (*crossly*) Oh, it's you.

Barnaby If I suddenly crushed you in my arms would you give a strangled cry?

Nancy You've been listening.

Barnaby Of course I have. I've been hiding behind that lifeboat. Did you know that my great-grandmother once met Harriet Beecher Stowe at a clam bake?

Nancy Don't be silly.

Barnaby My Uncle Willy knows Tennessee Williams' psychiatrist intimately. They get up to all sorts of mischief together.

Nancy I must go and type these notes.

Barnaby Does that old prune keep you at it all day long?

Nancy She's not an old prune. She's a wonderful woman and one of the most distinguished writers in America.

Barnaby You've got some freckles on your notes. I never noticed that before.

Nancy Well, it's very rude of you to notice them now.

Barnaby (*fiddling with his camera*) I love freckles – they send me. Just stand still for a moment. The light's perfect.

Nancy Why do you keep on taking photographs of me? I'm not in the least celebrated or important.

Barnaby How do you know? You might be the most important person in the world to someone some day.

He clicks the camera.

Nancy Well, I'm not now.

Barnaby Could I persuade you to give a brief, informal talk on sex and steel bands in the writing room.

Nancy No.

Barnaby Steel bands send me almost as much as freckles do. They make me think of coral reefs, bright coloured birds and you lying in my arms staring up through coconut palms at the tropical stars.

Nancy You've not only chosen the wrong girl, but the wrong cruise!

She turns to go.

Barnaby Everything's in the mind.

He catches her by the arm and begins to sing.

---

36 Tennessee Williams (1911–1983), born Thomas Lanier Williams III, was an American playwright and screenwriter, best known for such plays as *A Streetcar Names Desire* (1947) and *Cat on a Hot Tin Roof* (1955).

'Beatnik Love Affair'

Verse:

Why suffer from moral convictions?
Social restrictions?
Let's thumb our noses at
Cold wars and atomic predictions
They're merely waste of time.
Let's follow a vision
Now is the moment to – see clearly
And realise that really
We are on the brink of it
Come to think of it.

Refrain 1:

You and I could have an upright, downright, watertight, dynamite
Love affair
We could either play it up-beat, down-beat, off-beat, on-the-beat
Fair or square
Hey – for those flip calypsos
Ho – for that rhythmic din
Heig-ho – for those dopes and dipsos
Rum punch – coconuts – Gordon's Gin
Think if we tried out
Some little hide-out
On some tropical isle
Naked and warm
From dawn to moonrise
Somerset Maugham-wise
Blue Lagoon-wise
Every time we saw an evening star show
We could wonder if the same Jack Paar[37] show
Still was on the air
While we carried on with our on-beat, off-beat, beatnik love affair.

Refrain 2:

You and I could have an in-board, out-board, bed-and-board, overboard
Love affair
All we need's a little off-key, on-key, king-sized, organised
Time to spare
There – by the Caribbean
We'll – cross the Rubicon
We'll have – by the deep blue sea an
All-out, roustabout – carry-on.

---

37 American television host Jack Paar (1918–2004) hosted *The Tonight Show* from 1957 to 1962.

We'll get a 'man-tan'
Gargantuan tan
On those shimmering sands
Nothing to do but read and rest dear
We could get through 'By Love Possessed' dear
While we have a little good-night kiss I'll
Quite forget out last misguided missile
Just missed Gracie Square
And we'll carry on with our king-sized, organised, beatnik love affair.

At the end of the number, **Barnaby**, **Nancy** *and the* **Boys** *and* **Girls** *dance off.*

Verity, *who has been having a cool drink at the bar, comes back to her steamer-chair and settles down with her book.*

A **Steward** *passes from left to right banging the warning gong for lunch.*

A group of people, laughing and talking, come down from the upper deck and go off, presumably to the dining-saloon.

Mimi *enters from the left. She sees* **Verity** *and comes over to her.*

Mimi Would it drive you completely insane if I sat down for a minute?

Verity (*with a smile*) I don't think so. Why not try?

Mimi (*pulling up a chair*) You always look so cool and unruffled. I feel as if I'd spent my entire life in a super-market.

She sits down.

I've just escorted a merry throng of rubbernecks round the ship, engine-room and all. They ask the damndest questions.

Verity Can you answer them?

Mimi What I don't know, I invent.

Verity I certainly don't envy you your job.

Mimi Oh it has its points. I see the world and we well paid for it.

Verity Have you been doing it for long?

Mimi Ever since I retired from the stage – owing to popular demand.

Verity I had no idea you were an actress.

Mimi Neither had anyone else. That's why I ran away to sea. This is my seventh cruise in this gracious vessel. I'm beginning to feel as much a part of the ship as the funnel. What are you reading?

Verity (*holding up her book*) *Anna Karenina*. It's one of my standbys.

Mimi I saw a movie of that once. She throws herself under a train doesn't she? All for l'amour!

Verity Not only for l'amour, but because everything becomes too much for her.

Mimi Well let me know when the next train's passing. Everything is certainly becoming too much for me.

She rises.

There's been an angry scene about the deck tennis finals and our shuffleboard champion has developed a hernia.

Mimi *waves cheerfully and goes off.* **Mrs Lush** *comes on from the right dragging* **Alvin** *by the hand.* **Alvin** *is snivelling*

Mrs Lush It was all your own fault, Alvin. If you hadn't thrown the little girl's doll down the ventilator she wouldn't have hit you with the bat, and if you don't learn to be a good boy and behave yourself mother will have to have you analysed again.

Mrs Lush *and* **Alvin** *go off.* **Johnny Van Mier** *comes on from the left. He comes over to* **Verity.**

Johnny Mother and I wondered if you'd care to come and have a drink with us in the smoking-room before lunch?

Verity Won't that make us rather late? The Captain's a stickler for punctuality.

Johnny He's not coming down today. The Chief Steward told me.

Verity Very well. I'd love to.

She rises

Johnny Don't let's go for a moment.

Verity Why not?

Johnny I want to tell you something.

Verity (*sitting down again*)   What is it?

Johnny I want to tell you that I've never enjoyed anything in my life as much as dancing with you last night.

Verity (*lightly*)   That's very sweet of you, Mr Van Mier. I enjoyed it too.

Johnny You promised last night that you'd call me Johnny. All the people I really like call me Johnny.

Verity Very well – Johnny. But we mustn't keep your mother waiting.

Johnny She won't be there yet. She went down to her cabin to change. She always takes hours.

Verity That's a very smart jacket.

Johnny Mother says it's flashy.

Verity (*smiling*) Perhaps it is, a little, but you're tall enough to be able to carry it off.

Johnny Did I talk an awful lot of nonsense last night?

Verity No. You were very gay, and very charming.

Johnny It was the first time I've felt really happy since I came on board.

Verity I'm glad.

Johnny I'm not usually in the habit of pouring out my private troubles to people. But you were so sympathetic and – and sort of warm.

Verity I took it as a compliment.

Johnny I owe you a lot for being so understanding and – and so wise.

Verity It's easy to be wise about other people.

Johnny You look suddenly sad.

Verity How old are you, Johnny?

Johnny Twenty-six. Why?

Verity I just wondered.

Johnny Is age so important to you?

Verity (*with a laugh*) It's beginning to be.

Johnny (*putting his hands on hers*) I'm not a boy you know. I mean – I've been around quite a bit.

Verity (*drily*) Have you really?

Johnny Don't you believe me?

Verity (*gently withdrawing her hand*) You're a very handsome boy, Johnny. Handsome and attractive, and you dance beautifully – but –

Johnny But what?

Verity But I don't think you should encourage yourself to think – well – to think on the lines that you are thinking at the moment.

Johnny Why not?

Verity Because I'm a married woman, and considerably older than you.

Johnny Age again!

Verity Yes, age again. It does keep intruding, doesn't it?

Johnny (*very tenderly*) What are you so frightened of? What are you running from?

Verity I'm not quite sure. Myself I expect.

Johnny *gently takes her hand again and begins to sing.*

'Later than Spring'

Verse:

Have no fears for future years
For sweet compensation you may find
Make your bow
To the moment that is 'now'
And always bear in mind.

Refrain 1:

Later than spring
The warmth of summer comes
The charm of autumn comes
The leaves are gold
Poets say
That the blossoms of May
Fade away
And die.
Yet, don't forget
That we met
When the sun was high.
Later than spring
Words that were said before
Tears that were shed before
Can be consoled
Realise – that it's wise – to remember
Though Time is on the wing
Song birds still sing
Later than spring.

Refrain 2:

Later than spring
Though careless rapture's past
No need to gaze aghast
At days gone by
If you will – you can still
Feel the thrill
Of a new desire
Still – feel that glow
When you know
That your world's on fire
Later than spring
Remembered April showers
May bring our present hours
A clearer sky
We pretend – and pretend – it's the end

But the pendulum must swing
Nightingales sing
Later than spring.

At the end of the song, **Verity** *rises from her chair and stands looking at* **Johnny** *in silence for a moment. Then, with rather a tremulous smile, she takes his hands and they go off.*

The young man in running shorts, by now obviously in a state of exhaustion, trots laboriously on from the left, canters weakly round the deck again and trots off.

Joe *comes striding on from the right. He is intercepted by* **Sir Gerard** *and* **Lady Nutfield***, who come on from the left*

Sir Gerard   Purser.

Joe   Good morning, sir.

Sir Gerard   This *is* a British ship is it not?

Joe   Yes, sir.

Sir Gerard   Well, all I can say is, it doesn't feel like one.

Joe   I'm sorry to hear that, sir.

Sir Gerard   In the first place it's crawling with Americans.

Joe   The whole cruise is organised for the American trade, sir.

Sir Gerard   In the second place, the boat deck is covered in black smut from the funnel. My wife had to change her dress twice yesterday afternoon.

Joe   I'll speak to the Chief Engineer, sir.

Sir Gerard   And in the third place, I found a cockroach in my shower this morning.

Joe   I trust it was a British cockroach, sir.

Sir Gerard   I am not accustomed to impertinence. On a British ship I expect scrupulous politeness from members of the personnel.

Joe   Correct, sir. You are absolutely right, sir.

Sir Gerard   Thank you, Purser. Come, Mildred, it is time for luncheon.

The **Nutfields** *go off.* **Joe** *looks after them balefully. Two* **Stewards***,* **Carrington** *and* **Hoskins***, come on from the right. They begin to sing*

'The Passenger's Always Right'

Carrington
　The woman in cabin forty-nine has lost her diamond brooch.

Joe (*also singing*)
　Calm her, Carrington

    Charm her, Carrington
    That's the correct approach.

Hoskins
    A gentleman on the promenade deck just called me a lazy slob.

Joe
    Smile at him, Hoskins
    Smile at him, Hoskins
    That is part of your job.

Three other **Stewards** *appear. They sing in unison*

Stewards
    The three fat children in B deck 3
    Have thrown their bath-mat into the sea.

Three more **Stewards** *appear.*

Stewards
    The silly old broad in main deck 2 has dropped her dentures into the loo.

More **Stewards** *appear.*

Joe
    Passengers, since the world began
    Have been querulous, rude and snooty
    England expects that every man
    This day, should do his duty.

He jumps onto a small podium. All the **Stewards** *gather round him attentively.*

Verse:

Joe
    Weatherby?

Weatherby
    Here.

Joe
    Hoskins?

Hoskins
    Here.

Joe
    Green, Black, Richardson?

{ **Green, Blake, Richardson**
    Here. Here. Here.

Joe
    Crawford?

Crawford
    Here.

Joe
Shuttleworth?

Shuttleworth
Here.

Joe
Smith, Brown, Parkinson?

{ Smith, Brown, Parkinson
Here. Here. Here.

Joe
Where the devil are Bruce and Frome?

Weatherby
One's got shingles and the other's gone home.

Joe
Where's O'Reilley and Jock Macbride?

Weatherby
One got married and the other got fried.

Joe
Carrington?

Carrington
Here.

Joe
Brewster.

Brewster
Here.

Joe
Where's young Fawcett and Windermere?

Weatherby
Fawcett stayed home in bed
Poor old Windermere dropped down dead.

Joe
The start of each cruise
is the time I choose
To lecture each subordinate
You're not damned fools
And you know the rules
So see you all co-ordinate.

All
We've heard all this before
We can't stand any more.

Joe

    Bow – smile – charm – tact.
    Never forget one vital fact.

Refrain 1:

    The passenger's always right, my boys
    The passenger's always right
    Although he's a drip
    He's paid for his trip
    So greet him with delight
    Agree to all suggestions
    However coarse or crude
    Reply to all his questions
    Ply him with drink – stuff him with food
    The passenger may be sober, boys
    The passenger may be tight
    The passenger may be foe or friend
    Or absolutely round the bend
    But calm him
    Charm him
    Even though he's higher than a kite
    The passenger's always right.

Refrain 2:

    The passenger's always right, my boys
    The passenger's always right
    Those dreary old wrecks
    Who litter the decks
    Demand that you're polite
    Don't count on any free time
    Be kind to all the jerks
    And every day at tea-time
    Stuff 'em with cake – Give 'em the works
    The passenger may be dull, my boys
    The passenger may be bright
    The passenger may be quite serene
    Or gibbering with Benzedrine[38]
    But nurse him
    Curse him
    Only when the bastard's out of sight
    Remember, boys
    The God-damned passenger's always right.

---

38 Benzedrine was the brand name for amphetamine sulfate; a popular medication until the 1970s.

Scene Seven

The promenade deck.

The promenade deck stretches the entire width of the stage. A ship's rail comes half way on from each side indicating that the orchestra and the auditorium are the sea. In the centre where the rails do not quite meet there is a small bay in which there are a few steamer chairs. Behind these chairs is a door leading to the main hall.

When the lights fade in on the scene **Verity** *and* **Mrs Van Mier** *are occupying two steamer chairs in the centre.* **Mrs Van Mier** *is working at an embroidery frame and talking.* **Verity**, *with her book face downwards on her lap, is listening politely.*

Mrs Van Mier   – Of course, *I* knew the type of girl she was at the moment I set eyes on her – pretty, I suppose, in rather a common sort of way, but hard as nails and man mad.

Verity   An unattractive combination.

Mrs Van Mier   She also had a mania for dieting – like so many young girls nowadays – she sat through every meal picking away at a salad and smoking those nasty mentholated cigarettes. I remember saying to Johnny, the first time he brought her to the house, 'The poor thing looks half starved!' Of course he snapped my head off. Being a widow and the mother of an only son is no bed of roses I can tell you.

Verity (*absently*)   No – I don't suppose it is.

Mrs Van Mier   Of course if I had known then how unhappy she was going to make him I'd have thrown her out of the house neck and crop.

Verity (*with a slight smile*)   Wouldn't that have been a little drastic?

Mrs Van Mier   I'm afraid he takes after his poor father as far as women are concerned. Absolutely no discrimination. I remember when he was still at Harvard he fell in love with the most dreadful creature. I nearly went out of my mind with worry.

Verity   In what way dreadful?

Mrs Van Mier   Well. She was at least ten years older than he was to begin with and married to a psychiatrist. She kept on having nervous breakdowns and being given shock treatments and sending Johnny anguished telegrams. He soon got over that, thank goodness.

Verity   Did she get over it too?

Mrs Van Mier   I haven't the slightest idea. I expect she came to a bad end. That sort of woman always does.

Verity (*with a sigh, patting her book*)   Poor Anna.

Mrs Van Mier (*wrapping up her embroidery frame*)   Anna who?

Verity (*rising*)   Just an old friend of mine.

She smiles pleasantly.

We shall meet at dinner.

Verity *goes off on the right.* **Mrs Van Mier** *looks after her thoughtfully for a moment and puts her embroidery frame into her work bag. The young man in running shorts trots doggedly across the stage from right to left.* **Mrs Van Mier** *watches him with an expression of distaste.* **Johnny** *comes on from the left.*

Mrs Van Mier   That young man will strain his heart if he's not careful – like your poor Uncle Matthew.

Johnny   Shouldn't you be dressing for dinner?

Mrs Van Mier   I'm just going down. I've been having a little gossip with your Mrs Craig.

Johnny (*with a touch of irritation*)   Why do you call her 'my Mrs Craig', Mother? I don't own her.

Mrs Van Mier   Well, you must admit you've been fairly thick with her during the last few days.

Johnny   I like her. She's very attractive, good company, and she dances beautifully.

Mrs Van Mier (*rising*)   Those sorts of women always dance well. It's part of their stock in trade.

Johnny   Now what on earth do you mean by that?

Mrs Van Mier (*patting his check affectionately*)   You must forgive your poor old mother if she's a little over-wary. She's learnt in a hard school.

Mrs Van Mier *goes off through the centre door.* **Johnny**, *biting his lip with irritation, strolls down to the rail and looks out at the sea. The orchestra begins to play softly the first bars of the refrain of 'Sail Away'.* **Johnny**, *quietly and almost dreamily, sings the last few lines.*

Johnny (*singing*)
　　But when soon or late
　　You recognise your fate
　　That will be a great, great day.
　　On the wings of the morning
　　With your own true love
　　Sail away – Sail away – Sail away.

The lights fade on the scene.

Scene Eight

The sun deck. Night.

The deck is deserted. The bar is shuttered up and roped off. The moon is shining on the sea and there is the faint sound of the engines throbbing and the waves swishing against the side of the ship.

Mimi *comes on from the left. She looks rather peculiar because she is wearing elegant pyjamas and a fur stole. She is accompanied by her pug on a lead.*

Mimi There's no sense in dragging back, Adlai. You've been three times round the ship and it's time for you to go back to your basket and dream ghastly little dreams that make you twitch. Lift up your heart, Adlai, stop snuffling and look at those great big glorious stars. And if you are planning in your evil little mind to make the smallest wee-wee on this spotless deck, mother will wallop the living daylights out of you.

She and **Adlai** *go off.*

Nancy *comes down the companion-way from the upper deck, followed by* **Barnaby**. *He is in a dinner-jacket. She is in a simple, light-coloured evening frock*

Barnaby Why are you suddenly mad at me?

Nancy I just don't happen to like being pawed about.

Barnaby If you didn't expect to be kissed why did you come up onto the boat deck in the moonlight?

Nancy (*hotly*) I did *not* expect to be kissed. I expected you to behave yourself.

Barnaby How can you hope to wander about at night in a dress like that and not bring out the beast in men?

Nancy You're not a man. You're nothing but an overgrown schoolboy, and fresh at that.

Barnaby Will you have a Coca-Cola with me in the bar before lunch tomorrow morning?

Nancy No.

Barnaby Will you come to the movies with me tomorrow afternoon at four-thirty? It's *The Swiss Family Robinson*.

Nancy No.

Barnaby I knew it.

Nancy I knew it.

Nancy Knew what?

Barnaby You're crazy about me. But your sub-conscious won't let you admit it. You're scared.

Nancy I'm not in the least scared.

Barnaby Oh yes you are. You're scared that the naked, burning passion in my eyes might shrivel you up into a little freckled cinder!

Nancy (*witheringly*) Drop dead!

She goes off.

Barnaby (*left alone*)   She loves me!

He begins to sing.

Sings:

>Maybe I've found her
>Can this be she?
>Maybe I've found her
>The one for me
>Suddenly – suddenly – I wonder why
>Such a lot of extra stars
>Seem to shimmer in the sky
>Can this be my girl
>Do you suppose?
>This rather shy girl
>With freckles on her nose
>How can I prove to her
>Make her clearly see
>That she's the only love for me.

The music lifts and changes into waltz rhythm. **Barnaby** *dances romantically and exultantly on the deserted deck – as the lights fade.*

Scene Nine

Mimi's *cabin.*

Mimi's *cabin, which is in a state of considerable chaos. There is a large clump of coloured balloons in one corner,* **Adlai***, in his basket, in another. On the bed is laid out* **Mimi**'s *evening gown together with a number of paper hats and Cotillion favours. On the dressing table is a large leather-framed photograph of* **Skid Paragon** *wearing riding-clothes.* **Mimi***, with some butter muslin tied round her head and an Italian lesson-book on her knees, is seated making up before the mirror.*

Mimi (*to her own reflection*)   Io sono molta bella.

She glances at the book

Io *non* sono molta bella.

She looks back at the mirror

I was right the second time.

She turns to **Adlai***.*

Adlai – Lei è uno molto bellissimo pugalino, that's what lei è.

There is a knock at the door.

Come in.

Joe *comes in. He is carrying a corsage of flowers*

Joe   I've brought you some flowers. For the Captain's dinner.

Mimi (*jumping up and embracing him*)   Why Joe – that's just the sweetest thought I've ever known. You're an angel.

Joe   They'll bring out the colour in your eyes.

Mimi (*looking at herself in the mirror*)   Much better leave it where it is.

Joe   Come and have a drink in my cabin before the gruesome gala. Shuttleworth's wife's just had another baby. We're celebrating.

Mimi   Poor Shuttleworth. I can't think when he gets the time.

Joe   See you in about half an hour.

Mimi   Okay. Thanks for the flowers – you're a real pal.

He turns to go.

Joe *goes out. The telephone rings.* **Mimi** *picks up the receiver.*

Mimi (*at telephone*)   Pronto pronto – Ah Mrs Sweeny – Yes, Mrs Sweeny – No, Mrs Sweeny – by all means, Mrs Sweeny – Yes, the shuffleboard winners will be announced after the Captain's dinner and the prizes will be distributed in the main lounge at ten-thirty. – Yes, Mrs Sweeny, if the steward said they were porpoises they sure were porpoises, all our stewards are trained to recognise porpoises instantaneously. – Arriverderci, Mrs Sweeny.

She hangs up.

Mimi (*continues*)   Questa, Adlai darling, was la Signora Sweeny and entre le and Io she is a great big fabuloso cracking bore and brutto as sing into the bargain.

She reads from her book

'How much are these boot-trees?' – I'm sure I'm very sorry, Mrs Lush but it really was his own fault you know. He was getting in everyone's way and they were playing the finals. – Where did the rubber ring hit him? – Oh I see – poor little chat – we must all hope it goes down by the morning – No, Mrs Lush, they couldn't play deck tennis with soft rubber rings, they have to be hard. – No I am sure Mr Fluger didn't do it on purpose, he's a family man and devoted to children. – Very well, Mrs Lush.

She hangs up sharply

Basta – Basta – Basta – Mrs Lush. Vai and jump in the lago, Mrs Lush!

She hangs up and turns back to the book. She reads

'I fear that this washing-machine is of an inferior quality.'

She pitches the book across the room

Useful phrases, hey?

'Useful Phrases'

Verse:

When the Tower of Babel fell
It caused a lot of unnecessary Hell
Personal 'rapport'
Became a complicated bore
And a lot more difficult than it had been before
When the Tower of Babel fell.

The Chinks[39] and the Japs
And the Finns and Lapps
Were reduced to a helpless stammer
And the Ancient Greeks
Took at least six weeks
To learn their Latin grammar
The guttural wheeze

Of the Portuguese
Filled the brains of the Danes
With horror
And verbs, not lust
Cause the final bust
In Sodom and Gomorrah.

If it hadn't been for that
Bloody building falling flat
I should not have had to learn Italiano
And keep muttering, 'Si – Si'
And 'Mi chiamano Mimi'
Like an ageing Metropolitan soprano!

I should not have had to look
At this ghastly little book
'Til my brain becomes as soft as mayonnaise is
Messers Hugo and Berlitz
Must have torn themselves to bite
Dreaming up so many useless, useful phrases.

Refrain 1:

Pray tell me the time
It is six
It is seven
It's half past eleven
It's twenty to two
I want thirteen stamps

---

[39] This is a racial slur for Chinese culture and has been left in for context.

Does your child have convulsions
Please bring me some rhubarb
I need a shampoo
How much is this hat?
My mother is married
These boots are too small
My aunt has a cold
Shall we go to the opera?
This meat is disgusting
Is this the Town Hall?

Refrain 2:

How much is this ribbon?
It's cheap
It's expensive
What very fine linen!
What pretty cretonne![40]
What time is the train?
It is late
It is early
It's running on schedule
It's here.
It has gone.
I've written six letters
I've written no letters
Please fetch me a horse
I have need of a groom
This isn't my passport
This isn't my hatbox
Please show me the way
To Napoleon's tomb.

Refrain 3:

The weather is cooler
The weather is hotter
Pray fasten my corsets
Please bring me my cloak
I've lost my umbrella
I'm in a great hurry
I'm going
I'm staying
D'you mind if I smoke?
This man is the Purser
This isn't my cabin
This egg soup is too thick

---

40 A heavy cotton fabric.

Please bring me a trout
What an excellent pudding
Pray hand me my gloves
I am going to be sick.

Scene Ten

The promenade deck.

The deck is empty. It is about four o'clock in the morning. The noise of the sea is very loud.

Verity *comes on from the right. She is wearing a fur coat over her night things. She walks listlessly over to the rail and leans on it staring at the sea.*

Johnny *comes quietly down the companion-way from the deck above. He is wearing rubber-soled shoes, grey flannel trousers and a sports coat. He has a coloured scarf round his neck.*

He stands looking at **Verity** *for a moment before speaking, then he says, very softly –*

Johnny Verity.

Verity (*turning*) Oh – you made me jump.

Johnny (*coming over and leaning on the rail next to her*) Well met by moonlight.

Verity I couldn't sleep.

Johnny Neither could I. I've been up on the boat deck for hours. We're getting near land. I can sort of – feel it. A change in the air.

Verity Yes. I can feel it too.

Johnny A great deal seems to have changed for me – in the last twenty-four hours.

Verity I really must go back to bed – It will be dawn in a little while.

Johnny Don't go for a moment.

(*He looks at her pleadingly.*) Have a cigarette.

Verity No. I've smoked far too much already.

Johnny (*coming downstage and pointing to the sky*) Look – there's a shooting star. We must make a wish.

Verity There's no time. It went too swiftly.

Johnny (*looking at her*) I had time.

Verity (*lightly*) Did you, Johnny?

Johnny But the wish was already there. It's been there all evening.

Verity (*gently*) Good night, Johnny.

She makes a move to go

Johnny (*holding her with his eyes*) Please don't go.

Verity (*hesitantly*) This is very foolish.

Johnny The other morning when we were talking before lunch, you said, rather reprovingly, that you were a married woman and considerably older than me.

Verity It's true.

Johnny I noticed you didn't say that you were a happily married woman.

Verity Johnny. Please stop.

Johnny Are you – happily married?

Verity What makes you imagine that I'm not?

Johnny The expression in your eyes – when we were dancing last night.

Verity Please don't talk like that. I mean it – I really don't want you to.

Johnny It's true though isn't it? Something did happen when we were dancing. You can't deny it – please don't deny it.

Verity (*quietly, after a slight pause*) No – I don't deny it. I wish I could.

Johnny Why?

Verity (*with an attempt at lightness*) It's a little too complicated to explain.

Johnny I've fallen in love with you.

Verity (*looking down*) Have you, Johnny? – Have you really?

Johnny I know you've been unhappy and disappointed and disillusioned, but surely not enough to prevent you from ever loving anyone again – even for a little?

Verity (*with a sad little smile*) 'Even for a little!' A curiously practical phrase.

Johnny Verity – Oh my darling –

He takes her in his arms. She closes her eyes and surrenders to him. The music swells.

'This is a Night for Lovers'

> The clouds are following the moon
> The dawn will be breaking soon
> The stars are fading one by one
> The night is nearly done
>
> The mountains stand against the sky
> Watching the little clouds pass by
> Watching the shadows grow

Watching the shadows grow
On the sleeping world below.

This is a night for lovers
A night to be set apart
Forever in somebody's heart
This is a moment forever and above
This is a night for love.

Soon when the dawn discovers
Secret the night concealed
There'll be bright new hills
And a coloured sea
Instead of the delicate mystery
That the moon
Only half revealed.

When dawn is lighting up the sky
Watching the little clouds pass by
Watching the shadows grow
Watching the shadows grow
On the sleeping world below

This is a night for lovers
Set between yesterday's fears
And to-morrow's most probable tears
This is a moment forever and above
This is a night for love.

Scene Eleven

The sun deck (night).

The sun deck is gaily illuminated with coloured lights. The ship's orchestra is playing on a raised dais on the right. The deck is crowded with couples dancing. They are all wearing evening dress and most of them have paper caps on. **Mrs Van Mier**, *with* **Sir Gerard** *and* **Lady Nutfield**, *is seated at a table downstage sipping a liqueur and watching, with a keen eye,* **Johnny** *dancing with* **Verity**. *Just above them, at a table by herself,* **Elinor Spencer-Bollard** *is scribbling notes on a pad. She occasionally looks up with an expression of slight annoyance at* **Nancy** *who is dancing with* **Glen Candijack**. **Barnaby**, *who is leaning rather disconsolately against the ship's rail, finally cuts in. After he has danced with her for a short while, another young man cuts in and he retires scowling to the bar.*

The whole of this scene should be entirely choreographic and visual and there is no dialogue audible until **Mimi** *suddenly rushes on excitedly from the left and holds out her arms for the music to stop. The band tops with a crash of jangling chords.*

Mimi (*loudly*)   Land at last – Land at last! Look everybody – A bright light shining in a bad old world!

Everybody crowds to the rails and cheers. **Mimi** *starts to sing. This number is in the form of an up-beat Negro spiritual. Singly and in groups the* **Passengers** *and the* **Stewards** *join in until everyone on the stage is singing full out.*

At the climax, and at a signal from **Joe** *who is standing on the upper deck, all the coloured lights are switched off and, at the back, standing up majestically from the sea, the shadowy shape of the Rock of Gibraltar slides into view.*

Curtain.

First Act Finale

Introduction

Mimi
   Hail, pioneers! Hail, pioneers! Hail, pioneers!
   You have survived
   The mighty ocean's turbulence
   The sudden tempest's fearful roar
   The fury of the elements
   Until at last the welcome shore
   Rises against the star-filled sky
   To crown your glorious odyssey.

All
   Ah – Ah! Ah – Ah! Ah – Ah! Ah – Ah!

Mimi
   Give thanks to him, this blessed day
   To one above who set the course
   I am referring, need I say
   To Captain Wilberforce.

All
   All praise to him
   All praise to him
   We heartily endorse
   Your most appropriate salute
   To Captain Wilberforce.

Mimi
   You are about to land
   Tomorrow morning
   Upon an alien strand
   Your feet will tread

Accept from me I pray
A final warning
Remember what I say
Remember what I've said . . .

'You're a Long Long Way from America'

Refrain 1:

You're a long long way from America
You're a long long way from home
Let the standard guide books
Be your bedside books
And don't read sinde books
Like 'The Lays of Ancient Rome'
If you're not put off
By the continental coffee
That arrives on your breakfast tray
You will find you've learned a little from the bad old world
When you're back in the USA.

Refrain 2:

You're a long long way from America
Be prepared to face the worst
While guitars are strumming
'The Yanks are coming'
You'll find the plumbing
Rather frightening at first
Do not be surprised
If the milk's not pasteurised
And appears just a wee bit grey
You'll have learned something from the bad old world
When you're back in the USA.

Refrain 3:

You're a long long way from America
Be prepared for stress and strain
Don't expect hot showers
Or search for hours
To find fresh flowers
That are wrapped in cellophane
You need not suspect,
If you've had enough injections,
Every fish dish that comes your way
You'll have learnt some hints on cooking in the bad old world
When you're back in the USA.

Counter-melody:

> Get out the greenbacks
> Get out the greenbacks
> They will extricate us
> If we should go astray
> In ancient nations
> The populations
> Have learnt to count upon
> American donations
> Traveller's cheques can
> Do more than sex can
> To consolidate us
> Don't let the status quo go
> Hand out those dollar bills
> Be loyal and true
> To the traditions of the USA.

Act Two

Scene One

Tangiers.

The scene is a 'Place' in Tangiers.

On the right is a café with tables set up coloured awnings.

On the left is a shop stocked with Moroccan souvenirs, most of them leather, and all of them hideous.

At the back the mosques and Moorish buildings of the Kasbah rise up against the sky.

When the curtain rises there is a great deal of movement accompanied by wailing Arab music in the background. Beggars, rug-sellers, vendors of sweets and pistachio nuts, conjurors, shoeshine boys, etc. pass back and forth in front of the people sipping their apperitifs at the café tables.

After a little while **Ali** *detaches himself from the crowd. He is a disreputable-looking Arab dressed as a guide. He wears a shabby uniform coat, baggy trousers and a fez. He advances to the centre of the stage and blows three short blasts on a whistle. Immediately a collection of seedy characters of mixed breeds emerge from various directions and gather round him.*

One of them produces a small box on which **Ali** *mounts so that he can command attention.*

They are all gabbing and shouting at the top of their voices. **Ali** *blows his whistle again, their clamour dies away and he begins to sing.*

'The Customer's Aways Right'

Verse:

Ali
  Ibrahim?

Ibrahim
  Here.

Ali
  Stefanos?

Stefanos
  Here.

Ali
  Scarface Molyneux?

Scarface
Here, boss. Here.

Ali
Heinrich?

Heinrich
Ya.

Ali
Stanislas?

Stanislas
Da.

Ali
Levi Finkelstein?

Levi
Rah rah rah!

Ali
Where is Pedro the Portugese?

Ibrahim
In Gibraltar with a touch of DTS.

Ali
Where the devil is Wang-Hi-Chung?

Ibrahim
He's deported and his brother got hung.

Ali
Ismail?

Ismail
Here.

Ali
Abdul?

Abdul
Here.

Ali
Where's Mohammed Ben Al Kazir?

Ibrahim
He was caught forging cheques
Got religion, and changed his sex.

Ali
When a cruise ship comes
I expect you bums

To make your own deductions
Inspired by greed
You will all proceed
According to instructions.

Ali

The suckers land to-day
Hurray – Hurray – Hurray!

Ali

Cringe – beg – steal – whine
Never forget the famous line

Refrain 1:

The customer's always right, my dears
The customer's always right.
The son-of-a-bitch
Is probably rich
So smile with all your might
Be wiser than a monkey
Be on to all the tricks
If one of them's a junky
Give him a break – give him a fix.
The customer may be black, my dears
Or yellow or brown or white
He may have a yen for raw recruits
Or mountain goats or football boots
But smooth him
Soothe him
Pander to him morning, noon and night
The customer's always right.

Refrain 2:

The customer's always right, my dears
The customer's always right
They may pay a price
For curious vice
Or merely want a fight
They may have inhibitions
And yearn for secret joys
Obey your intuitions
Offer them girls – offer them boys.
The customer may be dumb, my dears
Or terribly erudite
Perhaps you can satisfy his needs
With strings of rather nasty beads
Compel him

Sell him
Anything from sex to dynamite
Remember, dears
The God-damned customer's always right.

When the vocal part of the number is finished they all embark on a grotesque dance which must be left to the supreme efficiency, humour and inventiveness of the choreographer.

When this is over **Mimi** *enters from the right with a group of tourists including the* **Candijack** *family,* **Mr Rawlings, Mr** *and* **Mrs Sweeny, Mary-Belle** *and* **Lollie, Mrs Lush** *and* **Alvin. Alvin** *is dressed in a cowboy outfit and carries a Tommy-gun.*

Mimi   We now come to the entrance of the famous Kasbah, known since time immemorial as the haunt of sinister and unpredictable characters –

Mrs Lush   Tell us the names of some of the characters, Mrs Paragon.

Mimi (*after a slight pause*)   Well, there was Haron al-Rashid and – Pépé le Moko –

Mrs Lush   Pépé le Moko came from Algiers not Tangiers.

Mimi   Perfectly correct Mrs Lush, but he used to spend his summers here.

Alvin (*pointing his Tommy-gun at her*)   Bang bang bang bang bang!

Mimi   Don't do that Alvin, dear. It interrupts my train of thought.

She consults her note-book

It is here, in the scented dusk, that veiled women flit furtively through the twisted cobbled streets, their eyes gleaming like crescent moons above their yashmaks –

Alvin   I want to ride on a yashmak.

Mimi (*patiently*)   People don't ride on yashmaks, Alvin, they wear them. You're probably thinking of a yak.

Alvin   What's a yak?

Mr Rawlings   Never mind now – stop yakking.

Mrs Lush (*turning on him*)   There's no necessity to be rude to the child just because he has an enquiring mind.

Mimi (*resuming*)   – It is at this sacred hour of the day that the Muezzin sounds from the minarets and all good Mohammedans turn their faces towards Mecca in the East and pray to Allah.

Alvin   What do bad Mohammedans do?

Elmer   Pick your pockets and face West.

He laughs uproariously

Maime Pipe down, Elmer.

Mrs Sweeny What is that white domed building like an inkstand?

Mimi That is a mosque, Mrs Sweeny. A mosque is an Arab church. Just like St. Patrick's on Fifth Avenue only you take your shoes off.

Elmer It's better with your shoes off!

He laughs again

Glen Oh, Dad, do shut up.

Alvin Bang bang bang bang bang!

Mimi Would you speak to Alvin, Mrs Lush? The dear little chap is driving me mad.

Mrs Lush The child's only enjoying himself.

Alvin I want a banana-split.

Mimi You'll have to wait until you get back to the ship. They don't make banana-splits in Morocco.

Alvin What do they make?

Mimi (*in steely tones*) Leather, Alvin, dear. They make great big knotted whips of leather. Come on all of you, we've got to get through that great big gorgeous Kasbah before lunch.

Alvin (*as they go*) Bang bang bang bang bang!

Johnny *comes on from the left and crosses to the café on the right where* **Verity** *is sitting, sipping a cup of coffee and reading a newspaper*

Johnny It's all right. I've found out where we can go. There's a beach only a few miles away and we can have lunch there on a terrace overlooking the sea.

Verity What about your mother?

Johnny She's going to the British Legation. Sir Gerard and Lady Nutfield are taking her. She loves legations and embassies. They feed her sense of importance.

Verity Didn't she want you to go too?

Johnny I said I had a headache and the beginnings of a sore throat and so I'd better stay on board.

Verity Oh Johnny. I really shouldn't encourage you to behave badly.

Johnny You look radiant. Beautiful as the day!

Verity (*looking up at him*) 'In delay there lies no plenty – Then come kiss me sweet and twenty'.

Johnny I will if you're not careful. Will you be all right here while I pop down to the hotel and arrange about the car?

Verity I expect I shall.

Johnny Stay quite still. Don't speak to any strangers. And try not to buy any carpets.

Verity Shouldn't you wear a hat? The sun is very strong.

Johnny Shouldn't you wear a yashmak? I don't like to think of anyone else looking at your face.

He blows her a kiss and goes off. She watches him go, then gives a happy sigh. The music starts in the orchestra and she begins to sing

'Something Very Strange'

Verse:

> This is not a day like any other day
> This is something special and apart
> Something to remember
> When the coldness of December
> Chills my heart.

Refrain 1:

> Something very strange
> Is happening to me
> Every face I see
> Seems to be smiling
> All the sounds I hear
> The buses changing gear
> Suddenly appear
> To be beguiling
> Nobody is melancholy
> Nobody is sad
> Not a single shadow on the sea
> Some magician's spell
> Has made this magic start
> And I feel I want to hold each shining moment in my heart
> Something strange and gay
> On this enchanted day
> Seems to be
> Happening to me.

Refrain 2:

> Something very strange
> Is happening to me
> Every cat I see
> Seems to be purring
> I can clearly tell

In every clanging bell
Some forgotten melody
Recurring
Tinker, tailor, soldier, sailor,
Beggar-man or thief
Every single leaf
On every tree
Seems to be aware
Of something in the air
And if only I were younger I'd put ribbons in my hair
Something strange and gay
On this romantic day
Seems to be happening to me.

Scene Two

The ship's nursery.

The ship is at sea again, steaming along the Mediterranean with Europe to port and Africa to starboard.

The ship's nursery is cheerfully designed for the benefit of the very young. There might almost be rabbits for other winsome animals frisking about on the wallpaper.

On the right is a rocking-horse and on the left a play-pen together with a contraption of coloured beads to fascinate and occupy the child mind.

There are also various toys and woolly animals and dolls scattered about.

The room is occupied by six children, the eldest of whom is **Alvin** *who is dressed as a Red Indian. The others consist of four little* **Girls** *of varying sizes and one other little* **Boy**. *The little* **Girls**, *if necessary, are called* **Cynthia**, **Irene**, **Lucille** *and* **Judy**. *The name of the little* **Boy** *is* **Cassidy**. *He is quite small and given to sniffling.*

When the lights fade in on the scene **Mimi**, *with bitterness in her heart, is groping about blindfolded. The* **Children** *are all shrieking and the noise is deafening. The game continues for a moment or two until* **Cassidy** *hits her a clout on the behind with a small cricket-bat. She whips off the bandage from her eyes and makes a grab at him but misses. He squeals with delight.*

Mimi (*sinking into a chair*)   That's quite enough of that. Be quiet all of you.

They continue to scream

Mimi (*continues*)   I said QUIET – MY DARLINGS!

They stop screaming and stand looking at her critically.

Cassidy   Your hair's all mussed up.

Mimi   Yes, dear – I know it is.

She pats at it hopelessly.

Now if you'll gather round me and keep still I'll tell you a story.

Alvin Not the one about the honeymoon couple?

Mimi No, Alvin . . . *Not* the one about the honeymoon couple.

Cassidy (*in a whining voice*) I don't want to hear a story. I want to play I'm in a space ship.

Mimi I wish to God you were – dear!

Alvin (*brandishing a toy tomahawk, capering about and shrieking*) Woolawoola woolawoolawoo – I'm going to scalp Cynthia.

Mimi You can scalp Cynthia later, Alvin. Just be a good boy and listen.

She recites:

'Once upon a time

In a big dark wood

Lived a dear little girl

Who was very very good –'

Alvin Aw, nuts!

Mimi What did you say, Alvin?

Alvin I said, 'nuts!'

Mimi (*with a sweet smile*) Well – just try not to say it again, dear.

She resumes

'One day a Prince came riding by

And what d'you think he did? –'

Alvin Spat in her eye!

He screams with laughter at his own jokes. The other **Children** *join in and applaud.* **Mimi** *snatches up a toy trumpet and blows a piercing blast on it. The* **Children** *fall silent. She begins to sing*

'The Children's A.B.C.'

Verse:

Mimi
A.B.C.D.E.F.G.
H.I.J.K.L.M.N.O.

Oh what a jolly little jocular
Group we are.

Alvin   Bla – Bla – Bla!

Mimi

Vocalise and harmonise
When your mother cries
One, two, three – go.
Try, if it's possible to keep on key
Sing the letters after me.

Children

Just how corny can you be?

Mimi

If you sing when you are blue
You find you
Never have to care a rap
When the skies are dark and grey
You just say –

Children

What a lot of crap!

Mimi

P.Q.R.S.T.U.V.
And W.X.Y.Z. or Zee
This is my personal recipe
For the Little One's A.B.C.

Refrain 1:

A. Stands for Absolutely Anything
B. Stands for Big Brass Bands
C. Stands for Chlorophil
D. Stands for Dexamil
E. Stands for Endocrine Glands
F. and G. don't suggest a thing to me
But after L. comes M. for Mother
And Mother's going to give you Hell.

Refrain 2:

A. Stands for Artichokes and Adenoids
B. Stands for Bolts and Belts
C. Stands for Cottage Cheese
D. Stands for Dungarees
E. Stands for Everything Else
G. Of course
Stands for Getting a Divorce

And F. sometimes stands for Fridge
But if I really were your mother
I'd throw myself from Brooklyn Bridge

Refrain 3:

A. Stands for Romeo and Juliet
B. Stands for Ku Klux Klan
C. Stands for Bethlehem
D. Stands for M.G.M.
C. Stands for 'So's Your Old Man'
F. And G. Stands for Home in Tennessee
And we know H. Stands for Stoats
But after L. comes M. for Mother
And Mother'd like to slit your throats!

Scene Three

The sun deck.

Over the rail can be seen, in the distance, the sweep of the Bay of Naples. It is late afternoon and the ship is due to sail in about an hour's time. 'Tenders' are still returning from the shore loaded to the gunwales with exhausted sightseers. The ship has remained in the Bay for two and a half days in order to give the passengers enough time to explore Pompeii, Vesuvius, the Amalfi Drive, Sorrento, Capri, etc., etc.

A group of people are clustered round the bar drinking and talking and making a good deal of noise.

Downstage on the left **Mrs Van Mier** *is seated in a steamer chair working at her embroidery frame. Next to her is seated* **Mrs Spencer-Bollard**. *She has, as usual, a notebook on her knees in which She occasionally scribbles when some brilliant thought occurs to her.*

Elinor People! Mrs Van Mier. People are the absorbing passion of my life. They are also of course my bread and butter.

She laughs complacently

That's why I never allow myself to be bored for an instant. There's a story in everyone if you are interested enough to ferret it out. For instance look at that man at the bar, the one in the peaked straw hat, how would you describe him?

Mrs Van Mier (*looking*)   Drunk.

Elinor (*triumphantly*)   Exactly! But why is he drunk?

Mrs Van Mier   Because he wants to be I suppose.

Elinor   It goes deeper than that – much, much deeper. He is escaping from something inside himself, some lonely area of discontent.

Mrs Van Mier   Well, I wish he could do it without making quite so much noise.

Elinor   Has it ever occurred to you that every single person travelling on this ship – with the possible exception of myself – is either escaping or pursuing? Take the mysterious Mrs Craig for example; so aloof, so outwardly sure of herself, but it is obvious from the haunted look in her eyes that she is also escaping from something, an unsatisfactory husband probably.

Mrs Van Mier   I think I would have described her as pursuing rather than escaping. She certainly seems to be setting her cap at my son.

Elinor (*laughing rather annoyingly*)   Aha! There's your Achilles heel, Mrs Van Mier. Your son. It sticks out a mile.

Mrs Van Mier (*irritably*)   I don't see how anybody's heel could stick out a mile.

Mimi, *looking hot and exhausted, comes up to them.*

Mimi   Whoever it was that said 'See Naples and die' hit it smack on the nose. I've seen Naples and I'm dying.

Elinor   You've been out all day, haven't you?

Mimi   Since eight-thirty this morning. A carefree, personally conducted tour. Thirty-three eager beavers squeezed into five automobiles and a picnic lunch on a hunk of lava. We've been round Vesuvius, up Vesuvius and down Vesuvius. Dear little Alvin Lush nearly fell into the crater but some spoilsport pulled him back.

Mr Rawlings, *the drunken man at the bar, staggers off his stool and comes unsteadily up to* **Mimi**.

Mr Rawlings (*loudly*)   She's back, boys! The Girl of the Golden West is back! Hallelujah!

He falls flat on the deck at her feet.

Mimi   There's been a slight technical hitch, ladies and gentlemen. We will not switch to Channel Five.

Three deck **Stewards** *rush forward and raise* **Mr Rawlings** *to his feet. He lurches towards* **Mimi** *again.*

Mr Rawlings (*thickly*)   I've grown accustomed to your face.

He tries to embrace her. She pushes him away and the **Stewards** *catch him.*

Mimi   Take him to his cabin, boys. Give him three Alka-Seltzers, a bucket of black coffee and, if necessary, a glancing blow with a baseball bat.

Mr Rawlings (*still held by the* **Stewards**)   You're a fine figure of a woman but you hold no mystery for me.

The **Stewards** *drag him away. He sings* 'I've grown accustomed to her face' *as he goes.*

Mrs Van Mier   That man hasn't drawn a sober breath since we left New York. It's disgraceful.

Mimi   We always get one of those on every trip.

She sighs

Well – me for a nice hot bath and a handful of Miltowns.

She smiles wanly and goes.

Nancy *comes on accompanied by three young men. She is wearing a bikini; the young men are in bathing-trunks. They are all laughing and talking at the top of their voices.* **Barnaby***, fully dressed, follows disconsolately behind. They all go off upstage without noticing* **Mrs Spencer-Bollard**.

Mrs Van Mier (*looking after them*)   I do hope your niece is proving herself to be an efficient secretary.

Elinor (*drily*)   I should be lost without her.

Mrs Van Mier (*putting her embroidery-frame into her work-bag and rising*)   Well, it's time for my rest. I've so enjoyed our little chat.

Mrs Spencer-Bollard *also rises. They are just about to go when* **Johnny** *and* **Verity** *come on. They look gay and happy.* **Johnny** *goes to* **Mrs Van Mier** *and kisses her.*

Johnny   We've had a wonderful day, Mother. We drove all the way to Positano and lunched in a little fisherman's restaurant.

Verity   You really should have come with us.

Mrs Van Mier   I'm afraid I didn't feel up to it.

Johnny   They gave us lobster cooked in garlic.

Mrs Van Mier (*with a slight shudder*)   Yes, dear. I gathered that.

Verity   I wonder if you and Johnny would dine with me tonight? I'll order a quiet table all to ourselves. I'm sure the Captain won't mind us forsaking him for once. He'll be on the bridge anyhow as we're sailing.

Mrs Van Mier   Thank you. That will be delightful.

Verity   Will you join us too, Mrs Spencer-Bollard?

Elinor   I think not, my dear, thank you all the same. I'll content myself with a little something on a tray in my cabin.

Mrs Van Mier (*forcing a cordial smile*)   Until later then?

She and **Mrs Spencer-Bollard** *go off. A group of people, laughing and talking and laden with straw hats and paper parcels bulging with souvenirs they have bought, pass along the deck.* **Johnny** *and* **Verity** *come downstage and stand together looking at the view. He reaches for her hand and squeezes it.*

Tenor *off-stage.*

Verity   It's beautiful isn't it? Look at the light on the sea.

Johnny That's Ischia away to the right and Capri straight ahead. It really does look like a goat, doesn't it?

Verity The sun will be setting in a few minutes and then the day will be over.

Mr and **Mrs Sweeny** *appear from the left and come up to them.*

Mrs Sweeny Hasn't it been a glorious day?

Verity Yes, it has.

She glances at **Johnny**.

Verity Indeed it has.

Mrs Sweeny Mr Sweeny and I have been summoning up our courage to ask you to take cocktails with us in the bar this evening before dinner. Haven't we, Edgar?

Mr Sweeny Yes sweetheart.

Verity There was no need to summon up your courage, Mrs Sweeny. I'd love to.

Mrs Sweeny Will you come too, Mr Van Mier?

Johnny (*shooting a quizzical glance at* **Verity**) Well – yes – thanks. It's very kind of you.

Mrs Sweeny That's just lovely. We shall look forward to it. Shan't we, Edgar?

Mr Sweeny We sure will, sweetheart.

They smile delightedly and wander away.

Johnny Verity, how could you? You know they're the ship's bores!

Verity I know, but they're a harmless old couple. It was a sudden impulse to give pleasure. I feel this evening that I want to be agreeable to the whole world.

Johnny Is that why you invited Mother to dine?

Verity (*with a slight laugh*) Partly. I know she doesn't approve of me but – but I feel grateful to her.

Johnny Grateful – why?

Verity (*looking at him tenderly*) Obvious reasons.

Johnny What would you do if I suddenly kissed you – here and now – on the public deck?

Verity Complain to the Purser.

Johnny I love you.

Verity I suppose there'll be an awakening – there always is – but oh – I don't want the dream to break just yet!

They begin to sing together.

'You and I'

You and I have wandered through a lovely day
And come what may
It belongs to us
We'll remember it when we are far away
And sirens sing other songs to us
We have moved together through a private dream
And even though we wake from it
Nothing can ever take from it
This memory we hold
It is ours alone
It is ours alone
Let our future be consoled
By the sweetest dream that we have ever known
You and I have wandered through a lovely day
And come what may
It belongs to us.

The sea is silver grey
And one by one
Down the pathway of the setting sun
Fishing boats steer
Far out across the bay
The shadows creep
Soon the vivid day will fall asleep
Night will be here
Why must the sunlight fade away
Hiding the sea and the shore
Couldn't the dark have stayed away
One minute more.
One minute more.

Scene Four

Taormina.

On the right there is a shop hung with coloured baskets, straw hats, vivid scarves, etc., below which is a wooden table piled high with various coloured espadrilles, inlaid boxes and other objects to catch the eye of the tourist. A little off centre there is a large archway through which can be seen, far, far down, the sea, with the SS Carolonia, *tiny in the distance, riding at anchor. On the left there is a café with a few tables set outside it on the street.*

When the light fades in on the scene it is early afternoon and nobody is stirring. The proprietor of the shop is fast asleep with a large hat over his eyes. At one of the tables outside the deserted café waiter is snoring with his head resting on his arms.

Suddenly there is the sound of a klaxon and the noise of a multitude of shrill voices. The shop owner and the waiter start to their feet. A few barefoot peasant children appear and a handsome young Sicilian with a guitar rushes through the archway and begins to tune up.

Following hotly on his footsteps a shrieking horde of Carolonia *tourists come milling through the archway. They fight their way into the souvenir shop, fill up the tables of the café and transform the peaceful little street into noisy chaos.*

This entire scene should be treated choreographically. At the end of it, the tourists disappear as quickly as they have come. There is not a single object left in the souvenir shop and a number of empty glasses cover the café tables. The street is littered with empty cigarette packs, bits of paper, the silver foil from film packs. The shop owner returns to the siesta he was enjoying at the beginning of the scene, the waiter does likewise. The young man with the guitar picks up a discarded copy of Life *magazine, places his guitar gently on the ground and settles himself comfortably against the archway – as the lights fade.*

Scene Five

Athens. The Parthenon. Day.

When the lights fade in on the scene, **Mrs Spencer-Bollard** *is seated on the ground with her back against a stone column.* **Nancy** *is beside her with a notebook in her lap.*

Elinor (*dictating*)   'How I wish that all of you – my dear readers – could be here with me at this moment' – Thank God they're not – 'gazing out from the Acropolis over the wine-dark Aegean' –

Nancy   How do you spell Aegean?

Elinor (*witheringly*)   The usual way. Where was I?

Nancy   Wine-dark Aegean.

Elinor (*continuing*)   'Behind me is the Parthenon where, step by step, stone by stone, month by month, year by year, the great Pheidas erected his immortal masterpiece, the Statue of Athena' –

Nancy (*singing to herself dreamily*)   Step by step, stone by stone, month by month, year by year, I'd like to build a Parthenon for you – Barnaby.

Elinor   What did you say, dear?

Nancy   Nothing, Aunt Elinor. I was just thinking out loud.

Elinor   Well, please don't. It's my business to think out loud and your business to take down what I think as rapidly and efficiently as possible.

Nancy   I'm sorry, Aunt Elinor.

Elinor   Let me see those notes.

Nancy (*flustered*)   You wouldn't understand them. They're in shorthand.

Elinor (*firmly taking them from her and looking at them*)   There's nothing written down here at all!

Nancy (*with a great display of innocence*)   Isn't there? I could have sworn there was. There must be something wrong with my pencil.

Elinor   Fiddlesticks!

Nancy   It's a dear little Greek pencil. I bought it at a cigarette store when we came ashore.

Elinor   Dear little Greek grandmother!

Nancy (*enthusiastically*)   A friend of mine in Westport, Connecticut had a dear little Greek grandmother – her name was Mrs Papadapolous.

Elinor (*ominously*)   Was it indeed?

Nancy *jumps up and begins to do a few haphazard dance steps, humming to herself as she does so.*

Nancy (*humming*)   Hour by hour, day by day, week by week, it is clear, I never really lived until I knew – Barnaby –

Elinor   Have you gone mad?

Nancy (*doing a pirouette*)   Yes, Aunt Elinor.

Elinor   You haven't taken down one word of what I have been dictating to you for the last hour.

Nancy (*blithely*)   Not a word.

Elinor   I think you'd better go back to the ship and lie down.

Nancy   I don't want to lie down. I want to fly through the air like a bird.

Elinor (*clapping her hands sharply*)   Nancy! Pull yourself together.

Nancy   I've fallen in love, Aunt Elinor.

Elinor   I was afraid this would happen.

Nancy   I was afraid it wouldn't!

Elinor   I must cable to your mother immediately.

Nancy   Dictate it to me now, Aunt Elinor. I'll just take it down properly, I swear I will. Just say – 'Nancy in love – wishes to fly through air like bird – wire instructions.'

Elinor   I assume it's that dusty young man with a camera who's always following you about.

Nancy   Yes, his name's Barnaby.

Elinor I gathered that from your recent vocal outbursts. What does he do?

Nancy He's going to be an architect – or an agriculturist. I forget which. I know it starts with an A.

Elinor Has anything happened between you – that shouldn't have happened?

Nancy I'm afraid not, Aunt Elinor. – Not yet.

Elinor Well, see that it doesn't.

Nancy (*suddenly stricken*) I've let you down, haven't I? I've betrayed your trust and taken advantage of your kindness. Will you ever forgive me?

Elinor Help me up.

Nancy (*doing so*) Are you terribly, terribly angry?

Elinor I never allow myself to be angry about inessentials. It's bad for the blood stream.

Nancy What are you going to do?

Elinor What I should have done in the first place if I'd had any sense. Buy a Dictaphone.

Nancy (*taking her arm*) Aunt Elinor?

Elinor What is it?

Nancy You won't send me home in disgrace, will you?

Elinor Certainly not. It would be far too expensive.

She turns to go.

Nancy Aunt Elinor.

Elinor What is it now?

Nancy I love you very much.

Mrs Spencer-Bollard *looks at her for a moment with an expressionless face and hands* **Nancy** *back her notebook*

Elinor Here. You can write out your own telegram. With your dear little Greek pencil.

She goes off.

Nancy, *left alone, suddenly laughs and then buries her face in her hands.* **Barnaby** *appears from behind a column. He goes to her.*

Barnaby Nancy –

Nancy (*startled*) Oh! You made me jump.

Barnaby I was behind a pillar.

Nancy You're always popping out at me from behind something or other. It makes me nervous.

Barnaby Were you laughing or crying?

Nancy I don't know.

Barnaby Where's she gone?

Nancy To buy a Dictaphone.

Barnaby You look wonderful against all this. Stand still just a minute.

He proceeds to adjust his camera.

Nancy If you take one more photograph of me I shall scream.

Barnaby I want to go taking photographs of you forever and ever – light and shade – night and day –

Nancy Stone by stone, step by step –

Barnaby What are you talking about?

Nancy The great Pheidias.

Barnaby Who's he? A vaudeville act?

Nancy He erected a famous masterpiece, the immortal statue of what's her name – You ought to know anyway. You're going to be an archaeologist.

Barnaby I'm not. I'm going to be an architect.

Nancy I knew it started with an A.

He suddenly lifts her in his arms, swings her round, sits her down on the base of a column and begins to sing.

'When You Want Me'

I'll have to get the bees and birds to tell you
That I've loved you from the start
I simply haven't got the words to tell you
What is truly in my heart
Joking apart

When you want me – if you want me
Call me – call me – if you care
When you need me – if you need me
Say so – say so – I'll be there
I've nothing but my heart to bring to you
No money but a questing mind
But if this little song I sing to you
Means a thing to you
Please be kind

When you're lonely – if you're lonely
Call me – call me – anyhow
If you want me – need me – love me
Tell me – tell me – Tell me how.

I'll love you longer than *The Forsyte Saga*[41]
And I'll tremble at your frown
I'd like to cable to Balenciaga
To prepare your wedding gown
Don't let me down.

When you want me – if you want me
Call me – call me – if you care
I've got an answer service
When you need me – if you need me
Say so – say so – I'll be there
I want to make my feelings clear to you
I've never felt like this before
I'd sacrifice my whole career to you
To be near to you
Evermore
When you're lonely – if you're lonely
Call me – call me – anyhow
You can reverse the charges
If you want me – need me – tell me now.

I really haven't any goods and chattels
But a beat-up Chevrolet
I only know I've got a heart that rattles
Every time you look my way
There's really nothing more to say
Except that I should like to stay
With you forever and a day.

When the number is over they dance off to the left.

Mimi *comes on from the right with her usual group of tourists including* **Mrs Lush**, **Alvin**, *the* **Candijacks**, *the* **Sweenys**, **Mr Rawlings**, **Marybelle**, **Lollie**, *etc.*

Mimi   This – mes enfants – is the most spectacular, the most sensational, the most famous ruin in the whole wide world. The Parthenon.

Elmer   Whoever built it must have had a good look at the Pennsylvania Terminal.

Maime (*reprovingly*)   Elmer!

---

41 A series of three novels and two interludes by English author John Galsworthy, published 1906–21.

Alvin (*shrilly*)   I'm a train. I'm a great big train. Whoo – whoo – whoo –

He proceeds to give an imitation of a train and charges back and forth banging into everyone.

Mimi (*with steely sweetness*)   Do you think, Mrs Lush, that you could persuade Alvin to be a great big train a little further off?

Mrs Lush   The child's only enjoying himself. He's naturally high spirited.

Mimi   We are all aware of that, Mrs Lush. He has been oppressively high spirited ever since we left Staten Island.

Alvin   Whoo – whoo – whoo –

He charges into **Mimi** *and stamps on her foot. She gives a cry of pain.*

Maime   Perhaps it would have been better to have left him on board, Mrs Lush. He is a little young to go sightseeing.

Mrs Lush   I brought my son on this trip to see Europe, Mrs Candijack, and Europe is what he's going to see. Quit being a train for a moment, Alvin, and be a brave Greek soldier.

Alvin   Greek soldiers look like sissies. They wear white skirts.

Elmer   Most of the sissies in our neck of the woods wear leather jackets and blue jeans.

He laughs loudly

Mr Rawlings (*singing drunkenly*)   Blue jeans – smiling at me.

He hiccoups and subsides.

Mimi (*reading from a guide-book*)   The name Parthenon, generally accepted since the fourth century BC was originally associated with the cult of Athena Parthenos, the virgin –

Elmer   Cult of the virgin hey? Your brother Fred sure would have appreciated this.

He nudges **Maime** *in the ribs.*

Maime (*exasperated*)   Will you lay off my brother Fred, Elmer. You're always making snide cracks at him. It was as much her fault as his anyway.

Mimi (*patiently*)   Whoever's fault it was, Mr and Mrs Candijack, could I have your undivided attention for just a few minutes. I've got to tell you all about Ancient Greece before lunch and it's nearly one o'clock now.

Alvin   What's a virgin, Momma?

Mrs Lush   You'll find out when you're older, dear.

Mr Rawlings   And when you do, son, just drop me a postal-card with the name and address.

Maime For shame, Mr Rawlings! In front of an innocent child!

Alvin (*capering about and shouting*) I want to know what a virgin is – I want to know what a virgin is –

Mimi A virgin, Alvin, is a lady who has not been married. And if your mother had not been married, you would not have been on this cruise, and if you had not been on this cruise, I for one would not be on the verge of a nervous breakdown.

Mrs Lush I resent your attitude to Alvin, Mrs Paragon. You're always picking on him.

Mimi The time has come, Mrs Lush, for me to cast discretion to the winds and give you a teensy weensy morceau of unvarnished truth. I *hate* Alvin.

Mrs Lush How dare you say such things. I shall complain to the Captain.

Mimi I think it only fair to warn you that the Captain hates Alvin too. In fact I cannot off hand think of one single living creature on the ship who doesn't long to kick the merry little fellow's teeth down his merry little throat.

Mrs Lush Mrs Paragon –

Mimi (*mowing her down*) He is a precocious, ill-mannered, noisy, spoilt little monster and I warn you here and now that if you go on encouraging him to make a rude, undisciplined little pig of himself, a day will dawn when he will bring your blue hair in sorrow to the grave.

Mr Rawlings (*loudly*) Hear, hear!

Mrs Lush (*to* **Mimi**) I'll report you for this. I'll have you thrown off the ship!

Mimi You'd be doing me a favour.

Mrs Lush (*to* **Alvin**) Come, honey – you and mother will go back on board and have ourselves a lovely chocolate malted.

Alvin I don't want a chocolate malted, I want a banana split.

Mrs Lush (*losing control*) You'll have what I tell you to have so shut up!

She gives him a cuff on the side of the head and drags him away screaming.

Elmer You're a courageous woman, Mrs Paragon, and I would like to shake you by the hand.

He does so.

Mimi Would you all go for a little ramble through the ruins and take some photographs for a few minutes? I'd like to be left alone.

Elmer Come on all of you. Let's do what she asks. If anyone's ever earned a breather, she has.

They all wander off chattering among themselves. **Mimi** *sinks down onto a stone and begins to sing.*

'Why Do the Wrong People Travel?'

Verse 1:

    Travel they say improves the mind
    An irritating platitude
    Which frankly, *entre nous*
    Is very far from true
    Personally I've yet to find
    That longitude and latitude
    Can educate those scores
    Of monumental bores
    Who travel in groups
    And herds and troupes
    Of various breeds and sexes
    Till the whole world reels
    To shouts and squeals
    And the clicking of Rolleiflexes.[42]

Refrain 1:

    Why do the wrong people travel – travel – travel
    When the right people stay back home?
    What compulsion compels them
    And who the hell tells them
    To drag their cans to Zanzibar
    Instead of staying quietly in Omaha?
    The Taj Mahal
    And the Grand Canal
    And the sunny French Riviera
    Would be less oppressed
    If the Middle West
    Would settle for somewhere rather nearer
    Please do not think that I criticise or cavil
    At a genuine urge to roam
    Buy why oh why do the wrong people travel
    When the right people stay back home?
    And mind their business
    When the right people stay back home
    With television
    When the right people stay back home
    I'm merely asking
    Why the right people stay back home?

---

42 A high-end camera made by the German company Franke & Heidecke.

Verse 2:

> Just when you think romance is ripe
> It rather sharply dawns on you
> That each sweet serenade
> Is for the tourist trade
> Any attractive native type
> Who resolutely fawns on you
> Is surely on the books
> At Mister Thomas Cook's
> There isn't a rock
> Between Bangkok
> And the beaches of Hispaniola
> That does not recoil
> From suntan oil
> And the gurgle of Coca-Cola.

Refrain 2:

> Why do the wrong people travel – travel – travel
> When the right people stay back home?
> What explains this mass mania
> To leave Pennsylvania
> And clack around like flocks of geese
> Demanding dry Martinis on the Isles of Greece?
> In the smallest street
> Where the gourmets meet
> They invariably fetch up
> And it's hard to make
> Them accept a steak
> That isn't served 'rear' and smeared with ketchup.
> It would take years to unravel – ravel – ravel
> Every impulse that makes them roam
> But why oh why do the wrong people stay back home?
> When the right people stay back home?
> And eat hot doughnuts
> When the right people stay back home
> With all that lettuce
> When the right people stay back home
> I sometimes wonder
> Why the right people stay back home!

Refrain 3:

> Why do the wrong people travel – travel – travel
> When the right people stay back home?
> What peculiar obsessions
> Inspire these processions
> Of families from Houston Tex:

With all those cameras around their necks?
They will take a train
Or an aeroplane
For an hour on the Costa Brava
And they'll see Pompeii
On the only day
That it's up to its ass in molten lava
Millions of tourists are churning up the gravel
While they gaze at St. Peter's dome
But why oh why do the wrong people travel
When the right people stay back home
And play canasta
When the right people stay back home
Won't someone tell me
Why the right people stay back home!

Scene Six

The Parthenon. Moonlight.

When the lights fade in on the scene, **Verity** *and* **Johnny** *are sitting leaning against a column. She is smoking nervously and staring into space. He is looking at her.*

Johnny   I wish I could understand.

Verity   I wish you could too. What I am trying to say isn't very easy.

Johnny   I don't know what you're trying to say. Your moods change so quickly, so suddenly.

Verity   Yes. – Yes, I suppose they do.

She gives a mirthless little laugh.

Johnny (*resting his hand on hers*)   The afternoon was so wonderful, and this should be the best of all, being here together in the moonlight in the most romantic place in the world – and yet you're unhappy.

Verity (*hopelessly*)   It's time we were getting back to the ship.

Johnny   Why – why are you unhappy? What has happened?

Verity   Don't you really know?

Johnny   Of course I don't. All I know is that we're alone together, we've been alone together nearly all day, and that I love you.

Verity (*suddenly getting up*)   The afternoon *wasn't* wonderful, Johnny. It was – somehow humiliating. That shabby little hotel and the woman at the desk smiling at us as we went upstairs.

She goes to him and touches his face with her hand.

I'm not blaming you, darling, truly I'm not. It's my own fault entirely for having been self-indulgent and foolish enough to let you make love to me in the first place.

Johnny Why was it so – so foolish?

Verity (*gently*) Because we can't go on with it – You must know that in your heart as well as I do. Please let's stop now, before it's too late, before everything is spoiled.

Johnny (*looking at her miserably*) Do you really mean that you don't want us to be – to be lovers any more?

Verity (*with her eyes lowered*) Yes, Johnny – dear dear Johnny. That is exactly what I mean.

Johnny But why – why? Have I failed you in any way?

Verity No. You haven't failed me. You've made me very happy, happier than I deserve to be. But it isn't the sort of happiness that could possibly last. I want, selfishly perhaps, to keep it as it is, something to be remembered always, without regret. I'm trying to behave well for once. Please help me.

Johnny Do you still love your husband?

Verity (*turning away*) Oh, Johnny, why did you ask that?

Johnny Do you?

Verity (*turning and meeting his eyes*) With a part of me – Yes. – I suppose I always will.

Johnny And you're going to divorce him?

Verity Yes – I expect so. I think he would really be happier if I did.

Johnny And you'll be alone?

Verity I think perhaps I deserve to be alone.

Johnny If I come to you then – will you see me?

Verity Yes, dear of course, of course I'll see you. But it won't be the same. Everything changes.

Johnny (*sadly*) You don't believe that I love you enough, do you?

Verity I do believe it. That's why I don't want to take advantage of it. I want us to say goodbye now as lovers. A tender, romantic goodbye in this ancient romantic place. As I said a moment ago, everything changes. But as far as you and I are concerned, I don't want to see the changes happening.

Johnny (*very gently*) I'm trying to understand, honestly I am – but – but it's dreadfully difficult –

She looks at him compassionately for a moment. The music starts in the orchestra. She begins to sing.

'This Is a Changing World'

Verse:

> The world was young
> So many years ago
> The passage of time must show
> Some traces of change
> Love songs once sung
> Much laughter – many tears
> Have echoed down the years
> The past is old and strange
> Each waning moon
> All dawns that rise – all suns that set
> Change like the tides that flow across the sands
> Each little tune
> That fills out hearts with vague regret
> Each little love duet
> Fades in our hands
> Don't stray among
> The moments that have fled
> New days are just ahead
> New words are still unsaid.

Refrain 1:

> This is a changing world my dear
> New songs are sung – new stars appear
> Though we grow older year by year
> Our hearts can still be gay
> Young love at best is a passing phase
> Charming and foolish and blind
> There may be happier, wiser days
> When youth is far behind
> Where are the snows of yesteryear?
> When winter's done and spring is here?
> No regrets are worth a tear
> We're living in a changing world by dear.

Refrain 2:

> This is a changing world, my dear
> New dreams are dreamed – new dawns appear
> Passion's a feckless cavalier
> Who loves and rides away
> Time will persuade you to laugh to grief
> Time is your tenderest friend
> Life may be lonely and joy be brief

But everything must end
Love is a charming souvenir
When day is done and night draws near
No regrets are worth a tear
We're living in a changing world, my dear.

When the song is finished he takes her in his arms. They stand there silently for a moment.

Mrs Van Mier walks on quietly from the left. They hear her step and turn. She stands looking at them in silence for a little and then speaks.

Mrs Van Mier (*icily*)   I have a taxi waiting down below. I would like you to drive me back to the Grand Bretagne Hotel, Johnny. I have removed our luggage from the ship. We are not continuing the cruise.

Johnny   What do you mean?

Mrs Van Mier   Exactly what I say. We are not continuing the cruise.

Johnny   But, Mother –

Mrs Van Mier (*ignoring him and turning to* **Verity**)   I consider, Mrs Craig, that it is time your unfortunate association with my son should come to an end.

Verity   You are too late. It has already come to an end.

Mrs Van Mier   Nevertheless I intend to take no risk of it continuing. I am sure you will understand my position. John is my only son and it is my duty to protect him from any undesirable influences. I am sure you may have your own reasons for your contemptible behaviour, but those are entirely you own affair.

Johnny   I forbid you to speak to Verity like that, Mother. It's cruel and unjust and you should be ashamed.

Mrs Van Mier (*turning on him*)   I am ashamed. I was also disgusted when I saw you and Mrs Craig coming out of that hotel together this evening.

Johnny   So you have been following us?

Mrs Van Mier   Certainly I have. I wanted to find out for myself whether or not there was any truth in the unpleasant rumours that have been spreading all over the ship.

Johnny (*furiously*)   I shall never forgive you for this, Mother, never as long as I live. The fact that I am your only son doesn't entitle you to spy on me and interfere with my private affairs – I –

Verity (*putting her hand on his arm*)   Johnny please – don't say any more. It isn't any use. Please, take your mother to the hotel as she wishes and tell the driver who brought us here to wait for me. I should like to be by myself for a little.

Johnny   Verity. I can't – I can't possibly leave you like this –

Verity Please, Johnny – please do as I ask – with all my heart I implore you to. Don't you see? There's nothing more to be said – there's nothing more that *could* be said between us now – after this.

She turns to **Mrs Van Mier**.

Verity Don't worry about your son, Mrs Van Mier. He is finer, kinder and wiser than you know. I can only hope that in the future you will prove yourself to be little more worthy of him than you have tonight.

She goes to **Johnny** *and kisses him.*

Verity Goodbye, my dear. Thank you for loving me – so sweetly –

Her voice breaks.

Johnny (*making an involuntary movement towards her*) Verity –

Verity (*near the end of her control*) No – No – No more. Go away – Go away now.

He gives her one hopeless look and then, in silence, takes his mother's arm and leads her away.

Verity, *left alone, walks slowly back to the column against which they were sitting at the beginning of the scene. She sings, very softly –*
Love is a charming souvenir
When day is done
And night draws near
No regrets are worth a tear –

Her voice breaks off and she leans against the column, burying her head in her arms, as the last chords crash out, and the lights fade.

Scene Seven

The promenade deck. Night.

When the lights fade in on the scene, **Verity**, *looking pale and drained, is leaning on the rail on the right, staring straight out in front of her. Her face is a mask of unhappiness.*

Barnaby *and* **Nancy** *come on. They are laughing at some private joke. They see* **Verity** *and come up to her.*

Barnaby Hallo, Mrs Craig. All alone?

Verity (*with an effort*) Yes – I was just looking at the lights of the town.

Barnaby The Parthenon looks wonderful from here, doesn't it?

Nancy It's the most beautiful place in the world. We're coming back here for our honeymoon.

Verity (*dully*) Honeymoon?

Barnaby Yes. We got engaged – just today. You're the first person we've told except Nancy's aunt. Won't you come up to the sun deck bar and have a nightcap with us – just to celebrate?

Verity It's very kind of you to ask me, but I really am terribly tired and I must go straight to bed.

Barnaby Too much sightseeing?

Verity Yes. Too much sightseeing.

She looks at them.

I wish you every possible happiness.

She suddenly kisses **Nancy**.

Verity And good luck.

Nancy (*smiling*) Thank you, Mrs Craig. Come on, Barnaby.

They go off hand in hand. **Verity** *watches them go and then turns back and continues to stare at the view. Her face is expressionless.*

A group of people come on from the left. Among them is **Mr Rawlings**. *Most of them are fairly 'high' but he, as usual, is very drunk indeed. As they pass along the deck he catches sight of* **Verity** *out of the corner of his eye. The others go off but he stays back and weaves his way over to* **Verity**

Mr Rawlings How about a little drinkie? Just one for the road.

Verity (*looking at him almost without seeing him*) No. No, thank you.

Mr Rawlings (*grabbing her arm*) Come on – be a pal.

Verity (*in a strangled voice*) Please go away and leave me alone.

Mr Rawlings One little kiss then – ere we part –

He suddenly seizes her and kisses her on the mouth before she has time to defend herself. She struggles free from him and gives him a ringing slap on the face. He staggers back.

Mr Rawlings (*angrily*) Who do you think you are anyway – Mrs High and Mighty Craig!

Verity (*quivering*) Go away from me.

Mr Rawlings (*unpleasantly*) I'd forgotten you only like 'em young. I'm the wrong age group! – Pardon the error.

He bursts into derisive laughter and staggers off after his friends. **Verity** *stands stock still for a moment with the back of her hand pressed against her mouth.*

Verity (*hopelessly almost in a whisper*) No – No – No! –

With a strangled cry she runs off the stage – as the lights fade.

Scene Eight

The sun deck. Evening.

The ship is lying in the bay of Villefranche. In the background can be seen, in the early evening light, the spectacular outline of the Côte d'Azur. Pastel-coloured houses, restaurants, apartment buildings and private villas catch the last rays of the dying sun.

At the bar, watched by **Fred**, *the barman, two men are listlessly throwing dice for drinks.*

Mr *and* **Mrs Sweeny** *are sitting at a table, staring silently into space. A party of tourists come on and pass across the deck, laughing and talking. When they have gone,* **Mrs Sweeny** *breaks the silence.*

Mrs Sweeny   So you just drifted into the casino while I was having my hair done?

Mr Sweeny (*gloomily*)   Yes, sweetheart.

Mrs Sweeny   And you just happened to sit down at the roulette table?

Mr Sweeny   Yes, sweetheart.

Mrs Sweeny   And you just happened to lose seven hundred and ninety-three dollars?

Mr Sweeny   Yes, sweetheart.

Mrs Sweeny   And you didn't happen to remember *before* drifting into the casino that I had particularly asked you to buy those table mats for Mrs Teitelbaum, the perfume for Louella and those three printed scarves that I picked out for the Pendleton girls?

Mr Sweeny   No, sweetheart.

Mrs Sweeny   I sincerely hope that God may forgive you, Edgar, for I never shall.

They begin to sing

'Bronxville Darby and Joan'

Verse 1:

> We do not fear the verdict of posterity
> Our lives have been too humdrum and mundane
> In the twilight of our days
> Having reached the final phase
> In all sincerity
> We must explain.

Refrain 1:

> We're a dear old couple and we HATE one another
> And we've hated one another for a long long time

Since the day that we were wed, up to the present
Our lives, we must confess
Have been progressively more unpleasant
We're just sweet old darlings who despise one another
With a thoroughness approaching the sublime
But through all our years
We've been affectionately known
As the Bronxville Darby and Joan.

Verse 2:

Our golden wedding passed with all our family
An orgy of remembrance and rue
In acknowledgement of this
We exchanged a loving kiss
A trifle clammily
Because we knew.

Refrain 2:

We're a dear old couple who DETEST one another
We've detested one another since our bridal night
Which was boring, unattractive and convulsive
And proved, beyond dispute,
That we were mutually repulsive
We're just sweet old darlings who torment one another
With the utmost maliciousness and spite
And through all our years
We've been inaccurately known
As the Bronxville Darby and Joan.

Sir Gerard *and* **Lady Nutfield** *come on from the right and pass along the deck.*

Lady Nutfield (*plaintively*)   We accepted, dear, and it's too late to back out now.

Sir Gerard (*irritably*)   *You* accepted. *I* did not.

Lady Nutfield   It *is* one of the loveliest villas on the Riviera and after all I was at school with her.

Sir Gerard   The fact that you were at school with her, Mildred, in no way alters the fact that she is extremely common and has a voice like a buzz-saw.

They go off. **Joe** *comes on followed by* **Lawford Craig**. **Lawford** *looks strained and anxious.*

Joe   Perhaps I could offer you a drink, sir?

Lawford   No, thank you. I should like to see the ship's doctor as soon as possible.

Joe   He'll be back in about an hour, sir. This is our last port of call and practically everyone's ashore.

Mimi *comes on from upstage. She sees* **Lawford** *and* **Joe** *and comes to them.*

Mimi   Mr Craig?

Lawford   Yes.

Joe   This is Mrs Paragon, sir. She knows much more about the whole business than I do.

Lawford (*shaking hands*)   It was you who sent me the cable?

Mimi   Yes.

Lawford   It was kind of you. I am most grateful.

Mimi   I thought it was the best thing to do.

Joe   I'll leave you to explain the situation, Mimi, while I go and arrange about Mr Craig's accommodation.

(*To* **Lawford**.) Fortunately a Mrs Van Mier and her son left the ship at Athens and so we have a vacant space.

Lawford   Thanks.

Joe *goes off.*

Mimi   Won't you sit down, Mr Craig?

Lawford (*ignoring this*)   Is she still on the danger list?

Mimi (*gently*)   No. Please don't worry. She's coming along fine. She's still in the sick bay of course. The doctor wants her to have complete rest and not see anyone.

Lawford   Can you tell me exactly what happened?

Mimi (*slowly*)   We none of us know exactly what happened. All we know is that she took an overdose of sleeping-pills.

Lawford (*quietly – after a pause*)   By accident? Or deliberately?

Mimi (*obviously embarrassed*)   I'm afraid I couldn't say.

Lawford   Please be as frank with me as you can, Mrs Paragon, without betraying any confidence. It – it means a great deal to me.

Mimi   I think – I think she was suddenly very unhappy –

She breaks off.

Lawford   Why? Do you know any specific reason?

Mimi   Yes, Mr Craig, I do. But I really can't say any more. It's none of my business. You do understand, don't you?

Lawford (*sadly*)   I appreciate your discretion.

Mimi I am sure she will explain everything to you when she's up and about again, which will be a few days' time. Meanwhile, will you forgive me if I make a small suggestion?

Lawford Of course. What is it?

Mimi Don't let her know you're on board until the doctor gives you the okay. And when you do see her, and talk to her –

She breaks off again.

Lawford Yes?

Mimi Don't ask too many questions. Don't make it too difficult for her. Try to be as – as gentle as you can.

Lawford (*with a wry smile*) I accept your suggestion, Mrs Paragon. It was kind of you to make it.

Joe *comes on again.*

Joe I've got you all fixed up, sir. Your cabin's ready for you.

Lawford Thanks. I'll come now.

Joe This way, sir.

He and **Joe** *move off*

Lawford (*turning to* **Mimi** *as he goes*) I am deeply in your debt, Mrs Paragon. Thank you so very much.

He follows **Joe** *off.* **Mimi**, *with a sigh, sinks down at one of the bar tables. She begins to sing softly.*

'Later than Spring'

Later than spring
Much disillusion comes
Sometimes confusion comes
You lose your way
Need it be – such unbearable sadness
To face the truth?
Love, with its passionate madness
Belongs to Youth

Later than spring
Our values change, my dear
It would be strange, my dear
If they should stay
Waste no tears
On the hurrying years

For whatever they may bring
Song birds still sing
Later than spring.

At the end of the reprise of 'Later than Spring', **Mimi** *goes off.*

Scene Nine

The promenade deck. Late afternoon.

Verity *is lying in steamer-chair. There is an open book faced downwards on her lap and her eyes are closed. She looks pale and wan.*

Marybelle *and* **Lollie** *come on from the right and pass across the deck.*

Marybelle (*as they go*)   I can't think what happened. I put in the filter, got the focus okay and set the shutter, and there he is, sitting on the steps of a cathedral with two heads.

They go off. After a moment or two **Lawford** *enters from the left. He comes over to* **Verity**'s *chair and stands looking down at her. He then, very gently, sits on the edge of the vacant chair next to her and puts his hand on hers. She opens her eyes*

Verity (*in a strained voice*)   Lawford – Oh Lawford!

She makes an effort to speak ordinarily.

How on earth did you get here?

Lawford   I fled from New York four days ago and joined the ship at Villefranche. I was worried about you.

Verity   You shouldn't have – really you shouldn't have. I'm perfectly alright.

Lawford   I should never have allowed you to come away on this damned cruise all by yourself anyway.

Verity   I expect it was all for the best, really. At least it's shown me up in my true colours. They're rather unattractive colours I'm afraid, shrill and garish and not in the best of taste.

Lawford   Don't say that. It isn't true.

Verity   I suppose they told you what – what happened?

Lawford   Nobody's told me very much. All I know is that you must have been in a pretty bad way to have – to have –

Verity (*wearily*)   It was just that everything suddenly became too complicated – too difficult. I made a hash of it of course. I always seem to make a hash of things, don't I?

Lawford   Don't talk about any of it now. Just relax and concentrate on getting well again. You don't have to explain anything at all, now or at any other time, if you don't want to.

Verity I made a fool of myself over a young man. It wasn't entirely my fault, but enough my fault to make me horribly ashamed. It's not a very edifying story but I think you have a right to know.

Lawford When we get back to New York the day after tomorrow I'm going to take you straight to the country. I've cabled them to open up the house and have everything ready. You will come, won't you?

Verity (*almost inaudibly*) Yes, Lawford. If you really want me.

Lawford I've come a long way to prove it to you.

Verity (*tremulously*) I've come a long way, too.

She begins to sing very softly.

'This is a Changing World'

This is a changing world, my dear
With each new day – new hopes appear
Age need not fill my heart with fear
So long as I can say
Somebody loves me enough to be
Gentle, forgiving and sane
Somebody has enough trust in me
To help me try again.
Gone are the ghosts of yesteryear
When you, my love, are standing near
No regrets are worth a tear
We're living in a changing world, my dear.

He takes her hand and gently kisses it. They walk off

Nancy *and* **Barnaby** *come on and stand at the rail looking out to sea.*

Barnaby (*after a pause*) This time tomorrow we shall be home.

Nancy (*listlessly*) I know.

Barnaby Don't you want to be?

Nancy I'm not sure. It's all been so wonderful and now it's all over.

Barnaby Not for us it isn't. For us it's all beginning.

He presses her hand, she smiles and they both look at the sea again. The **Candijack** *family come gloomily on from the left, lean on the rail and stare out at the sea.*

Elmer This time tomorrow we shall be home.

Maime Don't say that anymore, Elmer. We've got the message all right.

Elmer Have you finished the packing?

Maime (*wearily*) Everything's in except the mandolin and the yellow Arabian slippers for Grandpa. They had to be wrapped separately.

Elmer What about the Greek vase we got in Crete?

Maime I've wrapped it in your swim-shorts.

Elmer If that Greek vase is broken I shall never forgive you.

Maime It was already broken. Two thousand years ago.

Elinor *comes on from the centre.*

Elinor (*cheerfully*) Well . . . this time tomorrow we shall be home again.

Nancy Yes, Aunt Elinor.

Elinor I've just been listening to the news on the ship's radio.

'There Are Bad Times Just Around the Corner'[43]

Verse 1:

> They're nervous in Nigeria
> And terribly cross in Crete
> In Bucharest they are so depressed
> They're frightened to cross the street
> They're sullen in Siberia
> And timid in Turkestan
> They're sick with fright
> In the Isle of Wight
> And jittery in Japan
> The Irish roar and spout lads
> And so does everyone else
> Hooray hooray hooray
> Trouble is on the way.

Refrain 1:

> There are bad times just around the corner
> There are dark clouds hurtling through the sky
> And it's no use whining
> About a silver lining
> For we know from experience
> That they won't roll by.
> With a scowl and a frown
> We'll keep our spirits down
> And prepare for depression and doom and dread
> We're going to unpack our troubles from our old kit bag
> And wait until we drop down dead.

---

43 This is a revised version of a song Coward wrote in 1952.

Verse 2:

    They're morbid in Mongolia
    And querulous in Quebec
    There's not a man in Saskatchewan
    Who isn't a nervous wreck
    In Maine the melancholia
    Is deeper than tongue can tell
    In Monaco all the croupiers know
    They haven't a hope in hell
    In far away Australia
    Each wallaby's well aware
    The world's a total failure
    Without any time to spare.
    Hooray hooray hooray
    Suffering and dismay.

Refrain 2:

    There are bad times just around the corner
    The horizon's gloomy as can be
    There are blackbirds over
    The greyish cliffs of Dover
    And the vultures are hovering
    On the Christmas tree
    We're an unhappy breed
    And ready to stampede
    When we're asked to remember what Lincoln said
    We're going to untense our muscles
    Til they sag sag sag
    And wait until we drop down dead.

Refrain 3:

    There are bad times just around the corner
    We can all look forward to despair
    It's as clear as crystal
    From Baltimore to Bristol
    That we can't save democracy
    And we don't much care
    At the sound of a shot
    We'd just as soon as not
    Take a hot water bag and retire to bed
    And while the politicians nag nag nag
    We'll wait until we drop down dead.

Refrain 4:

    There are bad times just around the corner
    And the outlook's absolutely vile

You can take it from us
That when they atom bomb us
We are *not* going to tighten our belts
And smile smile smile
If we meet face to face
Some lout from outer space
Who appears in a rocket from overhead
We'll sing a verse and chorus of the old red flag
And wait until he drops down dead
A happy ending
Orpheus descending
Wait until he drops down dead.

Scene Ten

A part of the deck.

This is a 'cross-over' scene and should be treated entirely choreographically until the end when **Nancy** *and* **Barnaby** *sing a brief reprise of 'When You Want Me'.*

When the lights fade in on the scene there is a general atmosphere of bustle and excitement. **Stewards** *hurry back and forth carrying baggage.* **Passengers** *also pass to and fro along the deck, occasionally pausing for a moment to point out familiar landmarks as the ship moves nearer to New York. There is music underlying the whole scene and no actual dialogue is audible.*

Nancy *runs on from the left at the same moment as* **Barnaby** *runs on from the right. He seizes her and places her in a suitable homecoming pose with her hand in the air waving to nobody in particular. He crouches down and snaps a photograph of her. They then sing a reprise of 'When You Want Me'.*

'When You Want Me' (*Reprise*)

When you want me
Phone me – phone me
MU six two
Nine four three
We'll have a drink or something
If I'm not in
Try Algonquin
Four three thousand
We'll eat a snack and have a boozy time
I'm married to a damn good cook
It's really up to you to choose a time
If you lose it I'm
In the book
Try Filmore two
Six five four two

444   Sail Away

> That will find me
> Up to noon
> If not just leave a message
> It's been such fun
> Thanks so much, son
> Keep in touch, son
> See you soon.
>
> If you should need a little relaxation
> Why not drive down any night
> A hundred yards beyond the filling station
> Just before the traffic light
> Turn to the right.

Refrain 2:

> Dial TE two
> Four one three two
> That will get me
> Up to ten
> Or call me at the office
> Riverdrive six
> Eight two five six
> Branch extension
> Three two N
> All Saturdays are quite all right with us
> Drive over for a stirrup cup
> Maybe you'll stop and have a bite with us
> Spend the night with
> Just call me
> Let's meet one day
> Any Sunday
> Call me – call me
> Don't be shy
> You'll love to meet the children
> It's been swell, pal
> Give a yell, pal
> What the hell, pal!
> Bye – Bye – Bye!

The lights fade

The main hall.

The scene is the same as Act One, Scene One. The ship has docked and various including visitors are mingling with the outgoing passengers. **Mrs Spencer-Bollard**, **Nancy**, **Barnaby**, **Mr** *and* **Mrs Sweeny**, **Sir Gerard** *and* **Lady Nutfield**, **Mr Rawlings** *(still drunk)*, **Marybelle**, **Lollie**, *the* **Candijacks**, **Mrs Lush** *and* **Alvin** *all appear in due course and finally disappear down the gangway.*

Act Two, Scene Ten 445

Johnny *comes on from the gangway carrying a large bunch of roses.* **Joe** *intercepts him and they talk for a moment after which* **Joe** *goes back into his office and* **Johnny** *stands near the foot of the stairway looking rather disconsolate.*

Mimi, *carrying* **Adlai**, *comes out of the elevator.* **Skid** *rushes to her and wraps her in his arms. The photographers take a number of flashlight photographs and, accompanied by a cheering group of stewards,* **Skid** *and* **Mimi** *disappear down the gangway.*

By this time the crowd has thinned out a bit. **Lawford**, *with* **Verity** *on his arm, comes down the stairway. At the foot of it they stop as* **Johnny** *steps forward. He presents* **Verity** *with the roses. She looks startled for a moment and then, with a tremulous smile, accepts them. She introduces* **Johnny** *to* **Lawford**. *What is said cannot be heard. They chat for a moment politely and then* **Lawford** *and* **Verity** *go off down the gangway.*

Johnny *stands looking after them sadly. He moves slowly downstage, and sings the last phrase of 'Sail Away'.*

> When the wind and the weather
> Blow your dreams sky high
> Sail away – Sail away – Sail away.

A fresh influx of **Passengers** *and* **Stewards** *fills the stage.* **Johnny** *is moving towards the gangway as*:

The curtain falls.

The Girl Who Came to Supper

Critics' Notes

The work received a mixed response from American critics who, familiar with his straight plays that were revived in the same period, such as *Private Lives* (1930), struggled to define the elements of this large-scale musical. These elements included Broadway ballads, romantic duets, comic numbers and an imitation of the British music hall. Stephen Wattslondon of the *New York Times* drew significant comparisons between the brief performance of Tessie O'Shea, the Welsh-born Irish-named 'Cockney show-stopper' and the British music hall which was struggling to redefine itself in Britain of the 1960s. Wattslondon noted: 'Noël Coward was a London boy in his teens toward the end of the music hall's heyday, and no doubt the memory helped him to fashion Miss O'Shea's current song in so perfect a pastiche of the old days.'[1] His description of pastiche aligned with other American responses, which centred on the many different musical styles present in a single work.

Side-stepping musical discussions or critiques of the dramatic style, many critics instead focused on the performance of the show's leads, including Florence Henderson, 'who cavorts as an American showgirl involved in an affair with a Balkan ruler', as one of Broadway's newest leading ladies, alongside Barbra Streisand.[2] The star power cast could not, however, entirely quell critical responses to the work, including that of John Wilson.[3] Wilson lamented: 'Where are the innocence of heart and the faith in romance to make green again that oldest of sentimental tales about the prince and the girl of humble birth? Not, to be candid, in *The Girl Who Came to Supper* . . . Oh, there are pleasant nostalgic moments in this musical, which opened last night at the Broadway Theater. Some of Mr Coward's songs have a period glow . . . But the spirit that informed the Graustarkian fairylands of old does not irradiate *The Girl Who Came to Supper*. It struggles to make itself felt.'[4] Nevertheless, this work combines Coward's characteristically memorable tunes including the musical hall pastiche 'London is a Little Bit of Alright' along with 'This Time It's True Love' and 'Here and Now', both of which are reminiscent of *Bitter Sweet* and the Coward of 1930s London, with the glamour of the large-scale Broadway musical of the 1960s.

---

1 Stephen Watts, 'Sturdy Traditions: Tessie O'Shea's Local Triumph Stirs Memories of English Music Halls', *New York Times*, 16 February 1964.
2 Anonymous, 'Among the Newer Leading Ladies in Broadway Musicals,' *New York Times*, January 1964.
3 Howard Taubman, 'Theatre: Girl Who Came to Supper in Premier: José Ferrer is Star of Musical at Broadway', *New York Times*, 9 December 1963.
4 John S. Wilson, 'International Romance: An International Romance Set to Music Coward's Score', *New York Times*, 8 December 1963.

Running Order

Act One

'Swing Song'
'Yasni Kozkolai' (Carpathian National Anthem)
'My Family Tree'
'I've Been Invited to a Party'
'Waltz'
'I've Been Invited to a Party (Reprise)'
'When Foreign Princes Come to Visit Us'
'Sir or Ma'am'
'Soliloquies'
'Lonely'
'London'
'London is a Little Bit of All Right'
'What Ho, Mrs Brisket'
'Don't Take Our Charley for the Army'
'Saturday Night at the Rose and Crown'
'London Is a Little Bit of All Right' (Reprise)
'Here and Now'
'I've Been Invited to a Party (Reprise)'
'Soliloquies (Reprise)'

Act Two

'Coronation Chorale'
'How Do You Do, Middle Age?'
'Here and Now (Reprise)'
'The Stingaree'
'Curt, Clear and Concise'
'Tango'
'Welcome to Pootzie Van Doyle'
'The Coconut Girl'
'Paddy MacNeill and His Automobile'
'Swing Song (Reprise)'
'Six Lilies of the Valley'
'The Walla Walla Boola'
'This Time It's True Love'
'I'll Remember Her'

The Girl Who Came to Supper

Original Cast

Grand Duke Charles	José Ferrer[5]
Mary Morgan	Florence Henderson[6]
Queen Mother	Irene Brown[7]
Ada Cockle	Tessie O'Shea[8]
Simka	Murray Adler[9]
Peter Northbrook	Roderick Cook[10]
Tony Morelli	Jack Eddleman[11]
Colonel Hofmann	Chris Gampel[12]
Jessie Maynard	Marian Haraldson[13]
Baroness Brunheim	Lucie Lancaster[14]
First Girl	Donna Monroe[15]
Lady Sunningdale	Ilona Murai[16]
Major-Domo	Carey Nairnes[17]
Mr Grimes	Peter Pagan[18]
King Nicholas III	Sean Scully[19]
Second Girl	Ruth Shephard[20]
Violette Vines	Maggie Worth[21]

---

5 José Ferrer (1912–92) was a Puerto Rican-born actor and director. He was the first Hispanic actor to win an Academy Award in 1950.
6 Florence Henderson (1934–2016) was an American actor and singer. Her career included theatre, film and television roles, and she is best remembered for the role of Carol Brady in *The Brady Bunch*.
7 Irene Brown (1896–1965) was an English stage and film actor who starred in several Coward plays, along with the Vincent Youmans musical *No, No, Nannette*.
8 Tessie O'Shea (1913–95) was a Welsh character actor, born in Cardiff, and known for BBC radio broadcasts and her frequent performances at the London Palladium.
9 Murray Adler was an American stage actor.
10 Roderick Cook (1932–90) was born in London, and best known for his portrayal of Coward in the musical revue *Oh, Coward!* and as Count Von Strack in the film *Amadeus*.
11 Jack Eddleman (1940?–2011) was a notable actor and director, whose credits include *Oh! What a Lovely War!* (1964) and direction of Gilbert and Sullivan for the New York City Opera.
12 Chris Gampel (1921–2008) was a Canadian-born actor known for such films as *Annie Hall* (1977).
13 Marian Haraldson (born 1964) is an American stage actor known for such works as *One Upon a Mattress* (1964).
14 Lucie Lancaster (1907–98) was an American actor known for such works as *The Vagabond King* (1956) and *Pippin* (1972).
15 Donna Monroe is an American stage actor known for such works as *One Upon a Mattress* (1964).
16 Born Ellen Josephine Muray in Passaic, New Jersey, Ilona Murai was a soloist for the Metropolitan Opera Ballet. She appeared in such works as *The Seven Lively Arts* (1944).
17 Carey Nairnes was an American stage actor.
18 Peter MacGregor Pagan (1921–99) was an Australian actor known for such works as *The Overlanders* (1944).
19 Sean Scully (born 1947) is an Australian actor, best known for his work in such Walt Disney films as *The Prince and the Pauper* (1962).
20 Ruth Shephard played a number of minor roles on Broadway, including such works as *Subways Are for Sleeping* (1961) and *Mr President* (1962).
21 Maggie Worth was an American stage actor.

Dancers

Ivan Allan
Julie Drake
Robert Fitch
Sheila Forbes
Peter Holmes
Jami Landi
Sandy Leeds
Nancy Lynch
Carmen Morales
Ilona Murai
Scott Ray
Paul Reid Roman
Mari Shelton
Dan Siretta
Mike Toles
Mary Zahn

Singers

Jeremy Brown
Kellie Brytt
Jack Eddleman
John Felton
Carol Glade
Dell Hanley
Marian Haraldson
Barney Johnston
Elaine Labour
Art Matthews
Donna Monroe
Bruce Payton
Jack Rains
Ruth Shepard
Mitchell Taylor
Maggie Worth

Production Team

Musical Director	Jay Blackton[22]
Staging	Joe Layton[23]
Scenic Design	Oliver Smith[24]
Costume Design	Irene Sharaff[25]
Lighting Design	Peggy Clark[26]
Music Orchestrations	Robert Russell Bennett[27]
Dance Arrangements	Genevieve Pitot[28]
Vocal Arrangements	Jay Blackton
Production Stage Manager	Samuel Liff[29]
Stage Manager	Jerry Adler[30]
Producer	Herman Levin[31]

---

22 Jay Blackton (1909–94) was an award-winning music director and arranger. Work credits include *Oklahoma!* (1943) and *Two by Two* (1970).
23 Joe Layton (1931–94) was an American director and choreographer whose credits include *No Strings* (1962) and *George M!* (1968) with Joel Grey.
24 Oliver Smith (1918–94) was an American stage designer whose stage credits include *Guys and Dolls* (1955).
25 Irene Sharaff (1910–93) was an American costume designer whose credits include *The King and I* (1951) and *Hallelujah, Baby!* (1968).
26 Peggy Clark (1915–98) was an American lighting designer best known for her Broadway work including *Bells Are Ringing* (1956) and *Bye Bye Birdie* (1960).
27 Robert Russell Bennett (1894–1981) was an American composer and arranger whose credits include Broadway works like *Oklahoma!* (1943), *Kiss Me, Kate* (1948) and *My Fair Lady* (1956).
28 Genevieve Pitot (born 1920) is an American pianist, composer and dance arranger who worked with Jerome Robbins, Hanya Holm and Agnes de Mille.
29 Samuel 'Biff' Liff (1919–2015) was an American Broadway producer and stage manager. Credits include *Promise, Promises* (1968) with David Merrick.
30 Jerry Adler (born 1929) is an American theatre director, actor and producer best known for his work on *The Sopranos* and *The Good Wife*.
31 Herman Levin (1907–90) was an American producer whose work included *Gentlemen Prefer Blondes* (1949) and *My Fair Lady* (1956).

Act One

Scene One

The show curtain rises to reveal the back stage at the Majestic Theatre, London, the evening of 27 June 1911, the eve of the coronation of His Majesty George V.

'The Coconut Girl' is in progress; 'The Swing Song' is about to begin. In the foreground is **Jessie Maynard** *as* **Tina**, *the heroine, seated on the swing with the* **Girls** *grouped around her. In the wings, stage left and stage right, various members of the cast are awaiting their cues. An obligato[32] to the song is hummed by some of them while they are otherwise preoccupied by reading, eating fruit, making love, doing their fingernails, hair-dos, make-up, etc. Two of them are in kimonos singing along.*

As the curtain rises, we hear giggling of the girls in the play.

First Girl   It seems that Count Alexis is late.

Second Girl   Maybe he won't come at all.

Tina   He'll be here, my heart tells me so.

Third & Fourth Girls   Her heart.

They giggle as the other girls join in.

Tina   Yes, my foolish heart.

Bell tone in orchestra.

'Swing Song'

Tina
My foolish heart may yet discover
That all the dreams I have been dreaming are
In vain.

The girls in kimonos enter wings downstage right.

Girls
She has the air of one who's waiting for a love and
Who she's dreaming of we'll ascertain.

Tony Morelli *as* **Alexis**, *the hero, appears at the top of the stairs in the wings stage left with his* **Dresser**. *He is primping and getting ready for his entrance.*

Tina
No matter what the end may be here
In my
Golden reverie.

Alexis *starts down the stairs.*

---

32 A melodic section of a musical work that is integral to the whole; should not be omitted from the work.

As I swing to and
Fro high and low
High and low.

Girls
Would you permit Alexis for a while to stay with you?

Dresser *starts up the stairs.*

Tina
Maybe.

Girls
To share this beautiful day with you?

Tina
We'll see.

Tina	**Mary**
Not a cloud . . .	*(Entering the wings, half in her costume And singing very loudly one beat behind* **Tina**.*)*
Girls	Not a cloud . . .
Cloud . . .	In the sky . . .
Tina	**Alexis**
In the sky	S-h-h-h . . .
Girls	**Mary**
Sky . . .	Oh, I'm sorry, Mr Morelli! I was singing too loud . . . I just love that song, don't you? . . .

Tina
And the lark . . .

Girls
Lark . . .

Tina
Singing high . . .

Girls
High . . .

Tina
And the sound of the sea far below . . .

Girls
Below

Alexis	**Girls**
Appearing above onstage wall.	Ah . . .

Would you permit this fellow, who
Has nothing but a lonely
Heart to bring just to kiss
You as a swing to and
Fro?

There is a man standing behind her who turns out to be **Mr Grimes**, *the company manager, a seedy impresario in a matching dress suit.*

Mary
Hey, would you button me?

Grimes
S-h-h-h . . .!

Mary (*full voice*)
I'm sorry, Mr Grimes, I didn't . . .

Grimes
S-h-h-h-h . . .!

Mary (*whispering*)
Oh, I'm sorry, Mr Grimes – I didn't realise it was you.

Violetta Vines, *a dowager character actress, who plays the* **Marchesa** *takes her place in the wings.*

Girls (*continuing to swing*) Ah . . .	**Tina & Alexis** As we swing to and fro High and Low high And low All our Cares melt Away Like the cold Winter Snow.

Alexis
Would you permit this fellow for a while to stay with you?

Tina
Maybe . . .

Alexis & Girls
To share this beautiful day with you?

Tina
Mais oui!

Orchestra swollen tremolo[33] *as* **Tina** *and* **Alexis** *are about to kiss* . . .

Marchesa (*running on stage from the wings followed by* **Mary**)   Stop, I forbid it. He –

(*Indicating* **Alexis**.) – is an imposter. A rank fortune hunter!

Tina   Is – is this true

Alexis   No . . . !

Marchesa   The answer is written in his eyes. Look!

Tina *looks, and it is apparently a straight steer, because she utters a heartbroken moan.*

Mary   Count Alexis, you are a cad and a bounder. (*She kneels beside* **Tina**.)

All   Yes . . . Yes . . .

Mary   Come, Tina, we'll go back to Tallahassee in the morning. There you will forget. (*To the cast and chorus as she circles the stage*.) Dear friends, please leave this broken-hearted girl to her grief –

Tina (*wildly*)   No, no – the party must continue. Won't *somebody* dance with me?

A **Waiter** *near her drops his tray with a crash! He takes her in his arms and they dance around the stage until suddenly* . . .

Tina   Cy Mortimer! It's you!

Tina *faints, the* **Waiter** *gathers her up in his arms and carries her upstage.*

All
  Swinging to and fro
  Swinging to and
  Fro swinging to
  And fro
  Swinging to
  And fro
  Swinging to and
  Fro.

The act curtain falls. The **Company** *takes a bow. There is the accustomed backstage rush in foreground as it Rains takes the wall off stage left.*

Stagehand (*indicating the* **Marchesa** *who has taken her bow from the swing*)   Okay. Let her down.

She is lowered to the stage floor.

Grimes (*who has come down the stairs downstage left during the bows and now rushes onstage*)   All right – attention everybody! Line up for the presentation – His

---

33 A trembling effect in the orchestra.

Royal Highness and the gentlemen of his staff will be here in a moment. Principals over here –

Singers – ah – over there –

Ah – Dancers – you're dismissed! Don't forget your music for the Carpathian National Anthem!

Peter Northbrook, *an earnest and attractive diplomat, enters down stairs, stage left.*

Girl   Here it is. Here's the music.

She is distributing cards with the Carpathian National Anthem on them to the **Singers** *downstage right.* 'Coconut Girl' **Principals** *have words on papers in their pockets, concealed in bosoms, etc.*

Stagehand (*indicating swing which is to be flown*)   Take it up –

Another stagehand exits stage right to stage left with flat.

Grimes (*as* **Mary** *moves to the wrong side of the* **Principals**' *line*)   Over there. (*He pushes* **Mary** *to the other end of the line and then says to all* **Principals**:) All right – face this way.

(*He turns the line so that the* **Principals** *face upstage.*) Ready, Mr Northbrook!

Northbrook   Ready, Colonel Hofmann!

Hoffman   Ready, Your Royal Highness!

His Royal Highness, **Grand Duke Charles**, **Prince Regent of Carpathia** *enter downstairs stage left followed by* **Five Gentlemen** *in evening dress.*

Grimes   Welcome, Your Royal Highness.

Regent (*to* **Grimes**)   Most enjoyable. Light but entirely agreeable entertainment.

Grimes (*bowing*)   Thank you, Your Royal Highness. (*Indicates the waiting* **Principals** *and the* **Regent** *moves forward with him. In each presentation, the men bow and the women curtsey. The* **Regent** *handles them swiftly and apparently without effort.*) Your Royal Highness, may I present Miss Jessie Maynard . . .

Regent   So charming, Miss Maynard; and may I express the hope that you will find true happiness in the second act.

Grimes (*presenting the 'hero'*)   Your Royal Highness, Mr Tony Morelli . . .

Regent   A dashing fellow, your Count Alexis . . . most agreeable.

Grimes (*presenting 'Marchesa'*)   Your Royal Highness, Miss Violetta Vines . . .

Regent   A portrayal of unusual depth and feeling, Miss Vines.

Grimes (*presenting 'Waiter'*)   Your Royal Highness, Mr Stewart Addison . . .

Regent (*chuckling*)   How droll, your automobile song. We were very much amused.

Mary *has been bracing herself, and now it is her turn.*

Grimes (*with no enthusiasm*)   Your Royal Highness, Miss Mary Morgan.

Mary *sinks down in a curtsey so profound she seems to be headed for the basement and stays down.*

Regent   A notable vignette, Miss Morgan, of unusual charm.

Mary *is still submerged, so the* **Regent** *graciously adds something extra.*

Regent   A small role to be sure, but extremely well played.

Grimes, **Northbrook**, *others are gesturing for* **Mary** *to get up. She stays down.*

Regent   You may rise, Miss Morgan.

Mary   I can't, Your Majesty. My heel is caught in my skirt.

She extends a hand appealingly. It is **Grimes** *who yanks her up – angrily so that she is headed for the footlights until her course is blocked by the* **Regent***. He holds her for only a pneumatic moment.*

Mary   Thanks, Your Majesty. Excuse me –

Grimes   Get back in your place. (*To the* **Regent***:*) I beg Your Royal Highness' pardon.

Regent   It was nothing; entirely excusable.

Mary   Thank you, Your Highness. (*She curtsies again.*) You see I can do it fine. It was just hard luck getting my heel caught in my dress that way . . . and I'm sorry . . .

Labour, *leader of the group downstage right, blows her pitch-pipe.*

Mary   . . . I bumped into Your Majesty.

Grimes *snaps his fingers and the Carpathian National Anthem begins bringing everyone to attention.* **Mary** *smiles at the* **Regent**.

'Carpathian National Anthem'
'Yasni Kozkolai'

All
  Kraz-na klieg
  Spling az-ka do praz-lik
  Narn bal-achu vu
  Zveg-al az gab loot nyez kaz-ka biek-
  La vai Probst quas-ka-la-ka yaz-ni
  Yaz-ni ko-zko-lai.

The **Regent** *starts to relax but suddenly.*

  Klieg klieg
  Plach-a-vitz nyez

Nyez zla-ba-chai
Zla-ba-cai vai! Hey!

Grimes (*hustling the* **Company** *off and giving* **Mary** *a push for good measure*)

All right. Hurry with the change everybody

Mary *gives the* **Regent** *a big smile and starts up the stairs as he watches her progress.*

Stagehand   Bring in the Villa Marina!

Drop cloth comes down.

Regent (*as* **Mary** *exits, he's looking after her*)   So amusing those Americans and their musical shows . . . pity I can't take this opportunity to study their culture . . . Miss Morgan could help me . . .

Northbrook   Surely, sir, for research, you will find our British Museum has far better equipment.

Regent   Equipment, my dear Northbrook, is in the eye of the beholder. In the words of my uncle King Pavel of Carpathia, 'Tear down, if you will, the old libraries, but leave me the young librarians'.

Northbrook *laughs audibly, as the* **Five Gentlemen** *laugh very discreetly.*

Regent   Or, as it was put by my cousin Princess Teresa of Kroll – the most rewarding study of man – is men.

The **Five Gentlemen** *again laugh discreetly.*

Regent   And I might also mention my nephew, Prince Caspar of Bosnia, whose family motto is 'Smovolka dubroni', meaning, 'In the dark, all cats are grey'.

Northbrook   A most exotic family, sir, if I may say so . . .

Regent   You may, Northbrook, and on this subject, I will add a few words of my own.

'My Shady Family Tree'

Regent
My father was
Hungarian my mother
Came from Spain I've
Several aunts
In the South of
France and a
Grandmama
Maternal
Grandmama in the
Ukraine.

Northbrook
She went too far

Your grandmama
For it's cold in the old Ukraine.

Regent
My uncle a Bavarian
I've learned some tricks
Of his so if I'm not a
Polyglot
I should like to know who is.

Northbrook
So if you're not
A polyglot
I should like to know who is.

Five Gentlemen *dance.*

Regent
I was born in the shade of my family
Tree and I'm bound to admit
That it
Was pretty
Shady the
Dynasty
In 1033
Was found by Queen Eulalie
Who never exactly acted like a
Lady many a gaudy night she'd
Spend
With a troupe of strolling players
If her lovers were laid out end to
End
They'd stretch to the
Himalayas
She gave birth to such
Scads of illegitimate
Lads
With results that you can all too
Clearly see and one of those ultimate
Results was me
And my shady family tree.
My grandpapa on
Mother's side was far
More East than West he
Spent his life
With a Chinese
Wife in a mental
Home half-Oriental home
In Bucharest.

Northbrook
    What cruel fate
    I'd simply hate
    To be batty in Bucharest!

Regent
    The grandma on the other side was
    Russian to the core
    She danced in Kief but came to
    Grief
    In a brawl in Singapore.

Northbrook
    Oh what a blow
    To sink so low
    As to brawl in Singapore.

Regent *exits.* **Five Gentlemen** *dance.*

Regent
    I was born in the shade of my family tree and
    Believe it or not
    It's got
    A lot of
    Branches my
    Uncle Fritz
    Took leave of his wits
    And walked into the Hotel Ritz
    Attired in an evening dress of Cousin
    Blanche's one of my forebears took a
    Bride
    But because of interbreeding
    He tried and tried and tried and
    Tried without ever quite succeeding
    I've a grandmother
    Who went mad in 1832
    And drove, naked, to her diamond jubilee.

Five Gentlemen *start to exit.*

Regent
    Proving beyond all doubt you will
    Agree that I've been a very shady
    Judy O'Grady
    And the Colonel's
    Lady shady family
    Tree.

He exits

Blackout.

Scene Two

Mary (*disconsolate*)   I certainly gummed up the presentation. For once in my life I get to meet a real live Prince – and what do I do?

First Girl (*cynically*)   You think he was all that alive?

Mary (*defensive*)   I liked him; he was sweet.

Second Girl   You did all right, Mary. You were supposed to curtsey, weren't you?

Mary   Sure, but I wasn't supposed to throw in a flying tackle.

Grimes (*to* **Girls**)   All right, get on with it! There's a second act on . . . and you're in it. Hey, dear!

Mary *tries to sneak out with the others, still in her wrapper, as* **Northbrook** *steps in.*

Grimes   There she is, Mr Northbrook.

Northbrook   Miss Morgan, permit me to introduce myself. Peter Northbrook in the Foreign Service of his Britannic Majesty, temporarily attached to the suite of His Royal Highness, the Grand Duke Charles, Prince Regent of Carpathia.

Axed, **Mary** *sinks down in a profound curtsey.* **Northbrook** *is pained and comes down the stair.*

Northbrook   No – not to me. You need not curtsey to me, Miss Morgan.

Mary (*rising*)   I don't mind, and as long as I've got the knack of it now –

Northbrook   Miss Morgan, by command of His Royal Highness, I am empowered to invite you to supper this evening at the Carpathian Embassy.

Mary (*startled and after a long pause*)   . . . Me? With the Grand Duke and his Royal Carpathians? Are you sure he means me?

Northbrook   My instructions preclude any area of doubt or misunderstanding in this matter, Miss Morgan.

Mary   But – but what do I wear?

Northbrook   I had the impression that His Royal Highness admired the dress you wore when you were presented.

Mary   But that's not mine. I just wear that in the show. And if the Wardrobe Mistress caught me . . .

Grimes   Wear the dress, stupid.

And as **Mary** *looks up at* **Northbrook**.

Northbrook   I have nothing to add to that, Miss Morgan. I will remain to escort you to the Embassy at the conclusion of your performance.

Mary (*mechanically*)   Thanks.

As **Grimes** *and* **Northbrook** *exit, she looks stunned.*

Mary My God, wait until they hear about this in Milwaukee!

'I've Been Invited to a Party'

Mary
    I've been invited to a party . . . me!
    Everyone will say
    'Who's that pretty
    Girl?' as they see me
    Swirl round the
    Floor
    And before
    The night is through
    I'll be drinking champagne out of everyone's
    Shoe people will murmur
    'But she's
    Charming' what a lovely smile!
    What a sense of
    Style! Nobody
    Will guess that
    My dress
    Is the one that I wear in scene
    Three. And the whole royal
    Court will agree that the belle
    Of the ball – is me!
    The most entrancing waltz
    Will be the waltz the prince
    Will dance with
    Me and as we're
    Floating cheek to
    Cheek
    The pressure of his
    Hand will make me
    Understand
    There's really no necessity to
    Speak guests will
    Cheer
    And cry 'bravo!'
    As round and round and round
    We go and when the music comes
    To an end he'll say – 'hey
    You've found a friend!'

    I've been invited to a
    Party and when they've
    At last played the final

Dance someone will
Advance
And I'll wait till a
Stately
Limousine
Drives me back through the sunrise
To Camberwell Green[34]
And when I write
Home to
Milwaukee
Mom will have a
Fit when she reads
The bit
Saying that I danced with a
Prince and that since
I've been asked round to tea
Then she'll tell all the neighbours
With glee that the bell of the ball –
Was me!

Call Boy (Toles)   Please, Miss Morgan. Finale. Places, please for the finale.

Mary   Coming . . . (*She takes the dress off and passes the screen stage right.*)

Behind, principals and chorus of 'The Coconut Girl' are waltzing the finale of the show. **Mary** *appears, whispering to the girls on stage that she is 'going to a party'. She enters and does her part in the finale. The 'curtain' falls on 'The Coconut Girl' and* **Mary** *and the others take their bows, after which there is a frantic post-finale rush to get off and out.* **Mary** *turns to face the front, still apparently bemused as a* **Stagehand** *crosses left to right with a piece of scenery crosses in front of her. She continues singing.*

Mary
I've been invited to a
Party everyone will
Say

She takes off her right shoe.

Who's that pretty
Girl? As they see me
Swirl

Takes off left shoe.

Round the floor and

She starts to cross to the right.

Before the night is
Through I'll be
Drinking champagne
Out of everyone's shoe.

---

34 A park in South London.

She runs off and throws her shoe onto front of stage. The platform and steps of the dressing room have come on into position. **Ruth** *and* **Donna** *are in their 'street' costumes and are murmuring.*

Mary
People will
Murmur but she's
Charming what a
Lovely smile!
What a sense of
Style! Nobody
Will guess that
My dress
Is the one that I wear in scene
Three. And the whole royal
Court will agree that the bell
Of the ball – was me!

At the end of the waltz, **All** *strike curtain call pose; 'The Coconut Girl' act curtain comes down.*

Mary Hey, listen everybody . . .

Act curtain goes up again. **All** *strike call pose; act curtain falls.*

Girls, 'listen . . .

Everyone starts chattering and ignores her.

Siretta Take out two and three!

Mary Let me tell you what happened . . .

Gloria Just don't forget the coronation parade in the morning.

Siretta Set up from the top of the show!

Mary (*to* **Donna** *and* **Ruth**) Girls, you won't believe . . .

Donna We have to be at our window by 8 a.m.

Ruth Or the police won't let us through the line.

Everyone has exited except **Tony Morelli** *and* **Jessie Maynard** *who are arguing. They exit.*

Mary Okay. I'll be there but . . . (*She is alone onstage.*) You'd think one of them would listen.

Scene Four

The Royal Apartment, Carpathian Embassy, Belgrave Square, later that evening. It is a large, sumptuously furnished room, though the décor is heavy and Victorian.

Up centre, double doors lead to the main corridor. On extreme stage right there is a fireplace, above a screen covers the door to a bedroom, a buffet is against the wall, above hangs a large picture framed by two . . . A small stairway ascends to the Regent's bedroom. At extreme left, a chair and a small desk with telephone and lamp sit in front of the window. In front of the fireplace is an armchair. There is also a divan, behind which is a small table with a lamp.

As the table starts to turn, the **Major-Domo** *is leading eight* **Footmen** *(***John**, **Dell**, **Barney**, **Art**, **Bruce**, **Jack R**, **Mitch** *and* **Paul***) through the door who will end up on stage right. As they make their entrance they get into a two-line formation downstage left and sing:*

Footmen
    When foreign princes come to visit us
    Usually from the Balkans
    We send our time looking helpful and
    Solicitous and hovering about like
    Falcons.

Jack R
    If one of them wants a tra la la la la
    We have to set the stage for a seduction.

Bruce
    And what with the lighting

Mitch
    Champagne

Peter *and* **Ivan** *open doors upstage centre.* **Mike** *enters from behind the screen with a champagne bottle.*

Paul
    And caviar

Jack R *rolls the table from upper centre to downstage right position.*

Footmen
    It's certainly the hell of a production

Barney
    For emperors and czars
    Fresh flowers in every vase

Jack R, **Bruce**, **Mitch** *and* **Paul** *produce trick flowers.*

Dell *(crossing to centre, collecting the flowers from the other four in a vase)*
    And we introduce some spruce loose-covers

Art
    We also burn some scent
    In a spoon that's rather bent.

Mitch
  Essential for all potential royal lovers

Footmen
  Archdukes-grand
  Dukes rather out of
  Hand dukes
  Whose countries can't be found on
  Any map
  To inflame their tepid blood
  We release a gurgling flood
  Of cordon rouge and Châteauneuf-du-Pape.

Mike *allows the champagne cork to pop and the champagne splatters on the floor and furniture.*

Jack E   You silly ass!

Jack E *starts wiping the floor.* **Jack R** *turns the armchair and starts wiping it off.* **Mike** *exits and* **Art** *clears off the table, picks up two dish covers and crashes them like cymbals.* **John** *and* **Paul** *move the divan and test it together for softness.* **John** *exits stage left and* **Paul** *stretches out on the divan to sleep.* **Ivan** *exits upper left.* **Dell** *exits upper centre,* **Bruce** *and* **Peter** *exit upper left,* **Barney** *exits upper centre.* **Mike** *enters right with a mop and swings it around just missing* **Art** *who exits upper centre.* **Jack E** *supervises as* **Mike** *mops the floor and both exit right.* **Mitch** *enters left with lighted candles and places them on the table.* **Ivan** *enters upper centre with sheets followed by* **Peter** *carrying pillows, they exit upper left.* **Mitch** *exits upper left.* **Jack R** *blows out the candles and exits left.* **Paul** *sits up, sees the candle, lights them and exits right.* **Barney** *enters upper centre carrying a large tray of bottles and glasses, and outs it on the buffet.* **Jack E** *enters right with a perfume spray, crosses to centre, sees the candles are out, lights them and exits upper stage left.* **Jack R** *enters left, crosses to the window, closes drapes, shuts off light and exits upper centre.* **Barney** *takes a bottle and glass from the tray and sits on the divan. He starts to pour himself a drink when he notices the candles. He leaves the bottle and glass on the floor and crosses to the table, lights the candle and exits right.* **Mike** *enters right swinging an incense burner and exits upper left.* **Ivan** *enters upper left with a small stool, places it by the divan and exits upper centre.* **Bruce** *enters left, picks up a bottle and glass, takes a sip, giggles and exits upper left.*

Major-Domo *enters left, fixes the curtains, snaps the lights, pats the divan and blows out the candles when* **Simka** *enters upper centre followed by* **Ivan, John, Dell** *and* **Art** *carrying violin, two violas and a 'cello. They line up, bow and run their bows over the strings.* **Major-Domo** *signals to them to take their positions behind the screen. The musicians exit and the* **Major-Domo** *follows.*

As he exits seven men rush in and take the following positions. **Mike** *down right,* **Mitch** *down left,* **Jack E** *near table,* **Barney** *near buffet,* **Peter** *upper centre,* **Paul** *at divan,* **Jack R** *at window.* **Bruce** *enters upper left with four throw pillows. He throws* *one to* **Mike**, *one to* **Paul** *and one to* **Jack R**; *at the same moment all four throw pillows to the fireplace, on the divan, in front of the divan and on the chair at the window.*

The double doors are opened and the **Regent** *enters, crosses to a table and lifts a dish from it. He is humming a few bars of 'The Coconut Girl'. A* **Footman** *hands him a sword.*

Regent Not too many lights, Korovinsky. I'm not planning to read, or play cards.

Major-Domo *gestures for the lights to dim as the* **Regent** *signals for the uncovering of the tureen on the rolling table.*

Regent Caviar?

Excellent! (*dismisses the* **Footman** *and sees* **Hoffman**.)

Hoffman With respect, sir . . .

Regent Really, Hoffman, tonight I think I'm quite capable of guarding myself.

Hoffman Sir, the riots are continuing and are now reported even in the Capitol.

Regent (*ignores the sheaf of cables in* **Hoffman**'*s hand and crosses to the* **Major-Domo**) Please, Hoffman, tonight my mind is on higher things. (*To the* **Major-Domo**.) What is there to drink?

Major-Domo Champagne, Your Royal Highness, and of course vodka.

Regent I haven't the time. Just leave the vodka. Simka!

Simka *appears from behind the screen.*

Regent You will play on the usual signal. The cue for the music, please, Korovinsky.

The **Major-Domo** *hands a pillow to the* **Regent** *who sits on the couch while the* **Major-Domo** *turns out the table lamp.* **Simka** *plays.*

Regent No, no, no. Not a czardas. What sort of mood music is that? You'll have her leaping about and dancing all over the furniture.

Simka Forgive me, Your Royal Highness, I intended it only as an overture.

Regent I haven't the time. Once more.

The **Major-Domo** *turns on the lamp and instantly turns it off.* **Simka** *flares into a gypsy love song. The* **Regent** *pushes the pillow under the couch and listens enraptured. Then . . .*

Regent Enough, idiot. I don't need it. I don't even like it!

Simka *has stopped playing and slinks back to his place behind the screen.* **Nicolas** *appears flanked by bodyguards.* **Hoffman** *and all others bow low.*

Regent Good evening, Nicky.

Nicolas Good evening, Father.

Hoffman Your Majesty.

Regent What is it, my boy – What can I do for you?

Hoffman With respect, Your Royal Highness, I suggested this interview.

Regent Oh?

He looks from **Hoffman** *to* **Nicolas** *curiously,* **Nicolas***, fearful, is standing at attention.*

Hoffman Sir, pro-German elements are behind these riots and the name of King Nicolas appears in these reports as if His Majesty were in support of the demonstrations. (*Gives reports to the* **Regent**.) I felt His Majesty would appreciate an opportunity to explain.

Regent Is this true, Nicky?

Nicolas (*defiant, scared*) Yes, Father.

Regent For ten years I've been fighting their efforts to swallow us. And you've aligned yourself with *them* – against *me*?

Nicolas I'm sorry, Father. They have promised me the reforms *you* have refused.

Regent Promised!

Nicolas (*turned front*) I want my country to be free.

Regent Idiot, just because you've had a few German lessons, do you want them goose-stepping all over us?

Nicolas *moves away.*

Hoffman With respect, Your Royal Highness, if we act promptly to put down these riots . . .

Regent Riots, always riots! Don't my people know any indoor sports?

He beckons to the others, including **Nicolas***, and all exit; the* **Regent***, handing his sword to* **Footman**. **Bodyguards** *flank* **Regent** *as king follows,* **Hoffman** *brings up rear.*

Footman
 When foreign princes come to visit us
 Life is an exhausting
 Strain we long and pray
 For that happy, happy day.

Korovinsky When they bugger off home again.

The double doors are opened and **Mary** *and* **Northbrook** *appear.* **Mary** *is looking back timidly, around the room nervously.*

Major-Domo Sir, my Royal Highness wishes me to explain that urgent business with the Ambassador will detain him only a few minutes.

Northbrook Splendid, Korovinsky. (*He puts his hand on* **Mary***'s arm to keep her from curtseying. The* **Major-Domo** *and* **Footmen** *go.*)

Northbrook   I take it that you have thus far had little or no social contact with royalty, Miss Morgan? . . .

Mary (*defensively*)   Well, you know how it is . . . Milwaukee High School, then a year of clerking in the five and ten cent store . . . Where would I get a chance.

Northbrook (*with some despair*)   Tonight, when you were presented to the Regent, you addressed him as Your Majesty.

Mary   Oh, I thought he'd like that . . .

As **Northbrook***, pained, shakes his head.*

Mary   No good?

Northbrook   Most improper. Your Majesty may only be used if you should meet the Regent's son, King Nicolas, or the Queen Mother –

Mary   The Queen Mother? – is that his wife?

Northbrook   Oh no, the Regent is a widower. With your permission I will endeavour to explain. You see – he was born a prince of the royal house of Hungary. He married Queen Sophie of Carpathia, and at her death some years ago, their son, Nicolas, became king. Meanwhile, until His Majesty is of age, the Grand Duke rules as Regent – That's quite clear, isn't it?

Mary   Oh, sure.

Northbrook (*quickly*)   Now, as to the protocol . . .

Mary   What?

Northbrook   Protocol.

'Sir or Ma'am'

Northbrook
   The privilege of supping with a royal prince is
   Granted to a very few
   Allow me to give you one or
   Two hints as to what you may
   Say or do maintain a dignified
   Demeanour
   Be relaxed but not too
   Expectant and always
   Remember protocol . . .

Mary
   It sounds like a disinfectant

Northbrook
   Protocol my dear
   Is just a set of simple rules
   Designed to lubricate proconsular

Machinery for example it is wiser
When you talk with king or Kaiser
To confine your conversation to the
Scenery but I digress
The very first thing you must master is the
Method of address . . .
Sir or
Ma'am
Ma'am, or
Sir
One's addressed to him of
Course the others
Addressed to Her Majesty
Or Highness
May once in a while be used
But you'll notice a certain
Dryness if you get the terms
Confused ma'am or sir

Mary
Sir or ma'am

Northbrook
Accompanied by a simple bob
Not a profound
Salam don't have
A stroke
If a casual joke
Is received with funereal gloom
Another a curse
And in quick reverse
Back right out of the room.
Sir or
Ma'am
Ma'am, or
Sir
The mumbling of this simple
Phrase betrays the amateur
Royal condescension
May murmur a Christian name
But you'll notice a certain
Tension if you try to do the
Same

Mary
Ma'am or
Sir
Sir or ma'am

Northbrook
>Makes every royal personage as 'happy
>as a clam' if some remark
>Should go wide off the mark
>And you're suddenly conscious
>Of doom sink to the ground
>Swivel around
>And crawl right out of the room.

Do you think you can remember that, Miss Morgan?

Mary   I think so.

Northbrook   Good, very good.

A **Footman** *has wheeled in a supper table.*

Mary   Mr Northbrook!

Northbrook   Ah, supper!

Mary   Yes, supper. For how many?

Northbrook (*counting, then brightly*)   Two, isn't it?

Mary   Mr Northbrook, what kind of party *is* this?

As he is about to speak.

Never mind – I know.

She picks up her bag and gloves.

Northbrook   Miss Morgan, you must let me explain –

Mary   Mr Northbrook, I don't like to make a fuss or sound like a temperance poster. It's partly my own fault, for believing everything you told me – but that's how I am. I do believe everything. And if you left me alone here with His Majesty – by candlelight – I'd be a sitting duck.

Northbrook   Miss Morgan. What is more natural than that His Royal Highness should enjoy a quiet supper – quite innocently – with a lovely and charming young lady like yourself . . .

Mary   Mr Northbrook, just because I believe everything, that's no excuse for *telling* me everything.

Northbrook   Miss Morgan. (*Sonorously.*) Great events are shaping up in Europe today. Carpathia, though a small country, is most strategically situated and it is vital that her ties with England be strengthened. The great Bismark called Carpathia 'the cockpit of Europe'.

Mary   Did he?

Northbrook   And it was Prince Metternich who remarked, at the Congress of Vienna, 'who controls Carpathia is also the master of Herzogovina!'.

(*He finishes this like a trumpet call.* **Mary** *understandably looks at him blankly.*) But that's obvious isn't it?

Mary Sure.

Northbrook Miss Morgan, supper will occupy you for not less than three quarters of an hour – agreed? (*He goes right on.*) In precisely forty-five minutes I will come back and announce that a relative – your dear aunt – has been injured in an accident and that you must rush to her bedside.

Mary In Milwaukee.

Northbrook No, no. In London. You are utterly devoted to each other, and she travels everywhere with you.

Pause.

Please!

Mary (*speculating, looking around*) Well. Forty-five minutes . . .?

The problem is resolved by the entrance of the **Regent**, *preceded as usual by the* **Major-Domo**. *Forced to decision,* **Mary** *reluctantly puts down her purse and gloves, curtsies properly.*

Mary Hello!

Regent Good evening, Miss Morgan. How kind of you to accept my invitation on such short notice. And my apologies for being unable to receive you personally upon your arrival.

The **Major-Domo** *is still in attendance at the open door.*

Regent I expect you're looking forward to your night's rest. We have a very full day ahead of us.

Northbrook As a matter of fact, Your Royal Highness, I must clear the late cables at the foreign office.

Regent Ah, yes. Your devotion to duty is highly commendable, Northbrook.

Northbrook Thank you, Your Royal Highness. (*Backing out skilfully as* **Mary** *gestures to the clock. At the door he bows again.*) Miss Morgan . . . Sir . . .

The door closes.

Regent Please be seated.

Mary So late, and you still have to do homework?

Regent The burdens of my kingdom are heavy – and alas – I must bear them alone.

Mary First thing you'll know you'll have a nervous stomach.

Regent (*amused*) A nervous stomach, Miss Morgan, is the occupational disease of Balkan rulers. What remedy do you suggest?

Mary (*earnestly*) Sir, you shouldn't try to do more than two shows a day.

Regent I beg your pardon?

Mary I mean, you should relax.

Regent Thank you. I think that is excellent advice. Shall we start with a drink? I find that most relaxing.

Mary All right. (*Quite instinctively she gives him a warm sunny smile.*) What shall we have – Sir?

They laugh.

'Soliloquies'

Regent
    She looks quite sweet
    Perhaps a little young
    For me
    But still that youthful charm
    Will be a change
    I must arrange
    For Northbrook to
    Receive some sort of
    Minor decoration
    He's really done
    Exceedingly well and show
    – in fact
    Much tact
    Combined with shrewd
    discrimination.

Do you like vodka?

Mary I don't know. (*Apologetically.*) I don't drink very much – just a beer now and then with some of the musicians.

Regent (*pouring two small glasses.*) It's a Russian drink – quite refreshing. (*He hands her one of the glasses.*) Vechari prosnaya.

Mary
    He looks quite nice
    I'm not a bit afraid of
    The image that I
    Made of him was wrong
    His face is
    Strong but I
    Can see
    Some
    Tired little lines of
    Dissipation his eyes are kind and
    Just a bit sad
    I think – I'm glad
    That I'm the girl who had the invitation.
    Vechari prosnaya.

Regent An ancient Carpathian toast, 'Vechari' means vodka and 'prosnaya' (*Thinks a moment.*) it has something to do with good luck or long life but I'm not sure which. (*A sigh.*) Carpathian is a strange, difficult language, and I must admit with some shame that I have never quite mastered it. I looked it up.

Mary Oh, yes. You're Hungarian. (*Apologetically.*) I mean, Your Royal Highness is a Royal Hungarian. But your English is marvellous!

Regent I was educated at Eton and Oxford.

Mary (*impressed*) You went to *both*?

Regent I was young – perhaps foolish – (*Then briskly.*) Where were we?

Mary (*smiling*) Vechari prosnaya, Your Royal Highness.

Regent Excellent. You have a very good ear.

They touch glasses, she is about to take a sip when she sees him toss off the whole package.

Mary Like *that*?

Regent It is the only way. The Czar himself told me.

Mary Well, if it's a tip from the old feed-bag . . . (*She follows suit, looking quite pleased, then reacts visibly as the missile arrives on target.*) It doesn't smell of anything . . . what makes it burn?

Regent Who knows? . . . The Russians . . . such a devious mentality. (*As he starts to kiss her the telephone rings. The* **Regent** *looks at it, irritated, it catches him filling the vodka glasses again.*) Excuse me. They should not disturb me here. However – (*He crosses and picks up the phone.*) Yes. (*And then, in a pained voice.*) Now? (*And then.*) Very well, if she is on her way. (*He hangs up.*) My mother-in-law, the Queen Mother, wishes to speak to me –

Mary The Queen Mother. (*Running through her script.*) That's Your Majesty, or Ma'am. I curtsey, I don't speak unless spoken to, and I back out. (*Looking at him for approval.*) Okay?

Regent (*amused*) Her Majesty is quite deaf and rather vague so any minor breach of protocol you may commit is not likely to –

The doors at the centre open and the **Queen Mother** *sweeps in.* **Mary** *sinks down in a deep curtsey.*

Queen Mother Ah Charles, I was so anxious to speak to you –

Regent Yes, Mother – Perhaps in the morning would be –

Queen Mother Why, it's dear Elsa Herzogovina. My dear, you must have lost ninety pounds – how on earth did you do it?

Regent Mother, may I present Miss Mary Morgan.

Queen Mother Oh? Delighted to meet you. (*As* **Mary** *rises and extends her hand.*) Are you in London for the coronation?

Mary I'm in 'The Coconut Girl', ma'am, at the Majestic Theatre.

And as the **Queen Mother** *looks at her uncertainly.*

Regent (*loud*) Miss Morgan is an actress, Mother. And now, Mother, if I may –

Queen Mother (*heartily*) But of course! Did you not appear in our State Theatre in L'Aiglon of Rostand?

Mary No, ma'am.

Queen Mother You must come again. Ours is a provincial theatre to be sure, but we have recently had a visit from Madame Sarah Bernhardt; in fact she stayed with us. Oh my dear, the stories one hears about Miss Bernhardt's private life – are they to be believed?

Mary Your Majesty, I couldn't tell you – you see –

Queen Mother Quite right, I should not have asked. Forgive me.

Regent Yes, Mother – quite –

Queen Mother (*aside to the* **Regent**) Admirable discretion in one so young. (*And to* **Mary**.) Please remember me to Miss Bernhardt. And, I beg of you, don't tell her I was indiscreet. Entendu? Merci infiniment, ma chère. (*She turns to the* **Regent** *as if rebuking him for chattering.*) Now, Charles, I *must* speak to you, and it is a long time past my bedtime.

Regent Yes, Mother, I am at your service, Mother.

Queen Mother It's about Nick – (*And as the* **Regent** *stiffens.*) There – you've got that look in your eye already (*Pleading.*) Now, Charles, the boy is worried and upset, and I want you to be kind to him.

Regent You may be certain that I will do my duty.

Queen Mother Be sympathetic, Charles. He's young but so were we all. You were nearly young once yourself, Charles –

Regent Thank you for coming to speak to me about it, Mother. Goodnight.

Queen Mother Good night, Charles. (*Kisses his cheek.*)

Mary Good night, Your Majesty. (*She gets up to curtsey.*)

Queen Mother Goodnight, my dear.

Pause.

You should use more mascara, you know. When one is young, one should always use a great deal of mascara, and when one is older, *much* more.

Footmen *open doors. The* **Queen Mother** *exits. The* **Regent** *turns back.* **Mary** *rises from her curtsey and crosses to the right chair.*

Mary (*she sits*)   Oh, she's sweet – I mean, Her Majesty is sweet – and I loved meeting her – (*With a giggle.*) I can't wait to tell Sarah Bernhardt.

Regent (*pours drink and crosses to her vodka glass*)   Yes, let's drink to that. Your reunion with the divine Sarah.

They drink.

Mary   You know something – (*Holding up her glass.*) These Russians, they're on to a good thing here. They ought to bottle it.

Regent (*pours drink into her glass*)   I will certainly speak of it to the Czar. (*The telephone rings and this time the* **Regent** *is even more pained.*) This wretched telephone. My dear Miss Morgan – you must be starved there is our supper going to waste. (*He crosses to the phone as* **Mary** *pulls the table to her. Into the phone irritably –*) Yes? Who? (*Grudgingly.*) All right, connect him. Yes, Karlweis. Yes, yes of course I am alone.

Mary *reacts, turning to look at the* **Regent**.

Regent   Yes, Karlweis, the leader of the opposition has been arrested – yes, on my order. (*And then –*) The charge? Obstructing justice.

She sits. He continues carelessly.

Well, think of a better charge, and we'll change it.

Mary *is mildly horrified by this.*

Regent   I know he has a strong, militant following. Why do you think I had him arrested? (*With mounting impatience.*) I am not restricting his freedom of speech. He can go right on making speeches – he'll simply have to make them in jail from now on – that's all. (*Listens for a moment.*) Of course, the Americans will protest. They always protest. Don't we have a form-letter we send them . . .

Mary *crosses upstage to table for a drink, pours one, crosses back to the chair and sits.*

Well, you know the Americans – so smug and sanctimonious. Ask them how *they* got the Panama Canal. My dear Miss Morgan, let us hope this is the last of the interruptions. (*He replaces the phone, picks up the old mood and crosses with it to* **Mary**. *There is no mistaking the freeze.*) Is there something the matter with your supper?

Mary   Your Royal Highness. I am an *American*. (*Rising she says it rather like Nathan Hale on the scaffold.*) And proud to be one.

Regent   Oh. (*Pouring her a drink.*) How very tactless of me. I do apologise.

Mary (*loftily*)   Pray, do not bother, sir. And furthermore, if Your Royal Highness would like to know how we got the Panama Canal, I'll tell you, because I learned it in the civics class in Milwaukee. (*She crosses below him to the couch.*) We bought it, that's how. We paid cash, not only that, we wiped out yellow fever, which was caused by mosquito bites. (*Triumphantly.*) But nobody knew that until *we* bought the Panama Canal.

Regent   Admirable. I assure you my remarks were not intended to give offence. Please sit down.

Mary (*passionately*)   And the Bill of Rights! What about them, Your Majesty?

Free speech! For everybody – which includes even the leader of the opposition and free press, and free religion. I just love the Bill of Rights, don't you?

Regent   Oh, yes.

Mary   Article One. Congress shall make no laws respecting an established religion, or prohibiting the free exercise thereof; or abridging the freedom of speech or of the press; or the right of the people peaceably to assemble, and to petition the government for a redress of grievances.

Regent   Bravo! Jolly good show.

Mary   Two! A well-regulated militia being necessary to the security of a free state, the right of the people to keep and bear arms shall not be infringed.

Regent   Perfect . . .

Mary   Three. (*Confidentially.*) You know I never really like Three.

Regent   I can't say I entirely blame you.

Mary   Of course, I never said that to Mrs Applejohn.

Regent   Who is Mrs Applejohn?

Mary   My civic teacher in Milwaukee.

Regent   Oh, I say.

Mary   . . . one of the nicest women I have ever met in my entire life.

Regent   I'm sure.

Mary   How do you think I learned all about the Bill of Rights?

Regent   I was wondering about that. Four?

Mary   Four. You'll just love Four!

Regent   I know.

Mary   The right of the people to be secure in their persons, houses, papers and effects, against unreasonable searches and seizures, shall not be violated and no warrant shall be issued, but upon probable cause, supported by oath or affirmation, and particularly the place to be searched, and the persons or things to be seized. (*Warmly.*) Isn't that a great Four?

Regent (*gloomily.*)   Great! Perhaps a trifle long.

Mary   You think that's long. Wait till you hear . . .

And before he can protest.

Five. No person shall be held to answer for a capital or otherwise infamous crime, unless on a presentment of the indictment to a Grand Jury, except in cases arising in the land or naval forces, or in the militia, when in actual service in time of war or public danger; nor shall any person be subject for the same offence to be twice put in jeopardy of life or limb; nor shall be compelled in any criminal case to be a witness against himself; nor be deprived of life, liberty, or property, without due process of law; nor shall . . . (*wavering*) nor shall . . . (*She has run out of steam, the* **Regent** *noticeably perks up at once. She wails –*) Isn't that awful?

Regent No, no, not at all. (*He is busy comforting her.*) You are a credit to Miss Appleberg . . .

Mary What about Six or Seven. 'I have sworn on the altar of God eternal warfare against every form of tyranny over the mind of man.' Do you know who said that?

Regent (*mildly*) Thomas Jefferson.

Mary (*taken aback*) That's right. (*She starts to cry.*)

Regent My dear, I had no idea you found politics so moving. Perhaps I was wrong in what I said about the Panama Canal –

Mary (*delighted*) Oh! (*Impulsively she kisses him on the cheek.*) Thank you. Thank you for that! (*Suddenly horrified.*) Oh – I shouldn't have done that – excuse me – Your Royal –

Regent No, no. Under the circumstances perfectly natural.

Nicolas *enters.*

Nicolas Father! Father, I must speak to you.

Regent Must it be tonight, Nicky? I have a guest, as you see. May I present Miss Mary Morgan, my son, His Majesty King Nicolas.

Nicolas Good evening, Miss Morgan. It is delightful to meet you. Please sit down. (*Turning to the* **Regent**.) Father, I ask you to revoke the orders you have given Colonel Hoffman, and to release the leader of the opposition.

Regent Quite impossible, Nicky. And now I must remind you. . .

Nicolas Father, if you arrest two hundred agitators, six hundred will spring up in their place.

Regent In that event they will find themselves sleeping four to a cell, as I have no intention of enlarging our prices. That's quite enough now, Nicky. You have my permission to retire.

Nicolas Please, Father. I am the king and Colonel Hoffman is conducting this terror in my name.

Regent Colonel Hoffman, at my command, is merely preserving order.

Nicolas Father, I insist.

Regent (*not unkindly*)   This is foolish of you, Nicky. Never give an order you cannot enforce. Until you are eighteen, it is I who rule. Now . . . goodnight.

Nicolas   Yes, Father. (*He turns to* **Mary** *and is instantly smiling and polite.*) Goodnight, Miss Morgan. So very nice to have made your acquaintance. I do apologise for my intrusion.

Mary *curtsies.* **Nicolas** *turns to the* **Regent***, again stiff and subdued.*

Nicolas   Goodnight, Father.

Regent   Nicky.

Nicolas *exits.*

Regent   I'm so sorry.

Mary   Don't worry about me, Your Highness. Maybe you should go after your son – say something to make him feel better . . . (*Reaching for him.*) He'll be upset and all alone.

Regent   Alone? He has his bodyguards.

Mary (*shocked*)   His bodyguards! That's awful!

Regent   Why? He has his bodyguards, I have mine . . .

Mary   Do they *love* him?

Regent   Of course they love him. That's what they're paid for.

Mary   Oh, no! With respect, sir, that's not love at all. (*She kneels on the stool.*) The way you talked to your son reminded me of when I worked in the five and ten in Milwaukee and the floorwalker found a mistake in my cash register.

Regent (*the longest take*)   The connection seems remote.

Mary   No love, that's the connection.

Regent   No love . . . (*Aware of her warm sympathy.*) That's right, no love at all. My life is utterly empty of love. (*Reaching back for the lamp switch.*) It is love that I need. (*He switches off the lamp.*)

Mary   Oh you poor man.

Regent   Yes.

Mary   Oh . . .

Regent   I am resigned to it . . .

The solo gypsy violin starts soaring into the upper reaches of outer Magyar Weltschmers. He ignores it, naturally.

Mary   What's that?

Regent (*vaguely*)   One of my servants . . . heartbroken . . . mourning for a love lost long ago.

And as she nods in sympathy, other instruments are filling out the harmony. She looks at him surprised.

Regent   Naturally all his relatives are grieving with him.

Mary (*respectfully*)   One of them is a great arranger. It's lovely. Do you know the words?

Regent   Alas, only too well. (*Turns, leans to her and away.*)

'Lonely'

Verse:

> Imagine if you
> Can a solitary
> Man
> Eternally
> surrounded – yet
> alone

He straightens up and faces front.

> A royal
> Prince who
> Ever since
> He first began to dream
> Has lived within the shadow of a
> Throne pity him and think of him
> Weighed down by cases of state
> Hearing happy lovers laughing
> By weary and oppressed

To her:

> But maybe you have guessed
> The sad unhappy prince I am
> Referring to is I.

Front – She sits on the floor in front of him.

Refrain 1:

> Lonely
> Lonely a pawn
> Of destiny
> A sawdust puppet on a string
> No one near to me to know or even
> care
> That the heart behind this royal mask
> I wear beats out its melancholy days

> Proving the
> falseness of the
> phrase 'to be as
> happy as a king'

Waves to **Simka**.

> Only – only
> Swift moments here and
> There a brief illusion
> That I'm free
> I know too well true
> Happiness can never never
> Be
> For a solitary soul like me.

Leans back and right. The music continues.

Mary (*rising*)   You look so tired. Wouldn't you like to stretch out? (*She helps him.*)

Regent   My marriage was only a clause in the Carpathia Customs Treaty of 1893 yet it gave me comfort. But now I am alone, and it is too late.

Mary   Your Highness, please don't say that.

He sits again. She has difficulty focusing.

Regent   I must. It is the tragic truth.

Refrain 2:

He throws the pillow.

> Only – only

He pulls her to him.

> I hold deep in my heart
> That foolish dream that there
> May be just one last blossom
> Flowering
> On true love's eternal
> Tree for a solitary
> Soul like me.

The music continues under:

Mary (*turns away*)   Oh, Your Majesty, I wish I could help you.

Regent   You can, you can.

Mary   No I can't. You're practically a king and I'm only a bit-player – (*She turns away. Then, throwing caution to the wind.*) Well, what the hell. I can *try*!

She pulls his head from the couch. She kisses him. It is a prolonged, passionate embrace. The Sleeping Prince, coming to life with a vengeance, returns it ardently.

There is a discreet tap at the door, followed by a more vigorous knock, then a hammering.

Mary (*dreamily*)   What's that?

Regent   Oh, just some street noise.

He signals for the music to continue. The knocking resumes persistently. She kisses him again, achieving the same splendid results, but unfortunately **Northbrook** *enters at just this point. He is amazed by what he sees, and intimidated by the* **Regent**'s *oath, also by* **Mary**'s *reaction.*

Mary (*waggling her fingers cheerily*)   Oh, hi Mr Northbrook.

Northbrook (*the* **Regent** *is still glaring*)   Sir, with the deepest respect, my message was of such importance that I had no choice but to intrude.

The **Regent** *sits up.*

Northbrook   Er – Miss Morgan's aunt has been in a motor car accident. (*He steps in.*)

Mary (*giggles*)   What?

She looks at **Northbrook**, *then starts embrace.*

Northbrook   But her condition is serious and she is calling for you.

The **Regent** *starts to embrace her.*

Mary   Oh, tell her to take two aspirins and go to bed. (*She leans on the* **Regent** *who takes her hand.*)

Northbrook   Miss Morgan – she's in severe pain and is calling for you.

Mary   Oh, go away, you silly man.

She leans forward. She dismisses him with a royal gesture of her own.

Regent   Northbrook, I command you to leave us at once. (*He starts to embrace her.*)

Northbrook, *flustered, is about to turn to go.*

Mary   And kindly *back* out.

Regent *moves stage left.* **Northbrook** *closes the double doors in full flight.* **Mary** *rises and crosses to the* **Regent**.

Regent   Northbrook! (*Tenderly but firmly.*) Come . . .

Mary (*after a few yielding steps*)   Where are we going?

Regent   Does it matter?

Mary (*she realises she is being led to the adjoining bedroom*)   Oh – *there*. (*She frees herself gently and takes one step back.*) In a minute. Are you all right, Your Highness? You're swaying terribly.

*The **Regent**, of course, is perfectly sober, perfectly still.*

Regent   Come – I have so little time. (*Crosses to her, takes her hand.*)

Mary   Sure. I just want to tell you something first.

Regent (*taking her arm again*)   What is it? Say it.

Mary   If I take another few little steps – (*Indicating the bedroom.*) I'll be in love with you. It's always that way.

Regent (*gently*)   Always?

Mary   Every time . . . Twice – there I am, head over heels in love. (*As he takes her arm again.*) Do you understand? (*She crosses to him.*)

Regent   I understand.

Mary   Then that's fine . . . let's go.

She takes his arm and they are almost at the bedroom door, when suddenly her knees buckle, and she goes down.

Regent   My dear Miss Morgan! (*He bends over her.*)

Mary (*blissfully*)   M-m-m-m! You're so strong!

Regent   Please! (*Kneels beside her.*) Get up, get up at once. Don't you dare go to sleep.

*The **Regent** yanks viciously on a bell-pull. The **Major-Domo** enters, glances at the body on the floor, signals to waiters and footmen who come in, move with expert precision to pick up **Mary** and carry her to the bedroom.*

The unfortunate musicians have chosen this moment to make their music even more passionate.

Regent   Stop that infernal screeching!

Dim out.

Scene Five

*As the lights fade on the previous scene, the **Regent** is still heard yelling. He is answered by **Ada** still offstage.*

Regent   Korovinsky!

Ada (*off*)   Fish!

Regent   Korovinsky!

Ada   Fish!

*The scene has changed and the lights come up as a Cockney woman, **Ada Cockle**, enters from downstage right pushing her portable fish and chips stand in front of her.*

Act One, Scene Five   485

Ada   Fish! Here ya are! Get yer hot fish and chips here. Get 'em while they're hot.

At the same time, **Nicolas**, *concealed among a group of four people, enters from upper right and hides himself behind* **Ada** *and her stand. Two* **Secret Service Men** *enter upper right, push the crowd assembling onstage as they search frantically. One* **Girl** *drops her basket and she and her* **Boyfriend** *pick it up. The* **Secret Service Men** *split at centre and look right and left. Another group enters upper right, two of them cross the stage and exit upper left, and the other two come down centre as* **Ada** *calls to them.*

Ada   All right, ducks, get yer hot fish and chips here.

Londoner (Taylor)   One and one!

Ada   I hope you have a good spot to see the coronation. Here ya are. That'll be thruppence.

They take their fish and chips and start out left. The **Secret Service Men** *cross to cart to take a look.* **Ada** *holds up a newspaper to obstruct their view of* **Nicolas**. *They turn quickly and push off left ahead of the pair which just left* **Ada**.

Nicolas (*coming out*)   Thank you.

Ada   They nosed about a bit like a pack of bloodhounds and then 'opped it.

Nicolas   Thank you again, madame.

Ada   You don't 'ave no call to 'madame' me, dear. Ada Cockle's the name born and bred in London town. What are you up to? Running away from home?

Nicolas   Just for the evening.

Three **Londoners**, **Eddleman**, **Zahr** *and* **Morales**, *enter down left and at the same time another group,* **Haraldson**, **Felton**, **Matthews**, *enter upper right.* **Eddleman** *and* **Zahr** *exit upper left while the others line up at the cart. Musical underscoring starts at this point.* **Nicolas** *crosses down centre and looks off left.*

Ada   'Ere you are . . . (*She is calling to the crowd and serving at the same time.*) Get yer hot fish 'n' chips . . . that'll be thruppence . . . thank you . . . etc. (*Calling to* **Nicolas**.) 'Ere, come on boy – start learnin' yourself an 'onest trade.

Just wrap 'em like this and give 'em to the lady.

Nicolas *crosses to* **Ada***'s right and starts to wrap. The groups of* **Londoners** *cross upper right to upper left.*

Nicolas   Are they all going to the coronation already – er – Mrs Cockle?

Ada   They ain't exactly invited to Westminster Abbey, dear, but they'll get themselves a good place on the pavement. You can see the procession better from there anyhow. 'Ere, boy, 'ere's yer wages.

She brings him a paper full of fish and chips.

Nicolas Oh, this is marvellous.

Ada Of course they're marvellous, eat 'em up before they get cold.

Nicolas Hmm . . . they're good.

Ada Of course they're good.

Nicolas I've never tasted anything like it before.

Ada What? Fish and chips . . . they mean London to me, you see . . .

'London'

I was born and bred in
London It's the only city I
know
Though it's foggy and cold and
wet I'd be willing to take a bet

That there ain't no other place
I'd want to go, believe me.

'London Is a Little Bit of All Right'

London is a little bit of all
Right
Nobody can deny
That's true
Now bells – Big Ben
Up to the heath and down again
And is you should visit the monkeys in
The zoo bring a banana
Feed the ducks in
Battersea Park[35] or take a
Trip to Kew[36]
It only costs a tanner there and
Back watch our lads in the
Palace Yard[37] troop the colour
And change the guard
And don't forget your brolly and
Your mack and I'd like to mention:
London is a place where you can
Call right round and have a cosy
Cup of tea

---

35 A park on the south bank of the River Thames.
36 The location of the Royal Botanic Gardens in London.
37 The Palace Yard is a paved open space in the City of Westminster near the Palace of Westminster.

    If you're fed right up and got
    Tail right down
    London Town
    Is a wonderful place
    To be.

Scene Six

The St Martin's Lane drop rises to reveal Trafalgar Square. There are seven groups of **Londoners** *onstage waiting for the coronation procession. They have blankets, pillows, food baskets, camp stools, etc. with them. The group centre stage is actually cooking their meal over an open brazier.*

An eighth group enters down right and crosses to right of centre where they sit on a blanket. **Ada** *and* **Nicolas**, *pushing cart, circle upstage from left to right.*

All
    London is a little bit of all
    Right
    Nobody can deny
    That's true
    Now bells – Big Ben
    Up to the heath and down again
    And is you should visit the monkeys in
    The zoo

Ada
    Bring a banana
    Feed the ducks in
    Battersea Park or take a
    Trip to Kew
    It only costs a tanner there and
    Back watch our lads in the
    Palace Yard troop the colour
    And change the guard
    And don't forget your brolly and
    Your mack and I'd like to mention:

All
    London . . .

Ada
    . . . is a place where you can
    Call right round and have a cosy
    Cup of tea
    If you're fed right up and got
    Tail right down
    London Town

Is a wonderful place
To be.

Man (Barney) *playing the mouth organ enters downstage left.*

'What Ho, Mrs Brisket'

Dancers *downstage right begin first brisket dance. Then* **Ada** *lifts her skirts as if she was wading and sings.*

Ada
What ho, Mrs Brisket
Why not take a plunge and
Risk it the water's warm
There ain't no crabs
And you'll have a lot of fun among the
Shrimps and dabs
If for a lark
Some saucy old shark
Takes a nibble at your chocolate
Biscuit swim for the shore
And the crowd will roar

All
What ho, Mrs
Brisket! What ho,
Mrs Brisket
Why not take a plunge and
Risk it? The water's warm
There ain't no crabs
And you'll have a lot of fun among the
Shrimps and dabs

Ada
If for a lark
Some saucy old
Shark takes a
Nibble at
Your chocolate biscuit

All
Oh!

All
Swim for a shore
And the crowd will roar

All *remain silent, and* **Ada** *mouths the words 'What ho, Mrs Brisket'.*

All
What ho, Mrs Brisket
Why not take a plunge and

Risk it the water's warm
There ain't no crabs
And you'll have a lot of fun among the
Shrimps and dabs
If for a lark
Some saucy old shark
Takes a nibble at your chocolate
Biscuit swim for the shore
And the crowd will roar

Ada *ends up down right and does a little solo dance. The whole stage bursts into a wild dance.* **Barney** *plays the harmonica and* **Maggie** *starts serving tea to the group. During the dance* **Ada** *joins in at various times and weaving among the dancers works herself upper right, crosses upper left and finally down left to her cart. At the conclusion of the dance, the girls leap into the boys' arms. In so doing* **Sheila** *knocks over the stew pot while leaping to* **Mike**. *The crowd rises and yells in anger.* **Jack E** *and* **Jose** *grab* **Mike** *and drag him down right where they are met by* **Art**. **Maggie** *takes the box that she has been sitting on and moves it downstage and slightly left.* **Ada** *stands on the box and yells:*

Ada
Don't!
Don't take our Charley for the
Army he's a sensitive lad
And like his dad
His heart is far from
Strong he couldn't do
Route marches
On account of his fallen
Arches and is asthma's
Something terrible when the
Winter comes along.

He's a nice boy – one of the best
But when he gets a cold on his
Chest he coughs until he
Nearly drives us barmy
So nightie-night – close the
Door go back to the
Barracks and think some more
Before you take our Charles for the army.

All
Don't take our Charley for the
Army he's a sensitive lad
And like his dad
His heart is far from
Strong he couldn't do
Route marches

On account of his fallen
Arches and is asthma's
Something terrible when the
Winter comes along.

He's a nice boy – one of the best
But when he gets a cold on his
Chest he coughs until he
Nearly drives us barmy
So nightie-night – close the
Door go back to the
Barracks and think some more

Don't take our Charley for
The army he's a sensitive lad
And like his dad
His heart is far from strong;

At Saturday night at the Rose and Crown
Saturday night at the Rose and Crown
Is just the place to be
Tinkers and tailors
And soldiers and sailors
All cut for a bit of a spree
If you find that you be
Heavy of life

All
On Saturday night
At the R-O-S-E A-N-D

Ada   **All**
London   Crown
Is a little bit
Or all right nobody can
Deny that's true

                                           Boys
                                           What's the matter with
                                           A nice beef stew with greens
                                           And mashed potatoes

Big Ben, Bow Bells
Have a good laugh and
Watch the swells, treating
Themselves to a trot
On rotten row
Bring a banana

Boys
What ho, Mrs
Brisket why not
Take a plunge and
Risk it?

Girls	**Tenors**	**Basses**
Pa Pa	The water's warm there	Boom Boom
Pa Pa	Ain't no grass	Boom Boom

Girls and Tenors	**Basses**
And you'll have a lot of fun	Boom Boom
Among the shrimps and the dabs	Boom

Ada
Feed the ducks in Battersea Park
Or take a trip to Kew, it
Only cost a tanner
– There and

All
On –

Ada	**Girls and Basses**	**Tenors**
Back	Saturday night at the Rose and Crown	PA PA PA PA
	That's just	PA PA PA PA
		PA

All
The place to be

Ada and Boys	**Girls**
If you haven't a swanky club	Tinkers and tailors
Just pop into the nearest	And soldiers and sailors
Pub, a little of what you	All our for a bit of
Fancy does you good	A spree

All
And I'd like to mention

Ada	**All**
London	Don't take our Charley
	To the army
	he's a
	Sensitive lad and
	Like his dad his
	Heart I . . .

Ada
　And I'd like to mention London
　Is a place where

Girls and Tenors
　What ho,
　Mrs Brisket

　　　Basses
　You can call right round　　　　　　A nice beef stew
　And have a cosy cup of
　Tea

　　　　　　　　　　　　　　Girls and Tenors
　　　　　　　　　　　　　　　On Saturday

Ada and Basses　　　　　　　**Girls and Tenors**
　If you　　　　　　　　　　　　　Night
　Use your loaf a bit and　　　　　Don't take our Charley
　Know what's what　　　　　　　　For the ar-my

Ada
　Then London town

Tenors
　Saturday

Ada and Girls　　　　　　　　**Tenors**
　Lon -　　　　　　　　　　　　　　Night

　　　Basses
　-don town　　　　　　　　　　　　With greens and mashed
　London town　　　　　　　　　　　po-tat-oes

All
　So nighty-night close the door
　Go back to the barracks and
　Think some more

Ada and All
　It's a bloody good place

Ada
　To B-e-e-e-e

Ada　　　　　　　　　　　　　　**All**
　B-e-e-e　　　　　　　　　　　　　In London

Scene Seven

The Royal Apartment, Carpathian Embassy.

*The **Major-Domo** enters downstage right crosses to the couch, opens the draperies, crosses upper centre, claps his hands and eight **Footmen** (**Roman** and **Peyton**, **Homes** and **Matthews**, **Eddleman** and **Allen**, **Toles** and **Hanley**), carrying two breakfasts, enter upper centre, line up upper stage right as the **Major-Domo** inspects them. Satisfied, he leads them to the bedroom door upper stage left and they exit through it. Suddenly there is a terrible bellow.*

'Here and Now'

Mary (*she has crossed the room to sofa, she pats the seat and faces off left*)

    Here and now
    I've a wonderful secret that nobody knows
    Here and now
    I've got rings on my fingers and bells on my toes

Lifting her arms.

    When I woke as today was Dawning
    All the world seemed to glow

She smooths her hair.

    On the marvellous, magic morning
    Suddenly I know
    I'm in love
    I adore every moment that's hurrying by
    Up above

Pointing off left.

    There's a lovely new light in the sky
    When my prince appears
    I'll burst into tears
    And curtsey three times and bow
    Who could foresee
    That such happiness could happy to me
    Here and now?

She sits on the sofa.

    Here on this day

Lying down on the sofa on her back.

    Glorious day
    How can I keep my feet from Dancing?
    Some entrancing tune
    Makes me want to fly

She raises her arms.

> Higher than the moon
> In the sky

Turning over, lying on her stomach.

> Who can I tell?
> What can I say?
> How can I breathe and not Betray
> To every soul I see
> What today
> Means to me?
>
> Here and now
> I've a wonderful secret that nobody knows
> Here and now
> I've got rings on my fingers and bells on my Toes

Stepping off the sofa.

> When I woke as today was Dawning
> And the world seemed to glow
> On the marvellous, magic Morning
> Suddenly I know
> I'm in love
>
> I adore every moment that's Hurrying by
> Up above
> There's a lovely new light in the sky
> When my prince appears
> I'll burst into tears
> And curtsey three times and bow
> Who could foresee
> That such happiness could happy to me
> Here and now?

Regent (*entering from bedroom stage left*)   Hello, how do you feel?

Mary (*kissing his hand humbly, reverently to his surprise*)   That's how I feel – darling.

Regent   Miss Morgan, I think . . .

Mary   No, please, don't say anything. Just let me look at you. (*Impulsively.*) It was wonderful! I don't want to be anywhere – ever – but in your arms again.

Regent (*holding her off*)   Again?

Mary   And again and again and again and –

Regent   An interesting programme. A shade too exacting perhaps, but definitely quite interesting.

Mary (*pained*)   Darling, why are you so strange? After last night –

Regent   Last night – that star-crossed, never-to-be-forgotten last night, you took approximately three sips of vodka, and crumpled to the floor – *there*.

Mary   There?

Regent   Yes and for your further information, I spent the night there – (*Pointing to the room at right*) engrossed in Jaroslav's 'Footnotes to Carpathian Mythology', one of the dullest books I have ever encountered in any language.

Mary   Nothing happened?

Regent   Nothing . . .

Mary   But then why do I feel this way . . . all full of bird calls and forest murmurs.

Regent (*stiffly*)   I am very pleased that you so much enjoyed last night . . . (*Not without a tinge of frustration.*) I was unfortunately unable to be present.

Mary   All right, I passed out and you spent the night with somebody's Carpathian footnotes – it's happened anyway! (*Tenderly.*) I'm in love with you.

Regent   In love with me?

Mary   Yes.

Regent   Miss Morgan, has someone been giving you vodka again or do you usually suffer from these early morning hallucinations?

Mary   No good . . . ?

Regent   In love with me?

She is visibly hurt – he takes her arms but she pulls away.

Perhaps if you lie down for a few minutes . . .

Mary (*subdued*)   Yes, I see what you mean. . . (*She is backing out through the side bedroom door, awkwardly.*) Excuse me . . . (*At the door.*) Sir . . .

She is gone. The **Regent**, *bewildered, stands by the couch.* **Northbrook** *enters.*

Northbrook   Good morning, Your Royal Highness.

There is a pause.

Brilliant morning for the coronation, sir . . .

Regent (*another pause*)   Northbrook, I am not an unreasonable man. Faced with an unending round of official duties I sought to find for myself only a few moments of relaxation, and in this cause I called upon the Crown – through you, its delegate – for assistance. And what did you get me?

Northbrook   With respect, sir, a girl.

Regent   With respect, Northbrook, nothing of the sort. You got me an absurd, chattering child who regaled me with interminable reminiscences of life in a five and ten cent dime store – in Milwaukee – went on from there to patriotic speeches including a recital of the American Bill of Rights – in full – and furthermore – at what I shall refer to briefly as the crucial moment, she was rendered utterly insensible by an amount of vodka, which, in Carpathia, is normally added to the milk of four-year-old girls as a mild tonic. And you call that a girl?

Northbrook   Her appearance deceived me, sir.

Regent   I must concur. I, too, was taken in. Herr Gott, it was maddening. And to think that Lucy Sunningdale has been telephoning me constantly since my arrival, begging for a moment of my time.

Northbrook   But, sir, did you not remark the other day that you found Lady Sunningdale – 'old hat'?

Regent   True, Northbrook, but there is an ancient Carpathian proverb, 'Better an old hat than a bare hat.'

Northbrook   If I may make a suggestion, sir – perhaps Lady Sunningdale would be free this evening?

Regent   Tonight?

Northbrook   Sir! The Foreign Office ball is at ten . . .

Regent   Ah, yes.

Northbrook   A simple acte de presence on your part would suffice, and by midnight . . .

Regent   Yes, that's very good thinking, Northbrook. I will act upon it. In the meantime, get rid of her inconspicuously.

He exits. **Northbrook** *crosses to the other bedroom door, knocks.*

Mary (*entering*)   Oh. It's you. You've heard about my big night . . .

Northbrook   His Royal Highness mentioned it – in passing.

Mary   He's gone?

Northbrook *nods.*

Mary   Oh well, I'll wave when he rides by in the parade.

Northbrook (*steering her out*)   An excellent idea . . . Miss Morgan.

Mary   But you've got to get me something to wear over this dress – a raincoat, or something.

As **Northbrook** *looks doubtful.*

Mary   Look at me. I can't go out in this.

Northbrook *begins to exit, as the doors open –* **Nicolas** *enters as they bow.*

Nicolas   Good morning, Miss Morgan. Good morning, Mr Northbrook.

Northbrook & Mary Good morning, Your Majesty.

Nicolas Please sit down.

Northbrook If you will forgive me, sir, I must see about a car for Miss Morgan. (*Bowing out.*) Only a moment.

Nicolas (*going up the stairs and reaching for the doorknob*) Do sit down.

Mary If you're looking for your fa – I mean, His Royal Highness, he's already gone, Your Majesty. Mr Northbrook told me. I'm just hanging around until I get a raincoat or something to wear over this dress.

Nicolas Of course. I'm sorry about my intrusion last night.

Mary Forget it, Your Majesty. Anyway, I was rooting for you.

Nicolas Rooting?

Mary You know, if two teams are fighting it out, and you want one of them to win . . .

Nicolas Ah, I see . . . And you were – rooting – for me? Why?

Mary Because your father is a mean, stubborn tyrant and if Thomas Jefferson could get his hands on him, there'd be trouble.

Nicolas Yes, I dare say.

Mary You keep after him, Your Majesty. He'll like the twentieth century, once he gets used to it.

Nicolas I'll remember. Thank you, Miss Morgan. We're so very . . . to see you again. (*He starts to exit, turns at the door.*) You know, Miss Morgan, I like you better then any of my father's other mistresses.

Mary Hey, Your Majesty . . . You don't understand. Anyway, he liked me best.

'I've Been Invited to a Party (**Reprise**)'

I was Invited to a party
Though it wasn't quite
What I had in mind
I must be resigned
To the fact
That it lacked
That magic touch
That I'd over-romantically wanted so much
And when I get back
To the theatre
It will be a strain
Having to explain
How my pretty song

Went all wrong
And insisted on changing its key

Northbrook *enters, carrying an old raincoat.*

Northbrook Here you are, Miss Morgan. It's the only thing I could get. It belongs to one of the scullery maids.

Mary Oh, well, the lower classes have their useful moments.

She wraps the coat around her and they exit.

Scene Eight

The foyer of the Embassy.

The **Queen Mother**, *together with the* **Major-Domo** *and the* **Countess Brunheim**, *are descending the grand staircase. At stage right, the ladies and gentlemen of the court appear in a group.*

Queen Mother Is everybody ready and properly attired? Please remember, all of you, that the coronation is a religious ceremony and we must all conduct ourselves with the utmost dignity and decorum – General Vorkapich –

He bows.

Your sabre is sagging, General. Be careful not to trip on it.

The **General** *fixes his sword – the* **Queen Mother** *surveys the group.*

Queen Mother But where is the Countess Meissenbrun? Am I to go to the Abbey unattended, without my Lady in Waiting?

Major-Domo With Your Majesty's permission, I will enquire.

With a bow he exits up the stairs right, at the top of the landing. He is passed by **Mary** *and* **Northbrook** *in the process of sneaking out of the Embassy.*

Queen Mother (*about the* **Major-Domo**) Where is he going? (*To* **Baroness Brunheim**.) Why is everyone leaving me?

Baroness Brunheim (*quite loud*) He is going to look for Countess Meissenbrun, ma'am.

Queen Mother Don't shout, May. I can hear quite perfectly. It is only when people mumble . . . (*She sees* **Mary** *and* **Northbrook**.) Countess Meissenbrun! Come here at once!

Mary *and* **Northbrook** *freeze.* **Mary** *crosses to the* **Queen Mother**.

Queen Mother Why, it's Miss Morgan! My dear, how delightful to meet you again.

Mary Thank you, Your Majesty.

Queen Mother But that horrid manteau de voyage you are wearing – so unbecoming. Please take it off.

The **Queen Mother** *signals for a* **Footman** *to place a stool for her upper centre which she sits on.* **Mary***, with a helpless look at a stunned* **Northbrook***, takes off her raincoat and hands it to* **Northbrook** *who brings it down left and gives it to another* **Footman** *who takes it off.*

Mary   This dress, ma'am – I can explain – You see, I couldn't –

Queen Mother   Ah, better. Yes, much better. A lovely dress, and such a good colour for you. Please sit down.

Mary *looks around the chairless foyer and finally sits on the top step to the right of the* **Queen Mother***.*

Major-Domo   Your Majesty, the Countess Meissenbrun has suffered a rheumatic spasm and the court physician informs me it will be two days before she may leave her bed.

Queen Mother   That is most inconsiderate.

The **Major-Domo** *bows and stands on the steps to the right of the centre doors.*

Queen Mother   Very well. (*To the* **Baroness Brunheim**.) May, you shall be my Lady in Waiting.

The **Baroness Brunheim** *utters a slight groan of discomfort and bows. The* **Queen Mother** *has already turned to* **Mary***.*

Queen Mother   Je ne sais pourquoi mais les maladies des autres m'embêtent toujours – vous trouvez ça aussi.

Mary (*after a confused pause*)   Excuse me, Your Majesty, I didn't quite catch that.

Northbrook   I don't think Miss Morgan speaks French, ma'am.

Queen Mother   Nonsense! (*To* **Mary**.) Isn't he delicious? (*To* **Northbrook** *deliberately*.) If Miss Morgan does not speak French, Mr Northbrook, will you please explain to me how she has become the great friend of and disciple of Madame Sarah Bernhardt?

This rocks **Northbrook** *– the* **Queen** *continues conversationally with* **Mary***.*

Queen Mother   N'est-ce pas, ma petite? Je suis sur que vous parlez le Français mieux qu'une Française, et surtout d'une voix d'or.

She keeps looking at **Mary** *who looks to* **Northbrook** *for a prompt.*

Mary (**Northbrook** *pantomimes a 'oui'*)   Oui.

Queen Mother (*to* **Northbrook**)   There.

Northbrook *faces front. The* **Queen** *rattles on with* **Mary***.*

Queen Mother   Au sujet des maladies des autres, c'était La Rouchefoucauld, n'est-ce pas, qui a dit: dans l'adversité de nos meilleurs amis, nous trouvons quelque chose qui nous déplait pas?

Mary (*with eyes closed, just guessing*)   Oui.

Queen Mother (*heartily*)   Très bien, très bien, ma chère. (*To* **Northbrook**.) Most intelligent. (*Noticing the* **Baroness Brunheim** *beside her*.) May! Why are you jiggling about like that?

Baroness Brunheim   Ma'am, I would respectfully ask to be allowed to withdraw for a moment.

Queen Mother   Already? But how will you ever get through the religious ceremony? It is four to five hours you know.

She dismisses the **Baroness Brunheim** *who rushes off.*

Queen Mother   It is too annoying! Countess Meissenbrun and her rheumatics and now the Baroness Brunheim and her – curious condition. (*She is looking at* **Mary** *appraisingly*.) Mr Northbrook . . .

Northbrook   Ma'am?

Queen Mother   Mr Northbrook, please ask the steward to bring me my jewel case.

Northbrook *exits.*

Queen Mother   What are you playing now, my dear?

Mary   'The Coconut Girl', ma'am.

Queen Mother   Ah, something in English for a change. You are wise to do so. Let me see?

Is that Congreve or Sheridan?

Mary   No, ma'am. It's by Al Fleischberg, Buddy Maxwell and Joe Zink.

The **Footmen** *enter with the jewel case, led by* **Northbrook** *who gestures for the case to be brought to the left of the* **Queen Mother**.

Queen Mother   Oh! That is an evening dress you are wearing, isn't it?

Mary   Yes, ma'am, I could explain . . .

Queen Mother   Stand up a minute . . . (*She rises as does* **Mary**. *The stool is instantly taken away*.) Suitable . . . most suitable . . . (*Seeing the jewel case, to* **Northbrook**.) Thank you, Mr Northbrook. (*She takes a necklace out of the case*.) Now come here, my dear . . .

Mary *crosses to her and the* **Queen Mother** *places the necklace around* **Mary**'*s throat. The* **Queen Mother** *takes a tiara out of the case and places it on* **Mary**'*s head.*

Queen Mother   I am appointing you my Lady in Waiting for the day. (*She takes* **Mary** *down centre*.) You will ride with me in the coach – and accompany me to the Abbey.

Mary (*stunned, but holding on to the tiara*)   Westminster Abbey? Me? Oh, no, ma'am. I'd be arrested!

Queen Mother Arrested! (*A peal of laughter, to* **Northbrook**.) What a delicious sense of humour. (*To the* **Baroness Brunheim** *who has returned to her position at the left of the centre doors*.) May. You will be pleased to learn that you are excused from the Abbey. Please give her␣cape.

The **Baroness Brunheim** *happily bows and crosses down stage to* **Mary**. *The* **Queen Mother** *crosses to* **Northbrook**.

Queen Mother Ah, yes, that will be better . . . but something is lacking . . .

The **Baroness Brunheim** *has placed her sable on* **Mary** *who turns front – on air.*

Queen Mother Ah, of course, she must have an Order . . .

Northbrook But – Your Majesty, Miss Morgan is an actress.

Queen Mother Of course, she is. She is appearing in 'La Fille de Noix de Cocoa', de Fleischberg, Maxwell et Zink. (*Turning to* **Mary**.) N'est-ce-pas, ma petite?

Mary Oui.

The **Regent** *appears at the top of the stairs.*

Queen Mother Ah Charles! You're just in time.

The **Regent** *sees* **Mary** *and freezes. The* **Queen Mother** *crosses back to* **Northbrook**.

Present her to the Queen, while I find a suitable Order.

The **Queen Mother** *crosses to down right while the* **Regent** *turns menacingly to* **Northbrook** *down left*. **Mary** *crosses up to intercept the* **Regent** *who has begun to cross down left off the stairs.*

Mary Oh, honest to God, Your Royal Highness, it isn't my fault. (*She has stopped the* **Regent** *at the left of the stairs*.) I was trying to sneak out and I don't know what happened? –

The **Regent** *hasn't taken his eyes off* **Northbrook**.

Mary But I'm a Lady in Waiting and I'm going to Westminster Abbey.

This last is too much for the **Regent** *who goes headlong for* **Northbrook** *down left.*

Northbrook (*retreating*) With respect, sir, we must take our places.

Queen Mother (*turning front with an Order she has removed from General Vorkapich*) Ahm, here's that pretty mauve one – (*She holds it up for the* **Regent** *to have*.) Now hurry, Charles, or we shall be late.

Regent You realise, of course, that this Order is only given for a very special, personal service to the Head of State.

Queen Mother Oh, such hair splitting. No doubt she will do you one day.

(*To* **Mary**.) Take off your cape, my dear, the Regent is going to invest you.

Northbrook *crosses up stage and removes* **Mary**'s *cape. The* **Regent** *turns to* **Mary**.

Regent (*brusquely*)   Kneel!

Mary *crosses to a few steps to the left of the* **Regent**.

Regent   Here! (*Pointing to the spot directly in front of him.*)

Mary *rises from her half-kneel and crosses to the appointed place. She slowly kneels as the lights dim.*

Regent
    It's too absurd
    I can't protest – my hands are tied
    I'm trapped in this undignified
    Charade
    I find it hard
    On top of having
    Spent a night of amorous frustration
    To give this girl – for passing out cold
    An old
    Pure gold
    And really quite expensive decoration

The lights come to full, the **Regent** *faces* **Mary**.

Regent   For your services to the Crown, I hereby invest you with the Royal Carpathian Order of Perseverance – (*He crosses to her and lifts her to her feet.*) Second class! (*He pins it on her as the lights dim.*)

Mary (*when the lights have dimmed*)
    He looks quite cross
    His mouth is set – his eyes are grim
    But still I'm not afraid of him
    At all
    I knew I'd fall in love with him
    Which obviously wasn't very smart of me
    But even though I see him in this way
    I know
    He'll stay
    Forever in my heart a special part of me.

Queen Mother (*when the lights are full*)   Now kiss her, Charles, and we can be on our way.

The **Regent** *looks to the* **Queen Mother** *with discomfort and slowly turns to* **Mary** *who opens her arms full wide. He crosses to* **Mary**, *flings her arms aside, pushes her face down and kisses her ever so slightly on the forehead.*

Queen Mother   Splendid, now come everybody.

All prepare to leave through the centre doors. As the **Regent** *retrieves his hat for the General.* **Northbrook** *has met the* **Queen Mother** *at the top of the stairs and exits with her.* **Mary** *is still kneeling.*

Regent   Oh come along, you silly, infuriating creature.

Mary (*facing front as though he had uttered words of love*)   Oh, yes, my darling.

Mary *turns and follows up the stairs as the* **Regent** *retreats.*

The curtain falls.

End of Act One.

Act Two

Scene One

Westminster Abbey.

Before the coronation ceremony begins during the 'long wait'.

A section of the temporary seats, a stained glass window giving colour and light to the setting. In the foreground is the royal party of Carpathia, including **Mary**, *and as many peers, peeresses and visiting dignitaries as can be crowded into the setting.*

The assembled notables lament their boredom and the tedium of waiting for the ceremony to begin, a lament which is punctuated by bursts of glorious songs from **Mary**, *who is, by contrast, enthralled.*

Before and as the lights come up we hear a long fanfare. The assembled crowd looks to the left. A page enters, crosses right and takes his position. He is followed by the Maharajah and Maharani – the crowd follows them across the stage with their eyes. The Maharajah assists the Maharani to the top tier where she shoves the person sitting on the extreme right, who in turn shoves the person on their left and so on down the line, thus making room. The process is repeated with the Maharajah. When they have all settled, the entire line looks right and then front.

One noble, **Ivan**, *sleeps through the entire scene, and wakes only on given cues.*

All
> A coronation is spectacular
> And though as pageantry, not easy to
> Improve on to coin a phrase in the
> Vernacular
> We wish to God they'd get a
> Move on
> We hate the weight
> Of our robes of state
> And our jewellery weighs a ton

Nicolas
> And we'd sell our souls for some
> Nice hot rolls
> Or the smell of a Chelsea bun

All
> We rise at dawn and put our ermine on
> And then we squeeze into a freezing open landau
> To lift our trains will all this vermin on
> Requires the muscles of a Sandow

Women
  With stays too tight we sit
  Upright
  In a rigidly unyielding pew

Northbrook
  Even British oak
  Gets beyond a joke
  When you sit on it from nine 'til two

Ilona pokes Ivan, everyone looks.

All
  Part of a royal education is
  To be resigned
  To your behind
  Becoming numb
  The worst of every coronation is

Regent
  We always wish we hadn't come

All (*they yawn or slump*)
  OH-OH-OH-OH-OH-OH-OH here we sit

Maggie
  Exquisitely bored

All
  Hear our stomachs rumble
  As we watch latecomers
  Stumble up the nave

All
  Good lord!

Queen Mother
  Look at Cousin Maud
  Someone should have given her a shave

All
  Here we all elegantly squat

Queen Mother
  Praying that Aunt Xenia
  Won't give way to
  Schizophrenia again

All
  Great Scott!

Queen Mother
  Look at what she's got
  Dragging from the bottom of her train!

Mary
  It's all so wonderful – wonderful – wonderful
  It's like the most entrancing fairy tale I ever knew
  Diamonds, rubies and pearls
  As I can't quite believe it's true
  How shall I explain it to the girls?

  They'll think that having got into some awful scrape
  I'm trying – just by lying – to forget
  And when I start to tell about the sable cape
  They'll gape
  I'll bet

All
  Here we sit –

Bruse (*looking at* **Ivan**)
  Dummies in a row

Kellie
  Heaven knows how
  Many of us long to
  Spend a penny but
  We're stuck

All
  And so

Kellie
  Though it's all touch and go

All
  We shall simply have to trust luck

Mary	**All**
It was so wonderful – wonderful	Oh –
Ken	
Wonderful	Here we sit
	Women
It's the most	Here we sit
Lovely lovely lovely sight	
	Men
I've ever seen	Here we sit
	Women
All this glitter and gold	Dummies in a row
	Men
	Dummies in a row

All	
In my heart this will always be	Dummies in a row
Something to remember when I'm old	
	Tenors
	In a row
	Bass
	In a row
All	
I'll think of it each time I see	
A summer sky	
However sad and weary I may grow	
And every year another lovely	
June goes by	
I'll sigh	
Heigh-ho	**Bass**
It was so wonderful – wonderful	Ah
wonderful	
But it was long ago.	

Scene Two

*The **Regent**'s apartment.*

At dusk, after the ceremony. **Mary** *is removing her jewellery, the **Major-Domo** is helping her and putting it back into the jewel case.* **Northbrook**, *who sits on the sofa, is waiting.* **Mary** *finishes the song.*

Major-Domo *withdraws with the jewel case and a* **Footman** *puts stool onto the edge of the seat.*

Mary (*touching her Order*)   What about this?

Northbrook   Only the Sovereign or Head of State can revoke an Order of chivalry.

Mary   Well – from the look on his face when he pinned it on . . . (*She removes it slowly and puts it down affectionately.*) I guess I'm the only bit-player who ever wore a thing like this in real life, eh?

Northbrook (*not unkindly*)   On the contrary, history is full of them. Well, I guess I must find that raincoat if you're to get to the theatre on time. Excuse me.

He starts to go. **Nicolas** *enters.*

Nicolas   Ah, Mr Northbrook.

Northbrook   Your Majesty.

Mary   Hello, Your Majesty

Nicolas   Delightful to meet you again, Miss Morgan.

Mary   Thank you, Your Majesty, thank you! I'm just waiting for Mr Northbrook, then I have to get to the theatre –

Aware of **Nicolas** *glancing past her at the telephone on the desk.*

Mary   If you want to use the telephone, Your Majesty, I can wait outside in the hall.

Nicolas   Oh, no . . . please. (*Glancing at the telephone.*) In fact it may be possible for you to do me a great service.

Mary (*cheerfully*)   You name it, Your Majesty.

Nicolas (*after a glance around*)   If you would be kind enough to place a telephone call for me – Gerrard 374.

Mary *picks up the telephone.*

Mary   Hello, operator? Gerrard 374. (*And she extends the phone.*)

Nicolas   When they answer, ask for the Ambassador.

Mary *looks startled, but then complies.*

Mary   Hello, the Ambassador, please. What? Who's calling? The King of Carpathia, that's who.

Nicolas   Thank you, Miss Morgan. Thank you very much.

As she passes him the telephone, **Nicolas** *speaks urgently in German –*

Excellenz, Ich bin zu einem entshcheidung gekkomen. Ich werde ihre gesammten nach meine ruck-kehr empfangen, und sie in jedem weise unterstutzen die notigen nahmen zu treffen. Jawohl, met gewald, wenn mein vater nicht zustimmt. Das ist selbstverstandlich. Auf wiedersehn. Excellenz.

Mary, *listening, seems shocked by what she hears.* **Nicolas** *hangs up.*

Mary   Excuse me, Your Majesty, do you think that you should be getting mixed up in such monkey business?

Nicolas (*realising*)   Oh . . .

Mary   Well, I do understand German – from Milwaukee you know – (*She sits, troubled.*) Right now, I wish I didn't.

Nicolas   Miss Morgan, please trust me and go on rooting for me . . .

He steps back as the **Regent** *and* **Hoffman** *enter.* **Hoffman** *stays at the door as the* **Regent** *crosses down centre.*

Regent   Well, Nicky. I trust you had a stimulating talk with the German Ambassador. Unfortunately, we do not know what transpired as the talents of Colonel Hoffman and his staff do not extend to modern languages.

Ah, Miss Morgan. How very nice to see you again. And, as usual, in such pleasant circumstances.

Nicolas Father, Miss Morgan knows nothing whatever about this. She very kindly placed the call for me and . . .

Regent Yes, Miss Morgan has an undoubted flair for doing the wrong thing at the right moment. However, my concern is with you. I want the details of your conversation with the German Ambassador.

Nicolas (*defiantly*) No, Father.

Regent Charming! Barely sixteen, and already plotting against me. It must be your Hungarian blood. Hoffman!

Hoffman Sir!

Regent You will remain in close attendance on His Majesty.

Hoffman *bows.*

Regent Nicky, you are under house arrest and are not to leave the Embassy for the remainder of our visit.

Nicolas But, Father, the Foreign Office ball is tonight. You promised . . .

Regent You are indisposed.

Nicolas Yes, Father. Thank you, Father.

He exits, closely followed by **Hoffman**. *The* **Regent** *is downstage right and* **Mary** *is seated in the swivel chair.*

Mary (*with a weak smile*) Hello . . .

Regent (*flatly*) Goodbye!

Mary Yes, sir. I'm sorry about the telephone call, Your Highness . . .

Regent Miss Morgan, I am always willing to forgive . . . and in your case I am eager to forget.

Mary Yes sir. I'm just going – (*Not moving.*)

Regent (*staring out front*) Good.

Mary I returned all the jewellery, Your Royal Highness, the steward has it. Mr Northbrook was here – he counted it. You can ask him. He's just gone off to see if he can find that old raincoat for me again.

Regent (*flatly*) I wish him a safe – and speedy return.

Mary Yes, sir – I'll just wait outside . . . (*Still not moving.*)

Regent That perhaps would be best –

Mary Just one more thing – Sir . . .

Regent You did mention waiting outside . . .

Mary . . . about your son. You're handling him all wrong.

Regent Nonsense!

Mary Sir. He needs *you*, not Colonel Hoffman and those bodyguards.

Regent My son is having a completely normal upbringing. For your information, when I was a boy, I was terrified of *my* father. From the age of six onwards, when he kissed me goodnight, I stood at attention!

Mary But nowadays, things are different, Your Royal –

Regent They are *not* different, and I am not interested in nowadays.

Mary (*rising*) Well, sir, they're here to stay, and –

Regent Be still!

Mary (*sitting*) Yes, sir.

Regent I suppose it was your sympathy for my martyred offspring that led you to help him with this infantile conspiracy.

Mary I didn't know what was going on until I heard what he said to the German Ambassador and . . . (*Realising what she has said.*) Then I realised that . . .

Regent So! You understand German.

Mary (*weakly*) Oui.

Regent (*menacingly*) Ah ha!

Mary (*correcting herself and rising*) Naturlich . . . Now don't you try any rough stuff, Your Royal Highness, I am an American citizen!

Regent Miss Morgan, you have established your nationality beyond the shadow of a doubt. Now just tell me what my son said to the German Ambassador . . . (*She nods a refusal.*)

You refuse? You wicked, impudent girl – how dare you? (*Advancing to her.*)

Mary (*still backing away*) With respect, sir, I am no stool pigeon.

Regent (*baffled*) I beg your pardon?

Mary I mean, I can't tell you – it wouldn't be right.

Regent (*turning away and then, ingratiatingly, turning back to her*) Miss Morgan . . .

(*He extends a hand to her but she distrusts it.*) Miss Morgan . . .

She finally takes it and is led to the couch where they sit.

I promise you that if you give me this information, the incident will be forgotten and my son will not be punished.

Mary Excuse me, sir, but you talk about your son as if he were a convict.

Regent I will even let him go to the Foreign Office ball.

Mary What are you doing – restoring his good-conduct privileges? He's your only son –

Regent I know he's my only son. I've known it for years! But he's plotting against me! What am I to do – give him a reward?

Mary Well, I don't approve of his plotting against you – that's wrong!

Regent (*releasing her hands which he has held until now*) Well, thank you.

Mary And if you think he ought to be punished, then you do it. Like a father. Don't use that old Colonel Hoffman.

Regent (*rising, facing her*) Now, look here, this happens to be *my* household.

Mary (*rising to him*) In *my* family, even if my father walloped, I knew it was because he loved me.

'Love' turns the **Regent** *away.*

Mary We were real pals!

'Real pals' drives him further away. **Mary** *follows him.*

Mary My pop used to say us kids kept him young. Now you try it, Your Highness, you've got a young son, so you be young right along with him. If you love him, it'll be easy.

Regent Miss Morgan. I *do* love my son. Perhaps not in the mawkish fashion which seems to be one of the more nauseating manifestations of the American way of life, but I love him and will continue to do so. (*Shouting.*) As I see fit!

Mary Sure! You're spying on *him*; he's plotting against *you* – that's just a dandy relationship. Honestly, you tyrants are all alike.

Regent I am not a tyrant! (*To prove it, he has her by the shoulders and is shaking her violently.*) I am a benign and enlightened ruler –

Her vertebrae are jiggling.

– beloved by my people, because they know what is good for them.

–

He lets go of her, breathes heavily for a moment while **Mary** *pulls herself together, then indifferently:*

Regent You may go.

Mary (*frightened*) Excuse me, sir. (*She curtsies and is backing out.*) I'm sorry about the telephone call, Your Royal –

Regent You – may – go!

Mary Yes, sir. Thank you sir. I was just going . . . (*And she does – in haste.*)

Regent (*as the door closes*)

'How Do You Do, Middle Age'

What's wrong – what's wrong?
I'm behaving like an utter fool
I've always hitherto
See clearly what to do
And remained – restrained
And cool
But since this idiotic girl appeared
With her sentimental ignorance and youth
Though I merely asked her to sup with me
She's made me feel that the years are catching up
With me
And now that I must compromise slightly and politely
Face the truth

How do you do, middle age?
How do you do, middle age?
If you're planning to upset
And fret
And ultimately diminish me
Let – this wet
Soubrette – set to and finish me
Knowing that I'm
In my prime
And mellow season
Must I permit her
To twitter
Pure high treason?
Give me one reason
Can I still love now and then?
Shall I be sweet or gentle
Sane or mental?
Must I end my days
In a blazing rage?
Give me a clue
Over to you,
Middle age.

Comment ça va, middle age?
Qu'est-ce que tu as, middle age?
Autumn winds begin to blow
And so
I'd better unbend my mind to you

Though – you know
I'm not quite yet resigned to you
More relaxation
More ease
More time for snoozing
What consolation
Are these
For those amusing
Pleasures I'm losing
Shall I survive this decade
Or shall I nearly fade out
Done for – played out
What are your designs for the final page?
Give me a clue
Over to you
Middle age

It's too absurd
To let myself become morose
Disconsolate and lachrymose
And dull
Because a nattering, chattering ingenue
Is making me feel I'm ninety-two
Instead of a muscular forty-five
I've still got teeth – I'm still alive
My legs take me where I want to go
And so
I'm damned if I'll let this little whipper-snapper lay
Me low

A feather-brained, garrulous small part minx
Who never draws breath and seldom thinks
Who teases my amorous appetites
And then recites the Bill of Rights
And lectures me about my son
And heir
I swear
I'll not let this dizzy little busybody see I care
I care!

Why should I so upset myself?
Let myself
Get myself
In a state of acute dismay
Because some years have passed
Away?
Why should I crucify myself?
Sigh myself

By myself?
When I still feel bright
Of eye
Clear of brain
And ready to start from scratch all over again.

Don't jump the gun
Middle age
Life is still fun
Middle age
I'm not ready to kow-tow
Just now
And impotently unbend for you
Stay
Away
And wait until I send for you
Must taxes paid on the past be retroactive
Waves of self-pity
Are pretty
Unattractive
When you're still active
Don't be so dumb
Middle age
Spare me that glum recital
I'm still vital
I've enough bombast
For one last
Rampage
Leave it to me
Fiddle-de-dee
Middle age.

Scene Three

*The **Queen Mother**'s apartment.*

*The **Queen Mother** is seated on stage right settee rolling a skein of wool, held by the **Major-Domo** standing next to her, into a ball. The doors are opened by two **Secret Service Men** (**Fitch & Guitierrez**) ushering **Nicolas** into the room. They click their heels together, bow and exit.*

Queen Mother   Oh, Nicky, why *do* you consort with those dreadful men?

Nicolas   I'm under arrest, Grandma.

Queen Mother   Under arrest? Ridiculous! You can't be under arrest – you are the King!

Why would you dare do such a thing?

Nicolas Father.

Queen Mother Oh. Well, I'm sure it's only temporary . . .

The **Regent** *enters briskly, humming.*

Regent Ah, Mother! (*Kisses her cheek.*) I hope you didn't find the coronation too tiring . . . Nicky, I have decided to attach Colonel Hoffman from attendance on you. My dear boy, I should like to forget what happened between us a few moments ago. Well, don't just stand there at attention, Nicky!

Nicolas (*standing at ease with a loud stamp*) Yes, sir.

Regent Furthermore – since this is our last night in London – you may go to the Foreign Office ball.

Nicolas Thank you, Father, but I think not . . .

Regent You think not.

Queen Mother Splendid! Of course you'll go to the ball, Nicky. Who is to be your partner?

Nicolas I have no partner, Grandmother. I'm not going.

Regent You *are* going.

Queen Mother Of course. Don't worry, I will find you a partner.

Regent Take whom you like. I said that you're going, *and you're going.*

Queen Mother Baroness Brunheim?

Regent You're to dance and have a good time! That's an order! (*He exits.*)

Queen Mother There! You see how nice he can be. (*She crosses to* **Nicolas***, held back by the ball of yarn she is holding. She throws it to* **Major-Domo***.*) Now we must put our heads together and decide on a suitable partner for you . . . The young Duchess Brodny – no she is definitely retarded . . .

Mary *opens door.* **Mary** *slams it shut.*

Queen Mother Ah!

Mademoiselle Morgan!

Mary *enters.*

Queen Mother Quel plaisir . . .

Mary Excuse me, Your Majesties. I was just looking for an old raincoat.

Queen Mother My dear, that is an evening dress you're wearing, isn't it? Yes, of course. Such a good colour for you, and in quite exceptional taste. Yes, very nice. (*She gestures to* **Nicolas** *who steps forward.*)

Nicolas (*bowing*)   Miss Morgan, may I have the honour of your company at the Foreign Office ball this evening?

Queen Mother   Splendid! Now that is all arranged. Now, Nicky, you must go and dress at once or you will be late.

Nicolas *exits.*

Queen Mother   May! Where is that tiresome lady-in-waiting? May!

Baroness Brunheim *enters.*

Mary   Your Majesty – I do thank you, but I have to get to the theatre –

Queen Mother (*crosses to the* **Baroness Brunheim**.)   May, I will need my jewel case at once. And I will need your sable cape. (*She hurries the* **Baroness Brunheim** *out.*)

Mary   Oh my God!

Queen Mother   Qu'est-ce que tu as dit, petite?

Mary (*helplessly*)   Oui – I mean, not oui. No, ma'am, I must get to the theatre.

Queen Mother   Nonsense! We shall send someone to dismiss the audience, refund their ticket prices and tell them Mademoiselle Morgan will play another night.

Northbrook *enters with the raincoat.*

Queen Mother   Ah, here is Mr Northbrook. He will arrange everything.

Baroness Brunheim *enters with the jewel case and sable cape.*

Mary   Oh, Your Majesty – no. Mr Grimes would murder me!

Northbrook   Ma'am.

Queen Mother   Mr Northbrook, le question du théâtre, ça s'arrangera, ne'est-ce pas?

Northbrook   Oui.

Queen Mother (*crosses to the jewel case*)   Bon. (*To* **Mary** *as she pulls her right.*) Come here, my dear. *Music begins,* **Queen Mother** *puts a necklace, a tiara and, finally, a ring on* **Mary** *who smiles happily at last.*

Queen Mother   Ne t'inquiète pas, ma chère . . . ne t'inquiète pas . . .

Reprise: 'Here and Now'

Mary
   Here and now
   I've a wonderful secret that nobody
   Knows here and now
   I've got rings on my fingers and bells on my
   Toes though it ought to be quite alarming

Nicolas *enters, signals to* **Northbrook** *to take the ermine cape from the* **Baroness Brunheim** *and bring it to him.*

Mary
I'm not nervous at all
Arm and arm with my young Prince Charming

Nicolas *places cape on* **Mary**.

Mary
Going to the ball

The doors open. **Nicolas** *offers his arm to* **Mary** *and they exit. As the blue room set flies away and the scene shifts to the Foreign Office ball,* **Mary** *and* **Nicolas** *are seen waltzing in the ballroom setting. They dance off-stage right.*

Scene Four

The Foreign Office ball.

A scene of great splendour; a profusion of beautifully dressed women and men in uniforms, white ties and native dress from every corner of the Empire. From upper stage left a grand stairway curves across the upstage. A dance, 'The Stingaree', is in progress. The **Regent** *enters, beckons to* **Lady Sunningdale** *at top of the stairway.*

Dance Number: 'The Stingaree'

Regent (*as he dances with* **Lady Sunningdale**)   Lord Sunningdale is well I trust?

Lady Sunningdale   Yes, sir.

Regent   He was quite willing to let you come along?

Lady Sunningdale   Yes, sir.

Regent   Fine fellow!

Lady Sunningdale   Yes, sir.

The dance continues.

Regent   I have ordered supper in my apartment in an hour . . .

Lady Sunningdale   Yes, sir.

Regent   Caviar, champagne and, of course, vodka.

Lady Sunningdale   Yes, sir.

Regent   Just for two, so we can continue this delightful conversation.

The dance continues.

Regent   Do you like gypsy music with your supper.

Lady Sunningdale   Yes, sir.

Regent   With violins?

Lady Sunningdale   Yes, sir.

Regent   My leader, Simka, has been practising all day.

Lady Sunningdale   So have I!

Towards the end of the dance, they move off. He takes her to the foot of the stairway, bids her goodbye and moves through the arches. **Northbrook** *comes to the head of the stairs.* **Lady Sunningdale** *has exited.*

Regent   Ah, Northbrook, my dear fellow, there you are.

Northbrook *comes through the arches. The dance continues.*

Northbrook   Am I to assume, sir, that the necessary arrangements with Lady Sunningdale have been concluded?

Regent   But of course. What is involved, after all – two adults and a meeting of minds which is of crystal clarity. After all, we are not now dealing with some chattering female, my dear Northbrook, whose mind is constantly veering off on tangents. (*He looks with great interest at one of the girls dancing by.*)

Northbrook   No, sir, most definitely not.

Regent   A few words exchanged, a glance or two of some insignificance – et voilà.

'Curt, Clear and Concise'

Regent
    Curt, clear and concise
    Is the way that a lady should be
    I am not a perfectionist who seeks the sublime
    All I ask is a woman who won't waste my time
    I'm frankly sick to death of females who
    Procrastinate
    Who guard their virtue like a sort of Holy Grail
    I much prefer the type who's wiling to co-operate
    – concentrate
    Smack on the nose
    Bang on the nail
    Coy maidens who shed
    Bitter tears at the thought that they might
    Be misled and who faint dead away at the sight of a bed
    Soon find that my parting advice
    Can be curt, clear and concise

As **Footman** *enters with glasses.*

Regent
You must forgive me, Northbrook, if I should
Philosophise
At moments such as these
I find myself at ease
In matters of the heart, I'm sure our points of view
Indubitabley harmonise
You're quite a connoisseur

Northbrook
You're flattering me, sir.

Regent
I feel that really
You look on sex clearly
And factually
Which saves you quite a lot of time and tears
You have an air
Libertine – debonair

Northbrook
Well, sir, actually
I've been engaged for nearly seven years

Regent
You must excuse me, Northbrook, if I seem to minimise
The prevalent idea
That sex should be austere
I've always had a notion
Sensual emotion
Was a cracking bore
And as I mentioned before
Curt, clear and concise
Is the way that a lady should be
She should not sentimentalise the physical act
And believe she can dodge biological fact
I think it is behaving really indefensibly
To take exception to an amorous advance
Give me the kind of girl who mutters comprehensibly
– sensibly
Off with the lights
On with the dance
Though moralists say
That it's better to honour and love and obey
I have found that a casual roll in the hay
Without bridesmaids, confetti or rice
Can be curt, clear and concise

At the end of the song, the **Regent***, turning away, finds himself face to face with* **Nicolas** *and* **Mary***. She curtsies.*

Nicolas (*as the* **Regent** *is still staring at* **Mary**)   Miss Morgan was good enough to accompany me to the ball, Father.

Regent   Yes, Nicky. I am not that unobservant.

Nicolas (*enthusiastically*)   I've been waltzing with Miss Morgan, Father. It's ever so much more fun than doing it with Colonel Schwarzkopf. (*At her startled look.*) Colonel Schwarzkopf is the Royal Dancing Instructor.

Mary   More fun than Colonel Schwarzkopf . . . I am pleased.

Regent   That is not the Order with which I invested you this morning.

Mary   No, sir. Nicky, I mean, His Majesty gave me this. It's First Class.

Nicolas   I wanted her to have it, Father. (*At the* **Regent***'s startled, searching look.*)

Mary (*demurely*)   Just dancing, Your Royal Highness.

Music starts under.

Regent (*finally amused*)   Nicky, I think we should guard against the danger of having Miss Morgan become over-decorated, and bear in mind, also, that ours is a small country, and these Orders are expensive. And now, Miss Morgan, it gives me great pleasure to say . . .

(*He has extended his hand to her and she grabs it, and forces him to dance with her*) Good lord!

Scene Five

St Martin's Lane. Immediately following.

It is still coronation night. Resplendent in their ball finery are **Nicolas** *and* **Mary** *who enter downstage right.*

Nicolas   Isn't this marvellous – being out in the evening, without my aides?

Mary   I wouldn't know, Your Majesty, but I'll take your word for it. Won't Colonel Hoffman be having a fit?

They stop. **Nicolas** *glances at his watch.*

Nicolas   Yes, just about.

Mary   And your fath – I mean His Royal Highness.

Nicolas   It will soon be fourth of July – in Carpathia – then I will tell him what time to be home.

Mary *looks concerned.*

Nicolas   He will not be harmed – I promise you. He cannot continue to run the country as though he owned it outright. But he need only make a few concessions . . .

Mary   Somehow I don't think he's very good at that.

Nicolas (*enthusiastically*)   Just think – when my father is overthrown, I will be able to go to the theatre! I can see your play.

Mary   Well, it's not a bad little show, young man, but I wouldn't fight a war to get in.

Nicolas   I've only ever seen pantomimes and Punch and Judy shows – and your play, it's not like those, is it?

Mary   Oh, no. It's all about an American heiress who comes to Europe and falls in love with a nobleman who turns out to be an imposter, only finally it develops that he isn't an imposter at all. Now, Tina – she's the Coconut Girl because her father inherited this enormous coconut plantation in Florida from an old Indian Chief he befriended when he was a little boy, and he takes her to Europe – by the way, Tina's secretly in love with Cy Mortimer, a baseball player from Yale College.

Nicolas   What else happens?

Mary   Sit down, Your Majesty

He does.

I'll start at the beginning or you'll get confused. First of all –

She taps.

there's an overture

Chords from orchestra.

And then smacko – right into the opening chorus: Hello – how are you? How are you? Hello, hello, hello – m-m-ma! (*She throws a kiss.*)

Mary
Welcome to Pootzie Van Doyle
Who's made millions and millions from
Coconut oil
He's travelled by train
And the dear little coconuts paid for
His trip a man of the people
Hip, hip!

A man of the soil

Hooray!

All welcome to Pootzie Van Doyle
All welcome to Pootzie Van Doyle
Who's made millions and millions from . . .

Well, there are a lot more choruses, and now everybody is cheering (cheer, cheer, cheer) and milling around (mill, mill, mill) and that brings on Tina.

Nicolas The Coconut Girl!

Mary Right!

> I am known as the Coconut Girl
> Though my intimate friends call me Tina
> I'd be more contented
> If Dad hadn't rented
> Quite such a grand place as the Villa Marina the style is ornate
> We've logs of gold plate
> And my bathroom is m-m-mother of pearl
> But beneath all this show
> I'd just like to know
> That I'm simply – just simply – The Coconut Girl

Ha ha ha ha – hello, everyone! Hello, everyone! It's you! Here comes Cy Mortimer with his room-mate Bob Garfield. He's followed her to Europe in a terrible old automobile. And this is where they do their automobile number!

> Paddy McNeil
> Bought an automobile
> And invited his girlie for a spin
> Everything was fine and dandy for the first
> Few miles
> Until he let his clutch
> Right out and couldn't let
> It in
> As they drove at full
> Speed Paddy tried to
> Proceed with a little
> Original sin

> Paddy McNeil
> Bought an automobile
> And invited his girlie for a spin

> Everything was fine and dandy for the first
> Few miles
> Until he let his clutch right out
> And couldn't let it in
> As they drove at full speed
> Paddy tried to proceed
> With a little
> Original sin
> But he found he couldn't cuddle her with both hands
> On the wheel

Crash.

>That's why Paddy had to buy another
>Automobile!

Well, then, the car falls apart and the audience just screams! And that takes us into the serious part. By the way, we're in the garden of the Villa Marina now and there's a wall and a tree and a tree, and Tina is sitting in a swing right here. That's where Count Alexis finds her when he climbs over the wall.

Nicolas   The imposter!

Mary   Shhh – Your Majesty, that's supposed to be a surprise. Anyway, this is where they sing their famous swing song. It's a duet

Mary *sings both parts on a mock bass and soprano – first the bass.*

>Forgive me please for thus intruding
>Upon a lady who is fairer than the day
>Then –

Soprano:

>Kind sir if it should be
>To me you are alluding
>I must beseech you pray
>To go away

Bass:

>Be not unkind be not unfair
>Moments so sweet are all too rare

Soprano:

>As I swing to and fro
>High and low — high and low
>All my cares melt away
>Like the cold winter snow

Bass:

>Would you permit a stranger for a while to stay with
>You?

Soprano:

>Maybe

Bass:

>To spend this beautiful day with you?

Soprano:

   We'll see

Bass:

   Not a cloud

Soprano:

   AAH . . .

Bass:

   In the sky

Soprano:

   AAH . . .

Bass:

   And a lark

Soprano:

   AAH . . .

Bass:

   Singing high

Soprano:

   AAH . . .

She starts as a bass and gets confused and she changes to a soprano in the middle of the line:

   And the sound of the sea
   Far below

And this is where I say my line, 'Count Alexis, you are a cad and a bounder, etcetera, etcetera' and Tina throws herself into the arms of a passing waiter who turns out to be Cy Mortimer, and when she recognises him, she faints. And that's the end of Act One.

(*Chord.*) Wait till you hear Act Two.

(*Chord.*) And it opens with a sextette. I'm featured in it with five other girls. It takes place in the casino at Deauville . . .

   We're six lilies of the valley
   Rose, Maud, Kate, Jane, Marybelle
   And Sally
   We toil neither do we sin much
   But we find, in the casino, that we win much

More— by being gentles with the gentlemen
Playing at the tables
Often sentimental men
Give emeralds and sables
To Rose, Maud, Kate, Jane, Marybelle and Sally
Six pretty fillies
Far from being silly billies
Six lilies of the valley

Now, there's a second chorus, which is in harmony. I'll just do my part.

We're six lilies of the valley
Rose, Maud, Kate, Jane, Marybelle
And Sally
We toil neither do we sin much
But we find, in the casino, that we win much
More – by being gentles with the gentlemen
Playing at the tables
Often sentimental men
Give emeralds and sables
To Rose, Maud, Kate, Jane, Marybelle and Sally
Six pretty fillies
Far from being silly billies
Six lilies of the valley

Nicolas But what's happening? I mean, in the plot?

Mary Well, Count Alexis is heartbroken because he isn't really an imposter at all, and now he's working as a waiter and Cy Mortimer is engaged to Tina. This is where he goes to the roulette table, we all crowd around him and, as the table turns, he sings, 'Lady Luck, come to my aid. This is a game that must be played and won.' And we all sing, 'What fun, what fun, what fun'. Well, anyway, he wins – he wins again, and again and again, the excitement is terrific, and finally he breaks the bank. And we all sing:

That's marvellous, Count Alexis that's marvellous . . .

Nicolas Oh, it is marvellous!

Mary Yes, he's very pleased, because back home the coconut blight has struck Pootzie Van Doyle's plantation, and poor Tina is penniless. And then he throws the money – in cash – at her feet. And then she realises that he always loved her for herself alone and not for the coconuts.

Nicolas And is that the end?

Mary Almost. There is the Walla Walla Boola.

Nicolas What on earth is that?

Mary I'll show you

When you do the Walla Walla Boola Walla Walla Boola
You will find it more exciting
Than the Honolulu Hula
First you swing to the left
You swing to the right
It's got a bear that makes you want
To dance all night
Your hips start to wiggle
You give a little giggle
And begin to wish the temperature was cooler
So stand up and holler
Throw away your collar
Come on and do the Walla Walla Boola

When you do the Walla Walla Boola Walla Walla Boola
You will find it more exciting
Than the Honolulu Hula
First you swing to the left
You swing to the right
It's got a bear that makes you want
To dance all night
Your hips start to wiggle
You give a little giggle
And begin to wish the temperature was cooler
So stand up and holler
Throw away your collar
Come on and do the Walla Walla Boola
Walla Walla Boola
Walla Walla Walla Walla Boola!

When you do the Walla Walla Boola Walla Walla Boola
You will find it more exciting
Than the Honolulu Hula
First you swing to the left
You swing to the right
It's got a bear that makes you want
To dance all night
Your hips start to wiggle
You give a little giggle
And begin to wish the temperature was cooler
So stand up and holler
Throw away your collar
Come on and do the Walla Walla Boola
Walla Walla Boola
Walla Walla Walla Walla Boola!
Walla Walla Walla Boola!

Mary	**Nicolas**
Walla Walla Walla Boola!	Miss Morgan!
Walla Walla Walla Boola!	Miss Morgan
Walla Walla Walla Boola!	Miss Morgan!
Walla Walla Walla Boola!	

Oh! Blackout!

Scene Six

The Royal Apartment, Carpathian Embassy.

Mary *is again divesting herself of her borrowed finery, meanwhile diverting* **Northbrook** *with an account of her evening. He is not amused.*

Mary   . . . And then, after we had finished our fish and chips, it turned out His Majesty had never been on a London bus.

Northbrook   On a bus? Without his aides, or bodyguards?

Mary   Oh, I was right there all the time.

She has removed all her finery. Looks at it all laid out, suddenly saddened by the imminence of still another departure.

Well, that's it, Mr Northbrook. (*Indicating the jewels, etc.*) Everything but this . . . (*She touches her Order.*) . . . which I get to keep. Did you notice, I got promoted? Amazing, isn't it? This time last night I didn't even have *one* decoration and now . . .

The **Footmen** *have brought on a supper table, obviously set for two, with wine coolers, etc. She stares at it, then turns on* **Northbrook**, *kisses him impulsively in great delight.*

Mary   Oh Mr Northbrook!

Northbrook (*startled*)   Oh no, Miss Morgan.

And as she breaks away from him, heading for the bedroom.

Mary   I'll just go and wash off the fish and chips – they're delicious, but not romantic. And this is going to be romantic.

She blows the startled **Northbrook** *a kiss, vanishes.*

Northbrook   No, Miss Morgan, you do not understand. Oh God!

His prayer, if not precisely answered, gets action. The doors are opened, and the **Regent** *enters. He comes in briskly, ready for business.*

Regent   Ah, there you are Northbrook – I wondered what had become of you –

Northbrook *is agitatedly pointing to the door at left.* **Northbrook** *is shaking his head, points to the jewels and the fur cape. Then again at the door.*

Regent Oh, God!

Northbrook That, sir, was precisely my own reaction.

Regent But, surely, Northbrook, she does not expect to have supper with me.

Northbrook *timidly nods.*

Regent But what am I to do? Lady Sunningdale will be arriving in a few minutes.

Northbrook Sir, I will go downstairs to intercept her.

Regent Typical, Northbrook, typical. Cowardly to the core. (*He pours himself a slug of vodka, then with menace –*) You will stay, Northbrook. Think carefully and cleverly.

Northbrook Sir, you hold the solution in your hand.

The **Regent** *is uncomprehending for a moment.*

Regent Vodka?

Northbrook With respect, sir, precisely.

Regent Ah yes! Of course . . . vodka . . . Very good thinking, Northbrook. We'll act on that! Intercept Lady Sunningdale and entertain her briefly. Then in half an hour – make that twenty minutes – you may return to supervise the removal of Miss Morgan. She will be lying just about there. And, may I add, Northbrook, that I consider you a credit to the Foreign Office.

Northbrook Thank you, sir.

He exits, leaving the **Regent** *still bemused and intrigued by the plot. He still has his drink, he sips it with obvious pleasure. Then* **Mary** *enters from the bedroom, curtseying to the* **Regent***.*

Mary Oh, Your Highness, I nearly left . . . without seeing you . . . then I saw the supper table set for just us two again . . . I was thrilled. Please, Your Highness, can I have a drink?

Regent What?

Mary A drink, vodka, if you'll trust me with it just once more.

Regent Of course. With pleasure.

Mary Thank you, sir. Prosnaya something or other, Your Royal Highness, and then straight back with it. (*She drains the drink.*) More, please.

Regent More? Why are you drinking so much? It is most unbecoming in a young girl. However, if you insist . . .

Mary I'll be all right tonight, Your Highness, because I've already eaten fish and chips with His Majesty, the King.

Regent Fish and chips?

Mary Yes, and I got him the recipe so you can have them all the time when you get back home to the palace.

Regent In that event, I *myself* may join in the conspiracy against me.

Mary Oh, that. We cleared all that up over the fish and chips. (*She takes paper from her bosom.*) You can forget about it.

Regent What's that?

Mary It's a Proclamation. Listen! 'We, Nicolas, Hereditary King of Carpathia, hereby address this Royal Proclamation to Our People: Whereas all kinds of riots are going on all over the place, and whereas this is no way to run a country' – I helped him with some of the wording –

Regent Yes, yes, yes . . . Now get on with it.

Mary 'We, Nicolas, therefore call upon our loyal subjects to reject all outside propaganda of any kind and unite behind the leadership of our beloved father, the Regent, His Royal Highness . . .'

Regent *snatches the paper from her.*

Regent (*quickly reading the Proclamation*)   Very clever. Does he really believe me gullible enough to be taken in by this? And just who put him up to it?

Mary Oh. Your only son offers you something beautiful – his trust in you – and you examine it like a pawnbroker with a dollar watch.

Regent This is precisely why we have survived. When I became the Regent of Carpathia we had sixteen political parties, all of whom hated each other so violently that we had civil war the way other countries have four seasons. I also had an infant son, and this untidy, backward nation was his heritage. I did not see fit to hand it on to him in this lamentable condition so I devoted fifteen years of ceaseless, unremitting toil to the creation of something which is now worth destroying. So the conspirators creep out – and with them is my only son.

Mary But that isn't true. You've got that Proclamation in your hand . . .

Regent This? Do you think I trust an illiterate scrawl composed by an infant schoolboy and this immature actress? (*He tears the Proclamation.*) There's your Proclamation! There!

Mary Oh, I can just imagine what you've been through. But he does love you, and I told him I was positive that you love him.

Regent Miss Morgan, in your stunted and impoverished vocabulary, is there really no other word but love?

Mary Well, I admit, it does pop up quite a lot of the time, but, honestly, Your Royal Highness, that is your problem.

Regent Nonsense! I have transformed a squalid mittel-European ant heap into a country which is civilised, prosperous and at peace. Do you think love had anything to do with it?

Mary (*holding thumb and forefinger apart*)   Not even that much?

Regent No! It was done with power – used with cunning, treachery, guile and when necessary, brute force!

They kiss.

Mary I know just how you feel.

Regent No, no, no. Love is the enemy of all the cold, hard virtues that make a ruler or a king.

Mary I like that.

Regent Actually, that was first said by Caesar Augustus.

Mary Oh.

They kiss, the **Regent** *breaks away, rises and crosses and sits on the divan.*

Regent Love is dangerous for me. Kreislfinger in his definitive work establishes beyond the shadow of a doubt –

She lifts his legs, crosses behind the divan, snaps the light and the violin plays.

What's that?

Mary It's your servant mourning his lost love –

Regent Oh, that was a lie. They are professional musicians. It was a trick, to seduce you.

Mary It might work.

Regent But historical precedent proves that 87 –

They kiss.

– and 2/3 per cent of . . .

Her kiss has quieted him and **Mary** *sings from behind the couch:*

> There's nothing more to say
> Because at last your heart has beckoned
> In this brief fleeting second
> I know
> You really are a lonely man
> The one and only man

I dreamed of all my life ago

This time it's true love
This time it's real
Last night I knew love
Now I can feel
A lovely certainty at last has come true
I know you care for me as I care for you
This is no light love
No passing phase
This is the right love
No passing phase
This is the right love
For all my days
I need no violins
No moon nor stars above

I'll sure be glad to get out of this dress!

The lights dim out as the **Regent** *exits into the bedroom with* **Mary** *in his arms.*

Music bridges into the morning music as the light segue.

Scene Seven

The next morning.

At rise, the room is flooded with morning light and the **Footmen**, *under the supervision of the* **Major-Domo**, *are placing bowls of fresh flowers about the room. A breakfast table and two chairs are wheeled on and placed down stage right.*

Mary *enters from the bedroom and, taking a vase of flowers from the mantle, she rearranges the table.*

Northbrook (*entering from the* **Regent***'s bedroom*)   Good morning, Miss Morgan.

Mary   Oh, good morning, Mr Northbrook

Northbrook   Have you seen His Royal Highness this morning?

Mary   – not recently . . .

Northbrook   Mysterious forces are at work in the Carpathian Embassy, Miss Morgan.

Colonel Hoffman has been dismissed, the leader of the opposition has been released. Would you know anything about that, Miss Morgan?

Mary   I was sleeping.

Northbrook   Well, I must be off. His Royal Highness's train leaves in a short while.

Mary   Yes, I know.

Northbrook Goodbye, Miss Morgan.

Mary Oh, Mr Northbrook, could you please find me that old raincoat again.

Northbrook It's in the wardrobe – there – Oh, Miss Morgan, if you should ever consider giving up the stage, I think an opening could be found for you in our diplomatic corps.

Mary Thanks . . .

He bows to her and, in deference, backs out of the room. Three **Footmen** *have entered from the* **Regent***'s bedroom with a truck and two suitcases and exits.* **Mary** *is still concerned with the breakfast table.*

Mary
>This time it's true love
>All else apart
>Out of the blue love
>Has touched my heart

The **Regent** *has entered and heard the last line – and sings –*

Regent
>Dare I believe that one brief rendezvous
>You've grown to care for me as I care for you
>This is no light love
>Too well I know
>No fly-by-night love
>Could move me so

Both
>We need no violins, no moon nor stars above

Regent
>You are my own true love

Mary *curtsies,* **Regent** *lifts her up.*

Regent Oh, my dear. No.

Mary But I have to – it's protocol.

Regent It's a waste of time. As of this morning I have declared for the democratic way of life – and my son and I are now – (*with some difficulty*) – real pals. It is almost too much to face on an empty stomach!

Mary Won't you be late? . . . I mean . . . your train is waiting . . .

Regent It will wait. In some matters I am still a tyrant. My dear, it is really intolerable that we should be separated after just these few moments.

Mary Now I don't want you to worry about me. Besides, I have to get to the theatre anyway – I knew all along that you had to leave today . . .

Regent Be still – and listen to me. Mr Northbrook is arranging for your special passport . . .

Mary My special – what?

Regent – and your private car will be attached to the Orient Express.

Mary My private car!

Regent For your journey to Carpathia, idiot. And now will you please stop interrupting me? You will occupy the Smolny Villa; quite nice really, in a lovely garden by the sea, and it is easily run with a staff of only twelve – (*Aware that she is staring at him.*) Well, I must say, this is a fine time for you suddenly to become speechless!

Mary Are you sure? Do you really want me . . .

He rises to kiss her and the **Queen Mother** *enters.*

Queen Mother Ah, Charles! And Miss Morgan! Still at supper are you? Heavens, it's morning. Do sit down. Charles, I do thank you for what you've done for Nicky. He's so happy this morning. Are we really to have free elections? Oh, what fun! I shall do my part, of course, by making campaign speeches.

Regent Victory is assured.

Queen Mother At any rate, Nicky is in a marvellous mood this morning. You, Charles, you're looking especially well, too, Charles. Et toi, petite, tu as un mine superbe ce matin.

Mary *glances at the* **Regent** *who pantomimes 'Oui'.*

Queen Mother And such a pretty dress! Such a good colour for you! Quite exquisite taste, hasn't she, Charles? Always so soignée, whatever the occasion. Well, I mustn't dawdle, my chief lady-in-waiting Lady Meissenbrun is not fully recovered and that is such a nuisance. Au revoir, ma chère, you will bring your company to us soon, won't you? Do invite her, Charles. Perhaps we might have a joint season – you and Sarah Bernhardt! Just between us, my dear, now and again – just for variety – a little daytime dress – or perhaps a suit – nothing outré, of course. Entendu? Ma chère?

Mary (*with a curtsey*) Oui.

Queen Mother So sweet. Such fun we have had.

Mary Goodbye, Your Majesty.

Queen Mother Not goodbye, my dear. À bientôt . . . à bientôt . . . à bientôt!

Mary What did she say when she was leaving?

Regent À bientôt – it is a way of saying, in French, that one hopes to meet again – very soon. Her feminine intuition, no doubt . . .

Mary (*almost to herself*)   She just wants me to come because she thinks I'm a big actress, like Sarah Bernhardt –

Regent   Luckily, I know the truth – (*Crossing to her, mimicking her gesture in 'The Coconut Girl'*) Count Alexis, you are a cad and a bounder.

Mary   A small role, to be sure – Yes, yes, yes.

They laugh at the remembrance and embrace.

Nicolas *enters.*

Nicolas   Oh, excuse me, Father!

The **Regent** *and* **Mary** *break.*

Nicolas   I just wanted to say goodbye to Miss Morgan, Father.

Regent   Of course.

Nicolas   I want to thank you, Miss Morgan – for everything.

Mary   Your Majesty, it was a pleasure!

Regent   Would you two like to be alone?

Nicolas (*taking a gift box from his pocket*)   I've brought Miss Morgan a farewell gift, Father.

Regent   Well, give it to her, Nicky. You are now on the Council of State with me. You must learn to act with decision and confidence, my boy.

Nicolas   Yes, sir! It isn't very much, I'm afraid, but in all the excitement – (*With a look at the* **Regent**.) – nobody remembered to raise my allowance.

The **Regent** *accepts the dig and crosses to the breakfast table.*

Mary (*looking at the pin the King holds*)   Oh, it's beautiful.

Nicolas   With your permission, Miss Morgan.

He pins it on **Mary** *who is beaming.*

Mary   Thank you, Your Majesty. But it isn't really a farewell present. You see, I'm coming too.

Nicolas   With your company? To do the play? Oh, what fun!

Mary   No, not the company. They still have six weeks here in London.

Nicolas   Perfect. You see, for us, when we get home, there will be so much to do.

He has his hands on his back like his father. He stands proudly by the **Regent**. *He turns to face* **Mary** *and the* **Regent** *puts an arm on the boy.*

Nicolas   With those out of the way, we can really enjoy your play.

Mary *has wilted slightly.*

Mary Not the play, Your Majesty. Me. Just me.

Regent Nicky, Miss Morgan is coming alone . . .

Nicolas But that's even better! You'll be marvellous in recital.

Regent Yes, yes – Nicky, please see that your grandmother gets to the station safely. I'll join you very soon.

Nicolas Then I won't say goodbye, Miss Morgan – à bientôt.

Mary (*in a deep curtsey*) À bientôt, Your Majesty.

Nicolas Oh, no. Please.

He lifts her up. They face each other and **Nicolas** *kisses her and exits. Her mood is shattered.*

Regent My dear, the boy is young and inexperienced . . . when he knows, he will welcome you.

Mary I'd be no good in recital . . . even in a small theatre.

Regent I want you to come. I say that from the heart . . .

Mary My darling, thank you for that. This is the nicest dream I guess I'll ever have – and I made it on hardly any sleep. But if I went back home with you the whole dream would explode – I'd just be in your way there.

Regent Oh, my dear . . .

Mary It wouldn't seem funny or charming if you had to be explaining me, or apologising for me all the time – besides, some sneak is sure to tell your mother-in-law that I can't speak French.

Regent But – I was counting on you . . . There are worse dangers than the threat of home-made bombs.

Mary But we can be together. Make your throne secure for Nicky. And then –

Regent In eighteen months, my dear, do you know what can happen in that time?

Mary Sure. In eighteen months I will probably have learned Carpathian.

Regent You're talking trifles!

Mary Where shall we meet then? Paris? Paris would be fun, wouldn't it?

Regent You are the stubbornest, most irritating and most infuriating girl I have ever known.

Mary That's where I came in, isn't it?

Regent Night before last I met this funny, chattering American girl . . . argumentative, over-talkative, disrespectful, an irrepressible busy-body.

Mary (*ruefully*) I didn't think you noticed.

536   The Girl Who Came to Supper

Regent   I watched her closely and I even made notes. They'll be useful when I try to recall all the odd little details.

Regent
I'll remember her
How incredibly naïve
She was
I couldn't quite
Believe she was sincere
So alert
So impertinent
And yet so sweet
My defeat
Was clear
I'll remember her
Her absurd exaggerating
And her utterly deflating repartee
And the only thing that worries
Me at all is whether she'll
Remember me.

Mary   I'd better get that old raincoat. I can't go to the theatre looking like this – and if the girls see that I've been crying they'll think I didn't have a good time. (*She exits.*)

Regent
I'll remember her
In the evening when I'm
Lonely and imagining if
Only
She were
There I'll
Relive
Oh, so vividly
Our sad and
Sweet
Incomplete
Affair

Major-Domo *enters with* **Regent***'s hat.*

Regent
I'll remember her
Heavy-hearted when we parted
With her eyes so full of tears she couldn't see
And I'll feel inside a foolish sort of pride
To think that she remembers me

Regent *takes the hat.* **Major-Domo** *backs out.*

Act Two, Scene Seven   537

Regent *slowly exits as two* **Charwomen** *enter carrying fresh linen and dust covers and a* **Footman** *with a feather duster enters from a bedroom.* **First Charwoman** *covers furniture with dust covers;* **Second Charwoman** *takes flowers from vases around the room as* **Footman** *clears up breakfast table and begins dusting mantelpiece.*

Mary *enters from the bedroom in raincoat, looks around the barren room, takes some flowers from the bunch* **Second Charwoman** *has gathered and slowly exits through open doors centre.*

Curtain.

www.ingramcontent.com/pod-product-compliance
Lightning Source LLC
Chambersburg PA
CBHW071133300426
44113CB00009B/961